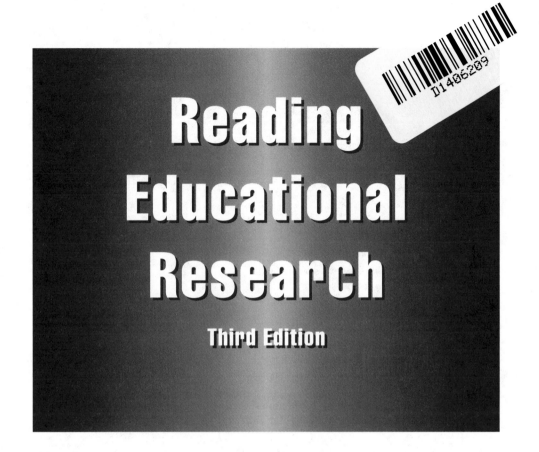

Reading Educational Research

Third Edition

Andrea Vierra

University of New Mexico

■

Judith Pollock

■

Felipe Golez

University of Minnesota

Merrill,
an imprint of Prentice Hall
Upper Saddle River, New Jersey   Columbus, Ohio

Library of Congress Cataloging-in-Publication Data

Vierra, Andrea.
    Reading educational research / Andrea Vierra, Judith Pollock,
  Felipe Golez — 3rd ed.
       p. cm.
    Includes bibliographical references (p. 357) and index.
    ISBN 0-13-680034-3 (alk. paper)
      1. Education—Research—United States.   I. Pollock, Judith.
  II. Golez, Felipe.   III. Title.
LB1028.25.U6V54   1998
370'.78'073—DC21   97-5516
                                      CIP

Cover photo: Susie Fitzhugh
Editor: Kevin M. Davis
Production Editor: Mary Irvin
Design Coordinator: Julia Zonneveld Van Hook
Text Designer: Eric Kingsbury
Cover Designer: Brian Deep
Production Manager: Laura Messerly
Director of Marketing: Kevin Flanagan
Marketing Manager: Suzanne Stanton
Advertising/Marketing Coordinator: Julie Shough
Production Coordinator: Holcomb Hathaway, Inc.

This book was set in Times Roman by Ash Street Typecrafters and was printed and bound by BookCrafters. The cover was printed by Phoenix Color Corp.

 © 1998 by Prentice-Hall, Inc.
Simon & Schuster / A Viacom Company
Upper Saddle River, New Jersey 07458

Earlier editions © 1992, 1988 Gorsuch Scarisbrick, Publishers

Printed in the United States of America

10 9 8 7 6 5 4 3 2 1

ISBN: 0-13-680034-3

Prentice-Hall International (UK) Limited, *London*
Prentice-Hall of Australia Pty. Limited, *Sydney*
Prentice-Hall Canada Inc., *Toronto*
Prentice-Hall Hispanoamericana, S.A., *Mexico*
Prentice-Hall of India Private Limited, *New Delhi*
Prentice-Hall of Japan, Inc., *Tokyo*
Simon & Schuster Asia Pte. Ltd., *Singapore*
Editora Prentice-Hall do Brasil, Ltda., *Rio de Janeiro*

Contents

Preface

As was the case with the previous edition of *Reading Educational Research*, the third edition is designed for use in an introductory educational research course. Its major goal is to prepare students to read educational research reports with understanding and to evaluate what they read. It will serve well not just students who take only this one course, but also students who go on to take additional course work in this area.

The book is divided into four parts, all of which have been updated and revised for the new edition. The introduction explains the role of research in science and orients the reader to locating and reading research reports. It also describes the two basic and very different kinds of research methods: quantitative and qualitative. The second and third parts of the book are devoted respectively to quantitative and qualitative, and to how quantitative and qualitative researchers collect and analyze data. With an emphasis on how the two methods necessarily complement each other, the fourth part of the book explains how both qualitative and quantitative research fit into complete research programs. Part IV also discusses practical limitations on the ways in which research is used.

Two of the book's strengths are its generous use of examples, some fabricated and many quoted directly from educational research literature, and frequent opportunities for readers to practice what they have learned. Examples are woven into the text and into the exercises; exercises are provided at frequent intervals within chapters (indicated by the symbol ■) as well as at the end of each chapter. In Appendix A, the complete texts of several research reports from educational journals are provided for summative practice. Responses to the exercises, against which readers may check their own responses, are given in Appendix C.

In teaching students about research, we have found that there is no substitute for actually reading the research literature in one's own field of interest. Thus, some of the exercises suggest that students find and read research reports in their fields. These exercises tend to be especially rewarding because students learn not only about research but about their professional fields. In these exercises, we structure ways for students to think about the reports they read, but we do not provide responses to these exercises; students' responses will depend on the material they read. Instructors may find it useful to organize class discussion around these open-ended exercises.

Because many of the terms used in educational research will be new to most readers, terms are highlighted and defined as they are introduced. A glossary of highlighted terms is included at the end of the book as well.

Acknowledgments

Acknowledgments in a book like this one can never be complete. We are indebted first to our students who, over the years, have taught us a great deal about how to teach research methods and who used and commented upon early drafts of the chapters and each edition of the text. The individuals who have provided the most direct help with this text are Cindy Gregory, Jesse Brooks, and Juliet Fisher, who located most of the examples we use from published research. We indicated that these examples are one of the book's strengths, and it is largely due to these individuals that this is true. We wish to thank Ophelia Miramontes, University of Colorado at Boulder; Gerard Giordano, New Mexico State University; Susan Gooden, University of Southern Indiana; and Flora Nell Roebuck, Texas Woman's University for their thoughtful reviews. The book is improved as a result of their suggestions.

Our most special thanks go to David Bachelor, without whom this book would not have begun, and to Kerry Eason, Byron Pollock, and John Humphreys, without whom it would not have been completed.

Part I
Introduction

This part of the book contains only one chapter. This chapter introduces you to the rest of the book. The chapter defines research and gets you started in the process of finding and reading research reports relevant to your own field in education. It also helps you understand how researchers choose their topics and how you can begin to evaluate the topics that are studied in the research you read.

An important part of this chapter is its introduction of the distinctions between two basic kinds of research: qualitative and quantitative. These two approaches differ in the kinds of topics that are pursued, the ways in which information about the topics is collected, and the kinds of knowledge that are obtained. This distinction is so basic that it will inform the remainder of the book.

There is some confusion in the literature on educational research methods about the best way to carve up the methodological pie and what to call the pieces. Most authors classify research methods as we do, into the two basic categories of quantitative and qualitative methods, although disagreement exists about what to call these two categories. Many authors also include a number of subclassifications, especially of quantitative research designs, that we do not. We do not omit these subclassifications because we think they are wrong; rather, we think that presenting them would require more detail than is appropriate for an introductory text. Throughout the book, we will note the more prominent instances of our lumping where others would split.

1

What Is Research?

SCIENCE AS A WAY OF KNOWING

Each of us has many ways of knowing, of gaining knowledge. I know, for example, that it is day, not night, because I perceive daylight through my window.

Other ways of knowing are more formal and organized. Logical reasoning is one example. If I am at my office and can't find my keys, I know my keys are not at home, because I had to have my keys to get to my office. A process of logical reasoning gives me the knowledge that my keys are not at home.

A common way to gain knowledge is to seek the opinion of people we believe to be experts about the matter in question. When a patient asks her doctor why she has a pain in her side, she is seeking knowledge about her physical health from someone she, as well as others, believes to be an expert about physical health.

Some academic disciplines are explicitly concerned with ways of knowing—with knowing about knowing. Philosophy and psychology are the two major examples. Philosophers and psychologists have created classifications of ways of knowing and study these classifications. The study of logic is a specialty of some philosophers; logicians are philosophers who study logic as a way of knowing. The study of perception is a specialty of some psychologists; perceptual psychologists are psychologists who study perception as a way of knowing.

Science, through what is called the scientific method, provides one of the major ways of knowing that academicians recognize; in fact, there is a branch of philosophy called the philosophy of science. The scientific method has a set of characteristics that distinguishes it from other ways of knowing. It is, for example, an empirical way of knowing; that is, scientific knowledge is based on observation in the real world of the events we want to know about. Some other ways of knowing are also empirical, but some are not. Expert opinion, for example, is not. When you ask a doctor about your health, the knowledge you gain is not based on your own observation of your physical condition but on your doctor's opinion.

In addition, the scientific method requires that these events be intersubjectively verifiable; that is, that reasonable people agree about the real-world events. The scientific method can tell us how many students attend a lecture, because reasonable people are likely to agree on the answer to this question; but it cannot tell us whether attending the lecture was the best use of these students' time, because reasonable people are likely to disagree on the answer to this question.

Science is also characterized by publicity in the literal sense. Scientists are expected to publicize their results—to offer their knowledge and knowledge processes for public scrutiny and criticism. Scientific meetings and publications are the primary vehicles whereby scientists meet this criterion of their profession.

One of the highest goals of science is discovering cause and effect relationships. Scientists want to know what causes the events they observe in the real world—events such as cancer, juvenile delinquency, automobile accidents, war, inflation, or the election to public office of certain individuals and the defeat of others. Science, then, is one way of knowing, but it is not the only way, nor is it the only way that is valid. There are many ways of knowing. Nonscientific ways of knowing have validity. Even scientists routinely use nonscientific ways of knowing. Because of its characteristics, science cannot provide all the answers—it can never be the only way of knowing that is required. One reason is that some questions of basic interest are simply not answerable through the methods of science.

Questions involving values are an example. Science can never tell us what we should do. For example, science cannot tell us whether the public schools should increase their emphasis on fine arts. However, science can sometimes provide information of use in answering such questions. It can tell us whether such groups as parents, students, and educators say that the public schools should increase their emphasis on fine arts. Science may also be able to tell us what will probably happen if the public schools do (or do not) increase their emphasis on fine arts. But science cannot tell us what we should do.

Even when science can provide direct knowledge about a question of interest, it does not provide the only valid knowledge. Consider a child who receives a low score on a math computation test but whose teacher believes that the child can do the kinds of computation that were tested. The test score only provides knowledge that for some reason the child's performance on the test—at the time, in the place, and under the circumstances that it was taken—was low. The teacher's beliefs about the child are based on many ways of knowing, which probably provide more valid information about the child's math ability than the test alone can. Questions have emerged in what is sometimes called the postmodernist period as to what knowledge is and whose knowledge we are talking about. Are there absolute truths? Can research ever be truly free of bias? For instance, by studying behavior management in a classroom, isn't the researcher already suggesting that behavior needs to be managed or dictated rather than learned and negotiated? To a novice this may seem to be hair splitting, but to contemporary researchers and philosophers of science this is a very important current issue. The issue involves whose interests are being served by science and research. We will return to this issue in chapter 11.

Although science is not the only valid way of knowing, it is an especially important way of knowing in some areas, including education. If you are a student of education, then you seek knowledge about education. Science is one of the most important means through which knowledge about education is obtained. Science cannot provide all the knowledge you require about education. Some questions of interest to educators do not lend themselves to scientific knowing; even when questions can be answered scientifically, other ways of knowing may apply and may also be valid. However, even if you are not sympathetic toward science as a way of knowing, as a student of education you need to be informed about science in order to make informed criticism of scientific knowledge about education.

■ EXERCISE 1

Imagine that you are ill and are trying to understand the cause of your illness. You have the following information about your illness. First, your doctor tells you that your symptoms may be the result either of a contagious virus or of food poisoning; she also indicates that symptoms of viral infection begin about three days after exposure, while symptoms of food poisoning begin about 36 hours after ingestion of the affected food. Second, you remember having been with a friend who was ill about three days before you became ill; and you remember having eaten some food with an "off" taste a few hours before you became ill. Do you think your illness is probably the result of a contagious virus or of food poisoning? What knowledge processes did you use in arriving at your decision? Did you use empirical evidence? Logical reasoning? Expert opinion? ■

RESEARCH: THE EMPIRICAL PART OF SCIENCE

This book is about research. Research is the empirical part of science—of seeking scientific knowledge. It is the part of science that involves systematic observation of events in the real world. Research is the process of collecting information about real-world events.

Research is only a part of science, but it is a very important part. Before they conduct research, scientists must decide what real-world events they want information about—what the research problem or question is. After the research is done—that is, after the information is collected—scientists must decide what the information means and what light the information they have obtained through research sheds on the original problem or question.

This book is primarily about research—about the process of collecting scientific data about the real world. However, we will also deal with research questions—with how scientists decide what it is that they want to do research about—and with analysis of research results—how scientists use research results to answer questions.

EDUCATIONAL RESEARCH

Past Influences of Research on Educational Practice

There has been a great deal of educational research over the years, as well as a great deal of research not explicitly labeled as educational but with implications for education. Many practicing educators are uninterested in educational research. They do not feel that it is relevant to what they do. However, whether they know it or not, research has dramatically impacted what they do.

For example, in much earlier times in Western culture, children were considered to be essentially small adults—to differ from adults primarily in stature. Thus, children were treated much as adults were treated: they consumed the same foods and beverages as adults, including alcohol and caffeine; they were put to work at adult tasks as soon as they were physically able; they were even imprisoned in the same facilities as adults, for the same offenses. Since then, research has shown that children's biological and psychological processes are different from those of adults. Partly as a result of research, we now treat children differently.

Research has shown, for example, that children's nutritional needs are different from those of adults; among other things, children require a diet with more protein than do adults. Some drugs affect adults and children differently; amphetamines, which have a stimulating effect on most adults, can have a calming effect on children. Children's cognitive processes are also different from those of adults. Very young children do not conserve in time and space; that is, for very young children, out of sight is literally out of mind.

Recent research in the behavioral sciences, including education, has greatly altered the ways in which practitioners work. Research done since the 1960s has demonstrated that proximity to an attachment figure is critical to normal personality development in young children. Human services agencies have changed their practices with respect to young children in light of this research. Unless a parent is severely abusive, it is more detrimental to a child's ultimate development to remove him from a troubled home than to leave the child with the parent to whom he is attached. This has caused human services agencies to redirect their efforts toward getting help for mildly abusive parents rather than removing children to foster homes.

Teachers use the results of research when they provide in-class time for sustained silent reading; research has shown that a good way to learn to read is to read. Special education teachers often use behavior modification with retarded and emotionally disturbed children; research has shown that many of these children do well in the highly structured environment, with immediate behavior contingencies, that behavior modification provides.

Research has changed educational practice and will continue to do so in the future. It is thus important for educators to be knowledgeable about research in their fields. This kind of knowledge requires reading professional literature, and in order to read such literature with understanding, it is necessary to know something about research itself.

Distinguishing Research Reports from Other Kinds of Professional Writing

In general, an item in the professional literature is a research report if it describes an attempt to obtain empirical information about a question of interest. It can, however, be difficult for beginning students to distinguish research reports from other kinds of professional writing. Many articles and books in the professional literature are not research reports. Some of these involve questions that are not empirically answerable. These tend to be questions with answers involving ethics, morality, or values. Examples of such questions are the following:

- Should the public schools become involved in moral education?
- Should most children in special education be mainstreamed?
- What should the standards be for admission to higher education?

Words such as *should* and *ought* provide good clues that the question under consideration involves ethics or values and thus cannot be answered empirically. Research can, however, provide information of use in answering such questions. For example, the following questions are empirically answerable and thus researchable. Their answers could be used in resolving questions of value.

- Do parents and teachers agree or disagree with a proposal to provide moral education in the public schools?
- What effects does mainstreaming have on children in both special education and regular classrooms?

■ What standards are currently applied in granting admission to higher education?

As you read the literature in your field in education, you probably will have little trouble spotting the articles that deal with values. However, there are also published works in education that deal with empirically answerable questions but do so in non-empirical modes. These can be harder to distinguish. An article titled "The Effects of Mainstreaming on Children in Regular Classrooms" is not a research report if it consists only of the author's opinions on the subject. Many other examples could be given of educational literature that does not result from research: articles and books describing curricula, educational programs, or teaching methods; books presenting educational philosophies; and articles by teachers reflecting on their classroom experiences. With a little practice, you will be able to distinguish research reports from other kinds of professional writing.

■ EXERCISE 2

Below are the titles of a number of articles published in educational journals. Which seem to be research reports and which seem to reflect other kinds of professional writing?

a. "Adolescents' Cognitions and Attributions for Academic Cheating: A Cross-National Study" (Evans, Craig, and Mietzel, 1993)

b. "Educational Research: A Personal and Social Process" (Allender, 1986)

c. "The Effects of a Self-Monitoring Process on College Students' Learning in an Introductory Statistics Course" (Lan, Bradley, and Parr, 1993)

d. "Issues and Trends in the Education of the Severely Handicapped" (Walker, 1984)

e. "Barriers to the Progress of Women and Minority Faculty" (Menges and Exum, 1983)

f. "The Short-Term Impact of Two Classroom-Based Preventive Interventions on Aggressive and Shy Behaviors and Poor Achievement" (Dolan, et al., 1993)   ■

Sources of Research Reports

Research reports are published in a number of types of sources. The most common vehicle for reporting research results is professional journals. The *American Educational Research Journal,* for example, is published by the American Educational Research Association and is one of the most prestigious research journals in the field of education. Subfields in education also have their own research journals: for example, *Reading Research Quarterly, Journal of Educational Psychology, Journal of Learning Disabilities, Sociology of Education, Educational Leadership, Anthropology and Education Quarterly, Health Education,* and *School Counselor.*

Research results are also reported in books. Major research projects can require a book for full reporting of results. An example is Gottfield's research on giftedness in young children, which was reported in a book titled *Gifted IQ: Early Developmental Aspects* (1994). Sometimes books containing research reports are anthologies, in which several different studies are reported under one cover. Malave-Lopez and Duquette (1991) edited such a volume called *Language, Culture, and Cognition: A*

Collection of Studies in First and Second Language Acquisition. The book contains articles by a number of different researchers.

The federally funded ERIC Clearinghouse also publishes research reports as well as other kinds of articles about education. Most academic libraries subscribe to ERIC.

Finally, a great deal of research is reported in theses, dissertations, and project reports, which are disseminated through the authors or sponsoring agencies. Libraries can assist readers who wish to obtain copies of such documents. Dissertation abstracts, for example, are available in most academic libraries, and copies of complete dissertations may be obtained for a fee. Government documents are also available through most major libraries.

With so many sources of research reports, it can be difficult for any individual to keep up with the sheer volume of research in a field of interest. The research community has responded to this practical problem by publishing what are called review articles. Review articles are written by respected scholars. They do just what their name suggests: review a given field. The author pulls together the most interesting and relevant research findings in a given area. Review articles can be enormously valuable to readers who are trying to keep up with the research in some educational area.

There are two major sources of research review articles in education: a journal titled *Review of Educational Research,* which is published quarterly, and a volume titled *Review of Research in Education,* which is published annually. In addition, annual volumes of research reviews are published in other fields that are sometimes of interest to educators: the *Annual Review of Psychology,* for example. Over a period of perhaps ten years, most subfields in education are reviewed in one of these sources. Titles of articles in recent issues of the *Review of Educational Research* and the *Review of Research in Education* include the following:

- "Restructuring the Classroom: Conditions for Productive Small Groups" (Cohen, 1994)
- "The Role of Volition in Learning and Performance" (Corno and Kanfer, 1993)
- "The Knower and the Known: The Nature of Knowledge in Research on Teaching" (Fenstermacher, 1994)
- "The Space Factor in Mathematics: Gender Differences" (Friedman, 1995)
- "Assessment and Diversity" (Garcia and Pearson, 1994)
- "The Organization of Effective Secondary Schools" (Lee, Bryk, and Smith, 1993)
- "Cooperative versus Competitive Efforts and Problem Solving (Qin, Johnson, and Johnson, 1995)

Using Academic Libraries

In the past decade, there has been a society-wide computer based revolution in the ways we deal with information. Because the primary focus of libraries is information, this revolution is particularly apparent in libraries. People who are not at least minimally computer-literate can still access information. For example, people who don't know how to use a computer word-processing program can still get by with typewriters. But it is almost impossible to use a modern library of any size, including academic libraries, without using a computer.

The first change that old-fashioned library users are likely to notice in academic libraries today is that the card catalog no longer exists. Now the link between a library user and the location of a particular book on the shelf is the computer. Fortunately, most computer catalogs are user-friendly—that is, they are easy for novices to use. And librarians are on duty to help users with any problems they encounter.

If you enter the library knowing the author and/or title of the book you want, you may think that your use of the library will not be computer-dependent. But you will need information from the computer about whether the library owns that book and, if so, whether it is already checked out. If the book is available, you can get its shelf location from the computer, go to that location, get the book, and check it out.

If what you want is a particular journal article, the process can be a little more complicated. Journals are usually in their own section of the library, and they have their own catalog. In addition to the author and/or title of the article, you need to know the title of the journal and the volume number or date of the issue in which the article appeared. You will then be able to use the journal catalog to find out whether the library has that journal and issue. If so, the catalog will tell you the shelf location. You can then read or copy the article or, if your library permits, check out that issue. If you elect to copy the article, you should check with a librarian about copyright laws.

Sometimes journal articles are available on the computer or on microfilm or microfiche as well as or instead of being available in hard-copy form. If you need to access a journal article in one of these ways, a librarian can help you. You can read the article on the computer screen or on a microfilm or microfiche reader; usually you can also print out a hard copy, though sometimes with articles on the computer this involves a fairly complicated "downloading" process.

When users find that the library doesn't have the journal issue or book they want, either because the library doesn't own it or because it isn't on the shelf, they often give up. This is unfortunate, since most libraries offer helpful services. If the item is checked out, libraries will often call it in or put a hold on it for you. If the item isn't available at that library, you can usually get it through an interlibrary loan service. These options take time, but if you can afford to wait, you can almost always get the item you want within a few weeks.

Searching for Information About a Subject

What is hard about using libraries isn't finding the shelf location of identified material—it's identifying that material in the first place. Often library users don't know the titles or authors of the material they want; all they know is that they want information about a particular subject. In this case they need to use the library's subject indexes to find the citations (author, title, etc.) for material that will be useful to them. The same computer catalog that indexes titles and authors is used to search for books on a particular topic. Using journal indexes is a little more complicated, but since most educational research is reported in journals, the ability to use journal indexes is a skill worth developing. With journal indexes, there are separate indexes for different academic fields. The most comprehensive computerized educational index is ERIC (Educational Resources Information Center), published by the U.S. Government. ERIC indexes journal articles, books, and unpublished documents, such as conference papers, educational association policy briefs, and school district studies. If you prefer to use a print version of the same index, ERIC publishes both CIJE (*Current Index to Journals in Education*) and RIE (*Resources in Education*). CIJE indexes journal articles, and RIE indexes all other ERIC documents.

Journal indexes in other fields are sometimes of interest to educators. Two examples are *Psychological Abstracts* and its computerized version, PsychLit, and *Social*

Sciences Abstracts, which is also available in print and computerized versions, both by the same title.

To find citations for books or journal articles that are relevant to a particular subject, you have to conduct a computer search of the book catalog or of an appropriate journal index. You must use key terms that the computer understands to describe the subject in which you're interested. If you use the wrong terms, you will not be able to find the information you need. In addition to determining the key terms a computer recognizes, you will want to narrow or broaden your search enough to retrieve the relevant information you are searching for. Otherwise, you may get too many or too few "hits." For example, suppose you're interested in finding research on professional organizations for teachers. You set up a search using the term *professional organizations.* But the computer hasn't been programmed to recognize this term so it doesn't find any matching items. You try the term *unions.* The computer has been programmed to recognize this term, but you get so many hits it would take you all day just to weed through them. The computer has found articles on any kind of union— truck drivers' unions, shipbuilders' unions, and so forth. If you use multiple key terms—for example, *teacher* and *union*—you will still get too many hits and most of the articles will not be research reports. In this case, you will need to use the multiple key terms *union, teacher,* and *research* to get just the information you want. You can also have the opposite problem. If you restrict your search too much, you may get too few hits. In this case, you need to broaden, rather than narrow, your search.

When setting up computer searches, you can use a free-text or thesaurus approach to choosing terms. With a free-text approach, you enter any terms that make sense to you. The trouble is, the computer may not have been programmed to recognize terms that make sense to you. If you're having problems with a free-text approach, it's worth the time it takes to learn to work from a thesaurus. A thesaurus is an index that helps you find terms the computer has been programmed to understand. A particular index usually has its own thesaurus, but you can also use the generic thesaurus, the *Library of Congress Subject Heading List.* A thesaurus can help you not only to identify terms the computer will accept but also to control the number of hits you get by identifying broader terms and narrower terms.

In addition to a thesaurus, there are two other sources of help in tailoring a search to get the hits you want. Both depend on your having already found at least one book or article about the subject you're interested in. If it is a book, you can use your library's computerized library catalog to look it up. You'll then need a librarian's help to call up the full record about that book. This record will contain the terms used to index that book. Using these terms in a search should get you to journal articles and other books about the same topic. If it is a journal article, you can check to see whether the article includes a list of terms used to index the article. Some journals typically include this information when they publish an article, and some don't. If you can find these terms, you can use them to set up a search for books or other journal articles.

The information you get from a hit depends on how you set up the search and on what options are available in the catalog or index you are searching. If you are searching a book catalog, you will usually get only the citation—such things as the author(s), title, year of publication, and publisher—and the shelf location. If you want to know whether the book is indeed relevant to your interests, you will have to find it on the shelf and look through it. If you are searching a journal index, such as CIJE, however, you can usually get an abstract as well as the citation. Reading the abstract often tells you if the article is likely to be useful to you.

The good news is that most or all of these services usually cost the user (that's you) nothing but time. When libraries began offering computerized services, they sometimes charged for librarians' help and/or for what are called "on-line" searches. Most academic libraries no longer charge for these services, except, perhaps, for on-line time. If your library does have an on-line charge, you may be able to avoid it for many searches by searching disks that are available at the library rather than doing on-line searches. Library personnel can provide you with information about costs.

Using a Personal Computer

For those of us who have access to a personal computer (PC), there is additional good news: we can now do library searches from our homes or offices. If you would like to do this, you will need to set up your PC for this kind of use. Typically, you need a modem and appropriate software (a computer program) so that your telephone line can be used for communication between your PC and the library's computer. You may have to buy a modem (although most newer PCs come with internal modems already installed), and the use of your telephone line may increase your phone bill, but otherwise, the service is usually free. Talk to a librarian at your university's library about the possibilities of accessing the on-line catalog and the computerized journal indexes.

Most of the time users spend in academic libraries nowadays is spent on computers; it is a real benefit to be able to do this computer work at any time of the day or night from your home or office. And if you are planning a trip to the library to check out only a few items, it's a good idea first to use your PC to determine whether those items are on the shelf. If not, you may be able to use your telephone or PC to have an item called in, to place a hold on an item, or to order an item through interlibrary loan. If so, you will have saved yourself a trip to the library.

■ EXERCISE 3

Ask three professors in your field to name the best research journals in your field. Go to the library at your university and find several back issues of these journals. Read the tables of contents in the journals. Some journals contain a mixture of research reports and other kinds of professional articles. Can you spot the research reports just by looking at the titles? Do any of the research reports seem relevant to your professional interests?   ■

■ EXERCISE 4

At an academic library, locate back issues of the *Review of Educational Research* and the *Review of Research in Education*. Look at the titles of the articles. Do any of them seem relevant to your professional interests?   ■

Reading Research Reports

Research starts with a question the researcher wants to answer. The research itself is the process of collecting empirical data to answer the question. After the data are collected, the researcher analyzes them to determine the answer to the question.

A simple example follows. Suppose a principal wants to know how many children purchase lunch at the school cafeteria. Every day for a week, the principal asks the cashier in the cafeteria to make a mark on a piece of paper each time a child pays the cashier for lunch. At the end of the week, the principal counts all the marks and divides the total by five. The result is 238. So the answer to the question is that for a given week an average of 238 children per day ate lunch in the school cafeteria.

In writing up her report on this research, the principal would say first what the question was, then what she did to get the answer, and finally what the answer was.

Many research reports in the educational literature are written in this format. There is an introductory section that indicates what the research question was; a middle section that describes the research itself—what was done to get an empirical answer to the question; and a final section about the answer that the process provided. In this sense, many research reports are written in a straightforward, predictable way.

What is presented within each of these sections, however, may be fairly complex. In fact, the remainder of this book is about the complexities of each of these stages of research: the question, the process, and the answer. The goal of this book is to help you do two things: to read about each of these stages of research with understanding and to evaluate each stage.

What Question Is the Researcher Trying to Answer and Why?

Research is the process of trying to answer a question empirically. In reading a research report, the first thing we need to know is what the research question was. In very brief research reports, the researcher may do little more than tell us this. In most reports, however, the researcher also explains why this question was asked—why the answer to this question is worth knowing.

What Did the Researcher Do to Try to Answer the Question?

This is often the longest section of a research report. Researchers explain, sometimes in detail, what they did to try to answer the question. This is important because our confidence in the answer the researcher gets largely depends on our confidence in this process. Without fairly complete information about the research process, we cannot be confident about the findings.

Suppose I tell you that I conducted research to answer the question, Do most children like school? Then I tell you that the answer I got is yes. Do you now believe that most children like school? Of course not. Whether you believe my answer depends on whether you think I did a good job of conducting my research: whether you believe that my research process was a valid one for answering this question.

In fact, this term—validity—is a critical one in research. Scientists talk about the validity of research at length and in detail. There are even named kinds of validity, which you will learn about later in this book. For now, you need to know that validity refers to the research process in this way: Was the process a valid one for answering the question that the researcher posed?

To return to the example of whether most children like school, what kinds of things will you want to know to evaluate my process and, ultimately, my answer? You will want to know almost everything there is to know about what my process was. Suppose I tell you that I asked children. Now do you believe my answer? Not necessarily. How I asked them is important—such things as who did the asking, how the question was phrased, and where the children were at the time.

Suppose I tell you that I had teachers ask the children in their classes to raise their hands if they like school. Now do you believe that my answer is valid? Probably not. You realize that children may not give honest answers to such a question in such a situation; they may slant their answers to what they think the teacher wants to hear or what they think will be acceptable to other children.

In evaluating my process, you will also want to know who these children were. Were they elementary-school children, high-school children, "normal" children, gifted children, learning-disabled children? Were they dominant-culture or culturally diverse children? Were they in public or private schools? And so forth.

The section of research reports in which researchers describe what they did to try to answer the research question is often the longest section because readers need to know a great deal about the research process in order to decide whether they believe the research results—or, more realistically, what reservations they have about the research results. In response to my study of whether children like school, you may decide to believe that these kinds of children, when asked in this kind of situation, say they like school, but not to believe that most children really like school.

What Answer Did the Researcher Get?

It may seem that the final section of research reports would, like the first section, be fairly brief. However, sometimes this section is lengthy. Research questions are often complex. The answer is usually not as simple as yes or no. Also, our research processes are never perfect; limitations in the process have to be discussed in terms of how they limit the answer. In this section researchers discuss the conclusions they think are defensible from the data they collected. They discuss reservations they have about the process and the answers it yielded. They discuss under what conditions they think the answers apply. And they often go on to say what they think the answers mean: such things as how these results fit into the bigger picture, what new questions were raised, and what directions future research might take to deal with problems encountered in this research or to check or expand on the findings of this study.

Figure 1.1 depicts the stages of research and the issues that are salient at each stage.

■ EXERCISE 5

Below are abstracts of several articles from educational journals. For each article, decide what the research question was; what the researchers did to try to answer the question (i.e., what the research process was); and what answer was obtained.

a. "Is the Medium the Message? An Experimental Comparison of the Effects of Radio and Television on Imagination" (Greenfield, Farrar, and Beagles-Roos, 1986, p. 201).

This study explored the hypothesis that radio would be more stimulating to the imagination than television. The hypothesis was tested using a within-subjects experimental design in which children at two different age levels (Grades 1–2 vs. 3–4) were exposed to one story in a television format, another in a radio format. Our measure of

FIGURE 1.1   Salient issues at each stage of research.

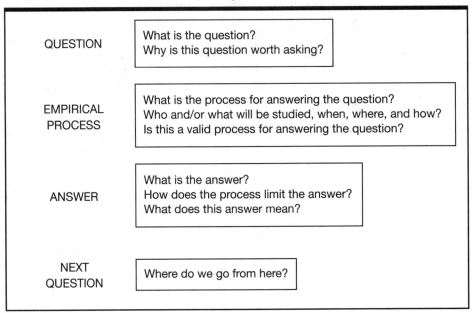

QUESTION	What is the question? Why is this question worth asking?
EMPIRICAL PROCESS	What is the process for answering the question? Who and/or what will be studied, when, where, and how? Is this a valid process for answering the question?
ANSWER	What is the answer? How does the process limit the answer? What does this answer mean?
NEXT QUESTION	Where do we go from here?

imaginative activity was the ability to complete an incomplete story by introducing original new elements that had not been part of the audiovisual or audio stimulus. In accord with the hypothesis, radio presentations led to more imaginative story completions than did television presentations. In addition, there was a carry-over effect such that a radio version at Time 1 led to more-imaginative responses to a televised story at Time 2, while a television story at Time 1 led to less-imaginative responses to a radio story at Time 2. As far as imagination is concerned, our results support Marshall McLuhan's (1964) thesis that "the medium is the message" (p. 23). While we found some specific effects on imaginative activity stemming from story content, all the more general effects are attributable to the medium in which that content is presented.

b. "Effectiveness of Cognitive/Relaxation Therapy and Study-Skills Training in Reducing Self-Reported Anxiety and Improving the Academic Performance of Test-Anxious Students" (Dendato and Diener, 1986, p. 131).

Forty-five test-anxious students were randomly assigned to one of four treatment conditions: (a) relaxation/cognitive therapy, (b) study-skills training, (c) a combination of relaxation/cognitive therapy and study-skills training, or (d) no treatment. Pretreatment and posttreatment measures were collected on self-reported state anxiety and classroom examination performance. The relaxation/cognitive therapy was found to be effective in reducing anxiety but failed to improve classroom test scores. Study-skills training had no significant effect on either measure. The combined therapy both reduced anxiety and improved performance relative to the no-treatment control condition and was significantly more effective than was either treatment alone.

c. "The Extended School Year: Implications for Student Achievement" (Pittman, Cox, and Burchfiel, 1986, p. 211).

Public policy makers have focused some attention upon extending the length of the school year. The current study investigated the following question: How does the number of days of school attended influence the level of student achievement on standardized tests? The achievement scores of students from two different school systems were analyzed. These students had experienced an interrupted school year of approximately 1 month due to severe weather in 1976–77. Yearly comparisons between the achievement scores of 1976–77 and other school years were made within and across groups. The results of the various comparisons suggested that simply increasing the length of the school year would not likely produce marked changes in test score performance.

d. "Developmental Stages and Institutional Structure: The Case of Continuing Education for Women" (Pitman, 1988, p. 139).

This article examines the responses of five women to their educational experience in a continuing education center. Through life-history interviews, the women's developmental stages or transitional statuses are defined and seen as influential in their response to the educational institution.   ■

■ Exercise 6

Locate several issues of the *American Educational Research Journal.* Read the abstracts of several articles that interest you (abstracts appear at the beginning of the article, right after the title). Can you tell from the abstracts what the research question was; what the researcher(s) did to try to answer the question (i.e., what the research process was); and what answer was obtained?   ■

RESEARCH QUESTIONS

Research is often conceptualized as either applied or basic. Applied research has the potential for meeting an immediate, perceived need of some group of practitioners (e.g., teachers, principals, or school counselors). Basic research has the potential for contributing to basic knowledge in some area of scientific interest (e.g., learning, social interaction, or creativity). Although basic knowledge can and often does ultimately lead to applied findings, this is not its immediate goal.

It is difficult to generalize about the sources of applied research questions, because immediate needs can come from anywhere. Many researchers employed by private businesses conduct applied research. For example, a publisher who is considering expanding into a new market will want to do research on the potential for sales and competition in that market. However, especially in a primarily applied field such as education, many researchers funded by federal, state, or local governments or by nonprofit foundations or private universities also do applied research. Practicing educators have immediate needs. How can gifted children be identified? How can reading problems be overcome? How can dropout rates be reduced? How can administration be improved? Practicing educators look to educational research for answers to some of their questions.

It is easier to generalize about the sources of basic research questions. Science and the scientific method offer some criteria, which are discussed below, for generating and evaluating the merit of basic research questions.

■ Exercise 7

Which of the following research questions seem to involve applied research (i.e., to have the potential for providing knowledge that will help meet the immediate needs of practitioners) and which seem to involve basic research (i.e., to have the potential for providing basic knowledge)?

a. Does a group of five-year-olds classify objects in a miscellaneous set on the basis of the form, function, or linguistic properties of each item?

b. Does the Occupational Unfitness Test (OUT) accurately identify job applicants who would perform unsatisfactorily if hired?

c. Does increased student-teaching time result in fewer problems during a teacher's first year of employment?

d. Does the repeated experience of failure that is beyond the individual's control precede clinical symptoms of depression?   ■

The Importance of Theory

Earlier in this chapter the point was made that one of the higher goals of science is the understanding of cause and effect relationships. One of the best tools in pursuing such understanding is theory. Theory is probably a word that you already have in your vocabulary, but it is likely that if you were asked to define theory you would find that you have only a vague notion of what it means.

A theory is a fairly comprehensive, causal explanation. Theory differs from lower-level, noncomprehensive explanations. To say that my child learned not to touch the stove by getting burned is a causal explanation; however, it is not a theory because it is not comprehensive. Reinforcement learning theory is a comprehensive causal explanation. It explains the causes of learning in terms of the consequences of behavior: Organisms learn to do things that have pleasant consequences; they learn not to do things that have neutral or unpleasant consequences. Social learning theory is also a comprehensive causal explanation. It explains the causes of learning in terms of observation and imitation of behavior: Organisms learn to do things by observing and imitating other organisms. These are comprehensive explanations because each applies to many kinds of learning, in many kinds of contexts, by many kinds of organisms.

The word *theory* is usually reserved for comprehensive causal explanations that go beyond what is already widely accepted to be true. Theories are thus, in one sense, merely proposed explanations that must be tested in order to be accepted or rejected. In actual practice, important theories are seldom definitively accepted or rejected. Instead, tests of a theory provide knowledge that is used to revise the theory. The revised theory then undergoes further testing and revision. Scientists often use the term *theory building* to describe their work, reflecting this ongoing process of testing, revision, and retesting. Theory is a useful tool for pursuing causal understanding because it has these two properties: It is comprehensive, and it has the potential for extending knowledge beyond what is already known.

One way to define research (some scientists argue that it is the only way) is to say that research is the empirical part of theory building. Theory comes, in part, from research: Scientists propose theories based on empirical observation. And research is used to test theory: Scientists observe empirical events to see whether they conform to theory.

Theory building typically begins with observation and pattern recognition. In observing events, scientists detect patterns in the events: When *X* happens, *Y* also tends to happen. For example, when an organism is hurt, it tends to avoid the source of discomfort, and when an organism is rewarded, it tends to seek the source of reward. From such observation and pattern recognition, scientists induce causal explanations: for example, that learning is caused by the consequences of behavior.

The word *induce* in the previous sentence is an important one. Philosophers use the term *induction* to describe one kind of reasoning: from the particular to the general. Causal explanation that is based on observation and pattern recognition is inductive. We observe particular events: a child who refuses to go near the stove after she is burned; a puppy who comes when called by the master who gives it a treat. Then we induce the general principle: Learning is caused by the consequences of behavior.

When induction results in a theory, the theory is considered to have been proposed, not proved. Scientists must then test the theory in further observation that is independent of the observations that generated the theory. This is because induction is not foolproof. The observed patterns may or may not reflect the operation of the general principle. Some apparent patterns are simply the result of coincidence.

Consider the following. If a researcher observes many characteristics of a particular group of people, he can almost always find coincidental "patterns" in a few of the characteristics. A researcher who has data on hundreds of physical measurements for a group of people (for example, eyelash length, neck diameter, tooth spacing, hair length, and so forth) will undoubtedly find that a few of these characteristics appear to pattern. In the group being studied, perhaps hair length appears to pattern with tooth spacing; that is, people with longer hair have more widely spaced teeth and vice versa. This would, however, be only a coincidence. If the researcher were to repeat the study on another group of people, hair length and tooth spacing would not appear to pattern, but some other characteristics would, also entirely coincidentally. This is why theories resulting from induction have to be tested on independent bodies of data.

Such tests of theory involve another kind of reasoning, which philosophers call deduction. Induction is reasoning from the particular to the general. Deduction is the opposite: reasoning from the general to the particular. With deduction, we begin with a general principle and deduce particular examples from it. If I begin with the general principle that learning is caused by the consequences of behavior, then I can deduce that my puppy should learn to come when I call her if I give her a treat.

Using deductive reasoning to test theory involves an if-then kind of reasoning: If this general principle is true, then this particular case should be true. If learning is caused by the consequences of behavior, then giving my puppy a treat should teach her to come when I call her. When we use deduction to make predictions about particular events based on theory and the predictions keep coming true, our confidence in the theory increases. When we make predictions deduced from theory and they do not come true, our confidence in the theory decreases.

Induction can be faulty because many events usually must be observed before previously unsuspected patterns can be seen. With so many events, coincidences can and do happen. Deduction does not have this weakness. With deduction, we predict in advance just which patterns we will and will not see. When a researcher makes a prediction in advance and then collects data that confirm the prediction, it is much less likely that the pattern is coincidental. If the researcher in the imaginary example above had predicted in advance that out of all the hundreds of possibilities hair length and tooth spacing would be related, it would be very unlikely that the confirmation of this prediction was a coincidence.

Theory building thus involves two kinds of research: inductive research, from which scientists hope to generate theory; and deductive research, with which scientists test theory. As was noted above, only after many years does research result in acceptance of a theory. Typically, deductive tests do not definitively confirm or disconfirm theory; rather, they suggest ways to modify theory. The modified theory is then subjected to further testing, further revision, and so forth. Over time, some theories come to be generally accepted. Reinforcement learning theory is an example. Most psychologists would now agree that the consequences of behavior are an important cause of learning.

Figure 1.2 depicts the relationship between research and theory building. The figure emphasizes that when research results in the generation of new theory, the relationship between the research and theory is inductive; whereas when research is done to test existing theory, the relationship between the theory and research is deductive. Inductive, theory-generating research results in new theories; deductive, theory-testing research is usually part of an ongoing process of modification and re-testing of existing theories.

■ EXERCISE 8

The following is often used as an example of a reasoning process:

All men are mortal.
Socrates is a man.
Therefore, Socrates is mortal.

If we alter the example as follows, it exemplifies a different kind of reasoning process:

Gasp. . . . Thud.
Oh my gosh, Socrates just died.
I wonder if all men are mortal.

Which of these examples involves inductive reasoning and which involves deductive reasoning?   ■

FIGURE 1.2   The relationship between research and theory.

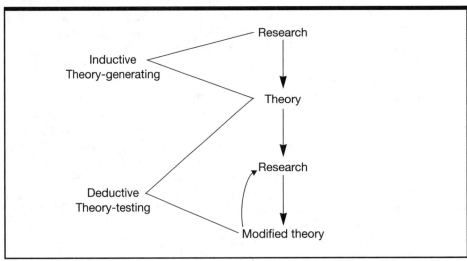

The community of scientists in a given area of knowledge—for example, learning—collectively evaluates the need for theory or the merit of a particular theory in that field by electing whether to do research to generate theory or to test a particular theory. If a substantial proportion of learning researchers elects to do deductive research on reinforcement learning theory, then reinforcement learning theory is considered to be an important theory of learning. An area of knowledge characterized by several important theories that researchers are deductively testing is likely to be a field in which causal understanding is developing at a relatively high rate. On the other hand, an area of knowledge that has few or no theories and in which most researchers are thus forced to work inductively is likely to be a field in which causal understanding is developing at a relatively low rate. Interestingly, applied research in education and the other behavioral sciences often falls into this latter category. We simply do not have many well-developed theories in some areas of great applied interest (for example, creativity and cognitive style).

The notion of theory also offers the scientific community a standard for judging the merit of research. Research that contributes to theory building in an important theoretical area is usually considered to be the best research. There is thus a tradition that deductive research is the highest form of research. This emphasis on deductive research can be misguided. When scientists in a field are fortunate enough to have several promising theories on which to work, deductive research is clearly the best use of resources. However, when a field lacks good theory, it seems obvious that resource allocation should emphasize inductive research to generate good theory rather than deductive research to test poor theory.

■ Exercise 9

Which of the following research topics seem to involve induction and theory generation and which seem to involve deduction and theory testing?

a. Differences between five- and ten-year-olds as to whether they classify objects in a miscellaneous set on the basis of the form, function, or linguistic properties of the items

b. Differences in the life histories of depressed and nondepressed persons

c. Differences in the cooperative behavior of children who have and have not viewed a videotape showing cooperative behavior

d. Observation in classrooms of two groups of teachers: those who have received high ratings from students and those who have received low ratings   ■

QUANTITATIVE AND QUALITATIVE RESEARCH

Another way to classify research involves the qualitative-quantitative distinction. These terms refer to the research process and to the kinds of data in which research results.

Quantitative research has quantifiable results. This means just what it seems to mean. Quantitative research involves numbers and counting. In a single study, quantitative researchers usually focus on a few, well-delineated things. Quantitative research tells us, for example, how many people who were studied have what IQ test scores and how many were men and how many were women.

Qualitative research is more difficult to define, partly because qualitative methods are less standardized than are quantitative methods. Qualitative research does not involve numbers and counting, and it usually has a broader focus than does quantitative research. Typically, it involves studying events in all or most of their complexity, rather than focusing on just a few aspects. Reporting qualitative research results involves describing what was observed, with little if any quantification. Qualitative research can tell us such things as what a typical day is like for an elementary-school principal—what he did, where, and with whom—or what happens in a high-school history class—how the teacher and students spend their time. It is intended to convey the flavor of real-life experiences, of "being there."

A researcher's choice of a qualitative or quantitative approach in a given study should depend on the kind of research question being asked. Some questions lend themselves to quantitative methods; others can be better pursued through qualitative methods. Sometimes a combination of qualitative and quantitative approaches can be used.

It might have occurred to you that qualitative research sounds like a good strategy when the purpose of research is to generate theory, and quantitative research sounds like a good strategy when the purpose of research is to test theory. This tends to be true. Qualitative research, with its broader focus, is often more appropriate when researchers are searching for patterns. Quantitative research is often more appropriate when researchers have narrowed their focus to one or a few patterns that they want to test.

The qualitative-quantitative distinction is so basic that it will inform the rest of this book. The methods used by qualitative and quantitative researchers to answer research questions are very different, and so are the kinds of answers they obtain.

■ EXERCISE 10

Which of the following topics seem to be candidates for qualitative research methods and which seem to be candidates for quantitative research?

a. Child-rearing practices of the Siriono people in Bolivia
b. Heart rates of children before and after 10 minutes of trampoline exercise
c. Percentage of elementary schools offering fine-arts instruction
d. The play content of four- and five-year-olds

LITERATURE REVIEWS

Most research reports begin with two related parts: a description of the question the researcher was trying to answer when he did the research; and an explanation of why this question was chosen—why it is important and worthwhile to pursue. This explanation involves what is usually called a review of the literature.

Students often consider literature reviews to be unimportant. In fact, a good literature review can be the most important part of a research report. It places the research question in the context of scientific thought: what is already known about this issue and what avenues of further investigation look promising to the scientific community.

If the research question is an applied one, with no theoretical claims, the researcher will usually review literature that documents a need for the kind of answer the researcher has tried to find. More often, however, researchers do make theoretical claims; they attempt to link the research being reported on with theory building. Occasionally such links seem tenuous, and it is tempting to conclude that the researcher has "invented" a theoretical rationale after the fact, in order to get his research funded or published.

If you already have a fairly sophisticated understanding of applied needs and of theory in your field of education, you will be in a good position to evaluate for yourself the contribution that a research report makes to knowledge. If you are a novice in your field, you may have difficulty making this kind of judgment until you gain more experience and knowledge.

SUMMARY

The scientific method is one of the means by which people acquire knowledge. The scientific method is distinguished from other ways of knowing by its empiricism, its requirement of intersubjective verifiability, and its emphasis on understanding cause and effect. Science is not the only valid way of knowing, and many questions of interest to educators cannot be answered scientifically. However, science is an important way of knowing in the field of education. Research is the empirical part of science—the process of collecting empirical data to answer a question. Research results influence educational practice in the most basic ways. Educational practitioners thus need to stay informed about research results in their fields.

Most educational research is reported in professional journals, although there are other sources of research reports as well. Articles reviewing research in particular fields are a valuable aid in keeping up with research findings.

The purpose of this book is to help you learn to locate, read, and evaluate research reports in your educational field. Research reports usually contain three sections. The first section specifies what the research question was and why it was investigated. The second section describes the research process—what empirical work the researcher did to try to answer the question. The third section discusses the answer that the researcher obtained.

Before research can be conducted, a research question must be formulated. Research questions can be either applied or basic. Basic research usually contributes to theory building. Most scientists agree that theory building is the most important kind of scientific work. Theory provides comprehensive causal explanations that go beyond already accepted knowledge.

There are two ways in which research is used in theory building. When scientists do not have good theory in an area of interest, they often do research in the hope of generating theory. Induction is reasoning from the particular to the general, so this is an inductive use of research; the scientists hope that their particular empirical work will suggest general theoretical propositions. When promising theory does exist, scientists do research to test the theory. Deduction is reasoning from the general to the particular, so this is a deductive use of research; scientists make predictions from general theoretical propositions about the particular empirical events they study. When research findings conform to theory, it seems likely that the theory is correct.

Research can be qualitative or quantitative. Quantitative research is usually highly focused and always involves some kind of enumeration of real-world events. Qualitative research is usually less focused and involves observation and reporting of real-world events in all their complexity. Qualitative research is often inductive and associated with the generation of theory. Quantitative research is often deductive and associated with the testing of theory.

In the first part of a research report, the researcher usually states the question and reviews the literature—that is, specifies what the research question was and why it was worth studying. If the research was applied, the researcher will usually document the need for an answer to the question. If the research was basic, the researcher will usually describe the role of this particular study in theory building.

SUMMARY EXERCISES

1. Excerpts from several published articles and a book are reprinted below. Decide whether each excerpt is from a research report or from some other kind of professional publication. If the excerpt is from a research report, answer the following questions: Was the research quantitative or qualitative? Was the research basic or applied? If the research was basic, was it inductive, theory-generating research or deductive, theory-testing research?

a.   "Factors Promoting Secure Attachment Relationships Between Employed Mothers and Their Sons" (Benn, 1986, pp. 1224–1225).

It has been consistently shown that mothers of infants judged securely attached are distinguished by their "sensitive responsiveness" and emotional availability, and mothers of infants judged insecure by the anger and rejection underlying maternal actions (Ainsworth, Blehar, Waters, & Wall, 1978). Recent findings (Egeland & Farber, 1984) suggest, however, that underlying maternal affective and personality states may be more accurate predictors for promoting stability in secure attachment patterns than are care-giving characteristics. Several investigators who have begun to look at the inter-relations between discrete aspects of parenting and general assessments of affective personality integration also advocate that such latter measures may provide a richer basis for understanding parent-child interaction and individual differences in child development (Brunquell, Crichten, & Egeland, 1981; Heinecke, 1984; Sameroff, Selfer, & Zax, 1982). . . .

It is proposed that a broad-band construct, such as "maternal integration," that integrates individual differences among working mothers along a host of dimensions of maternal work functioning would provide a more powerful means of relating child attachment outcomes to maternal behavior than would specific, less-organizational type variables. In addition, information regarding how secure attachments are promoted between infants and their employed mothers would be more clearly understood.

The purpose of this study was to assess the relative effect of maternal psychological functioning—reflected in the conceptualization of maternal integration—on the quality of mother-son attachment. . . .

Thirty Caucasian mothers and their firstborn sons aged between 17 and 21 months participated in this study.

b.   "Human Diversity and Pluralism" (Gordon, 1991, p. 99).

In this article, I define and distinguish between diversity and pluralism, suggesting that diversity speaks to the characteristics of persons and pluralism to the multiple criteria persons must meet in a changing society. Differences in learning styles are discussed as an example of challenges facing educators if students are to meet the changed demands for competence in the 21st century.

c.   *Inside High School: The Students' World* (Cusick, 1973, p. v).

This book is my attempt to describe the way a number of students behave in high school and to explain the way their behavior affects themselves, the teachers, administrators, and the entire school organization. It was undertaken with the hope of developing a clearer understanding of the way these students see and act in high school, and subsequently to develop a better understanding of why they do what they do. The information-gathering procedure was based on the assumption that any group of individuals will develop a reasonable way of behaving in their environment, and if one wishes to understand that behavior, he can do so by joining them, submitting himself to the routine, rules, and regulations that structure their world, and recording everything that goes on.

I gathered the descriptions during a six-month period in which I attended a high school daily, associated myself with some students, went to class, ate in the cafeteria, and took part in the informal classroom and corridor activity. After becoming accepted, I even joined in their out-of-school social life for the purpose of comparing what they did in school with what they did out of school.

d. "Predicting Academic Success for American Indian Students" (Dingman, Mroczka, and Brady, 1995, p. 10).

Given the difficulties inherent in assessing children with instruments normed for another culture, the failure of early efforts to devise culture-fair tests, and the lack of predictive validity for noncognitive measures for American Indians, finding a means for predicting academic success for this population remains problematic. This investigation found that one important measure of academic success for [the] American Indian students [in this study], quarters of college enrollment, was a significant covariate of performance of three tests of simultaneous processing (Localization, Form Completion, and Orientation). It is suggested that these, or similar sorts of tests, may be valid predictors of academic potential for the American Indian population. These tests are seldom included in the most widely used standardized intelligence tests.

e. "The Birth Order Factor: Ordinal Position, Social Strata, and Educational Achievement" (Travis and Kohli, 1995).

The relationship between birth order and academic attainment of 817 men and women from a variety of socioeconomic backgrounds in the United States was explored. . . . Although some studies report the absence of a significant birth order effect. . . , other studies have found a direct association. . .and an indirect association between ordinal position and educational attainment.

The two explanations most often offered are (a) the confluence hypothesis and (b) the resource dilution hypothesis. In the first instance, emphasis is on dilution of the intellectual milieu; in the second, on the dilution of such factors as economic resources. . . .

[Our] findings support a resource-dilution hypothesis.

2. Find three reports of research in your field in educational journals. Is the research qualitative or quantitative? Is it basic or applied? (If you think the answer is both, you may be right. Some research is both basic and applied.) If the research is basic, is it inductive, theory-generating research or deductive, theory-testing research? (If you are a beginning student and do not yet have a good understanding of theory in your field, you may find it difficult to answer the last question.)

3. Think of three research questions to which you would like to know the answer. Conduct a search for research reports that might answer these questions.

SUGGESTED READINGS

Gage, N. (1978). *The Scientific Basis of the Art of Teaching.* New York: Teachers College Press.

Travers, R. (1983). *How Research Has Changed American Schools.* Kalamazoo, MI: Mythos.

Part II
Quantitative Research

Chapter 1 introduced you to the research process, including how researchers choose their topics. Most of the remainder of this book is about how researchers pursue the topics they have chosen: how they collect and analyze empirical information bearing on the questions they have asked.

There are basic differences between qualitative and quantitative research methods in how information is collected and analyzed. These differences are so basic that they will inform the rest of this book. We will deal first with quantitative and then with qualitative research. The special characteristics of qualitative research will come into focus more clearly when you can compare it with quantitative research. To do quantitative research, researchers must make four kinds of decisions: what information is required, how it should be collected, on whom or what it should be collected, and how it should be analyzed. Part II consists of seven chapters that take up these issues. Chapters 2 and 3 concern the information researchers collect. Chapter 4 concerns how it is collected. Chapter 5 concerns who or what is studied. Chapters 6, 7, and 8 concern how the information is analyzed.

Each of these aspects of research has implications for the validity of the answer that the researcher obtains to the question being asked. In order to accept the answer the researcher proposes, we want to know that the researcher collected appropriate information, in an appropriate way, and on appropriate people or things to answer the question. Then we want to know that the researcher analyzed the results appropriately. Each of the chapters will help you to understand and evaluate these aspects of the research process.

SUGGESTED READINGS

Babbie, E. (1992). *The Practice of Social Research*. Belmont, CA: Wadsworth.

Gall, M., Borg, W., and Gall, J. (1996). *Educational Research: An Introduction*. White Plains, NY: Longman.

Gay, L. (1996). *Educational Research: Competencies for Analysis and Application*. Englewood Cliffs, NJ: Prentice-Hall.

Kerlinger, F. (1986). *Foundations of Behavioral Research*. New York: Holt, Rinehart and Winston.

Pedhazur, E., and Schmelkin, L. (1991). *Measurement, Design, and Analysis: An Integrated Approach*. Hillsdale, NJ: Erlbaum.

2

Variables and Hypotheses

In chapter 1, we pointed out that quantitative research questions focus on things that can be enumerated. These "things" are called *variables*. Variables constitute the focus of quantitative research; variables are what quantitative researchers ask questions about. In order to read quantitative research with understanding, you need to know what a variable is.

VARIABLES AND CONSTANTS

A variable, conveniently enough, is something that varies, that has more than one value. People's weight is a variable; individuals have such values of this variable as 92 pounds, 133 pounds, and 178 pounds. IQ test score is a variable; people have such values of this variable as 93, 101, and 118. Whether people sleep with their socks on is a variable, having the values yes and no.

The opposite of a variable is a *constant*. A constant is something that doesn't vary, that doesn't have more than one value. The number of seconds in a minute is a constant; it always has the value 60. The number of days in a week is also a constant; it always has the value 7. An important thing to realize, however, is that in research many things can be either variables or constants, depending on the context. Age, for example, is usually a variable; but in a study of day-old infants, age is a constant. Similarly, grade in school is a variable when a researcher studies all the children in a middle school, but grade in school is a constant when a researcher studies only seventh-graders. Constants and variables represent characteristics of the people or things a researcher studies; sometimes these characteristics are constant, and sometimes they vary.

Categorical and Continuous Variables

An important thing to understand about variables and constants is that their values do not have to be expressed as numbers. In fact, in educational research many variables do not have numerical values. Gender is a frequently studied variable, having the values male and female. Ethnicity is a variable that has such values as Anglo, Hispanic, and American Indian, or perhaps White and Black. Depending on their purposes, researchers define variables and their values in different ways. Counseling method is a variable, having such values as directive and nondirective.

Variables that have numerical values are called *continuous variables,* because their values are on a numerical continuum; variables that have named values are called *categorical variables,* because their values represent non-overlapping categories. Weight is measured on a continuum, from zero pounds up. Male and female, on the other hand, are non-overlapping categories.

Some researchers use other names for the types of variables we have just described. Categorical variables are sometimes called *nominal* or *discrete variables.* Continuous variables include what are also referred to as *interval* and *ratio variables.* In addition, there are what are called *ordinal* or *semicontinuous variables.* Semicontinuous variables have numerical values, but the numbers represent order or rating or rank rather than quantity. If you were asked to rate this book on a scale from one (terrible) to five (terrific), your response would be a semicontinuous value.

When you read research reports, it usually will be fairly easy to figure out whether a variable is categorical, semicontinuous, or continuous. But researchers sometimes treat potentially continuous variables in a categorical way. This can be confusing! The variable age, for example, usually has values on a numerical continuum—perhaps from 20 to 70, depending on the ages of the youngest and oldest people in the study. However, a researcher may decide to treat age as a categorical variable by labeling people in the study as young, middle-aged, or elderly. If you keep in mind that this may happen, it is usually not too difficult to figure out what's going on.

The fact that quantitative research involves numbers is due to the fact that quantitative research focuses on variables. It is the values of variables that are enumerated. Even non-numerical values can be counted: For example, a researcher can report how many of her subjects were women and how many were men, or how many received the treatment and how many did not.

■ Exercise 1

Which of the following can be variables and which are always constants?

a. Number of days in a month
b. Number of months in a year
c. Number of days in a year
d. Test score
e. Leadership style
f. Native language
g. Heart rate
h. Hair color
i. Number of cents per dollar
j. Number of pesos per dollar
k. Gender of National Football League players   ■

■ Exercise 2

Which of the following variables are probably categorical and which are continuous or semicontinuous? What might be some of the values of the categorical variables? How might a researcher make the continuous variables categorical?

a. Test score
b. Leadership style
c. Native language

d.   Heart rate

e.   Performance rating (1–10)

f.   Program participation

g.   Age

h.   Years in program (one or two)   ■

Subjects and Cases

Quantitative researchers collect empirical data on the values of variables. This is another way of saying that they ascertain the values of variables for particular people or things. People whom a researcher studies are usually called subjects; things are usually called cases. A researcher studying children's test scores would refer to the test scores of her subjects; a researcher studying dropout rates at various schools would refer to the dropout rates for his cases.

In this book the following format will be used to represent the results of quantitative research:

Subject or Case	Variable Value
a	1
b	2
c	3
d	4

The two examples given above can be formatted as follows:

Subject	Test Score	Case	Dropout Rate
Alice	78	Lincoln High	12%
Joe	85	Central High	36%
Maria	92	Beltway High	4%
Leroy	79	Freedom High	17%

Of course, real research usually involves more than four subjects or cases; this is an abbreviated format.

Educational research involves both variables and constants, but while researchers often use the term *variable* when referring to their research, they rarely use the term *constant.* Constants in research are usually referred to as characteristics of the research subjects or cases. For example, a researcher interested in the test scores of a group of fifth-graders would refer to test score as a variable in his study, but he would not refer to grade in school as a constant in his study; rather, he would simply describe his subjects as fifth-graders.

Figure 2.1 exemplifies the focus of quantitative research on subjects or cases and variables.

■ EXERCISE 3

The following examples were taken from published research. What variables did the researchers study? Can you tell what the values of the variables were? Who were the subjects of the studies (i.e., what were their characteristics)?

FIGURE 2.1   The focus of quantitative research: characteristics and variable values of subjects or cases.

```
                     SUBJECTS OR CASES

                  Characteristics (Constants)
            ┌──────────────────────────────────┐
            │              Examples             │
            │     Profession:  teacher          │
            │     Level taught: high school     │
            │     Type of school:  inner city   │
            └──────────────────────────────────┘


                   Variables and Values
            ┌──────────────────────────────────┐
            │              Examples             │
            │     Gender:  female or male       │
            │     Years taught: 1–10            │
            │     Subject taught: required or elective │
            │     Score on burnout scale: 1–25  │
            └──────────────────────────────────┘
```

a. Single fathers were surveyed about their experiences as homemakers (Risman, 1986).

b. Subjects were physically active men and women (Heyward, Johannes-Ellis, and Romer, 1986).

c. Female and male heterosexual dating individuals (86% White, 9.7% Black, 4.3% other ethnicities) reported on power balances or imbalances in their romantic relationships (Felmlee, 1994).

d. Twenty-one pairs of third-grade children and their mothers were observed performing a series of solvable and unsolvable tasks (Hokoda and Fincham, 1995).

e. College students' ratings of instructors were examined in required and elective courses (Cranton and Smith, 1986).

f. White adolescents living in two-parent families provided information on parental employment patterns, school grades, and family characteristics (Bogenschneider and Steinberg, 1994).   ■

RELATIONAL AND NONRELATIONAL QUESTIONS

There are two basic kinds of quantitative research questions: relational and nonrelational. Nonrelational questions simply ask for a report on the state of some variable. Examples of nonrelational questions follow:

■ What methods of counseling are employed at the University of New Mexico Student Health Center?

■ What is the average Graduate Record Examination (GRE) score of 1997 college graduates?

■ What percentage of students drops out before high-school graduation?

Do you see that each of these questions asks for a report on the state of some variable? The first question asks what the values of the variable *counseling method* are at a particular counseling center. The second question asks about the average value of the variable *GRE score* for a certain group of students. The third asks what proportion of students has the value dropout, as opposed to nondropout, of the variable *dropout status*.

Relational questions ask about the relationship between two (or more) variables. Examples of relational questions follow:

- Is directive counseling more successful than nondirective?
- Do people who had higher GRE scores earn more money?
- Does a higher percentage of culturally diverse than of Anglo children drop out of high school?

Do you see that each of these questions asks about the relationship between two variables? In the first question, the variables are method of counseling and success of counseling. In the second question, the variables are GRE score and income. In the third question, the variables are ethnicity and dropout status.

In the educational literature, relational research reports greatly outnumber nonrelational ones. In fact, in some fields nonrelational reports are a rarity. This is because relational research, as we will see, has the potential for yielding understanding of cause and effect. As was pointed out in chapter 1, understanding cause and effect is one of the higher goals of science. When researchers can profitably ask relational research questions, they prefer to do so.

When you have identified the research question in a quantitative research report, ask yourself whether the question involves at least two variables and whether there is the suggestion of a relationship, often causal, between these variables. If so, the research is relational. You must, however, exercise some caution in applying this rule. It is possible for nonrelational research to involve two or more variables—for example, what are the heights and weights of certain people? Unless it is clear that the researcher will be trying to relate the two variables, these are simply two separate nonrelational questions in one study.

■ Exercise 4

Which of the following research questions are relational and which are nonrelational?

a. What is the native language of each child in Mr. Montoya's kindergarten class?
b. Does weight affect the running speed of NFL quarterbacks?
c. Are successful school principals more democratic in their leadership styles than unsuccessful principals?
d. What are the IQ test scores of children in this study?
e. Is physical punishment used more often in larger families?
f. Do blondes have more fun?
g. For each Palo Alto public-school teacher, what is the highest degree held and how many years of teaching experience does the teacher have?
h. Are lawyers who scored higher on board exams rated as better lawyers on a scale from 1 to 10?

i. What was the average exchange rate in December for pesos and dollars?

j. Is there a relationship between alcohol consumption and clarity of speech?   ■

Relational researchers are interested in finding out whether there is a relationship between two or more variables. We say that there is a relationship between two variables when subjects or cases who have the same or similar values of one of the variables tend also to have the same or similar values of the other variable. This criterion is met in the following example.

Subject	Method of Counseling	Outcome of Counseling
a	Directive	Successful
b	Directive	Successful
c	Nondirective	Unsuccessful
d	Nondirective	Unsuccessful

With results like those above (on a larger group of people, of course), a researcher would be able to conclude that there is a relationship between the two variables *method of counseling* and *outcome of counseling*, because people who have the same value of the method variable also have the same value of the outcome variable.

There is also a relationship between the variables in the following example.

Subject	Cigarette Smoker	Heart Beats per Minute
a	No	70
b	No	75
c	Yes	90
d	Yes	95

People who do not smoke have similar (lower) heart rates, while people who smoke have similar (higher) heart rates.

The example below, however, shows no relationship between the variables, because subjects who have the same value of the first variable do not tend also to have the same or similar values of the second variable.

Subject	Hair Color	Having Fun
a	Blonde	Yes
b	Blonde	No
c	Brunette	Yes
d	Brunette	No

Some blondes have fun, and some don't; some brunettes have fun, and some don't. Blondes and brunettes are equally likely to have or not have fun. There is thus no relationship between hair color and having fun.

One of the interesting things about relational research is that relationships can be demonstrated only between two variables; it is impossible to demonstrate a relationship between two constants or between one variable and one constant. The following examples demonstrate why.

Imagine that you read this headline in your daily newspaper: "Marijuana Use Linked to Heroin Addiction." The article under the headline reports that a researcher has interviewed 100 heroin addicts and found that all of them used marijuana before becoming addicted to heroin. Many people would be convinced by such a report. However, the headline might just as well have said, "Attending School Linked to Heroin Addiction." After all, each of the 100 heroin addicts interviewed probably would also have reported that he or she attended school before becoming addicted to heroin, if the researcher had asked that question. In fact, with this research technique, we could easily "link" any number of things to heroin addiction: drinking milk, having a mother, or wearing sneakers, for example.

The problem is that the research, as conducted, attempts to link two constants. All the people interviewed had used marijuana and all were heroin addicts, so these were constants, not variables. Obviously, it is impossible to demonstrate a relationship between two constants.

It is also impossible to demonstrate a relationship between a variable and a constant. Suppose the researcher had interviewed 100 heroin addicts and found that 50 of them had used marijuana and 50 hadn't. The researcher would have one constant, heroin addiction, and one variable, marijuana use. Here is an abbreviated look at the results of this research.

Subject	Marijuana Use	Heroin Addiction
a	No	Yes
b	No	Yes
c	Yes	Yes
d	Yes	Yes

Would the researcher be able to claim a relationship between the two? Of course not; heroin addiction was present whether marijuana use was present or absent.

Relationships can be demonstrated only between two variables. If the researcher had interviewed 50 heroin addicts and 50 nonaddicts and found that all or most of the addicts had used marijuana while none or few of the nonaddicts had used marijuana, then there would be a relationship between the two variables. This situation can be conceptualized as follows.

Subject	Marijuana Use	Heroin Addiction
a	No	No
b	No	No
c	Yes	Yes
d	Yes	Yes

Now people who share the same value of the marijuana-use variable also share the same value of the heroin-addiction variable.

■ EXERCISE 5

In which of the examples below is there a relationship between the two variables (that is, in which of the examples do subjects or cases having the same or similar values of the first variable also have the same or similar values of the second variable)?

	Subject	Gender	Self-Disclosing
a.	a	Female	Yes
	b	Female	Yes
	c	Male	No
	d	Male	No

b.

Subject	Months in Program	Health Behavior
a	1	Poor
b	2	Good
c	8	Good
d	9	Poor

c.

Subject	In Special Education	Self-Esteem
a	Yes	Low
b	Yes	Low
c	No	High
d	No	High

d.

Subject	Anxiety Level	Test Score
a	4	99
b	6	91
c	8	86
d	10	78

e.

Subject	Instructional Program	Test Score
a	Old	45
b	Old	64
c	New	47
d	New	63

Independent and Dependent Variables

Often relational research is an attempt to demonstrate not just a relationship but a causal relationship. The existence of a relationship between the method of counseling employed and the outcome of counseling suggests that the method of counseling employed is one of the causes of the outcome of counseling. The existence of a relationship between cigarette smoking and heart rate suggests that smoking is one of the causes of higher heart rates. Researchers use special terms to distinguish between variables that are thought to be causes and those that are thought to be effects. Causal variables are called *independent variables* and effect variables are called *dependent variables*.

This makes sense if you think about it. Effects depend on causes; the values of effect variables depend on the values of causal variables. If counseling method were the total cause of counseling outcome (that is, if all directive counseling were successful and all nondirective counseling were unsuccessful), then the value of the counseling outcome variable for any individual would depend on the value of the counseling method variable for that individual; if we knew that someone had received directive counseling, we would also know without even checking that his counseling had been successful. In the real world, of course, one variable is rarely the total cause of another. Counseling outcome has many causes; method of counseling is just one of them.

It is important for you to realize that what is a dependent variable in one study may be an independent variable in another. One researcher may investigate the effects of marijuana use on heroin addiction, while another investigates the effects of heroin addiction on criminal activity.

Cause Versus Association

An important caution is required here. Not all relational research is about causal relationships. There are noncausal relationships, as well as relationships in which cause is in doubt; the term *association* or *correlation* is often used to refer to such relationships. Careful researchers distinguish between true cause and simple association or correlation. Consider the following example.

Imagine that a researcher (for reasons about which we will not inquire) has demonstrated the following relationship between two variables.

Case	Ice Cream Sales	Deaths by Drowning
October	Low	Few
November	Low	Few
December	Low	Few
January	Low	Few
February	Low	Few
March	Low	Few
April	Moderate	Some
May	Moderate	Some
June	Moderate	Some
July	High	Many
August	High	Many
September	High	Many

Clearly, in the months when ice cream sales were low, deaths by drowning were few; and as ice cream sales increased, so did deaths by drowning. Does this mean that there is a causal relationship between drowning deaths and ice cream sales? How would such a relationship work? Do ice cream sale levels affect drowning incidents? Perhaps people eat too much ice cream, go swimming, get cramps, and drown. Or do drowning death rates affect ice cream sales? Perhaps people assuage their grief over the drowning deaths of friends and relatives by eating ice cream.

Obviously, neither of these explanations is very likely. What is likely is that the relationship between the variables is not causal but simply associational. In this case, the association is due to the fact that both variables under consideration are in fact caused by the same third variable: weather. Ice cream sales are causally related to weather: As temperatures increase, so do ice cream sales. Drowning deaths are also causally related to weather: As temperatures increase, more people swim, and therefore more people drown. However, ice cream sales and drowning deaths are not causally related to one another.

Distinguishing between cause and association can be a serious problem in research. Often our research methods can tell us only that variables are associated; they cannot tell us whether the relationship is causal. Researchers are sometimes tempted to infer cause when only association has been established. It is not at all uncommon, for example, for a researcher to use the terms independent and dependent variables, which imply cause and effect, when the researcher knows that the relationship is merely correlational. It is up to you to be wary of such inferences. In chapter 4 you will learn about the techniques that are available to researchers for distinguishing true cause from simple association and how to evaluate their use.

Proxy Variables

The use of proxy variables is a special case of associational research. Many researchers have demonstrated a relationship between the "independent" variable, household composition, and the "dependent" variable, school performance. Overall, children from single-parent households do not do as well in school as children from two-parent households. Clearly, however, this is not a causal relationship. There is nothing inherent in single-parent households that makes a child do poorly in school; some children from single-parent households do well in school.

Household composition is a proxy variable; it is related to, and thus in a rough way can stand in for, the true causal variables. We assume that the true causal variables involve extremely complex configurations of events in a child's life—for example, dysfunctional family patterns that contributed to the parents' divorce and persist after the parents' divorce; or economic stresses that contribute to the single parent's being less physically and/or emotionally available to the child.

Proxy variables can be useful when true causal variables are not well understood or are difficult to measure. Even though household composition does not affect school performance directly, it is associated with school performance. Information about a child's household composition can thus be used to help understand the child's school performance. If a child's school performance begins deteriorating, understanding the cause of the deterioration will be important to the child's teacher in deciding how best to help the child. If the teacher learns that the child's parents have recently been divorced, the teacher will probably assume that emotional, rather than cognitive or physical, factors are contributing to the child's difficulties in school. In seeking help for the child, the teacher will then send the child to the school counselor, not to the special-education teacher or nurse.

Although proxy variables can be useful, there is danger in considering them to be true causes. Researchers do not always identify proxy variables; you will want to be alert to the possibility of their use and avoid making assumptions about cause.

Predictor and Criterion Variables

Some educational research is explicitly designed to provide information about non-causal associations between variables. College entrance examinations and grade-point averages are a good example. Research has demonstrated an association between people's scores on certain tests and their grade-point averages in college: People who do well on the tests tend to get better grades, and people who do poorly on the tests tend to get poorer grades. College admissions officers sometimes deny admission to people with low test scores on the grounds that such people are not likely to graduate. However, no one believes that the test scores themselves actually cause grade-point averages. The test is a proxy for the truly causal variables.

When research is done as a basis for making such predictions, researchers often use special terms for their variables. What would usually be termed independent variables are instead labeled *predictor variables,* and what would usually be termed dependent variables are instead labeled *criterion variables*. When researchers use these terms they are explicitly saying that any relationship between the variables is thought to be not causal but simply associational. College entrance tests are predictor variables and grade-point average is a criterion variable.

It is conventional to use X as a symbol for an independent/predictor variable and Y as a symbol for a dependent/criterion variable. Figure 2.2 depicts the types of quantitative research questions and answers.

■ Exercise 6

For this problem, use the relational research questions (*b, c, e, f, h,* and *j*) from Exercise 4. For each question, identify the independent and dependent (causal) or predictor and criterion (noncausal) variables. Do any of the independent variables seem to be proxy variables rather than true causes? ■

Hypotheses

Relational research questions are usually stated as hypotheses. A hypothesis is a prediction about the relationship between two or more variables. The following are examples of hypotheses.

- There will be a difference in the outcomes of directive and nondirective counseling.
- People with higher GRE scores will have higher incomes.
- There will be no difference in the dropout rates of culturally diverse and Anglo children.

Researchers restate their relational research questions as hypotheses because hypotheses can be subjected to empirical test. We cannot empirically answer a question. We can, however, change the question to a prediction and then find out whether or not the prediction is empirically confirmed.

■ Exercise 7

For this problem, again use the relational research questions (*b, c, e, f, h,* and *j*) from Exercise 4. State each question as a hypothesis—that is, change each question into a statement that makes a prediction about the relationship between the variables. ■

Interaction Hypotheses

So far we have dealt with single variables or with relationships between only two variables. However, single studies often involve relationships between more than two variables—almost always one dependent variable and two or more independent variables. This is because researchers are ultimately interested in understanding cause and effect, and most effects have more than one cause. Not only that, but causes sometimes have different effects when they combine with other causes from when they operate alone.

FIGURE 2.2   Types of quantitative research questions and answers.

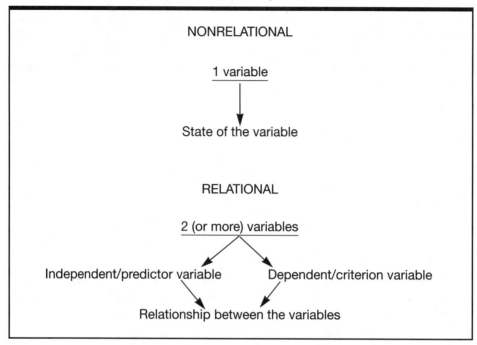

Consider the following example. Suppose that you were stuck in a traffic jam but were not in a hurry. You would probably not mind too much. But if you were stuck in a traffic jam when you were on your way to an important appointment, you might get angry. Just being stuck in a traffic jam wouldn't make you angry, and just being on your way to an important appointment wouldn't make you angry; it's the two together that would make you angry.

When researchers are interested in the ways that causes work together, they collect data on all variables of interest for the same subjects. They can then study the combined effects of the independent variables on the dependent variable (usually called *interaction effects*), as well as the effect of each of the independent variables alone on the dependent variable (usually called *main effects*).

Many educational researchers are interested in understanding the causes of test performance. One of the things that is known to affect test performance is test anxiety. How would you guess this relationship works? Most people would probably guess that anxiety has a negative effect on performance—that people who are more test anxious get lower test scores than do people who are less test anxious. If this was your guess, you are only partly right. Test anxiety doesn't operate in a vacuum; many other variables also affect test performance, and some of them interact with anxiety in interesting ways.

One of the variables that is known to interact with test anxiety is test difficulty. On difficult tests, anxiety does have the effect that most people would predict: It lowers performance. But on easy tests anxiety has the opposite effect: It improves performance.

The best explanation that researchers presently have for this is that a little anxiety is a good thing, because it increases task attention. When low-anxious people see that a test is easy, they get even less anxious and don't attend to the task as well as they could. On the other hand, a lot of anxiety is a bad thing because it decreases task attention. When high-anxious people see that a test is hard, they get even more anxious—in fact, so anxious that the anxiety absorbs most of their attention.

Order of Interaction Effects

More than two independent variables may be studied at the same time. When this happens, there are various levels of possible interaction effects. For example, with three independent variables, there are three possible main effects and the following possible interaction effects: those between all combinations of two independent variables (called *first-order interactions*) and that between all three independent variables (called a *second-order interaction*).

A researcher might, for example, study the relationship between the independent variables *test anxiety*, *actual test difficulty*, and *perceived test difficulty* and the dependent variable *test score*. He would look at three main effects—for test anxiety, actual test difficulty, and perceived test difficulty; three first-order interaction effects—for test anxiety and actual test difficulty, test anxiety and perceived test difficulty, and actual test difficulty and perceived test difficulty; and the second-order interaction between test anxiety, actual test difficulty, and perceived test difficulty.

It can be very difficult for beginning students to figure out what is happening when more than two variables are studied at one time. Sometimes researchers treat each independent variable separately, analyzing its relationship with the dependent variable alone.

In this case the research simply involves a number of separate hypotheses, one for each independent variable with the dependent variable—for example, test anxiety will affect test score, and test difficulty will affect test score. More often, though, researchers also test hypotheses about the combined effects of the multiple independent variables on the dependent variable—in this example, that test anxiety and test difficulty will interact to affect test score.

To make matters more complicated, researchers may test hypotheses about several different dependent variables in one study, and these dependent variables may be analyzed with the same or different independent variable(s). In a single report, a researcher might discuss all of the following hypotheses.

- Main effect of test anxiety on attention
- Main effect of test difficulty on attention
- Interaction effect of test anxiety and test difficulty on attention
- Main effect of test anxiety on test score
- Main effect of test difficulty on test score
- Interaction effect of test anxiety and test difficulty on test score

Occasionally you will encounter research in which all the variables in an analysis are continuous. In this case, researchers combine the independent/predictor variables in order to study their combined relationship with the dependent/criterion variable, but they usually do not use the terms main effects and interaction effects; instead they do something called multiple-regression analysis. We'll discuss this more fully in chapter 7. The thing to keep in mind when you are trying to identify the hypotheses in a research report is that what can seem to be a bewildering variety of variables usually can be boiled down to either main-effect or interaction hypotheses, each almost always having one and only one dependent variable.

Figure 2.3 summarizes the information on quantitative research questions and answers that we have presented in this chapter. In the figure, IV stands for independent variable, and DV stands for dependent variable.

■ EXERCISE 8

Each of the following sets of variables contains one dependent variable and multiple independent variables. Indicate the main and interaction effects that could be studied. For each interaction effect, indicate whether it is a first- or second-order interaction.

a.   Student achievement, student ethnicity, teacher ethnicity
b.   Type of reinforcement, learning, strength of reinforcement
c.   Age, highest degree obtained, years of experience, teaching skill   ■

SUMMARY

Quantitative researchers answer research questions by ascertaining the values of variables for particular subjects or cases. Variables can be either categorical or continuous. Categorical variables have named values; continuous variables have numerical values.

Although nonrelational research questions occasionally appear in the research literature, most research reports involve relational research. This is because relational research has the potential for demonstrating cause and effect. Not all relationships are causal, however. Variables labeled as independent may be merely proxies for the truly causal variables. When there is only an association or correlation between variables—that is, when a documented relationship is not causal—knowledge of the relationship can still be worthwhile, however. Predictor variables can permit us to make useful predictions about criterion variables.

Researchers usually phrase their relational research questions as hypotheses. A hypothesis is a prediction about the relationship between variables. Researchers formulate their relational research questions as hypotheses because of the requirements of proof. We cannot prove the answer to a question; we can, however, empirically test predictions.

Relational research questions usually involve only one dependent variable but often have more than one independent variable. This is because most effects have more than one cause, and causes often operate differently in the company of other causes. When there is more than one independent variable, researchers often analyze both main and interaction effects. A main effect involves the relationship between one independent variable and the dependent variable. An interaction effect involves the combined effects of two or more independent variables on a dependent variable.

SUMMARY EXERCISES

1.   Several abstracts of articles from research journals follow. For each, identify the variables and subject characteristics (constants). Is each variable categorical or

FIGURE 2.3 Summary of the types of quantitative research questions and answers (IV = independent variable; DV = dependent variable).

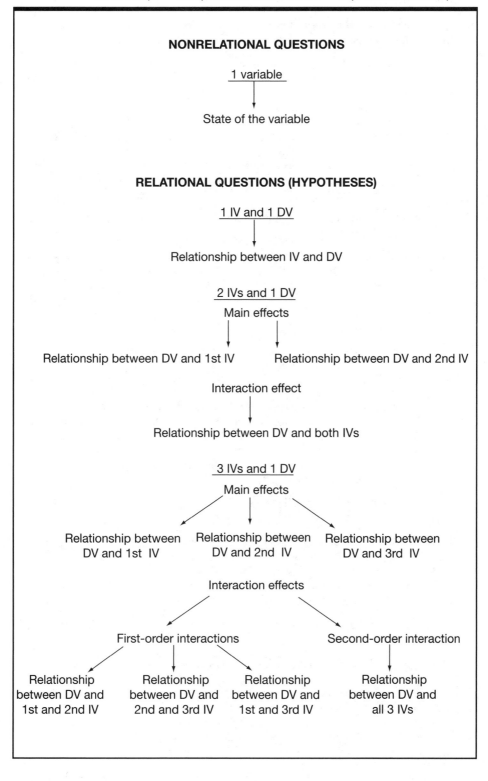

continuous? Is the research relational or nonrelational? If it is relational, identify the combinations of independent and dependent variables that were analyzed, including interaction effects if any.

a. "The Effects of a Self-Monitoring Process on College Students' Learning in an Introductory Statistics Course" (Lan, Bradley, and Parr, 1993, p. 26).

Sixty-nine graduate students enrolled in a statistics class participated in this study, which investigated the effects of self-monitoring on learning and attitudes toward learning. With protocols designed for this study, subjects in a self-monitoring condition recorded frequency and intensity of their learning activities and rated self-efficacy of solving statistical problems. Subjects in an instructor-monitoring condition evaluated the instruction provided in the class. Subjects in a control condition took the course without any research activity.

Scores obtained from class examinations and attitude inventories were the dependent variables. As predicted, the self-monitoring group performed better than did the instructor-monitoring and control groups. No attitude difference was found.

b. "Formal Operations and Academic Achievement" (Mwamwenda, 1993, p. 99).

Although Piaget's theory of cognitive development has been extensively researched cross culturally, not many studies have addressed the question of how it is related to university students' academic performance. The purpose of the present study was to examine the relationship between formal operations and academic achievement among Canadian university students. The results show a statistically significant relationship between cognitive development and academic achievement; students who had fully attained formal operations performed better than those who had not.

c. "The Relationship between Chicano Children's Achievement and Their Teachers' Ethnicity" (Vierra, 1984, p. 285).

Educators are often encouraged to provide minority teachers for minority students; yet empirical evidence about the academic effects of such a practice is limited. This study compares the reading achievement of Chicano students with Anglo teachers and Chicano students with Hispanic teachers. Subjects were 2,129 third- and fourth-graders in Title I schools in a large, urban, southwestern school district. An analysis of covariance, controlling for pretest scores, shows no difference in posttest scores between the two groups of children at either grade level.

d. "Snacking Patterns and Nutrient Density of Snacks Consumed by Southern Girls" (McCoy et al., 1986, p. 61).

We obtained information on the . . . nutrient contributions that snacks made to the total diet of 1,224 adolescent girls living in eight southern states. . . . [S]nacks contributed 52%, 43%, and 39% of the respective Recommended Dietary Allowance (RDA) for riboflavin, vitamin C, and thiamin and notable amounts of other vitamins, minerals, proteins, carbohydrates, and fats.

e. "Differential Effects of Sex and Status on Evaluation of Coaching Ability" (Parkhouse and Williams, 1986, p. 53).

The present study tested whether sex bias favoring males exists in the evaluation of basketball coaching ability for male and female coaches varying in professional status (defined by won/loss records and coaching honors). Subjects were male ($n = 80$) and female ($n = 80$) high school basketball athletes. Subjects evaluated written coaching philosophy statements from a hypothetical male and female coach. . . . The coaches were evaluated with semantic differential scales which assessed knowledge of coaching, ability to motivate, player's desire to play for, and predicted future success. . . . A sex of athlete by sex of coach interaction effect on the four . . . dependent variables indicated strong sex bias favoring males. Overall, male and female subjects rated the male coach the same and always higher than the female coach while male subjects rated the female coach even lower than did female subjects.

f. "The Effects of Gifted and Talented Programs on Academic Self-Concept: The Big Fish Strikes Again" (Marsh et al., 1995, p. 285).

Participation in gifted and talented (G & T) programs is predicted to have negative effects on academic—but not nonacademic—self-concept on the basis of social comparison theory and Marsh's big-fish-little-pond effect (BFLPE). In two studies, students in G & T programs experienced systematic declines in three components of academic self-concept (Reading, Math, School) over time and in relation to matched comparison students in regular mixed ability classrooms, but not in four components of nonacademic self-concept (Physical Appearance, Peer Relations, Parent Regulations). In both studies, these results were consistent over gender, age, and initial ability level. Selection criteria, program strategies, and advice to parents are proposed to counteract this BFLPE and to maximize the benefits associated with G & T programs.

2. Locate at least three quantitative research reports in your field. For each report, identify the variables and constants. Is each variable categorical or continuous? Is the research relational or nonrelational? If it is relational, identify the combinations of independent and dependent variables that were studied, including interaction effects.

3. For the research questions you made up for Summary Exercise 3 in chapter 1, identify the variables and constants. Is each research question relational or nonrelational? If relational, identify the combinations of independent and dependent variables.

3

Operational Definitions and Measurement Validity

In chapter 1 we introduced the concept of research validity—that is, whether the research process is a valid one for answering the question the researcher posed. If the process is valid, then the answer should be valid. Researchers distinguish two basic kinds of validity—internal and external. *Internal validity* refers to whether the research process yields a result that is valid in the research context—that is, whether the answer to the research question is valid for the people on whom the research was done, at the time the research was done, in the place the research was done. *External validity* refers to whether the answer to the research question is valid in a larger context—for other people, at other times, in other places. Internal validity has two components: *measurement validity,* which is what the rest of this chapter is about; and the *validity of causal argument,* which we will take up in chapter 4. External validity will be dealt with in chapter 5.

MEASURING VARIABLE VALUES

When a quantitative researcher has decided on the variables he wishes to study, a method must be found for measuring the variables—that is, for determining the value of each variable for each of the subjects or cases that will be studied. For example, if gender is one of the variables of interest, the researcher must decide on a method for determining whether each subject is male or female; if intelligence is a variable of interest, then a method must be found for deciding how intelligent each subject is.

There are often many possible methods for measuring a variable. Gender may be measured by what is called self-report; that is, each subject is simply asked to indicate whether he or she is male or female. Gender may also be measured by checking written records; school records, for example, indicate whether students are male or female. Gender may also be measured by what is called observation; that is, the researcher (or someone else designated by the researcher) may simply look at the subjects and decide whether each is male or female.

Similarly, intelligence may be measured in many ways. There are a number of standardized tests that are considered to be tests of intelligence; any of these might be used. Intelligence could also be measured by asking students' teachers; teachers might, for example, be asked to assign each student in their classes a value of above average, average, or below average in intelligence.

Operational Definitions

This process of deciding how to measure a variable must ultimately result in what is called an *operational definition*. An operational definition of a variable specifies the operations that will be performed to measure the variable. Operational definitions are thus very precise; in fact, one of the characteristics of operational definitions is that they give such complete information about how a variable is measured that other researchers can use them to replicate the method of measurement for a given variable.

Here are some operational definitions of gender. Note that each one gives complete information on the operations that will be performed to measure the variable, which would permit anyone who wished to replicate the measurement method.

- The subject's answer to the following question on an anonymous questionnaire: What is your gender, male or female?
- The gender of the subject, male or female, as reported on his or her school enrollment card.
- The classroom teacher's designation of the subject as male or female.

Here are some operational definitions of intelligence.

- The subject's score on the Wechsler Adult Intelligence Scale.
- The classroom teacher's response to the following question: Indicate whether you feel each student in your class is above average, average, or below average in intelligence.

Obviously, researchers must operationally define their variables in order to measure them; if they didn't, they wouldn't know what their subjects' values of the variables are. Ideally, all research reports should include these operational definitions. In practice, however, some do not. This may be due to restrictions on the length of the report, to carelessness, or to many other reasons. Sometimes, for example, a researcher may operationally define a variable by creating a test or questionnaire especially for the study. If this instrument is very lengthy, it may not appear in the research report. Another researcher who wished to replicate the study, or a reader who wished to evaluate the instrument, would be unable to do so. However, in such cases the researcher who designed the instrument will usually send a copy to people who request it.

At other times, researchers may omit reporting their operational definitions because they seem obvious. Consider a researcher who is investigating the relationship between gender and certain attitudes. The researcher reports that a questionnaire was administered to measure the attitude variables but does not mention the operational definition of the gender variable. A reader is probably safe in concluding that the questionnaire also contained an item asking the subjects to indicate their gender.

Treatment Variables

There is one exception to the rule that variables must be measured and therefore operationally defined: *treatment variables*. Teaching method, with the values lecture and discussion, is an example of a treatment variable. This kind of variable is frequently encountered in educational research. One of the things educators are most interested in is the efficacy of different kinds of educational treatments: lecture versus discussion, special education versus mainstreaming, reward versus punishment. Treatment variables are almost always categorical; their values are the different conditions of treatment administered to the subjects in a given study.

Sometimes one of the values of a treatment variable is no special treatment at all. People who have this value of a treatment variable—that is, people who are in the study but are not receiving any treatment—are called *controls.* Researchers often refer to *treatment groups* and *control groups* in their studies. *Treatment* and *control* are values of the categorical treatment variable. In a study in which some subjects received counseling and some did not, the treatment group would consist of the subjects who received counseling; the control group would consist of the subjects who did not receive counseling.

The terms *measurement* and *operational definition* usually are not applied to treatment variables. Instead of measuring treatment variables and providing their operational definitions in research reports, researchers describe what the treatment conditions were and how they were administered. The remainder of this chapter, which is about the validity of operational definitions, does not, for the most part, apply to treatment variables. However, there are issues around the validity of treatments; we will deal with these at the end of this chapter.

■ EXERCISE 1

Which of the following variables is operationally defined (not necessarily well defined, but defined)? Do any of the variables seem to be treatment variables? Save your answers; you'll need them for a later question.

a. Gender: whether the subject is male or female
b. Math achievement: subject's score on the CTBS math subtest, form U, level 2
c. Religious affiliation: parent's designation of the child as Catholic, Jewish, Protestant, other, or no preference
d. Anxiety: subject's level of anxiety
e. Intelligence: test score
f. Feedback: researcher either gives subject feedback on his or her performance or does not give subject feedback
g. Counseling outcome: client's rating at termination of therapy of therapeutic success, from 1 (unsuccessful) to 7 (successful)
h. Amount of fun being had: minutes per hour that subject smiles   ■

■ EXERCISE 2

Write down at least three realistic ways to define operationally the variable seventh-graders' ethnicity, having the values Anglo, Black, Hispanic, Native American, Asian, and other. Be sure that each definition is complete enough to permit replication by another researcher.   ■

Validity of Measurement

Quantitative research questions are about variables. In order to study variables, researchers must operationally define them. If an operational definition of a variable is invalid, can the answer to the research question about that variable be valid? Of course not.

As a simple example, imagine that a researcher is interested in how much a group of children knows about math. The researcher operationally defines math knowledge in terms of a test, but the test is written at a level that is beyond the children's ability to read. The researcher gives the test, sees that the children do poorly on it, and concludes that the children know little about math. Is this answer valid? No. The operational definition did not validly measure the variable of interest, so the answer to the research question about that variable is not valid.

Operational definitions are thus extremely important. Research cannot be useful if its operational definitions are inadequate. As a consumer of educational research, you must become skilled at locating and evaluating the operational definitions that are given in research reports. In this chapter, you will learn some criteria that will help you evaluate operational definitions; however, the ultimate judgment is yours. If an operational definition does not make sense to you, then the research will not be of use to you.

Evaluation of operational definitions involves something called *measurement validity*. This term means just what it seems to mean: Does a researcher's operational definition provide valid measurement of a variable of interest? Does the measurement instrument actually and accurately measure what it is supposed to? Rulers provide a good example of reasonably valid measurement. Rulers are supposed to provide a measure of length in inches and feet; if used with reasonable care, that is in fact what they do, with reasonable accuracy.

Measurement can present validity problems in any field, but in education and the other behavioral sciences, valid measurement is especially difficult. This is because many of the variables in which educational researchers are interested are not directly observable. Someone's height is directly observable; someone's intelligence or attitude is not. The only way to measure variables that are not directly observable is by inference, and inference can be wrong.

To infer is to make a guess about something that is not known based on something that is known. If two children are presented with a problem and one of the children solves the problem more accurately or more quickly, we may infer that that child is more intelligent than the other. However, it may also be true that the child is more knowledgeable about the problem or more motivated to solve the problem, rather than more intelligent. Most math tests are supposed to measure math ability or achievement, but even when they are used with reasonable care, they may not in fact measure math ability or achievement. They may instead measure reading ability or test motivation or test anxiety or test-taking skill or cultural knowledge.

Educational researchers are interested in understanding such things as how people think, how people's attitudes are formed, and how attitudes affect behavior. Many variables of interest to educational researchers tend not to be directly observable. Valid measurement is thus one of the biggest challenges faced by educational researchers. How would you like to have to come up with a valid way to assign values of thought and attitude variables to subjects in a study?

The first criterion to keep in mind when you are evaluating operational definitions is that no matter what variables a researcher claims to be studying, he or she is really studying only the variables as they were operationally defined. Consider a research report titled "Effects of Counseling on Anxiety." Such a title suggests that the research is about anxiety. However, anxiety must be operationally defined. If anxiety is defined as the subjects' scores on a paper-and-pencil test, then the research is not really about anxiety but about people's scores on a paper-and-pencil test. You must decide whether you are willing to accept the test as a definition of anxiety. If anxiety is defined as the subjects' perspiration rates as measured by a galvanic skin response machine, then the research is not really about anxiety but about perspiration rates. You must decide.

The fact that variables can be measured in so many ways accounts for many of the apparent contradictions that can be found in the research literature in many fields. It would be a simple matter to find six different research reports involving the relationship between counseling and anxiety, with six different operational definitions of anxiety and six different sets of results.

On the other hand, using different operational definitions of the same variable can also be a good thing. No operational definition is perfect; each has some weakness. Using multiple operational definitions of the same variable allows one definition to compensate for the weakness of another; when research results are similar, even though different operational definitions were employed, our confidence in the findings tends to be strengthened. For example, if similar relationships are found between self-esteem and school performance using several different operational definitions of both self-esteem and school performance, then we are more likely to believe that there really is a relationship between self-esteem and school performance.

Researchers sometimes use multiple operational definitions of a single variable in a single study, hoping to enhance confidence in their findings. Each operational definition then functions as a separate variable.

■ EXERCISE 3

Look at the operational definitions that you identified in Exercise 1, parts *b, c, e, g,* and *h.* Do you see any possible validity problems with these operational definitions?

■

METHODS OF MEASUREMENT

Although there are various ways to operationalize most variables, this variety can be classified into a limited number of categories of measurement methods. Most educational variables are operationally defined in terms of the following categories.

"Objective" Tests

Tests, usually of the paper-and-pencil variety, are the most commonly employed method of measurement of cognitive variables, and they are occasionally used to measure other kinds of variables as well. From your own experience as a student and elsewhere, you are already familiar with this method of measurement. Intelligence tests, achievement tests, aptitude tests, and some personality and attitude tests fall into this category. Most mastery or criterion-referenced tests are also in this category; this includes many of the teacher-made tests given to students at all levels of the educational system for purposes of checking mastery and assigning grades.

These tests are not truly objective; that is, they are not free from bias. They are often, however, called objective tests to indicate their relative freedom from scorer bias. They are "right-answer" tests, which are or can be scored with a key. A given subject's test result or score will be the same no matter who or what does the scoring; that is, any reasonably intelligent, literate person or any properly programmed machine that scores such a test will assign the same scores to individuals as would any other reasonably intelligent, literate person or any other properly programmed machine.

Bennett (1993) suggests that we call instruments in this category *highly constrained,* since an individual's choice of responses to these instruments is restricted, rather than open-ended. Often, the conditions under which these tests are administered are also "constrained"—i.e., standardized.

The frequency with which these tests are used in educational research is due in part to their objectivity, in this limited sense, relative to other methods of measurement. It is also due in part to their practicality; relative to other methods of measurement, these tests can be administered quickly and inexpensively to large groups of subjects, usually without extensive training of test administrators and scorers. Many of these tests are also widely known and used; this promotes comparability of operational definitions across a large number of studies.

Some objective tests provide fairly direct measurement of variables of interest to educational researchers. If we want to know whether children can spell certain words correctly or add two-digit numbers correctly, objective tests are a reasonably direct way to find out. But many objective instruments are based heavily on inference. The Bem Sex Role Inventory, for example, designates subjects as masculine, feminine, androgynous, or undifferentiated on the basis of their self-ratings from 1 to 7 on such questions as whether they love children. This does not provide direct measurement of sex-role identity. Sex-role identity is a personality variable, and personality exists in the brain. At this time, we have no means of directly measuring personality. We must infer it from behavior, such as the answers people give about themselves to questions on tests, and such inferences may not always be valid.

Mass-administered, paper-and-pencil instruments may not always adequately measure many of the variables which they purport to measure—for example, intelligence, personality, knowledge, and attitudes. Many educators believe that such tests are culturally biased, or are biased in favor of more literate subjects, even when they purport to measure variables that are conceptually independent of literacy, such as intelligence. Despite their drawbacks, they continue to be widely used in educational research—probably overused—because they are expedient (i.e., relatively quick and inexpensive) and provide comparability between studies.

Interviews and Questionnaires

Interviews and questionnaires are another common method of measurement in educational research. They are most often employed to measure demographic and attitudinal variables. Demographic variables refer to subjects' backgrounds; age, gender, ethnicity, income, education, and residence are examples of demographic variables.

In one sense, the only difference between interviews and questionnaires is who asks the questions and records the answers. In an interview, a person called the interviewer poses questions to the subject and records the subject's answers. With questionnaires the questions are read by the subject, who then records his or her own answers. The same questions may be asked using either method.

In another sense, however, interviews and questionnaires are very different from one another, because the presence and characteristics of an interviewer can affect a subject's answers for better or worse. Subjects, for example, are more likely to be candid about such things as their sexual orientation and racial/ethnic attitudes when responding to an anonymous questionnaire than to a person. On the other hand, interviewers can clarify a question that a subject finds ambiguous. They can also make decisions about such things as when to probe more deeply into a particular question or when subjects seem to be avoiding particular issues.

Both kinds of instruments may contain either closed or open-ended questions. Closed questions are those that give the respondent fixed choices in answering. Open-ended questions permit the respondent to phrase his or her own answers. The same question may be asked in either way. Here is an example of a question that might appear on a questionnaire or interview schedule:

- How would you feel if your child were placed in a special-education class?

If the respondent were permitted to supply any answer she wished, the question would be considered open-ended. If, however, the respondent were instructed to choose one of the following answers—*positive, neutral,* or *negative*—the question would be considered closed.

Open-ended questions can facilitate getting at a subject's true feelings, while closed questions often force a subject to choose an answer that does not reflect his or her true feelings. However, closed questions have the advantage of facilitating classification of subjects' responses and comparisons between subjects. How would you like to have to classify the following answers to the open-ended question, "What is your ethnicity?"

Black
Anglo
Indian
African
None
American

Are Black and African the same? Are Anglo and American the same? How can one have no ethnicity? Does Indian mean American Indian or from India? Sometimes researchers try to compromise by asking closed questions, after which subjects are encouraged to make any comments they wish.

Although both interview schedules and questionnaires may contain both open and closed questions, in actual practice interview schedules tend to have more open questions and questionnaires tend to have more closed ones. In interview situations even closed questions can take on an open flavor, because interviewers can respond to subjects and questionnaires cannot.

An advantage of interviews and questionnaires is that they are fairly direct; they permit subjects to speak for themselves. Other methods of measurement often require a great deal of inference. Suppose a researcher is interested in parents' attitudes toward school integration and operationally defines the attitude variable as parents' responses to school integration. Do parents attempt to block such integration methods as busing? Do parents withdraw their children from integrated schools? Do parents move out of integrated neighborhoods? This sort of operational definition requires researchers to infer parents' attitudes from their behavior, and such inferences may not be valid. Parents who attempt to block busing may not object to integration but may feel that children should attend local, neighborhood schools. Parents who withdraw their children or move away may have reasons other than negative attitudes toward integration.

Interviews and questionnaires permit subjects to speak for themselves. On the other hand, we cannot always be sure that they are speaking candidly or that they even know the "true" answer; many people over- or underestimate their own characteristics and situations.

On the practical side, questionnaires tend to be relatively inexpensive to administer, although not as inexpensive as most objective tests. Interviewing, on the other hand, can be fairly expensive, since interviewers' time usually must be paid for. A disadvantage of both interviews and questionnaires is that most researchers design their own instruments; this does not promote comparability of operational definitions across a large number of studies.

Observation

Scientists often refer to any operational definition as an observation: We "observe" people's test scores; we "observe" their questionnaire responses; we even "observe" their pulse rates. However, one method of measurement relies on what is specifically referred to as observation. In this method, the researcher or someone delegated by the researcher assigns values of a variable to subjects or cases after observing their behavior, behavior products, or characteristics directly.

Observation can provide fairly direct measurement of educational variables. If a researcher is interested in how many times children raise their hands, the most direct way to measure that would be observation. More often, however, observers are required to make inferences. Observational research thus often relies heavily on observer judgment.

A researcher interested in educational administration might employ the following operational definition of leadership style: An evaluator will observe each principal leading a faculty meeting and will afterward judge the principal's leadership style to be democratic or authoritarian. A leadership style that appears authoritarian to one observer, however, may appear democratic to another.

A researcher interested in sexism in education might employ the following operational definition of sexism: An evaluator will observe each teacher interacting with students for one hour; during this period the observer will record whether each teacher-initiated interaction with a student is directed toward a male or female student. However, evaluators may disagree about just what constitutes a teacher-initiated interaction.

Sometimes, instead of observing behavior directly, it is the products of behavior that are observed. A researcher who is interested in the effects of a particular art curriculum on children's creativity might operationally define the dependent variable as follows: Trained judges will evaluate the creativity of children's drawings before and after the children have participated in the art program. However, evaluation of creativity may be a very subjective process.

Researchers who rely on observational methods of measurement often go to great lengths to minimize the subjectivity of observer judgment. Observers are trained to be more objective, tested, retrained, and retested, until their objectivity meets the researcher's standards. The problem, of course, is more acute when multiple observers are used, each observing different subjects. Researchers want observers to assign values of a variable to subjects in a way that reflects actual differences in the behavior of the subjects, rather than differences in the judgment of observers. Therefore, when multiple observers are used, they must be trained not only to be consistent in their own observations, but also to be consistent with other observers.

Sometimes observers are simply asked for their opinions, as in the example above of asking a teacher to rate the intelligence of children as above average, average, or below average. It is assumed that teachers' opinions are based on their observations of the children involved, but the researcher exercises no control over the observation process. More often, however, observers are equipped with forms for recording their observations. These forms may be checklists, on which the observer simply checks off the occurrence of listed characteristics and behaviors. Observers in one of the examples above would use a checklist. Each time a teacher initiated contact with a student, the observer would place a mark in the appropriate place on a checklist to indicate whether the contact was with a male or female student.

Often, however, more complex forms, called rating scales, are used. With rating scales, observers must decide not only whether a particular characteristic is present, but also to what degree it is present. In another of the examples above, observers might use a rating scale to indicate the degree of authoritarianism in a principal's leadership style. Such observers might be required to assess the principal with a scale like the following:

DEMOCRATIC   *1*   *2*   *3*   *4*   *5*   *6*   *7*   *AUTHORITARIAN*

Rating scales tend to require more observer judgment than do checklists.

A few observational instruments are widely known and used, much as standardized tests of ability, knowledge, and personality are widely known and used. Often, however, researchers design their own checklists and rating scales. This does not promote comparability of operational definitions from study to study. Because observers usually must be paid, observation also tends to be a relatively expensive method of measurement.

Written Records and Other Documents

Sometimes out of necessity and sometimes by choice, many researchers use existing records to provide a measure of variables. Researchers interested in past events are often limited to historical documents for information on the values of variables. Other researchers use existing records to avoid the cost of collecting new information: for example, if IQ test score is a variable of interest, a researcher may be able to use school records of a previously administered test rather than administer the test again. Archives typically provide a very inexpensive method for operationalizing variables.

The disadvantage of archival operational definitions is that the researcher does not control the measurement. If a researcher controls the administration of an IQ test, he can vouch for the competence of the test administrator, the suitability of the test environment, and the accuracy of scoring and recording. If a researcher uses existing IQ test records, he may have no information on such matters.

Using archival records, researchers also may have to modify their operational definitions to suit the information available. A researcher may wish to define intelligence operationally in terms of IQ test *A,* which she feels is the best instrument for a particular group of children; the only records available, however, may be of scores on IQ test *B,* which the researcher feels is an inferior instrument. However, the choice may not be the researcher's; the principal at the children's school may not be willing to authorize the administration of a new test when IQ scores are already available. The researcher will thus be obliged to change the operational definition of the intelligence variable from IQ test *A* to IQ test *B.*

Figure 3.1 summarizes the advantages and disadvantages of the four methods of measurement.

■ EXERCISE 4

What is the method of measurement in each of the following operational definitions: objective test, interview/questionnaire, observation, or archives?

a. Gender: subject's answer to the question, Are you male or female?

b. Reading level: subject's score on the CTBS Reading subtest, form U, level 2

c. Gender: subject's gender as recorded on his or her school enrollment card

FIGURE 3.1 Advantages and disadvantages of the four methods of measurement.

	ADVANTAGES	DISADVANTAGES
Objective Tests	Comparability across studies Usually inexpensive Objective scoring	High inference for some variables
Interviews/ Questionnaires	Questionnaires usually inexpensive Usually low inference	Lack of comparability across studies Interviews usually expensive
Observation	Most direct way to measure some variables Only way to measure some variables	High inference for some variables Usually expensive Lack of comparability across studies
Archives	Only way to measure some variables Usually inexpensive	Researcher's lack of measurement control

d. Student teacher's skill: master teacher's rating of student teacher's performance from 1 (poor) to 5 (excellent)

e. Anxiety: subject's score on the SCARED test

f. Attitude: subject's response to the following statement: I (strongly agree, agree, disagree, strongly disagree) that taxes should be raised to provide more money for education.

g. Criminal act: whether or not the subject has been convicted of a misdemeanor or felony in the town in which he or she resides

h. Fluency in Spanish as a second language: native Spanish speaker's rating of subject as good, fair, or poor Spanish speaker ■

■ Exercise 5

Write down two realistic operational definitions of the variable classroom atmosphere, having the values informal/unstructured and formal/structured. One of the operational definitions should reflect an interview/questionnaire method of measurement; the other should reflect an observational method of measurement. What strengths and weaknesses do you feel each definition has? ■

■ Exercise 6

Several examples of variables and their operational definitions from published research reports follow. For each study, indicate the method of measurement. How validly do you feel the researchers have measured their variables? Why do you suppose the researchers chose these operational definitions? Are the operational definitions complete enough that another researcher could replicate the method of measurement?

a. Engelberg and Evans (1986) studied children with three "levels of achievement": learning disabled, normal-achieving, and gifted. Here is their operational definition of achievement level (p. 92):

Subjects from both the learning disabled and gifted samples had been previously identified by the school system and were involved in special programs designed to supplement regular classroom curriculum. In addition, 100 normal-achieving students were drawn from intact classes.

b. Stockwell and Dye (1980) studied "counselor touch" (p. 443).

Touch was defined as physical contact between the hands and wrist of a counselor and the hands, arms, shoulders, and upper back area of a client. The specific mode of touch used in this study was a "squeeze" (at least 4–5 seconds of firm contact).

c. DeBeer-Keston, Mellon, and Solomon (1986) studied "personal space invasion" at a bank of public telephones (p. 408).

In the experimental (invasion) condition, the confederate approached the phone next to the subject and engaged in conversation using that telephone. In the control (non-invasion) condition, the confederate remained at the observation site with the other experimenter, the site being a table behind a column, 15 ft away from the phone bank.

d. Shreeve et al. (1985), in a study responding to a proposed school-prayer amend-
    ment to the U.S. Constitution, operationally defined "the attitudes of public
    school teachers toward school prayer" (p. 33).

    [Teachers] voluntarily completed a seven-page [survey of] their personal religious
    practices and beliefs, their attitudes towards the proposed amendment and their atti-
    tudes towards the general concept of school prayer.

e. Sorsdahl and Sanche (1985) studied elementary children's self-concepts using
    the Piers-Harris Children's Self-Concept Scale.   ■

COMPONENTS OF MEASUREMENT VALIDITY

This chapter has stressed the importance of operational definitions. One point especially bears repeating: No matter what variables a researcher claims to be studying,
he is really studying the variables only as they are operationally defined. You, as a
consumer of research, must become skilled at locating and evaluating operational
definitions. If an operational definition does not make sense to you, then the research
is not likely to be of use to you.

In part, your evaluation of operational definitions will be a personal, idiosyncratic process. If you are absolutely convinced that paper-and-pencil IQ tests do not
measure native intelligence, then you will not be interested in research about native
intelligence that employs paper-and-pencil IQ tests. Someone else, with a different
view of such tests, may feel otherwise, of course.

There are, however, some objective standards by which to evaluate operational definitions. Many research reports contain evidence for validity of measurement. Some of
this evidence involves technical terms and concepts that you need to understand.

Reliability

Reliability is one very limited and specific component of measurement validity. *Reliability of measurement* refers to whether the measuring instrument consistently gives
the same answer to the same question. That may sound silly, but here's an example
that will demonstrate to you how reliability can be a problem.

Suppose that you wish to order a window shade. You go into your sewing box (or
the sewing box of someone you know) and retrieve a cloth tape measure, the kind
used to determine the size of someone's waist or hips. Using this cloth tape measure,
you determine that the width of your window is 30 inches. When you call the store to
order the shade, the salesperson stresses the importance of having absolutely accurate
measurement. You decide to measure once more to be sure, again using the cloth tape
measure. To your surprise, this time the window seems to be only 29 3/4 inches wide.
You try again. Now the window seems to have gotten wider—30 1/4 inches. The
problem is that you are using an unreliable measuring instrument. Cloth tape measures stretch slightly. If you pull the tape very tight, the window will seem to be
slightly narrower than if you leave a small amount of slack in the tape. The cloth tape
measure is an unreliable instrument, because it does not consistently give the same
answer to the same question: What is the width of this window?

Similarly, some of our instruments for measuring education variables are, or
under certain circumstances can be, unreliable. A multiple-choice test that is much

too hard for subjects is usually unreliable. Subjects often guess on such tests. If the same test were given to the subjects two days in a row, they would guess differently each day. Today Judy may be a lucky guesser who gets 25 questions right. Tomorrow she may be an unlucky guesser and only get 15 questions right. Clearly, in such a situation we are not consistently getting the same answer to the same question: How many of these questions can Judy answer correctly?

Reliability is linked to an important concept in measurement: *measurement error.* Because humans and the devices they invent are fallible, we assume that there is some error in all measurement, although we sometimes are able to see to it that the error is very small. Even a yardstick, which is a fairly reliable measuring instrument, yields imperfect measurement. Using a yardstick, it would be nearly impossible to measure accurately the difference between 1¹⁄₆₄ inches and 1²⁄₆₄ inches.

Educational measurement is subject to all sorts of errors. Even a very reliable test does not consistently give exactly the same answer to the same question. Even if the multiple-choice test is not too hard for Judy, she will probably guess on a few items. She may also be feeling better and thinking more clearly today than tomorrow and thus get an additional question or two right. Perhaps today she will get 25 questions right and tomorrow only 23.

We have ways to estimate mathematically the error associated with a given measurement instrument. We also have ways to estimate mathematically the related issue of the reliability of a given instrument. In reading research reports, you will often see statements like the following:

Reliability of the SAT is .91.

Test reliability was established to be .84, using the split-half method with a
    Spearman-Brown correction.

Such statements will always involve a number between 0 and 1.0, called a *coefficient of reliability,* with 1.0 representing perfect reliability.

You may wish to use the following rules of thumb in interpreting reliability coefficients. A coefficient greater than .90 represents very good reliability. A coefficient between .80 and .90 represents acceptable reliability for most educational research purposes. A coefficient below .80, however, may be considered acceptable when the variable is known to be very difficult to measure reliably. A coefficient below .60 is usually considered inadequate.

Often researchers use the term *reliability coefficient;* sometimes, however, they use other terms to represent this concept—terms such as *consistency* or *agreement.* If a researcher says that her test has a test-retest consistency coefficient of .77, this is a reliability coefficient.

There are ways to increase the reliability of most instruments. When a test is being developed, these methods are employed. In its initial form, a test may yield a reliability coefficient of only .72. By the time the same test is in its final form, reliability may be .91. These methods take time and money, however. Most commercially available tests have good reliability; the publishers couldn't sell them if they didn't. On the other hand, a researcher who has developed an instrument especially for her own study may have to be satisfied with a reliability coefficient of .81.

Sometimes when researchers use commercial tests, they don't bother to specify the reliability. They probably feel that the reader will assume that the reliability of such tests is good. This assumption is usually safe. If, however, you wish to check on the reliability of a nationally known test, you can refer to the publisher's literature or to the *Mental Measurements Yearbook* (Buros, 1995), which is usually on the reference shelf in academic libraries.

One point is worth keeping in mind. A reliability coefficient is established by actually administering the test to a group of subjects. The resultant coefficient is valid for the subjects on whom the reliability data were collected. This coefficient may or may not represent the test's reliability for different groups of subjects, however. For example, a college entrance test is standardized by administering it to a large group of subjects who are considered to represent all college applicants in the United States. Reliability coefficients for such tests are derived from these norming groups. A researcher who uses such a test on a group of subjects who are substantially different from the norming group may not be safe in citing the reliability coefficient for the norming group. A test that is reliable for the norming group may not be reliable for a group of culturally diverse subjects or learning disabled subjects, for example.

In this regard, reliability coefficients that are established by researchers themselves, on the basis of data collected from their research subjects, may be preferable to the coefficients established by test publishers. Researchers' own coefficients, although usually lower, are at least representative of their subjects.

Interobserver Reliability

Operational definitions that involve an observational method of measurement present a particular reliability problem. Assume that a researcher wishes to measure the variable *teacher organization*. The researcher operationally defines the variable as follows. Trained observers will observe 50-minute lectures. At the end of each lecture, they will rate the teacher's overall organization on a scale from 1 (disorganized) to 5 (organized). The research will be conducted simultaneously in two cities. Thus, two different observers will be employed.

Such a researcher must establish *interobserver reliability* (sometimes called *interrater* or *intercoder reliability* or *consistency* or *agreement*)—that is, the degree to which each observer gives the same answer to the same question. Martha observes George lecturing. Martha gives George a rating of 4 on the organization scale. If Sam had also observed George giving that lecture, would Sam also have given George a rating of 4? If not, then the ratings that the two observers give to all the teachers in the study may not reflect differences in the teachers but differences in the observers. This is not what the researcher wants to measure at all.

There is only one way to establish interobserver reliability; that is to have the various observers actually view and rate the same subjects. The researcher in this example would have to do a pilot study, bringing the two observers together, having them view and rate the same teachers, and then mathematically determining their interobserver reliability coefficient. If the coefficient were low, the researcher would have to train the observers and repeat the pilot until the coefficient became acceptably high. Then the actual research could be undertaken with confidence that the observers' ratings reflect differences in the teachers, not in the observers.

When you see interobserver reliability coefficients in the educational research literature, you will know that the researcher has actually compared the observers' ratings on a single group of subjects. The coefficients are to be interpreted just as are other reliability coefficients: they range from 0 to 1.0, and higher is better.

■ Exercise 7

What evidence would you like to see of the reliability of the following operational definitions?

a. Three judges grade 300 students' essays; each judge evaluates the work of 100 children.

b. The Bem Sex Role Inventory, for which the publisher reports reliability coefficients ranging from .78 to .94, is administered to recent immigrants from Southeast Asia.

c. The Iowa Test of Basic Skills, forms 7/8, levels 9–14, for which the publisher reports reliability coefficients ranging from .97 to .98, is administered to a group of predominantly middle-class, Anglo children.   ■

TYPES OF MEASUREMENT VALIDITY

Reliability is a component of measurement validity. An unreliable instrument cannot be valid: If an instrument does not consistently give the same answer to the same question, then it cannot be validly measuring anything. However, a reliable instrument may still be invalid: It may consistently give the same answer to the same question, but the question may not be the one we want to answer. Most standardized tests are reliable, but many of them may not be valid for particular purposes. IQ tests are reliable, but it is an unanswered question whether they are valid tests of native intelligence. Because they are reliable, we assume that they are measuring something—perhaps reading ability, or cultural skills, or other learned behavior; unfortunately, that is not what we want them to measure. It is thus important that researchers establish the reliability of their measuring instruments. However, once done, this still leaves a large part of the instruments' validity open to question.

There is another difference between reliability and validity. Reliability, being a mathematical concept, can be estimated with some precision. The broader concept of validity is much less precise, more complex, and more relative.

Imagine, if you will, that you have designed a test that you intend to be a test of reading ability. What could you do to establish its validity? Well, you might review the test, item by item, and argue, first, that each item contains material that is thought by reading experts to relate to reading and, second, that all of the components of reading skill thought to be important by reading experts are proportionally represented in your items. You would argue that some of your items are vocabulary items, some comprehension items, some speed items, and so forth. If I challenged you, you might refer me to certain publications by reading specialists to support your claims about the skills that are important in reading.

What else could you do? You might take an easier route and simply submit the test for evaluation by three people who are thought to be reading experts. If they all evaluate your test as good, you have another kind of support for its validity.

What else could you do? You might administer your test to a group of subjects and then also administer to the same group of subjects another test that is already accepted by reading specialists as a valid reading test. If you get similar results using your test and the accepted test, you have another kind of support for your test's validity.

Is there anything else you might do? How about administering your test to a group of subjects who have taken a course in reading improvement? If the results of your test agree with the grades students received in the course (if people judged by your test to be better readers got higher grades in the course and vice versa), you would have another kind of support for your test's validity.

In fact, all of these methods and more are employed by researchers in trying to establish the validity of their operational definitions. Different methods yield different kinds of evidence for validity. Thus it has come about that different kinds of validity have been identified and named. The most common kinds of validity are described briefly below.

Content Validity

Content validity involves analyzing the content of an instrument to determine whether the content represents the quality that the instrument is supposed to measure. An analysis of the way in which each item on a reading test relates to what is known about reading skills represents an effort to establish content validity.

Studies of content validity are usually done by people thought to be experts in the field in question. The weight of content validity studies thus depends on two things: the reputation of the people doing the studies and the merit of their arguments. Both of these, of course, are matters on which reasonable people might well disagree. Unless you are highly skilled in the field in question, you may feel unable to evaluate content validity claims. This puts you at the mercy of the experts.

Criterion Validity

Criterion validity involves how well the results obtained by administering an instrument agree with some criterion—that is, with the results obtained from administering some other measure to the same subjects. There are two kinds of criterion validity, with two different purposes.

Concurrent Validity

Concurrent validity involves whether the results obtained by administering an instrument concur with the results obtained from administering another, presumably valid, measure to the same subjects. A comparison of a group of subjects' scores on your reading test with their scores on other reading tests, or with their grades in a reading course, represents an effort to establish concurrent validity. Concurrent validity can usually be estimated with the same kind of precision as reliability. That is, researchers can compare subjects' scores on two tests and calculate a coefficient representing the degree of similarity in the two sets of scores. Such coefficients are to be interpreted much as reliability coefficients are: They range from 0 to 1.0, and higher is better.

Of course, the weight of concurrent validity studies depends entirely on the validity of the existing measures. If an attempt is made to validate a new IQ test by establishing its concurrent validity with existing IQ tests, you will not be convinced if you feel that existing IQ tests are invalid. Similarly, results of a new paper-and-pencil test of anxiety might be compared with judgments of the subjects' anxiety by a group of psychiatrists who interviewed them. If you do not trust psychiatrists' ability to distinguish levels of anxiety, you will not be impressed by such a concurrent validity study. You may not feel knowledgeable enough to evaluate the validity of existing measures; if not, you will again be at the mercy of the experts.

Predictive Validity

Predictive validity is the second kind of criterion validity and is a very specialized kind of validity. Many instruments used in educational settings are designed for the express purpose of predicting educational outcomes. College entrance examinations are a classic case in point. They are designed to predict how well a student will do in college; they are used to screen out students who probably will do poorly and to select students who probably will do well.

The obvious way to validate such instruments is to try them and see if they work. If an instrument does in fact have a good success rate in predicting outcomes, then it is said to have good predictive validity with respect to these outcomes. Predictive validity, like concurrent validity, can usually be estimated mathematically. Predictive validity is, however, a very limited kind of validity. An instrument with good predictive validity for certain outcomes is only valid in one way: as a predictor of those outcomes. Its validity for other purposes must be established in other ways.

The Scholastic Aptitude Test (SAT) and the American College Test (ACT) are college entrance examinations that are usually administered to students in their last year or two of high school. These tests have some validity as predictors of students' college success, but it is inappropriate to use them to evaluate secondary-school teachers or programs (although they are not infrequently used in these ways). Their validity for these purposes has not been established.

Construct Validity

Construct validity can be a difficult concept for beginning students. Constructs are variables that we cannot directly observe, although we have indirect evidence of their existence. Intelligence is an example of a construct.

We have theories about constructs. Part of contemporary theory of intelligence, for example, is that heredity influences an individual's intelligence. When researchers attempt to measure a theoretical construct, one way to assess the validity of the measurement instrument is to compare the results of the measurement with theory about the construct. The fact that children's measured intelligence tends to be similar to that of their biological parents is an argument for the construct validity of the instrument used to measure intelligence.

However, another part of contemporary theory of intelligence is that level of overall intelligence does not differ across races of people. The fact that the level of measured intelligence does differ across races is an argument against the overall construct validity of the instrument used to measure intelligence.

There is a trend toward discussion of construct validity issues in research reports. However, mention of construct validity in research reports is still rare compared to mention of the other kinds of named validity that we have described.

■ EXERCISE 8

Decide whether the following situations involve content validity, concurrent validity, or predictive validity.

a.   An employer requires all job applicants to take a test.

b. A university requires all students scoring below 18 on the ACT math subtest to take remedial math.

c. The Educational Testing Service asks education professors to evaluate proposed items for the National Teachers' Examination.

d. A researcher reports that 80% of the people identified as hypochondriacs by her test were diagnosed by their physicians as having no apparent physical illness.

■

OTHER KINDS OF VALIDITY ARGUMENTS

Sometimes researchers will explicitly address the issue of measurement validity, using such terms as measurement validity, or concurrent validity, or predictive validity. Sometimes, however, these terms will not be available to cue you that the researcher is addressing the issue of the validity of the operational definition of a given variable.

For example, assume that you are reading a research report. One of the variables in the report is secondary students' evaluations of teachers, defined in terms of an evaluation form developed by the researcher. You come to a passage containing the following information. The author declares that she submitted the form to two of her colleagues in her university's department of secondary education, who judged it suitable for use in secondary schools.

You have just read an argument for the validity of the author's operational definition, although no terminology was used expressly to tell you so. As with the more formal kinds of validity statements, you must use whatever information is available to decide whether you feel the operational definition is valid or not. In this case, you may feel that the author and her colleagues, being university professors in secondary education, are probably able to judge competently whether an instrument is suitable for use in secondary schools. Or you may feel that most university professors are out of touch with the real world of education, and that some practicing secondary teachers should also have been consulted. You may need to include what you know about the students in the study in order to evaluate the validity argument. If the students are typical, you may be satisfied with the professors' judgment. If, however, they are special in some way (e.g., have a learning disability) you may wish that the author had consulted some special education experts. Of course, if the author has said nothing about the actual items on the instrument and you are not familiar with it, you may also wish to examine the items yourself.

As another example, suppose that you are reading another research report. One of the variables of interest is mathematics achievement, measured by a paper-and-pencil test. The subjects are inner-city elementary-school children. The author indicates that instructions for taking the test were read aloud by the teacher and that children were encouraged to ask the teacher to read them any questions that they were having trouble reading themselves. Again, you have just come across a validity argument. The author is trying to establish that the test, as administered, provided a valid measure of mathematics achievement rather than measuring reading ability.

In order to enhance sales of their tests, test publishers usually commission elaborate validity studies. Testing libraries have reports on these studies. The *Mental Measurements Yearbook* (Buros, 1995) also summarizes available information on the validity of most nationally known tests.

Figure 3.2 summarizes formal measurement validity considerations.

FIGURE 3.2   Measurement validity considerations.

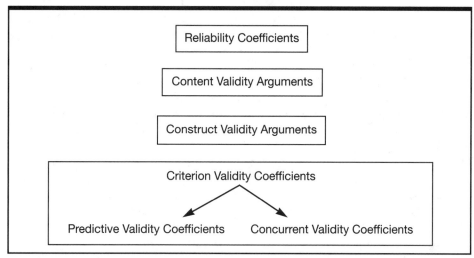

EVALUATING MEASUREMENT VALIDITY

Learning to evaluate arguments for the validity of measurement is a matter of being informed about two things: the concept of measurement validity and the variables being measured, including certain predictable problems in their measurement. You can then not only recognize and evaluate validity arguments when you see them but also decide what additional validity problems you think the author neglected to address. As you become more knowledgeable in your field in education, and as you read more educational research in your field, your skills in this area will increase.

Sometimes researchers simply do not mention anything about the validity of their operational definitions. As we pointed out earlier, there can be many reasons for such an omission. If the publisher insists that the entire research report be presented in two pages, there is simply no space for any but the minimum information about the study. Or the operational definition may be so straightforward that the researcher feels no defense is necessary. If a researcher tells you that the variable *gender* is defined in terms of information on the children's school enrollment cards, are you seriously going to question the validity of this definition?

Another point we made earlier in this chapter is that researchers often employ several different operational definitions of a single variable in a single study. This is usually because the variable is difficult to measure validly. In such cases, researchers employ a variety of operational definitions, each with its own particular validity problems, hoping that the various definitions will compensate for each other's validity problems. For example, a researcher interested in students' intelligence may operationalize intelligence in two ways: a paper-and-pencil IQ test score and teacher's assessment. This researcher may reason that IQ test scores are at least partly invalid due to such factors as students' reading ability or test anxiety, so teachers are encouraged to assess students irrespective of these factors. On the other hand, teachers may be influenced by such things as students' attractiveness or industriousness; the test does not have these biases.

The researcher has really posed two separate research questions, one for each of the two operational definitions of the intelligence variable. Each of these questions must be answered separately. If, however, each answer is the same (e.g., these students' IQ test scores are low, and teachers rate these students' intelligence as low), then the researcher is more comfortable in concluding that these students' intelligence has been accurately assessed. Of course, it is still possible that the test and the teachers share a bias—e.g., cultural bias—that the researcher has not considered.

A special note is required here about treatment variables. We pointed out earlier that treatment variables are not measured but administered, and that research reports describe these administrations rather than provide their operational definitions. Thus, the kinds of validity issues we have dealt with in this chapter do not apply, strictly speaking, to treatment variables. However, when research involves a treatment variable, it is worth asking some of the same kinds of questions we ask about the validity of measured variables—in particular, whether the treatment was described fully enough that you can evaluate it and another researcher could replicate it; and whether the administration created the variable the researcher intended to create.

Suppose, for example, that a researcher wishes to study the effects of learned helplessness on subjects' performance of some task. Before measuring their task performance, she attempts to induce learned helplessness in some of her subjects by having them work on an unsolvable problem. This research is supposed to be about the effects of learned helplessness, but it is really about the effects of working on an unsolvable problem. You need to evaluate whether having subjects work on an unsolvable problem indeed induces learned helplessness.

As another example, suppose that a researcher manipulates a treatment variable involving reward and punishment. The researcher reports that he asked one group of teachers to reward children for appropriate behavior and another group to punish children for inappropriate behavior. The issue is whether the teachers in fact implemented the researcher's request. This research is supposed to be about whether children received reward or punishment; in fact, it is really only about whether their teachers were asked to administer reward or punishment. In order to accept the manipulation as valid for the variable that the researcher says is being studied, we would want to have some evidence that the teachers actually did what the researcher requested.

In some fields, this kind of problem is very common. Subjects are given different kinds of treatment: Some children receive reward and some punishment; some receive a new reading program while others receive the traditional program; some teachers receive an inservice program that other teachers do not receive. The researcher, of course, wants to see whether there is what is called a treatment effect—that is, whether the treatment makes a difference in such things as classroom discipline, reading ability, or teaching effectiveness. Often, however, it is not the researcher who implements the treatment; and, unless the researcher takes steps to guard against this possibility, it may be that the treatment was not in fact implemented as the researcher had intended. In these situations, researchers should include evidence about the implementation of treatments in their research reports. In the example in which teachers were asked to administer reward or punishment, the researcher would have had to send trained observers into the teachers' classrooms to document that the teachers were doing what the researcher requested.

Now we would like to ask you to try to step back and take the long view on operational definitions. No matter what variables researchers say they are studying, remember that they are really only studying the variables as operationally defined. Many educational variables, unlike many variables in the "hard" sciences, are notoriously difficult to define validly. Thus, two research reports, each claiming to investigate the same variables, often represent, in fact, quite different studies. Allegedly similar variables often differ in method and reliability of measurement, and each has its own validity problems. And so far we are dealing with only one of several problem areas in doing research: operational definitions. Consider this the beginning of your understanding of why good, replicable research in education is so hard to do (and find).

Figure 3.3 provides a model for evaluating measurement validity.

■ EXERCISE 9

What would you like to know in order to assess the validity of the following operational definitions (don't forget about reliability)? What strengths and weaknesses do you see in the definitions?

a. Teachers' ratings of principal's leadership ability
b. A paper-and-pencil test of creativity
c. Number of fisherpersons present each year as an index of the number of fish in the lake
d. A nationally standardized achievement test to measure science knowledge
e. Interviews with parents about child-rearing practices
f. Observer's assessment of the affective content of teacher-student interactions
g. Camp commanders' reports on the health status of prisoners of war ■

SUMMARY

In order to measure variables, researchers must define them operationally. Operational definitions specify the operations that the researcher will perform to ascertain the values of variables for the subjects or cases in a study. Because replication is

FIGURE 3.3 Steps in evaluating the validity of treatments and operational definitions.

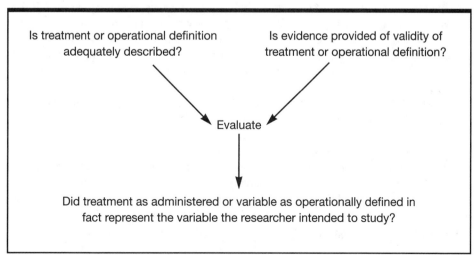

important to the development of knowledge, operational definitions that appear in a research report should be complete enough that other researchers can replicate them.

There are often many possible ways to define a given variable operationally. And, because measurement is an inexact science, different operational definitions may yield different variable values. This accounts for some of the discrepancies that can be found in the research literature. Two researchers who claim to be measuring the same variable but use different operational definitions may get different results. On the other hand, using different operational definitions can be a good thing. All operational definitions have some weakness, but different definitions tend to have different weaknesses. One definition can thus compensate for the weaknesses of another. If research results are similar using several different operational definitions of a variable, then our confidence in the research results is increased.

Four kinds of operational definitions are commonly used in educational research. Objective tests are often employed to operationalize cognitive, and sometimes affective, variables. They are relatively inexpensive and fast to use, and their wide use enhances comparability of operational definitions between studies. However, they cannot provide direct measurement of cognition and affect and are thus usually high-inference measures. Interviews and questionnaires are often employed to operationalize demographic and attitudinal variables. They are relatively fast to use and inexpensive, although not quite as much so as objective tests. They provide the most direct method we have to measure many variables of interest; they have the advantage of letting subjects speak for themselves. However, researchers tend to develop interviews and questionnaires for their own studies; this does not promote comparability of operational definitions between studies.

Observation is sometimes employed to operationalize behavioral variables. It is a relatively slow and expensive method of measurement, but some variables of interest are difficult to define validly in other ways. Observation often requires a great deal of observer judgment, so observer qualifications are important.

When researchers are interested in past events, records of these events often provide the only possible method of measurement. At other times, using existing information saves the cost of collecting new data. However, researchers who use records to operationalize variables cannot control the circumstances of original data collection.

The usefulness of operational definitions depends on their validity. We need to know whether the operational definitions that researchers employ validly measure the variables in which we are interested. Reliability is one component of validity. Reliability involves the consistency of measurement—whether an operational definition consistently yields the same answer to the same question. Reliability can be determined mathematically. Reliability coefficients range from 0 to 1.0, and higher is better. In observational studies using multiple observers, interobserver reliability is critical.

Many of the things researchers do to validate their operational definitions cannot be readily classified. However, some kinds of validity have been named. Content validity involves analysis of the content of operational definitions, usually by people considered to be experts about the variable being measured. Concurrent validity tells us whether an operational definition results in variable values that concur with values obtained in other ways that are accepted as valid. Predictive validity indicates whether an operational definition can be used to make accurate predictions. Construct validity refers to whether an operational definition results in variable values that "behave" in ways that are consonant with theory about the construct being measured.

Treatment conditions are not measured but administered. Instead of describing their operational definitions of treatment variables, researchers describe how their various treatment conditions were administered. Although the kinds of measurement validity concerns that have been dealt with in this chapter do not strictly apply to treatment variables, there are issues surrounding the validity of treatments. In evaluating a researcher's description of a treatment variable, we need to ask whether the treatment conditions were described fully enough that we can evaluate them, and whether the treatment conditions as administered in fact represent the variable the researcher intended to study.

The most important thing to remember about operational definitions is that no matter what variables researchers claim to be studying, they really are studying only the particular operational definitions that they used.

SUMMARY EXERCISES

1. Below you will find excerpts from published studies. For each study, identify the variables. Which of the variables is operationally defined in the excerpt? What is the operational definition? Can you classify the operational definition in terms of one of the methods of measurement described in this chapter (objective test, interview/questionnaire, etc.)? Was any independent variable manipulated by the researcher(s)? If so, briefly describe the manipulation. What evidence did the researchers offer of the validity of the operational definition/manipulation? Can you classify the validity evidence in terms of one of the types of named validity described in this chapter (content, criterion, etc.)? Why do you think the researchers chose this operational definition? Do you feel the operational definition is valid? Why or why not?

a. White, Labouvie, and Bates (1985) studied sensation-seeking and delinquency among middle-class adolescents (p. 201).

Self-report questionnaires provided the data for this study. Self-report is an accepted indicator of delinquency by most researchers in the field (Hindelang et al., 1981) and provides a more direct measure of delinquent behavior than do measures based upon official law enforcement records (Huizinga and Elliott, 1981). The level of delinquency reported by our respondents parallels the amount of involvement found in other surveys of predominantly middle-class adolescents (Linden, 1978; Levine and Kozak, 1979; Richards et al., 1979).

b. King and Cooley (1995) studied the imposter phenomenon, which is an "intense feeling of intellectual inauthenticity experienced by many high-achieving individuals" (p. 304).

Clance's IP Scale (1985) is a 20-item self-report instrument designed to assess the extent to which an individual experiences the imposter phenomenon. The items measure imposter attributes and feelings, such as fear of failure despite past successes, dread of evaluation, fear of not being able to live up to the expectations of others, and attributions of success to error or luck. Clance's IP Scale has been found to identify imposters in both clinical and non-clinical settings (e.g., Holmes, Kertay, Adamson, Holland, & Clance, 1993). The internal consistency of Clance's IP Scale was reported to be .96 (Holmes, et al., 1993) (p. 307).

c. Wang and Nguyen (1995) had two research questions: whether the experience of passionate love would change as a consequence of development throughout adulthood, and whether highly anxious people would be especially motivated to seek passionate love relationships (p. 459).

The Passionate Love Scale (PLS; Hatfield & Specher, 1986) is a 30-item questionnaire that asks the respondent to think of a person whom they love (or loved) passionately. The PLS has three subscales: Cognitive (e.g., "Sometimes I feel I can't control my thoughts; they are obsessively on _____"), Emotional (e.g., "Sometimes my body trembles with excitement at the sight of _____"), and Behavioral (e.g., "I eagerly look for signs indicating _____'s desire for me"). On a 9-point Likert-type scale ranging from *not at all true* (1) to *definitely true* (9), respondents indicate how accurately each statement describes their experience of passionate love. All items on the PLS are scored in the positive direction.

The PLS possesses high internal consistency (coefficient alpha = .94), and test items are largely uncontaminated by social desirability factors (r = .09 with the Social Desirability Scale; Hatfield & Sprecher, 1986). Construct validity of the PLS was also established; it correlated more highly with Rubin's Love Scale (1970) than with Rubin's Liking Scale (1970). The validity of the PLS has been corroborated by other researchers (Hendrick & Hendrick, 1989) using factor analytic techniques.

d.   Sorsdahl and Sanche (1985) developed the Classroom Meeting Behavior Rating Scale (CMB) for a study of fourth-graders' classroom behavior (p. 51).

The CMB is a measure of interpersonal behavior during classroom meetings. It consists of 10 items that allow teachers to rate children on classroom meeting behaviors such as attentiveness, tolerance for the views of others, tact and manners, participation, obedience to rules, and ability to achieve or participate in the consensus of the meeting. Each item is scored on a 5-point scale ranging from almost always to almost never. Sample items include "refuses to agree, prevents consensus," "tactless, rude, socially inappropriate," and "behavior often requires a review of rules or removal from the meeting."

The split-half reliability coefficient for the CMB is .88, "well beyond the .60 that Salvia and Ysseldyke (1981) considered a minimum standard."

e.   Fishbein et al. (1990) studied time of learner's questioning, tutor's response, and learner's learning in tutoring sessions. The researchers set up different tutoring conditions. Some subjects had their questions answered while they were learning; others did not. Some subjects had their questions answered while they were trying to demonstrate what they had learned; others did not.

f.   Greenbaum (1985) studied conversation in American Indian and Anglo upper-elementary classrooms (pp. 106–107).

Two videotape cameras were used to record each class session. No data were used from initial recordings in any of the classes. . . . One camera provided a wide field of view of the teacher and the class, while the second camera individually recorded the listener-gaze of 18 students. . . . Verbatim transcripts were made of teacher and student utterances. . . . From these transcripts, classroom interactions were divided into four categorical sequential events, which collectively constituted a turn taking round, or exchange, between the teacher and the class. These were (a) teacher utterance, (b) class turn-switching pause, (c) class utterance, and (d) teacher turn-switching pause. An utterance was considered to be the time it took a speaker to emit all the words that speaker was contributing to a particular exchange (cf., Matarazzo & Wiens, 1972); a turn-switching was the latency period between the end of one speaker's utterance and the start of another's (cf., Jaffe and Feldstein, 1970). Two observers used a .01 second stopwatch to measure the duration of each event. . . .

Gaze behaviors of the 18 sampled students were gaze duration and gaze direction measured during 12 randomly selected teacher utterances. Gaze duration was measured with a .01 second stopwatch, and gaze direction was classified as one of three mutually exclusive categories: teacher-, peer-, or object-directed. For each of the sampled intervals, the percent gaze in each of the three directions was calculated.

To assess interobserver reliability on the objective speech measures, one of the 11 class sessions was scored by both observers. The reliabilities for listener-gaze were derived by having both observers score the gaze of the same three students, one from each student group (reservation Indian, public school Indian, public school non-Indian). Among the data scored by both observers, there were no significant mean differences on any of the five measures ($t < 1.00$). The observed Pearson correlations ranged from .97 to .99.

g. Paulsen (1991) investigated a number of variables as predictors of high-school seniors' participation in collective action. Collective action involved participation "in at least one protest or demonstration . . . or community problem-solving event" (p. 103). Predictors included socioeconomic status (ranging from 2 to 96), leadership (coded as 0 or 1), grades (from A = 4 to F = 0), college preparatory courses (0 or 1), urban school (0 or 1), student participation (1 = none to 4 = a good deal), gender, race, and political efficacy (0 or 1).

In his study, Paulsen utilized data that he obtained through the Interuniversity Consortium for Political and Social Research. The data were collected by Jennings and Niemi from 1965–1973 as part of their Youth-Parent Socialization Panel Study. Paulsen focused on 1,063 subjects who were high-school seniors in 1965.

h. Morrison, Ross, Gopalakrishnan, and Casey (1995) studied the effects of feedback and incentives on achievement in computer-based instruction. There were five feedback conditions (answer until correct, knowledge of correct response, delayed, no feedback, and no questions) and two incentive conditions (task and performance). "Results showed an overall effect favoring performance incentives across all levels of . . . feedback conditions)" p. 32.

Subjects were 346 undergraduates enrolled in one of two introductory required courses in teacher education. One course taught basic applications of technology while the other dealt with educational psychology and human development (typically taken before or with the technology course). Subjects from the technology course ($n = 148$) participated in the study as a required activity for a regular course unit on instructional objectives. This group of subjects was considered to be working under performance incentives. The only difference between the research context and typical instructional procedures was that the particular instructional unit, with minor content modifications, was converted from lecture and print material to a CBI [computer-based instruction] program. . . .

Subjects in the educational psychology course ($n = 98$) used the same CBI program but were offered credit toward their course grade for participating in an "outside" experiment. They were encouraged to "do their best," given the purposes of the study. They were also told, however, that their level of performance would have no bearing on the amount of credit received. This group of subjects was considered to be working under task incentives.

Subjects were randomly assigned within classes (i.e., performance- vs.-task-incentives conditions) to one of five feedback groups (p. 35).

2. Locate at least three quantitative research reports that look interesting to you in research journals in your field. For each report identify the variables that were studied. Were the operational definitions of these variables specified in the articles? If not, why do you think the researchers omitted them? If so, what were the operational definitions? Do the methods of measurement fit one of the four categories (objective tests, interviews and questionnaires, observation, and archives) that were described in this chapter? Do the researchers offer evidence of the validity of their operational definitions? If not, why do you think they omitted such evidence? If so, evaluate the evidence. Whether or not evidence was provided, do you think the operational definitions are valid? Why or why not? Why do you think the researchers chose these operational definitions?

3. For the research questions you made up for Summary Exercise 3 in chapter 1, try to define the variables operationally. What validity issues do you see for your operational definitions?

4. Construct a brief questionnaire on some topic of interest to you. Administer the questionnaire to five people and get their feedback on how you might improve the questionnaire.

SUGGESTED READINGS

Aiken, L. (1994). *Psychological Testing and Assessment.* Boston: Allyn and Bacon.

Anastasi, A. (1988). *Psychological Testing.* New York: Macmillan.

Foddy, W. (1993). *Constructing Questions for Interviews and Questionnaires: Theory and Practice in Social Research.* New York: Cambridge.

Thorndike, R., and Hagen, E. (1977). *Measurement and Evaluation in Psychology and Education.* New York: Wiley.

4

Quantitative Research Design and Causal Argument

In chapter 3, we introduced the concept of internal validity. Recall that internal validity refers to whether the research process yields an answer to the research question that is valid for the context in which the research was done. Internal validity has two components. One of them is validity of measurement, which was covered in chapter 3. The second component of internal validity is the validity of causal argument, which is the subject of this chapter.

Most quantitative research in education focuses on relationships between variables, and most, though not all, of these relationships are thought to be causal. However, as chapter 3 cautioned, we cannot make assumptions about causation in the absence of causal evidence. It is time now to look at what constitutes a causal argument in quantitative research.

CONFOUNDING VARIABLES

The history of causal argument—i.e., the development of scientists' thinking about causal argument—is an interesting one and has been treated in many sources. Most quantitative researchers now follow a model for causal argument that was first proposed by John Stuart Mill (Cook and Campbell, 1979, p. 18).

Rephrasing what Mill had to say in contemporary terms, we can argue that variable X is causally related to variable Y in a given study only if all of the following conditions are met:

1. X precedes Y in time.
2. X and Y are related.
3. No other variable is related to Y.

These conditions are necessary for the following reasons.

1. X must precede Y in time because causes have to come before effects. You yell after you grab the hot handle of the pot on the stove, not before.

2. X and Y have to be related. For a group of individuals, when the value of the causal variable is present, the value of the effect variable must also tend to be present; and when the value of the cause variable is absent, the value of the effect variable must also tend to be absent. Consider the causal variable *having unprotected sex* and the effect variable *getting pregnant.* For women, when the value of the causal variable is present (i.e., they do have unprotected sex), the value of the effect variable

also tends to be present (i.e., they do tend to get pregnant); and when the value of the causal variable is *absent* (i.e., they do not have unprotected sex), the value of the effect variable also tends to be *absent* (i.e., they tend not to get pregnant). Having unprotected sex is related to pregnancy because women who have unprotected sex tend to get pregnant, and women who do not have unprotected sex tend not to get pregnant.

3. No other variable can be related to *Y*, because if another variable is related to *Y*, then it, instead of *X*, may be the cause of *Y*. Imagine that a researcher measures two variables with the following results.

X	*Y*
No	No
No	No
Yes	Yes
Yes	Yes

The researcher is certainly in a position to conclude that there is a relationship between the two variables. However, as was pointed out in chapter 2 for ice cream sales and drowning deaths, such results alone do not permit the conclusion that the relationship is causal. It is quite possible, for example, that both *X* and *Y* are caused by a third variable and thus have no direct causal relationship with each other.

Imagine that the researcher in fact identifies and measures such a third variable, with the following results.

X	*Y*	*Z*
No	No	No
No	No	No
Yes	Yes	Yes
Yes	Yes	Yes

On the basis of this evidence, the researcher cannot demonstrate that *X* causes *Y*, because *Z* may cause *Y*. In this example, *Z* is called a *confounding* (or *extraneous* or *intervening* or *nuisance*) *variable* because it confounds the relationship being investigated—that between *X* and *Y*.

As a real-world example, assume that a researcher has demonstrated the following relationship between self-esteem and school achievement.

Self-Esteem	*Achievement*
Low	Low
Low	Low
High	High
High	High

This researcher would like to be able to conclude that self-esteem is causally related to school achievement—that low self-esteem causes students to do poorly in school, and high self-esteem causes students to do well in school. What happens to the researcher's causal argument, however, when the following confounding variable is discovered?

Self-Esteem	Achievement	Intelligence
Low	Low	Low
Low	Low	Low
High	High	High
High	High	High

It is now obvious that there may be no causal relationship between self-esteem and achievement. Achievement may be caused by intellect instead.

In the real world, many causes operate simultaneously on a given effect. In order to argue that one variable causes another, researchers must create an artificial situation in which only one independent variable is allowed to operate on the dependent variable; if other independent variables are allowed to operate, we cannot be sure which one is causing the effect on the dependent variable. In order to argue that X causes Y, a researcher must be able to argue that in her study no other variable was related to Y—that she has controlled for potentially confounding variables.

Figure 4.1 summarizes causal argument.

■ EXERCISE 1

Imagine that a researcher has demonstrated a relationship between shoe size and reading ability in a group of elementary-school children. Do you think this is a causal relationship? If not, what confounding variable(s) do you think accounts for this relationship?   ■

Controlling Confounding Variables

Holding Constant

A quantitative researcher has four ways to control a potentially confounding variable in a given study. The first is not to let it vary—to keep it constant. This can be conceptualized as follows.

X	Y	Z
No	No	Yes
No	No	Yes
Yes	Yes	Yes
Yes	Yes	Yes

FIGURE 4.1   Components of causal argument.

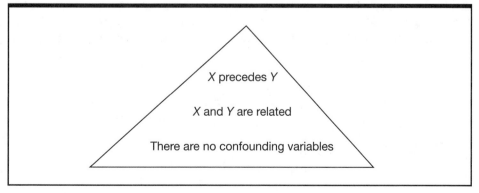

X precedes Y

X and Y are related

There are no confounding variables

In chapter 2 we pointed out that a relationship between a variable and a constant cannot be demonstrated. When Z is kept constant it cannot be the cause of Y, because it is not related to Y.

To continue with the self-esteem example, a researcher who wished to control the potentially confounding variable *intelligence* could do so by keeping it constant.

Self-Esteem	Achievement	Intelligence
Low	Low	High
Low	Low	High
High	High	High
High	High	High

Now intelligence does not confound the relationship that the researcher wishes to study, between self-esteem and achievement. Because intelligence is not related to achievement in this study, it cannot be a cause of the achievement differences that were found in this study.

Matching

The second way a researcher can control a potentially confounding variable is to allow it to vary, but in such a way that it is not related to Y. This can be accomplished as follows.

X	Y	Z
No	No	No
No	No	Yes
Yes	Yes	No
Yes	Yes	Yes

When potentially confounding variables are controlled in this way, they cannot be causes of Y because they are not related to Y.

This method of controlling variables is called matching. How matching is done can be a bit difficult to understand at first. A good way to get a handle on it is to think of it in the following way.

A researcher who wishes to control a potentially confounding variable by matching begins by identifying a pool of potential subjects (or cases). He then ascertains the values of the independent variable for these potential subjects. Next he divides the subjects into groups based on shared values of the independent variable. Let's imagine that a researcher has identified a potential-subjects pool, measured their values of X, and divided them into groups based on shared values of X, as follows:

	Subject	X
	a	No
	b	No
Group 1	c	No
	d	No
	e	No

	f	Yes
	g	Yes
Group 2	h	Yes
	i	Yes
	j	Yes

Group 1 consists of all the potential subjects who share one value (no) of the independent variable, and group 2 consists of all the potential subjects who share another value (yes) of the independent variable.

Now the researcher must match the two independent-variable groups on Z, the variable to be controlled. To do this he first ascertains the subjects' values of Z. Imagine that the results are as follows:

	Subject	*X*	*Z*
	a	No	No
	b	No	No
Group 1	c	No	No
	d	No	Yes
	e	No	Yes
	f	Yes	No
	g	Yes	No
Group 2	h	Yes	Yes
	i	Yes	Yes
	j	Yes	Yes

From this pool of potential subjects, the researcher now selects actual subjects in matched pairs. A pair consists of one subject from each of the groups; matching is done on Z. This means that for every subject in the first group who has a particular value of Z, there must be a subject in the second group who also has that value of Z. Subjects who cannot be matched in this way must be excluded from the study. In this example, matching could be done as follows:

	Subject	*X*	*Z*
	a	No	No
	b	No	No
Group 1	d	No	Yes
	e	No	Yes
	f	Yes	No
	g	Yes	No
Group 2	h	Yes	Yes
	i	Yes	Yes

Subject *a* in group 1 has the value *no* of the variable to be controlled; subject *f* in group 2, who also has the value *no* of this variable, matches subject *a*. Subject *b* in group 1 has the value *no* of the variable to be controlled; subject *g* in group 2, who also has the value *no* of this variable, matches subject *b*. Similarly, subjects *d* and *h* and *e* and *i* are matched. Subjects *c* and *j,* who were in the original pool, could not be matched and are no longer in the study.

Groups 1 and 2 are now matched on the variable to be controlled. As you will see if you look at the last example, the net result of matching is that X and Z are not related; thus, Z cannot be a confounding variable in this study.

Now the researcher can proceed to measure the dependent variable, Y. If it turns out that X and Y are related, Z will not be a confounding variable, because Z is not related to X:

Group	X	Y	Z
1	No	No	No
1	No	No	Yes
2	Yes	Yes	No
2	Yes	Yes	Yes

Intelligence could be controlled this way in a self-esteem study. The results would look like the following:

Self-Esteem	Achievement	Intelligence
Low	Low	Low
Low	Low	High
High	High	Low
High	High	High

Now intelligence does not confound the relationship that the researcher wishes to study, between self-esteem and achievement. Since intelligence is not related to self-esteem in this study, it cannot be a cause of the achievement differences that were found in this study.

Statistically Controlling

A third way that researchers can control potentially confounding variables involves statistics, which we'll get to later. For now, suffice it to say that if a researcher has identified and measured a potentially confounding variable, it is possible to control it statistically as well as by keeping it constant or matching. A researcher might, for example, report finding a relationship between self-esteem and achievement when the influence of intelligence on achievement was statistically controlled.

Treating as Independent Variable

Often researchers deal with a potentially confounding variable in a fourth way: by including it as an additional independent variable and studying the way it interacts with the other independent variable(s) to affect the dependent variable. This makes sense, if you think about it. A potentially confounding variable probably is a cause of the dependent variable; if it weren't, the researcher wouldn't be worried about it. Most techniques for controlling confounding variables require identifying and measuring them. At that point, it is often little additional trouble to go ahead and treat them as independent variables.

This accounts, in part, for the fact that so much educational research involves multiple independent variables and interaction analyses. When you are reading a research report involving multiple independent variables, you will often get the feeling that the researcher is really more interested in some of them than in others. You may be right. The researcher is probably primarily interested in one or two of the independent variables; she essentially views the others as confounding variables but is dealing with them by building them in rather than controlling them out.

Figure 4.2 depicts the four techniques available to researchers for controlling potentially confounding variables.

■ EXERCISE 2

In each of the following examples, decide whether the confounding variable has been controlled and, if so, whether it was controlled by being held constant or by matching.

a. X	Y	Z		b. X	Y	Z		c. X	Y	Z
1	1	1		1	1	1		1	1	1
1	1	1		1	1	2		1	1	1
2	2	2		2	2	1		2	2	1
2	2	2		2	2	2		2	2	1

■ EXERCISE 3

For each of the following examples, create a table like those in Exercise 2 to show what the research data might look like.

a. A researcher studies the effect of highest degree held (master's or doctorate) on principal's leadership style (democratic or authoritarian); gender is controlled by being held constant.

b. X = native language (Spanish or English), Y = SAT score, Z = IQ (matched).

Researchers thus have at their disposal four ways to control potentially confounding variables. The problem isn't finding ways to control them but that there are so many of them to control. Consider a researcher who investigates the effects of reinforcement by teachers on children's social skills. She finds that reinforced children develop more social skills than do nonreinforced children. But there are so many potentially confounding variables that might also have accounted for her results: children's intellect, age, gender, social experiences outside the classroom during the research, motivation, level of social skill on entering the program, cultural background, language ability, nutritional status, physical impairment, learning style. These

FIGURE 4.2   Four techniques for controlling potentially confounding variables.

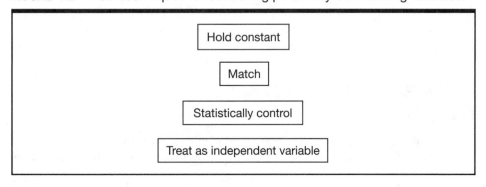

and many other variables might have influenced the subjects' social development. How can a researcher ever deal with them all?

One way is actually to attempt to identify and control all such potentially confounding variables. But even if the researcher is successful in identifying them, they must be measured in order to be controlled. It is not difficult to ascertain the gender, age, and perhaps the cultural background of most subjects. The researcher can then control them by holding them constant—by using only subjects who are of the same age, gender, and cultural background; or by matching—by assigning equal proportions of boys and girls of various ages and of various cultural groups to be reinforced and not reinforced. Such variables as intellect, social skill on entry, language ability, nutritional status, motivation, learning style, and physical impairment can also be measured (although with varying degrees of validity) and controlled, but this can be an expensive proposition. And what about such things as social experience outside the classroom during the program? How is a researcher ever able to be sure of what a child's social experience is, day in and day out?

■ EXERCISE 4

Several examples of research situations follow. For each example, identify the potentially serious confounding variable(s). It may help to format the examples as follows:

X	Y	Z
?	?	?
?	?	?
?	?	?
?	?	?

a. A researcher wished to know whether computer-assisted instruction is effective. He compared the learning of two groups of children. One group, fifth-graders taught by Mr. Vincent, received computer-assisted instruction; the other group, third-graders taught by Ms. DiMarco, received regular classroom instruction. The computer-assisted group learned more.

b. A researcher wished to know whether health education is effective. She compared the health practices of two groups of subjects. One group volunteered for and received health education; the second group did not volunteer for and did not receive health education. The group receiving health education had better health practices.

c. A researcher wished to know whether reinforcement increases task attention. He compared the time on task of Ms. Almari's kindergarten classes. The morning class was not reinforced; the afternoon class was reinforced. The classes spent about the same amount of time on task. The researcher concluded that reinforcement was ineffective in increasing task attention.   ■

EXPERIMENTAL AND NONEXPERIMENTAL RESEARCH

A researcher's ability to solve the problem of confounding variables depends in part on whether the research is experimental or nonexperimental. In experimental research, the researcher determines the values of the independent variable; in nonexperimental research, the researcher uses naturally occurring values of the independent variable.

Research methodologists usually classify nonexperimental research approaches into several different types, although there is disagreement about how many types there are and what to call them. Names that are used include *ex post facto, survey, correlational, descriptive,* and *quasi-experimental research.* We do not feel it is necessary to deal with these various classifications in an introductory text. The basic issues in nonexperimental research are common to all the types, and our treatment of nonexperimental research is general enough to apply to all of the types.

We have defined experimentation in terms of researchers' determining subjects' or cases' values of the independent variable. This definition of experimentation overlaps with the notion of treatment variables, which we introduced in chapter 3. All experimental variables are treatment variables; it is the conditions of treatment that the researcher dictates. But not all treatment variables are experimental; a researcher may study treatment conditions that she does not dictate. Then the research is nonexperimental.

Often a given independent variable can be studied either experimentally or nonexperimentally. Perhaps a researcher is interested in knowing whether open classrooms enhance children's self-concepts; that is, whether children in open classrooms have higher self-concepts than children in traditional classrooms do. The researcher can determine the values of the independent variable, by assigning some children to open classrooms and other children to traditional classrooms; or the researcher can use naturally occurring values of the independent variable, by finding some children who are already in open classrooms and other children who are already in traditional classrooms.

The values of some independent variables, however, cannot be determined by researchers, for either ethical or practical reasons. Most of what are called demographic variables fall into this category. These are variables reflecting subjects' backgrounds (e.g., age, gender, ethnicity, occupation, and income). Although it would be possible for a researcher to dictate people's occupations and incomes, there are both ethical and practical reasons for not doing so; and it is simply impossible for researchers to control people's ethnicity, age, or gender. Some research, therefore, simply cannot be done experimentally.

At other times, researchers may prefer to do experimental research and experimentation may not be ethically or practically precluded, but the researcher may simply be unable to find cooperative subjects. Often educational researchers must elicit consent and cooperation from principals, teachers, parents, or students. Such people sometimes have understandable reluctance about allowing researchers to determine the values of variables in educational settings. Ideally, a researcher may wish to decide which children in a given school are placed in open classrooms and which are placed in traditional ones. The principal, however, may be unwilling to give up the prerogative of assigning children to classrooms.

■ EXERCISE 5

Which of the following independent variables must be studied nonexperimentally? Which may be either nonexperimental or experimental? What would be the practical and ethical implications of studying these latter variables experimentally?

a. blood type
b. test anxiety
c. self-esteem
d. native language
e. intelligence
f. teaching method   ■

Random Assignment

The implications of this aspect of research design—that is, whether the research is experimental or nonexperimental—are enormous, because experimentation offers researchers a powerful tool for controlling confounding variables and thus demonstrating that a relationship is causal. The tool is called random assignment. Experimental researchers determine the values of the independent variable for the subjects or cases in their studies. If the independent variable is type of counseling, with the values *directive* and *nondirective,* the researcher decides which subjects will receive directive and which will receive nondirective therapy. On what basis does the researcher make these decisions? The best basis for causal argument is usually random assignment.

Here's an example of how such a researcher would randomly assign. Let's assume that the researcher has 100 subjects. She wishes to assign randomly 50 of them to receive directive counseling and 50 to receive nondirective counseling. She can simply toss a coin for each subject; the "heads" will go into one group, and the "tails" will go into another group. In this case, if the coin comes up heads, the subject will receive directive counseling; if it comes up tails, the subject will receive nondirective counseling. (In fact, researchers usually use tables of random numbers for such purposes, but the principle is the same.)

The reason that random assignment is such a useful strategy for controlling potentially confounding variables is that random assignment makes it very probable that potentially confounding variables are effectively matched; and if variables are matched, they can't confound causal argument.

Suppose that the group of 100 subjects contains 60 women and 40 men. If the subjects are randomly assigned to the two treatment groups, it is very likely that each group will contain close to 30 women and 20 men—that gender in the two groups will be matched. For every, or nearly every, woman in directive therapy, there will be a matching woman in nondirective therapy; and for every, or nearly every, man in directive therapy, there will be a matching man in nondirective therapy.

The beauty of random assignment is that it maximizes the probability that any potentially confounding variable is effectively matched, whether it was identified as a potentially confounding variable or not: physical health, education, employment, attractiveness, affluence, what subjects had for breakfast, whether they like classical music or jazz, and so forth. (Random assignment does not guarantee control of all variables. Unlikely things do happen. For example, it is possible, though highly improbable, that in the example given above random assignment of subjects to directive and nondirective therapy groups would have resulted in a predominantly female directive therapy group and a predominantly male nondirective therapy group. This points up the value of replication. Improbable things can happen once, but it is even less probable—much less probable—that they will happen twice, and still less probable that they will happen three times.)

Random assignment thus offers researchers maximal control over variables that have the potential to confound causal argument. In reading experimental research, however, you must evaluate whether the researcher has used the potential of experimentation to best advantage. Although most experiments involve random assignment, occasionally one does not: The researcher determines the values of the independent variable but uses some basis other than randomness to assign subjects or cases to treatment conditions. In such a situation, of course, the advantage of random assignment is lost, and potentially confounding variables cannot be considered controlled.

■ EXERCISE 6

Following are data on 50 imaginary subjects. After the imaginary data were created, a table of random numbers was used to assign the subjects by identification number to two groups. If these subjects were now assigned to two independent variable groups, random assignment should make it probable that any potentially confounding variable has been effectively matched between the two groups. Assume that gender, ethnicity, and educational level are potentially confounding variables in the study in which these data will be used. Check to see whether random assignment did, in fact, effectively match the two groups on all three of these variables; that is, check to see whether groups 1 and 2 contain approximately equal numbers of males and females, Anglos and Hispanics, and college graduates and non-college graduates. If random assignment matched these three variables, do you see that it probably matched other variables as well, even those we haven't identified or measured?

Group	Subject I.D. Number	Gender	Ethnicity	College Graduate
1	3	F	A	No
1	5	F	A	No
1	6	F	A	No
1	7	F	A	No
1	8	F	A	No
1	9	F	A	No
1	12	F	A	No
1	16	F	A	Yes
1	17	F	A	Yes
1	20	F	A	Yes
1	21	F	H	No
1	22	F	H	No
1	24	F	H	No
1	28	F	H	Yes
1	31	M	A	No
1	34	M	A	No
1	37	M	A	No
1	40	M	A	Yes
1	41	M	A	Yes
1	42	M	A	Yes
1	44	M	H	No
1	45	M	H	No
1	46	M	H	No

1	47	M	H	No
1	50	M	H	Yes

Group	Subject I.D. Number	Gender	Ethnicity	College Graduate
2	1	F	A	No
2	2	F	A	No
2	4	F	A	No
2	10	F	A	No
2	11	F	A	No
2	13	F	A	No
2	14	F	A	Yes
2	15	F	A	Yes
2	18	F	A	Yes
2	19	F	A	Yes
2	23	F	H	No
2	25	F	H	No
2	26	F	H	No
2	27	F	H	No
2	29	F	H	Yes
2	30	F	H	Yes
2	32	M	A	No
2	33	M	A	No
2	35	M	A	No
2	36	M	A	No
2	38	M	A	No
2	39	M	A	No
2	43	M	A	Yes
2	48	M	H	No
2	49	M	H	Yes

■

■ EXERCISE 7

Ascertain the values of four or five categorical variables for at least 30 people (perhaps your classmates). Be sure the variables aren't embarrassing (whether they ate breakfast this morning is okay; whether they like X-rated movies isn't). Randomly assign the people to two groups, perhaps by tossing a coin. Did random assignment effectively match the two groups on each variable? ■

Control of Potentially Confounding Variables in Nonexperimental Research

Because random assignment affords particularly good protection from potentially confounding variables and thus enhances causal argument, many researchers would prefer to assign randomly. However, as was pointed out earlier, the values of many independent variables of interest to educators cannot be dictated by researchers. In some educational subfields, the problem is especially serious. Researchers interested in biological causes of human behavior (for example, biologically based differences between male and female behavior) cannot do experiments; neither can researchers interested in socialization as a cause of behavior (for example, differences in the behavior of children of alcoholic and nonalcoholic parents).

Such researchers cannot randomly assign subjects to be biologically male or female or to be socialized by alcoholic or nonalcoholic parents. Thus the possibility that confounding variables will confound causal argument looms large in nonexperimental research. A great deal of research has shown that men achieve more highly in mathematics than women do. Does that demonstrate a biological basis for math achievement? Of course not. It is quite possible that males are socialized to be better at math than females—that socialization is a confounding variable in the demonstrated relationship between biological sex and math achievement and that biological sex is merely a proxy or predictor variable for math achievement.

Because nonexperimental researchers cannot randomly assign, they must rely instead on identifying and controlling potentially confounding variables. As was pointed out earlier, this can be very difficult to do. Such variables are often hard to predict. Even when they can be predicted, they are often hard to measure, and even when they can be measured, such measurement is often expensive.

Nonexperimental researchers sometimes go to great lengths in attempting to control subject or case characteristics. For example, researchers interested in biological differences between male and female behavior cannot ethically or practically control people's gender-role socialization; but if this variable is not controlled, it is almost certain to confound the study. In such situations, researchers have few options. One is to study differences in the behavior of newborn males and females. When such differences are found (and they are), researchers are in a good position to argue that they must be biologically caused rather than learned through differential socialization. However, this strategy places severe limitations on the behavioral differences that can be studied, because a newborn's behavioral repertoire is very limited. Certainly it is not possible to study differences in newborn males' and females' math achievement.

A nonexperimental researcher is faced first with the problem of identifying all subject or case variables that pose a serious threat. Another way of thinking about this is as follows: Nonexperimental researchers must identify all variables that may be causally related to the dependent variable being studied. This is a difficult proposition, because most dependent variables of interest to educational researchers have multiple causes that are not entirely understood. How would you like, for example, to have to identify all the causes of mathematics achievement, or delinquency, or typing skill, or self-esteem?

Once these variables are identified, they must be controlled. The four ways to do this were described earlier in this chapter. All of them involve the expense of validly measuring potentially confounding variables, which is sometimes difficult to do no matter how large a budget the researcher has. Some of them also involve additional, nonmonetary costs. Sometimes the easiest way to control a potentially confounding variable is to keep it constant. Thus you will often see research reports in which all subjects are male (or female), first-graders (or eleventh-graders), or beginning (or experienced) teachers. The problem with this solution is that it limits the generalizability of the study's results. Chapter 5 is devoted to generalizability. For now, suffice it to say that if a study is conducted on males only, researchers are often unsure as to whether the study's results apply to females as well.

Matching causes similar problems. Often, in reading research reports, you will see a statement like the following: Groups were matched for age, gender, and intelligence. This means that the researcher measured potential subjects' age, gender, and intelligence, as well as their values of the independent variable and dependent variables. Then the researcher made sure that for every male in independent-variable group 1, there was a male in independent-variable group 2 (and often in additional independent-variable groups; there are frequently more than two); for every 13- year-old in group 1, there was a 13-year-old in group 2; for every subject with an IQ of 115 in group 1, there was a subject with an IQ of 115 in group 2; and so forth. As you can see, this quickly gets tedious. It also affects generalizability, because some potential subjects cannot be matched and must be excluded.

■ EXERCISE 8

Imagine a school district in which federal funds are available to provide special services to low-income children who are achieving poorly in school. A researcher receives a contract to evaluate the federal program. She informs program personnel that, in order to control potentially confounding variables in the study, she would like to assign the eligible children randomly to treatment and control groups—that is, to receive and not to receive the program. Program personnel, however, are unwilling to give up their prerogative of deciding which children to serve. They explain to the researcher that treatment and control groups already exist. Because there are not enough funds to serve all the children who are eligible, federal-program teachers select only certain of the eligible children to receive services. If the researcher uses these preexisting treatment and control groups, what confounding variable poses a serious threat to causal argument in her study? That is, if the researcher finds that eligible children who receive services show more improvement in school achievement than do eligible children who do not receive services, can she conclude that the program is effective?   ■

Within-Subjects Designs

When random assignment is not possible, an important tool for controlling potentially confounding variables is lost. One clever way for either experimental or nonexperimental researchers to get around this problem is to use subjects as their own controls for potentially confounding variables. This is sometimes called a *within-subjects* (or *repeated-measures*) *design.* A researcher might, for example, measure children's learning in their regular classrooms in the fall and then measure the same children's learning in a special program in the spring. Instead of having two groups of children, each group having a different value of the independent variable, the researcher uses only one group of children, having two different values of the independent variable over two periods of time. Such research is set up as follows.

Subject	Special Program	Learning
a	No	Less
b	No	Less
a	Yes	More
b	Yes	More

Notice that each individual subject appears twice. If, as represented above, the children learn more in the special program than in their regular classrooms, the researcher would like to be able to conclude that the special program caused the higher rate of learning.

Is such research vulnerable to confounding variables? In many respects, no. Most potentially confounding variables are automatically matched when subjects are used as their own controls. Gender, for example, cannot be a confounding variable because it is matched over the two groups—it has to be, since the two groups are the same children. Many other variables are similarly controlled—the children's nutritional status, learning styles, and intelligence, for example, are unlikely to have changed over the school year.

However, using groups as their own controls usually introduces confounding variables into the research. For example, if the children learn more in the spring, perhaps it is not due to the special program but to the time of year. Or perhaps children learned things in the fall that helped them to learn more in the spring.

It is also possible that some characteristic of the subjects changed, quite coincidentally and without the researcher's knowledge, in a way that confounds the study. For example, if the school happens to introduce a parent-involvement program at the same time that the researcher introduces her special program, subjects' greater learning may be caused by increased parent involvement rather than by the program the researcher is investigating.

Measurement of the dependent variable also becomes a problem. The same test cannot be used to measure the children's learning during both periods. It is known that children tend to do better on an achievement test the second time they take it simply because they have learned something about the test by taking it the first time. Therefore, different tests have to be used. How is a researcher to be sure that the second test isn't easier than the first one? This would make it appear that the children learned more when they didn't.

Even though these problems exist, researchers sometimes elect to use within-subjects designs because they do head off problems with many potentially confounding variables. Such researchers usually use two (or more) different groups of children, each serving as its own control for most variables and both serving to control such things as time of year and test difficulty. One group, for example, might be in their regular classrooms in the fall and in the special program in the spring. The other group would be in the special program in the fall and in their regular classrooms in the spring. If both groups learn more in the special program, then this cannot be due to time of year.

With these kinds of controls on potentially confounding research variables in place, within-subjects designs can provide good causal argument, because most potentially confounding variables are obviously controlled. Unfortunately, many independent variables of interest to educational researchers do not lend themselves to within-subjects designs. If a variable cannot be studied experimentally, there is a good chance it also cannot be studied using a within-subjects design. Demographic variables are the most obvious example.

Demographic variables cannot be studied experimentally because researchers cannot control things like people's gender, age, ethnicity, and socioeconomic status. Nor can these be independent variables in a within-subjects design; the same individual cannot be male at one time and female at another, or Anglo at one time and Hispanic at another.

■ Exercise 9

Nonsense-syllable pairs are often used in memory research. A group of subjects is shown a set of nonsense-syllable pairs (e.g., *bim-gar*); the subjects are then shown only the first syllable of each pair (*bim*) and asked to remember the second syllable. Imagine a study of the effectiveness of imaging in aiding memory that is conducted as follows. A group of subjects is first shown a set of 10 nonsense-syllable pairs and simply asked to remember them. Next the same subjects are shown another set of 10 pairs and asked to remember them, but this time the subjects are asked to use imaging to help them remember. The subjects remember more pairs after being asked to use imaging than before. What kinds of subject variables have been controlled by this research procedure? What confounding variables have actually been created by this research procedure? Make and fill in a table like the one below to show what the results of this research might look like.

Subjects	Imaging	Pairs Remembered	Controlled and Created Confounding Variables			
?	?	?	?	?	?	?
?	?	?	?	?	?	?
?	?	?	?	?	?	?
?	?	?	?	?	?	?

Single-Subject Designs

Whether they compare two or more groups of subjects at one point in time or the same group of subjects at two or more points in time, most research designs are group designs. Occasionally, however, researchers employ what are called *single-subject designs*. The name, single-subject, implies that only one subject is studied. In fact, one or a few subjects may be studied. The important thing is that subjects are not grouped; each subject is studied separately.

Most researchers usually prefer group over single-subject designs. Some research situations, however, do not lend themselves to group designs; group designs, for example, don't work well when there are too few subjects per group. Perhaps the most common reason for the use of single-subject designs is that too few subjects are available for a group design. Sometimes this is unavoidable—for example, when the phenomenon of interest is very rare.

Occasionally, however, single-subject designs are preferable to group designs even though a group design would be feasible. This is especially likely to be true when researchers are just beginning to study a phenomenon of interest. In such situations, we can sometimes learn more by intensively studying one or a few individuals than by grouping similar individuals for study. When we don't know very much about a situation, grouping people may obscure a lot of interesting things that are going on.

Sometimes researchers make causal argument in single-subject studies. With respect to evaluating causal argument, single-subject designs are probably best viewed as variations on within-subjects designs.

Within-subjects designs provide excellent control of most of the subject variables that could otherwise confound a study. This is because the researcher studies the same group of people at different times—times when they have different values of the independent variable. Any change in the people's value of the dependent variable when their value of the independent variable changes is probably because their value of the independent variable changes, not because of some change in other characteristics of the people—most of their characteristics stay the same over time.

This is also a strength of single-subject designs. In single-subject studies, researchers begin by establishing what is called a *baseline*. Baseline refers to the subject's "normal" values of the independent and dependent variables. Once the baseline has been established—i.e., once the researcher knows what the subject's normal values of the variables are—the value of the independent variable is changed, either by the researcher (in which case the study is experimental) or in a naturally occurring way (in which case the study is nonexperimental). If the subject's value of the dependent variable changes when the value of the independent variable changes, it is likely that the two variables are causally related.

Sometimes, as a double-check on causal argument, researchers add a third stage to single-subject studies. In the third stage, the subject's value of the independent variable is returned to baseline. If the subject's value of the dependent variable also returns to baseline during this third stage, it is even more likely that the two variables are causally related. You will occasionally see designs referred to as *A-B* or *A-B-A* designs. These letters stand for values of the independent variable, *A* for baseline and *B* for change. In an *A-B* design, the same subject is studied at two points in time— first baseline and then change. In an *A-B-A* design, the same subject is studied at three points in time—first baseline, then change, then return to baseline.

Experimental researchers can use random assignment to maximize the probability that most potentially confounding variables have been controlled, whether or not they have been identified. Within-subjects designs offer both experimental and nonexperimental researchers another way to deal with these variables, whether identified or not; however, this solution to the problem of confounding variables is not often used, because most research questions do not lend themselves to this approach. Most often, then, nonexperimental researchers must rely on their ability first to identify such variables and then to control them in one of the four available ways: holding them constant, matching, statistically controlling them, or building them in as bona fide independent variables.

Random assignment of subjects to independent-variable groups takes place at the beginning of the data-collection stage of research. After this time, confounding variables can be introduced into the research. Imagine, for example, a researcher who randomly assigns subjects to directive and nondirective counseling groups, and then assigns the directive group to an experienced therapist and the nondirective group to an inexperienced therapist. The variable *therapist's experience* is now totally confounded with the independent variable. If the directive group does better, it may be because they had an experienced therapist, not because they received directive therapy.

Random assignment of subjects to independent-variable groups offers no protection from this kind of eventuality, because it cannot affect variables that arise later. Both experimental and nonexperimental researchers must rely on identifying and controlling such variables. However, experimental researchers usually have the edge over nonexperimental researchers in this regard as well. In experimental research, the researcher controls the values of the independent variable. If he is in a position to do this, he is also likely to be able to control other variables in the research situation, such as teacher competence, physical environment, and materials used. In fact, some experimental research is done in laboratories, where researchers even have control over such things as room temperature, humidity, and lighting.

Nonexperimental research is usually done not only on naturally occurring values of the independent variable but also in other natural conditions. Often a researcher who cannot control the values of the independent variable in a study also cannot control such other variables in the research situation as teacher competence, physical environment, materials used, and so forth. All of these then become potentially confounding variables.

Both experimental and nonexperimental researchers must attempt to identify and control potentially confounding variables in the research situation, but this is often easier to do when the research is experimental. If a researcher has the ability and permission to control the values of the independent variable, it is likely that he also has the ability and permission to control other variables in the research situation. However, if a researcher cannot obtain permission to control the independent variable, it is unlikely that he can obtain permission to control other variables. If, in a study of open and traditional classrooms, a principal will not allow a researcher to determine which children go to which kind of classroom, how likely is she to allow the researcher to determine the materials that the children use, the characteristics of their teachers, and the temperature of their classrooms?

Sometimes researchers use the principle of randomness to try to control potentially confounding variables that may arise in the research situation. They do this by randomly assigning independent-variable groups to potentially confounding conditions in the research. To continue with the example given above, directive and nondirective therapy groups could be randomly assigned to therapists, to therapy times, to therapy rooms, and so forth. This would not guarantee control of these potentially confounding variables, but it would make their effects random rather than systematic. With this strategy, it would be unlikely that either the directive or nondirective group consistently received the more favorable aspects of therapy—the better therapists, the better times of day, the better rooms, and so forth.

Figure 4.3 summarizes the information we have presented on techniques for confounding variable control. Figure 4.4 contrasts the ways that experimental and nonexperimental researchers can use these techniques.

SOME CLASSIC DESIGN PROBLEMS

Packaged Variables

A phenomenon that makes the problem of confounding variables particularly difficult is the existence of what are called *packaged variables*. This name refers to the fact that the values of certain variables tend to be packaged together. A common example of this is provided by the case of biological sex and gender identity. The values of these variables tend to be packaged together. Biological males usually have male gender identities, and biological females usually have female gender identities. This, of course, is because biological sex usually determines the gender identity that an individual will learn. Biological females are usually socialized as females, and biological males are usually socialized as males.

Although packaged variables tend to have values that are packaged together, they are separate variables and can have separate effects. Biological sex, for example, affects such things as an individual's ability to become pregnant; men cannot become pregnant, but most women can. Gender identity affects such things as people's choice of clothing; in the United States most women wear dresses at certain times, but most men never wear dresses.

FIGURE 4.3 Confounding variable control.

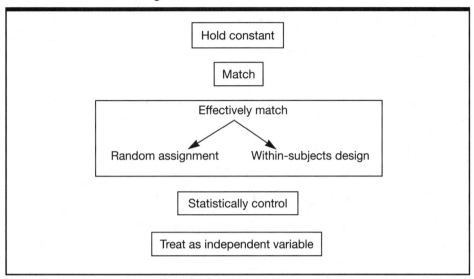

The problem with packaged variables is that whenever one of them is the independent variable of interest in a study, the other will almost always be a confounding variable. In studies of gender identity as an independent variable, biological sex almost always will be a confounding variable; and in studies of biological sex as an independent variable, gender identity almost always will be a confounding variable.

This is a serious problem, because it is often important to know which of two packaged variables is the true cause of some dependent variable of interest. To continue with the above example, it is important to educators to know whether biological sex or gender identity is the true cause of males' tendency to outperform females in mathematics. If the cause is biological sex, then the effect cannot be changed. But if the cause is gender identity, the effect can be changed; gender identity is learned, and schools can help teach girls to do as well as boys in math.

Packaged variables can be insidious, because we are not always aware of their existence. If a study appears to provide excellent causal argument, we will conclude

FIGURE 4.4 Techniques available for controlling potentially confounding variables in experimental and nonexperimental research.

NONEXPERIMENTAL
Identify and control potentially confounding variables
Within-subjects designs

EXPERIMENTAL
Identify and control potentially confounding variables
Within-subjects designs
Random assignment

that the independent variable is a cause of the dependent variable. However, if some unidentified variable is packaged with the independent variable, it may be the true cause. Even random assignment cannot offer protection from unidentified packaged variables; packaged values of the confounding variable are assigned right along with the values of the independent variable.

It can be very difficult to design research that deals with packaged variables. The techniques for controlling potentially confounding variables that you have learned about in this chapter are typically of no avail when variables are packaged. All of these techniques require that the researcher identify and unpackage the variables. We can never be sure we have identified all the possibilities; and even when we have identified a packaged variable, unpackaging it can seem impossible. To unpackage biological sex and gender identity, for example, a researcher would have to have subjects whose biological sex and gender identity were different—biological males socialized as females and/or biological females socialized as males.

While it would be possible to do such an experiment on humans, there would be enormous practical difficulties; and, even if the practical difficulties could be overcome, it would be extremely unethical for researchers to manipulate children's gender socialization. In situations like this, researchers have only one option: to try to discover what are sometimes called "natural experiments."

This term refers to naturally occurring situations in which variables which are usually packaged have been unpackaged. To return to the example of gender, researchers have been able to locate a few naturally occurring situations in which people's biological sex and social gender differ. These studies tend to support social gender, not biological sex, as the cause of most of the differences between women's and men's behavior (see, for example, Archer and Lloyd, 1985).

However, such natural experiments tend to be very rare. The very fact that a situation is so unusual may restrict its relevance to the mainstream of scientific knowledge. And, because they are so rare, researchers who are lucky enough to find natural experiments can't be too choosy about details; for example, the situation that the researcher finds may not lend itself to the study of the dependent variables in which the researcher is most interested. Finally, since natural experiments are not, in fact, experiments, they tend to present the usual problems of nonexperimental research: that is, even though the packaged variables have been unpackaged, there are often other confounding variables.

Even with all these drawbacks, however, natural experiments make important contributions to knowledge; they give researchers the opportunity to isolate for study variables that would otherwise be hopelessly confounded.

Maturation Effects

Much research takes place over time. Groups of children are placed in different educational programs for nine months; pre- and posttests are administered to determine which group learned more during the year. Groups of clients are placed in different counseling programs for a year; pre- and post-measures are administered to determine which group improved more in mental health during the year.

The danger in such studies lies in attributing all of the children's learning or the clients' improvement to the educational or counseling program. In fact, over time, children learn a great deal whether or not they are in special educational programs;

and many people's mental health improves over time without counseling. Such phenomena are known as *maturation effects;* the term signifies that people change over time just by virtue of leading normal lives.

Suppose that, in the first example given above, children learned more in special program A than in special program B. If the research was well done and successfully replicated, should we seriously consider implementing program A in our schools? Not necessarily. It is possible that both special programs were in fact inferior to the regular school program—that children would have learned as much or more if they had been left in their regular classrooms (or, for that matter, if they had not attended school at all) than they learned in program A. In terms of the second example, it is possible that clients' mental health would have improved as much or more if they had not received any counseling at all.

Control Groups

The solution to this problem is the use of control groups. Control groups are groups of subjects who do not get any special treatment during the research; they simply lead their normal lives. For control groups, the value of the independent variable is *leading normal lives.* The imaginary researcher in the first example above could have used three, instead of two, groups of children in his research: children in special program A, children in special program B, and controls—that is, children in their regular classrooms, leading their normal lives. In the second example, three groups of clients could have been employed: clients in counseling program A, clients in counseling program B, and controls—that is, people receiving no counseling therapy, leading their normal lives. If educational or counseling program A is superior not only to program B but also to the control condition, then we can conclude that the maturation effect is not responsible for the success of A. It may then be worthwhile to adopt A as our program of choice. Often when control groups are used, there are only two values of the independent variable: treatment and control. A researcher will investigate whether some single educational program is better than no special program at all (e.g., whether sending slow learners to a resource room for special help is better than leaving them in their regular classrooms, or whether children in summer school learn more than children who spend their summers away from school).

Expectancy Effects

Using control groups of any kind, however, creates a special confounding variable called *expectancy.* It is known that people's behavior can change simply because they, or someone else, expect it to change. This effect has been documented most dramatically in medical research. Patients can get better just because they, or their doctors, expect it. When control groups are used, expectancy effects pose a real threat. Treatment groups in research are getting some special treatment; this can set up the expectation of positive results. Control groups, however, are not getting any special treatment; for them, there are no special expectations for improvement. If the treatment group does improve more than the control group, how can we be sure this is due to the differential treatments and not just to the differential expectations set up by the different treatments?

Hawthorne and Pygmalion Effects

One kind of expectancy effect was documented and named by educational researchers. This involves the effect that the expectations of others can have on research subjects. Rosenthal and Jacobson (1968), in a now-famous study, demonstrated that teacher expectations can affect student achievement. They simply told teachers at the beginning of the year that some of their students had been identified as having great intellectual potential. The students who were named had, in fact, merely been randomly assigned to be named. At the end of the school year, many of these students did better than those in the control group, who had not been named. Rosenthal and Jacobson called this the *Pygmalion effect,* borrowing the name from a well-known piece of British literature in which a commoner becomes an aristocrat because people believe her to be an aristocrat.

Another named expectancy effect also comes from the social sciences. It was demonstrated that factory workers' productivity can increase due to the workers' expectations. This research came to be known as the Hawthorne study, and any subject expectancy effect is now called a *Hawthorne effect.* Sometimes the term *halo effect* is also used.

Placebos and Double-Blind Research

In medical research on the efficacy of drugs, expectancy effects are controlled by using placebos. Placebos are substances that look like real drugs but are not—pills made of sugar, for example. Medical researchers usually use at least three treatment groups: one getting the real drug, one getting a placebo, and one true control group that gets no pill at all. Neither the patients nor their doctors know which is the real drug and which the placebo. If patients taking the drug improve more than patients taking the placebo, researchers can be confident that the result is not due to expectation. This strategy is called *double-blind research,* because both the patients and doctors are "blind" to who is getting the real drug and who is getting the placebo. This controls both Hawthorne and Pygmalion effects.

In educational research, it can be more difficult to control expectancy effects. It is relatively easy to disguise a drug, but it can be difficult to disguise a special educational program. If some children are left in their regular classrooms and some are pulled out for a special program, how can an educational researcher keep the children, their parents, and their teachers from having expectations? Often educational researchers make some effort to disguise the existence of treatment and control groups. If treatment students are to be pulled out of their regular classrooms, then control students are also pulled out. During the pull-out, however, control students receive their regular lesson. Such a ploy may control student and parent expectations, but teacher expectations may still vary.

Researchers may also try to control expectations in the measurement of dependent variables. Consider a researcher who wishes to study the effect of some treatment on children's play. The dependent variable, play, may be operationally defined in terms of observation; that is, observers will be used to evaluate the children's play. Such a researcher will want to be sure that the observers do not know which children got the treatment and which were controls, because this knowledge might set up observer expectations influencing their evaluation of the children's play.

For similar reasons, it is often important that researchers not be directly involved in the implementation of the research they design, because researchers know what they expect to find. A counseling researcher investigating differences between two types of therapy may conduct both kinds of therapy himself. If subjects receiving therapy type *A* improve more than subjects receiving type *B,* it may be due simply to the fact that the researcher/counselor expected this result.

■ EXERCISE 10

Excerpts from two research reports are printed below. In each study, the researcher dealt with a potentially confounding variable in the research situation. Decide what the variable is and how the researcher dealt with it.

a. Keating and Bai (1986) studied "Children's Attributions of Social Dominance from Facial Cues" (p. 1269).

Stimulus photographs depicting adults with lowered brow expressions or without smiles were hypothesized to appear dominant relative to photographs showing adults with raised-brow expressions or with smiles, respectively. Each adult was photographed in two different poses: first with brows lowered and then with brows raised or first without a smile and then with a smile.

b. Hong and O'Neil (1992) studied "Instructional Strategies to Help Learners Build Relevant Mental Models in Inferential Statistics." In their experiment, they introduced students to an important topic in statistics, hypothesis testing. In presenting this material they varied the presentation sequence and mode to see whether these variations would affect the students' learning of the material.

The subjects were 27 graduate and 29 undergraduate students who were taking introductory statistics courses at a California research university. Introductory hypothesis testing was a topic in the subjects' statistics courses. The experiment took place before the subjects covered hypothesis testing in the courses. The subjects were grouped into blocks according to their educational level (graduate or undergraduate status), and a random assignment to each treatment condition was made separately for each block of subjects (p. 153). ■

EVALUATING CONFOUNDING VARIABLE CONTROL

Where does all this leave you, the consumer of educational research reports? In fact, it sometimes leaves you in a difficult position. When you read a research report, you must decide whether the researcher is trying to demonstrate a causal relationship between variables. If so, you must evaluate the researcher's control of potentially confounding variables. When random assignment has been used, you have the comfort of knowing that most of the potentially confounding variables in existence at the time of random assignment probably have been controlled. There is always the possibility that something has sneaked through the defense of randomness; replication is the cure for this, unless what sneaked through is a packaged variable. You must still, however, evaluate the researcher's control of variables that occurred after random assignment was made.

When you read nonexperimental research (or, rarely, experimental research without random assignment), you must evaluate control of all variables. This involves evaluating two things: the researcher's predictions about potentially confounding variables and her methods of control. In other words, you must first decide whether the researcher has identified all of the potentially confounding variables that pose a serious threat. This can be very difficult, because it involves being able to predict all of the probable influences on the dependent variable. If you are a novice in your field, you will not be very confident in your ability to do this.

Evaluating the researcher's control of the identified variables is easier. In order to control potentially confounding variables, researchers must validly measure them. You can evaluate this measurement just as you learned in chapter 3 to evaluate the measurement of any variable. Once measured, variables can be controlled in only four ways: by holding them constant, by matching, by statistically controlling them, or by building them in as independent variables.

Figure 4.5 summarizes the process of evaluating causal argument.

FIGURE 4.5   Evaluating control of potentially confounding variables.

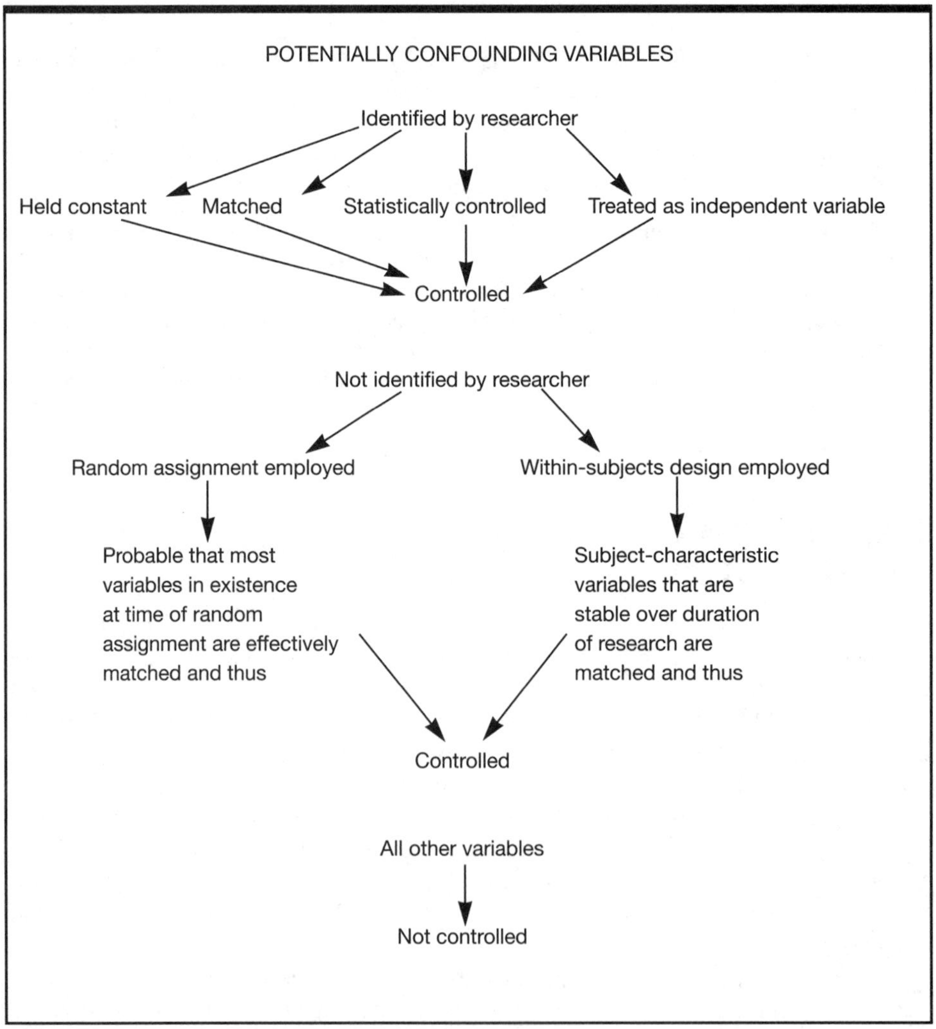

SUMMARY

Demonstrating causation is one of a researcher's most difficult tasks. In a given study, we can demonstrate that X caused Y only if X preceded Y in time, X and Y were related, and no other variable was related to Y. Other variables that relate to Y in a given study are called confounding variables. In order to demonstrate cause, potentially confounding variables must be controlled.

There are four ways to control potentially confounding variables: by holding them constant, by matching, by statistically controlling them, and by building them in as independent variables. All of these solutions require identifying the variable and validly measuring it. This process is never foolproof, because we never can be sure that we have identified all of the potentially confounding variables in a study. Even when we do identify them, we may not be able to control them, because it may be impossible or impractical to measure them validly and/or control them.

Experimental research usually affords good control of potentially confounding variables. Experimental researchers control the values of independent variables. If researchers exercise this control by randomly assigning subjects or cases to independent variable values, it is probable that most potentially confounding variables are effectively matched. Because experimental researchers are able to control the values of the independent variable, they are likely to be able to control potentially confounding variables that arise after random assignment as well.

Nonexperimental researchers use naturally occurring values of independent variables. They cannot randomly assign. Confounding variables thus tend to pose a much greater threat to causal argument in nonexperimental research than in experimental research. Within-subjects designs, including single-subject designs, take care of many potentially confounding variables, but they usually introduce confounding variables into the research situation; these must then be controlled.

Packaged variables present a serious threat to causal argument. Often, discovering a natural experiment is a researcher's only possible way to "unpackage" the variables and solve this problem. Research done over time is vulnerable to the maturation effect; the use of a control group prevents researchers from attributing normal change in subjects to the independent variable in a study. Expectations of subjects and others involved in the research are known to affect research outcomes; unless expectations are controlled, expectancy effects also threaten causal argument.

Evaluating confounding variable control is a two-stage process. First, the researcher's identification of potentially confounding variables must be evaluated; it is possible that the researcher overlooked potentially serious confounding variables. Then the researcher's control of identified variables must be assessed.

SUMMARY EXERCISES

1. Several examples from the published research literature follow. For each example, determine what the independent and dependent variables were and what potentially confounding variable(s) the researchers dealt with and how. Do you feel the attempted confounding variable control was adequate? In some of the examples, the researchers actually created uncontrolled confounding variables. Can you spot them? Evaluate causal argument in the study.

a. King and Cooley (1995) studied the relationship between the imposter phenomenon and subjects' family achievement orientation and achievement-related behaviors. The imposter phenomenon is "an intense feeling of intellectual inauthenticity experienced by many high-achieving individuals" (p. 304). Overall, subjects with greater family achievement orientation had higher levels of the imposter phenomenon. Female subjects with higher levels of the imposter phenomenon had higher GPAs and spent more time on academics.

b. Klein, Erchul, and Pridemore (1994) randomly assigned subjects to one of six groups representing learning condition (individual or cooperative) and reward condition (task, performance, or none). Cooperative individuals were further randomly assigned to particular triads for cooperative work. All subjects worked on the same instructional TV lesson. Subjects who worked alone performed better on a posttest and experienced more continuing motivation than did subjects who worked cooperatively. Type of reward did not affect posttest performance or motivation.

c. Jowett (1986) studied the effects of two different kinds of preschools on children's behavior, achievement, and adjustment to school. Five schools offering each type of program were selected; the two groups of schools were matched on

> . . . significant characteristics. . . . Within these schools, children were matched on sex, age, father's occupation, ordinal position in family and family structure (e.g., single parent, step-parent, etc.) (p. 22).

d. Butts and Crowell (1985) investigated

> . . . the effect of caffeine ingestion on submaximal endurance performance of 15 females and 13 males. . . . For the caffeine (C) trials, 300 mg of caffeine was added to 250 ml of decaffeinated coffee and ingested one hour prior to the exercise. The decaffeinated (D) trial involved consuming 250 ml of decaffeinated coffee an hour prior to the test (p. 301).

Neither the subjects nor those who carried out the experiment knew which subjects received the caffeine.

e. Dolan et al. (1993) studied the short-term impact of two classroom-based preventive interventions on children's aggressive and shy behaviors and achievement. Comparison classrooms received no special attention.

> The design for a preventive trial of this type must provide for an estimate of leakage or spillover effects that might happen if all or part of the intervention strategies were adopted in the comparison classrooms. The problems were addressed in the research design by having both internal control classrooms that did not receive any special intervention within the intervention schools as well as external control classrooms within the nonintervention schools (p. 323).

f. Pianta and Ball (1993) studied the relationship between maternal support (which involved the amount of support the mother received from her social network including her husband) and two variables (behavior and competence) reflecting child adjustment in kindergarten. They also measured maternal background (which involved education, occupation, and age at birth of first child); child intelligence; child risk (which involved medical and/or developmental difficulties); and child gender. Statistical analysis was used "to assess the extent to which maternal social support predicted child adjustment when maternal background, child intelligence, child risk and child gender were controlled" (p. 113). Then, in a second group of analyses, maternal background, child intelligence, and child risk were treated as independent variables to determine whether they interacted with maternal support to influence child adjustment.

g. Hebbeler (1985) investigated

   . . . the impact of Head Start participation . . . by comparing the [fourth-, eighth-, and twelfth-grade] performance of students who attended Head Start with a group of comparison students who applied to Head Start but were not admitted to the program (p. 208).

h. Travis and Kohli (1995) studied the relationship between birth order and academic attainment. They compared the relationship between these variables across four social-origin groups: "rich, comfortable, meager, or poor" (p. 504). They found that birth order had a strong negative relationship with educational achievement within the comfortable group, but not within the other three groups.

i. Leak (1980)

   . . . compared the relative effectiveness of two methods of group counseling with incarcerated felons. Eighty subjects were randomly assigned to either a new, highly structured method that used specific counseling exercises, a more traditional nondirective group method relatively low in structure, or a waiting-list control group (p. 520).

   Both therapy conditions were implemented by the same counselor.

j. Nichols and Miller (1994) studied the relationship between learning context and student performance and motivation in high-school algebra.

   Sixty-two students were randomly assigned to either a cooperative learning or traditional lecture group" (p. 167). Students were enrolled in the control (15 males, 15 females) or experimental group (16 males, 16 females) as part of the normal enrollment procedure from a pool of approximately 390 Algebra II students. The school counselors assigned students to section via computer, without regard to previous algebra performance and without knowledge of the treatments. Barring scheduling conflicts with other courses requested by students, assignment was quite random. A pretest of Algebra I knowledge was used as a covariate in the analysis of achievement differences between groups in order to control entering achievement differences. The groups did not differ significantly on the pretest (p. 169).

2. Locate at least three relational, quantitative research reports on topics of professional interest to you in research journals. Select reports in which the researcher attempts to demonstrate a cause and effect relationship between variables, not just a predictor-criterion relationship. Also select at least one nonexperimental study and at least one study with random assignment (not random sampling, which we deal with in the next chapter). Evaluate the researchers' causal arguments. What did the researchers do to control potentially confounding variables? Were the researchers' control efforts successful, in your opinion? Why or why not? Did the researchers identify all of the potentially serious confounding variables in the study?

3. For the relational research questions you made up for Chapter 1, Summary Exercise 3, think about causal argument. Do you believe there is a causal relationship between the variables? If so, could you use random assignment or a within-subjects design? If not, what variables might well confound causal argument? What might you do to control them?

SUGGESTED READINGS

Kirk, R. (1968). *Experimental Design: Procedures for the Behavioral Sciences.* Belmont, CA: Brooks/Cole.

Meyers, L. and Grossen, N. (1974). *Behavioral Research: Theory, Procedure, and Design.* San Francisco: W.H. Freeman.

Montgomery, D. (1991). *Design and Analysis of Experiments.* New York: Wiley.

5

External Validity
in Quantitative Research

The previous two chapters dealt with internal validity—that is, with validity of measurement and confounding variable control. Internal validity involves whether the research results validly reflect the research situation. Research might, for example, indicate that there is a causal relationship between cognitive style and school performance. Internal validity deals with whether the relationship is, in fact, causal (i.e., with confounding variable control) and is, in fact, between these two variables (i.e., with validity of measurement).

But even if internal validity questions have been dealt with, and we believe that the independent and dependent variables of interest were validly measured and potentially confounding variables were controlled, we know only that the research results are valid for the situation in which the research was done—that in the example above a relationship exists between cognitive style and school performance for these subjects, at this place and time, and in this context. This is a problem built into all research. Because research is empirical, it must always be carried out on particular people or things, at particular places and times, and in particular contexts. However, our interest in the findings is rarely limited to the research situation. In order for research findings to interest us as practitioners, we must be convinced that the results are likely to apply to the situations in which we work; and part of scientists' interest in research findings is understanding the additional situations to which particular research results can be applied.

Research can be internally valid, with independent and dependent variables well defined and potentially confounding variables well controlled. However, unless the research has external validity—unless the results apply to a larger context than the one in which the research was done—most people will not be interested in the results.

This issue involves what is called the external validity of research: whether a study has validity external to itself. Research has external validity if its results can be generalized beyond the research situation, to other people, at other times and places, and in other contexts. And generalizability depends on representativeness: Research results can be generalized to other contexts if the context in which the research was done is representative of these other contexts.

SUBJECTS OR CASES

The subjects or cases on whom research is done greatly affect the generalizability of the research results. Suppose that a researcher wishes to test the hypothesis that students with better school attendance records have higher grade-point averages (GPAs).

The researcher goes to a nearby high school and, from school records, finds the values of these variables for 100 students. Suppose that the research results do not support the hypothesis.

At this point, what can the researcher safely conclude? Only that, for these 100 students, there is no relationship between attendance and GPA. If the researcher were to publish these results, would you be interested in them? Probably not. And the reason would be that you are not likely to be interested in these particular students. If you are a teacher, you are interested in a possible relationship between attendance and GPA for the students who are and will be in your classes. If you are a principal, you are interested in all students who are and will be in your school. If you are the Secretary of Education for the entire country, you are interested in all the students in the country.

If you work with poor, inner-city, elementary-school children, and you read a research report that indicates that there is no relationship between attendance and achievement for a group of 100 middle-class, suburban, high-school students, would you be likely to conclude that it doesn't matter whether your students come to school or not? Of course not. You would realize that the factors affecting the achievement of your students and the research subjects are likely to be different. On the other hand, if you work with middle-class, suburban, high-school students, it is very possible that such research results would apply to your students.

POPULATIONS AND SAMPLES

To get around this problem, researchers usually consider their subjects or cases to be samples of some larger group, which, of course, they are. Any group (or even individual) is a sample of any larger group whose characteristics it shares. Two 30-year-old American men are a sample of each of the following groups: all people; all men; all Americans; all 30-year-olds; all 30-year-old men; all 30-year-old Americans; and so forth. Researchers use the term population to refer to the larger group. Any three first-graders are a sample of the population of first-graders.

A very important thing to understand, however, is that samples of populations do not necessarily represent those populations. You are a sample of the population of all humans. You probably represent the population with respect to species-specific biological characteristics, such as how your circulatory system works, but you certainly do not represent the population with respect to personal values or hair color or gender. We usually want to be able to generalize research findings from the sample on whom the research was conducted to some population. But if we are to do this, the sample must represent the population. Whether a research sample can be considered to represent a population depends heavily on the research question involved. If the research question involves the effect of vaccination on smallpox, then almost any sample of people can probably be considered representative of all people. If the new drug is found to prevent smallpox in almost any sample of people, then we will probably be willing to conclude that it is likely to work with all people. (We will assume for the moment that the sample is sufficiently large; we discuss sample size a little later in this chapter.)

If, however, the research question involves the effects of different political advertising campaigns on people's candidate preferences, a sample composed only of men cannot be considered representative of all people. It is known that men's and women's voting preferences are influenced by different things. If one kind of advertising campaign is found to be superior in influencing some men's candidate preferences, we cannot conclude that it is likely to be superior in influencing other people's (including, of course, women's) preferences. We may, however, be willing to conclude that it is likely to be superior in influencing the preferences of other men.

Figure 5.1 depicts the relationships between populations, samples, and generalizability, showing that not all samples are representative and that only representative samples allow a researcher to generalize about a population.

One way for researchers to get around the problem of sampling is to do research on the entire population of interest. You will occasionally come across research of this sort. The superintendent of a small school district, for example, may request that her staff collect data on all students in the district. If the rest of the research is validly done, there is then no question that the research results apply to all students in the district. However, for obvious reasons, such results are usually only of local interest. Most educational researchers work and publish for a wider audience. It is usually impossible for researchers to identify, much less study, all members of a population of interest.

Random Samples

Another way for researchers to get around the problem is to do research on a *random sample* of the population of interest. This is because random samples (of adequate size) are likely to represent the populations from which they are drawn. Random means without pattern. If a sample is selected from a population by choosing all men,

FIGURE 5.1   The relationships among populations, samples, and generalizability.

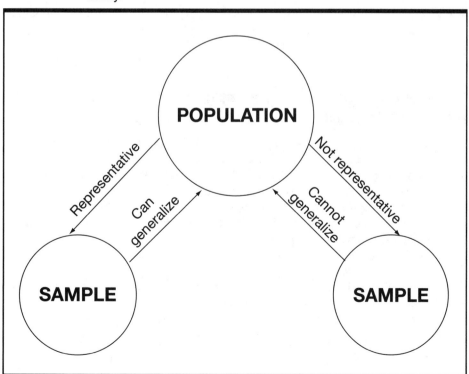

then the sample has been selected according to a pattern; if a sample is selected by choosing all eighth-graders, then the sample has been selected according to a pattern. Such samples obviously would not be representative of populations of both genders and all ages. Similarly, if a sample is selected from a population by taking the first 100 names from an alphabetized list, the sample has been selected according to a pattern. This sample also may not be representative of the population. Perhaps there is a tendency for members of a particular ethnic group to have names that begin with the letter *A*. This ethnic group would then be over-represented in the sample.

In a random sample, no pattern is employed in selection. Technically, each time a subject is randomly selected into the sample, all members of the population have an equal chance of being selected. We approach random sampling in "real life" when we play cards. If you shuffle and cut cards, you approximate a random sample. Ideally, each time you deal a card, every card in the deck has had an equal chance of being in that card's position. Similarly, raffles approximate random samples. When a number of raffle tickets are placed in a drum and rotated, and the winning ticket is drawn by a blindfolded person, we assume that each ticket has had an equal chance of being selected. Researchers select random samples by using what is called a table of random numbers (or by having a computer use a table of random numbers). Each member of the population is assigned a number in any way the researcher desires. Then a table of random numbers is consulted. Such a table is simply a list of numbers arranged without pattern. Perhaps the first three numbers in the table are 16, 84, and 59; the researcher will select subjects 16, 84, and 59 for the sample and will continue using the table until enough subjects have been identified. If a random sample is large enough, it is likely that it represents the population no matter what the research question is. If, for example, a population contains 500 men and 500 women, a random sample of 100 subjects from that population is very likely to contain close to 50 men and 50 women. If the same population contains 600 Democrats and 400 Republicans, it is very likely that the sample will contain close to 60 Democrats and 40 Republicans. This is true for any characteristic of the population that we can think of, and even those we can't.

The Difference Between Random Sampling and Random Assignment

A word of caution is in order here. Chapter 4 introduced the concept of random assignment. Many students confuse this with random sampling. The two are, in fact, quite distinct, and you need to understand the difference between them.

Random sampling is employed to select subjects or cases for research. Its purpose is to maximize the probability that the research sample represents a given population and thus to increase our confidence that the research results can be generalized to that population. Random sampling enhances external validity.

Random assignment is employed after the research subjects are selected to determine which subjects will have which value of the independent variable. Its purpose is to maximize the probability that subject characteristics are matched between the experimental groups and thus that potentially confounding variables are controlled. Random assignment enhances the internal validity of research.

Random sampling and random assignment are independent of one another; that is, in a given piece of research, either may be employed with or without the other.

■ EXERCISE 1

Which of the following examples involve random sampling and which involve random assignment?

a.   100 students at Central High were randomly selected to participate in a study.

b.   In a group of 50 principals, 25 individuals were randomly designated to receive training on evaluating teachers; the remaining 25 principals did not receive such training.

c.   50 children of divorced parents and 50 children of non-divorced parents were randomly chosen to participate in a study.   ■

Sampling Error and Sample Size

We expect the characteristics of random samples to be similar to the characteristics of the populations from which the samples were drawn, but we do not expect them to be exactly the same. If we drew a random sample of 100 people from a population containing 500 men and 500 women, we would expect our sample to contain about half men and half women, but we would not be surprised if it failed to contain exactly 50 men and 50 women. We might easily get 48 men and 52 women, or 51 men and 49 women. This difference between numbers of men and women in our sample would not reflect differences in the population but would be due to what is called *sampling error.*

With a sample size of 100, however, we do not expect sampling error to be very large. We would be surprised if one-fourth of our sample—25 people—were men and three-fourths—75 people—were women. Although it is possible for random samples of this size to differ this much from populations, it is not very probable; that is, it doesn't happen very often.

On the other hand, if we drew a random sample of only four people from the population of 500 men and 500 women, we would not be terribly surprised if one-fourth of our sample—one person—were male and three-fourths—three people—were female. How much sampling error we can expect from a random sample is thus a function of sample size: In smaller samples, larger sampling error is more likely.

Even a random sample cannot be assumed to represent a population if the sample is too small. This is because, in a small sample, the influence of one or a few individuals is relatively greater. Suppose a researcher wishes to know the average income of a population of 1,000 people, and the population contains 999 middle-income persons and one millionaire. If the researcher selects a random sample of 500 people, it will not matter much whether or not the millionaire is selected; the average income of the sample will be fairly representative of the population either way. If, on the other hand, the researcher selects a random sample of five people, whether or not the millionaire is selected will greatly affect the average income of the sample. If the millionaire is in the sample, its average income will be much greater than that of the population.

What is an adequate sample size? Techniques are available to researchers to help them answer this question; such techniques are linked to the statistical techniques that the researcher will use to analyze his results (more on this later). The adequacy of sample size depends in part on how many variables and values will be studied; more variables and values require more subjects. As a rule of thumb, samples of 25 to 30 subjects are usually considered adequate for research involving one independent and one dependent variable, and even smaller samples are frequently encountered. Other things being equal, however, representativeness is a function of size. When they can afford to, researchers often opt for the security of samples of several hundred or even several thousand subjects. After a point, however, diminishing returns set in. The difference in representativeness of samples of 500 and 1,000 subjects is very small.

■ Exercise 2

Below are two examples from the research literature. For each example, describe the sample that was employed, including the sample size. Did either of the studies involve an entire population of interest? Was either of the samples random?

a. Mendelson, Aboud, and Lanthier (1994) studied "Personality Predictors of Friendship and Popularity in Kindergarten." The participants were 70 children (34 girls and 36 boys) who ranged in age from 61 to 74 months (m = 68 months) at the beginning of the study. They all attended one of five kindergarten classes in two public schools that served a white, middle-class suburb of a large city (p. 417).

b. Osborne (1986) compared passing rates of students in all Catholic and Protestant schools in Northern Ireland on state-required examinations (p. 43). His study was sponsored by

    . . . the Northern Ireland Fair Employment Agency, a statutory body charged with eliminating discrimination and ensuring equality of opportunity in employment between those of different religious beliefs (Osborne, 1980). To assist in its work, the FEA has sought a benchmark measure of the proportions of Protestant and Catholic school leavers' examination attainments against which to judge patterns of employment and recruitment in Northern Ireland. ■

■ Exercise 3

Take a random sample of half the people from Exercise 7, chapter 4. Does the sample represent all the people with respect to each of the variables? ■

Nonrandom Samples

Random sampling is a good research strategy. With random sampling, researchers can study any variables for a manageable number of subjects or cases with great confidence that their results represent a larger population. Unfortunately, however, random sampling has one severe drawback; every member of the population must be identified and available for research. This drawback often puts the technique beyond most researchers' means. Consider a researcher who is interested in the population of inner-city first-graders in the United States. It would take so long even to identify the members of the population that by the time the researcher was ready to do the study, the subjects would be in the second grade.

In practice, most researchers can neither study their entire populations of interest nor randomly sample them. They must, therefore, rely on arguments for the representativeness of their samples. One of a researcher's important tasks is thus to identify characteristics of the potential sample that may affect its representativeness. The sample can then be selected so that it represents these characteristics of the population. Consider, for example, a researcher who wishes to study the effects of two different mathematics curricula on children's mathematics achievement. If curriculum *A* proves superior for the children in the research sample, the researcher wishes to be able to generalize these results beyond the sample, to conclude that curriculum *A* would also be superior for other children. Perhaps the researcher wishes to be able to generalize these results to the population of "ordinary" or "typical" children in the United States. This researcher must identify the characteristics of the potential sample that may affect its representativeness of the population with respect to mathematics learning. These characteristics are such things as age, grade in school, gender, ethnicity, socioeconomic status, intelligence, and prior mathematics achievement, because these things are known to affect math learning. The researcher would then try to select a sample that represents the population with respect to these variables. Shoe size, however, is not likely to affect math achievement. The researcher would not, therefore, feel obliged to select a sample with shoe sizes that were representative of those in the population.

Suppose the ultimate sample were composed of equal numbers of sixth-, seventh-, and eighth-grade girls and boys, with ages, IQ scores, and mathematics achievement levels appropriate to these grades, who are predominantly middle-class Anglos, and who reside in Wichita. The researcher might then argue that his sample should be considered representative of the population of typical, Anglo, middle-class, middle-school children in the United States. Of course, we might argue back that the math learning of children in Wichita may differ from that of children in larger cities or smaller towns or rural areas.

As a consumer of research, you must learn to evaluate the evidence researchers provide about their samples. You will make these evaluations, of course, in terms of your own interests, and your evaluations may differ from someone else's. As was pointed out earlier, you will want to know whether research results can be generalized to the situations in which you work. If you are an educator in a rural area, then some of the studies done on suburban children may not be of interest to you, even if the samples seem to be representative of suburban children. What you must always keep in mind is that the representativeness of samples depends on the nature of the research question. There may be no important differences between rural and suburban children when the research question involves the effects of nutrition on learning, but a great deal of difference when the question involves the effects of drug education on delinquency. Figure 5.2 depicts the evaluation of a sample's generalizability.

■ EXERCISE 4

Below are descriptions of samples from the educational research literature. What limitations do you see on the generalizability of the research results; that is, what characteristics of the subjects may affect the research results?

a. Hegarty, Mayer, and Monk (1995) recruited 38 undergraduates from the psychology subject pool at the University of California, Santa Barbara, and asked them to try to solve an arithmetic word problem involving basic arithmetic operations and reasoning. They then compared the problem-solving strategies of the successful and unsuccessful problem solvers.

FIGURE 5.2   Evaluating a sample's generalizability.

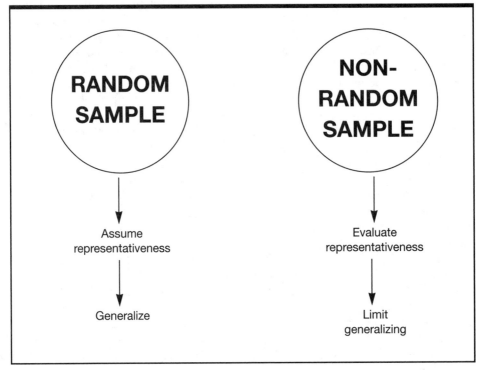

Unsuccessful problem solvers base their solution plan on numbers and keywords that they select from the problem, whereas successful problem solvers construct a model of the situation described in the problem and base their solution plan on this model (p. 18).

b. Cranton and Smith (1986) studied the effects of course characteristics on student ratings of instruction at two universities. "Data were collected in 1,777 classes in five departments at all levels of instruction over 3 years" (p. 117).

c. Rothschild et al. (1986) studied the effects of television commercials on subjects' EEG recordings, recall, recognition, and affective response. "The subjects were 83 middle-class adult women, ranging in ages from 20 to 50. All were members of a church group" (p. 197).

d. Hong and O'Neil (1992) studied "27 graduate and 29 undergraduate students who were taking introductory statistics courses at a California research university" (p. 153). They investigated the effects of two kinds of presentation sequence and two kinds of presentation mode on the students' learning of an important concept, statistical hypothesis testing. The kind of presentation sequence and the kind of presentation mode did affect the students' learning. ■

Cluster Samples

Because the difficulty of identifying and gaining access to members of populations usually makes bona fide random sampling difficult, researchers sometimes employ a strategy called *cluster sampling*. With this technique, relevant characteristics are identified and then successively sampled. A researcher interested in administering a questionnaire to a representative sample of teachers in the United States might first draw a representative sample of states. He would then identify school districts in the sampled states only and draw a representative sample of districts within these states. Then he would identify schools within the sampled districts only and draw a representative sample of schools within these districts. He could then contact this fairly small number of schools about distributing the questionnaire to all teachers in the school. Figure 5.3 illustrates this example of cluster sampling.

This would be a reasonably representative sample, obtained at relatively little expense. Obtaining a bona fide random sample would require trying to ascertain the name of every teacher in the country, drawing a random sample from these names, and then trying to obtain the addresses of sampled teachers, each of whom teaches in a different school. With cluster sampling, the researcher only has to identify school districts within a limited number of states and schools within a limited number of districts; all of this information is a matter of public record.

■ EXERCISE 5

An example of cluster sampling (Hannon and McNally, 1986, p. 239) is provided below. Identify the successive stages in the sampling procedure. (It might help to create a diagram like the one in Figure 5.3.) Why do you suppose the researchers chose these particular stages?

> All the children in the study came from three primary schools, chosen with the aid of LEA [London Education Authority] advisers, whose head teachers agreed to assist the research. One school, situated in the middle of a large council estate, was expected to be predominantly working-class, a second in the outer suburbs of a city was expected to be predominantly middle-class, and it was known that in the third school, in an inner-city area, about three quarters of the pupils were from Asian immigrant families. It was decided to sample three groups of 24 children in the appropriate age range with equal numbers of each sex—a middle-class group, a working-class group, and a group of children for whom English was a second language (ESL). Questionnaires were sent home with all first year juniors to discover, amongst other things, the parents' occupations. Response rates of 65%, 96% and 80% were obtained; no attempt was made to prompt non-respondents. Children were assigned to Social Classes I to V on the basis of the replies received. Children in classes I to III–M were considered as middle-class, those in III–N to V, working-class. The identification of children (at the third school) as members of families where English was a second language was made by school staff, including a specialist ESL teacher.
>
> From the working-class children 12 boys were selected at random and an equal number of girls, matched in age as closely as possible to the boys, was selected to make up the working-class group. The middle class and ESL groups were created by selecting children matched as closely as possible by age and sex to the working class group. ■

Stratified Samples

If a researcher is testing a hypothesis with a categorical independent variable, it is sometimes desirable to have equal or nearly equal numbers of subjects or cases with

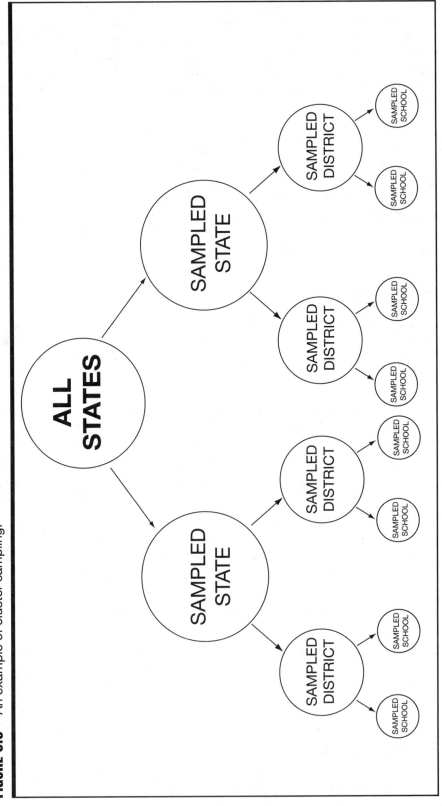

FIGURE 5.3   An example of cluster sampling.

each value of the variable. For example, a researcher may wish to test the hypothesis that there is a difference between boys' and girls' time on task. Such a researcher may need to have equal numbers of boys and girls in her sample. This is because some statistics that are used to test such hypotheses require equal numbers. If the researcher has identified a population (e.g., special-education students) that is predominantly male, she has a problem. She cannot have both a representative sample of such a population and equal numbers of boys and girls in her sample, because a representative sample will be predominantly male. In this case, the researcher may elect to employ what is called stratified sampling. The population is first stratified or grouped in terms of the variable of interest—in this example, gender—and then each stratum or group is sampled independently of the others. In this example, the researcher would first stratify the sample into two groups, one of boys and one of girls; she would then draw samples of equal or nearly equal size from each of the groups, perhaps 50 boys and 50 girls.

If stratified samples are representative, researchers can safely generalize their stratified results to the population; if, for example, girls' time on task in a representative, gender-stratified sample is significantly longer than that of boys, the researcher is warranted in concluding that it is likely that girls' time on task is also greater than boys' in the population. However, not all of the data available to the researcher can be generalized. The average time on task of all children in the sample does not, for example, represent that in the population; the population contains a higher proportion of boys, and boys spend less time on task, so the average time on task in the population will be less than in the sample. Figure 5.4 illustrates this example of stratified sampling.

■ EXERCISE 6

Following is a description from the published research literature of stratified random sampling. How did the researchers stratify their population before sampling? Which of the researchers' results will generalize to the whole population? Which will not?

Robison-Awana, Kehle, and Jenson (1986) studied self-esteem and sex-role perceptions as a function of academic achievement (p. 180).

A stratified random sample of 140 seventh-grade students representing three distinct levels of academic competence was selected from a predominantly middle class junior high school in a large urban area. The subjects' mean age was 13.2 years. The three groups that comprised the study were as follows:

Below average. This group consisted of 21 boys and 19 girls in the seventh grade English and reading class. The below average group was composed of students who generally performed 2 years below grade level on the Iowa Tests of Basic Skills and, according to teacher report, could not maintain an adequate position in a regular classroom. The students in the below average group did not qualify for assistance under Public Law 94–142.

Average. This group consisted of 25 boys and 25 girls from a regular seventh grade English and reading class. The average group was composed of students who performed within a year above or below grade level on the Iowa Tests of Basic Skills.

Above average. This group consisted of 25 boys and 25 girls from a seventh grade accelerated English and reading class. All of these students performed in the top 15% on the Iowa Tests of Basic Skills and were generally at least 2 years above grade level.

■

FIGURE 5.4 An example of stratified sampling.

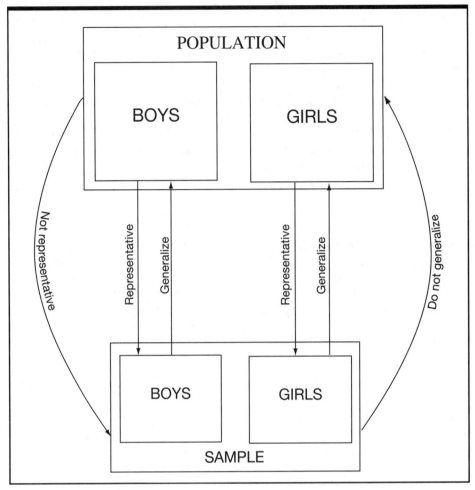

Convenience Samples

Practical difficulties in obtaining good samples abound. For subjects, participating in research takes time and is sometimes inconvenient. Researchers cannot coerce subjects to participate; they must obtain their cooperation. Also, to set up and implement research, researchers often must be in contact with subjects. If subjects are scattered over a wide geographic area, the research usually will be much more expensive and time-consuming than if they are concentrated in a locale near the researcher. The makeup of many samples is thus ultimately dictated as much by practical considerations as by generalizability considerations.

Consider a researcher who wishes to have teachers administer a test to a sample of 100 children in a large school district. Consent typically must be obtained from the principals of the schools the children attend, as well as from the children's teachers and parents. If the researcher identifies a bona fide random sample, the sampled children will be located at many different schools, in many different classrooms. Consent will have to be sought from literally dozens of principals and teachers. Not all of these people will be willing to cooperate, so the sample will no longer be random.

When the researcher has finally identified enough cooperative principals and teachers, she will have to coordinate the obtaining of parental consent and the actual test administration with each principal and teacher involved. Again, not all parents will give consent, so the representativeness of the sample will be further eroded. If, however, the researcher obtains her sample of 100 children by testing all the children in four classrooms in the same school, consent and coordination will only involve one principal and four teachers. It is not surprising that many researchers opt for this second strategy, making use of what are known as convenience samples. The trouble with convenience samples, of course, is that they tend to restrict generalizability. Individual schools tend to be relatively homogeneous with respect to characteristics that affect generalizability. Socioeconomic status (SES), for example, is known to affect many educational variables. Most schools are relatively homogeneous with respect to students' SES. If research is conducted in one school, most subjects are likely to be from middle (or high, or low) SES families. Much educational research done on only one SES group cannot safely be generalized to other SES groups.

Populations as Samples

Occasionally, researchers identify populations and employ bona fide random samples but still make arguments for the generalizability of their results. This is because the identified population is not, in fact, the real population of interest. A researcher might, for example, indicate that her population is all the elementary principals in Chicago and that she has randomly sampled this population. She might then go on to argue that all the elementary principals in Chicago in fact represent all elementary principals in large cities in the United States. This is because her real population of interest is not all the elementary principals in Chicago but all the elementary principals in the United States.

In such a case, you must evaluate the evidence provided and decide whether the study population is itself a representative sample of the population of interest to you.

Figure 5.5 depicts the evaluation of the various sampling strategies we have discussed.

Data Banks

Representative sampling of large populations of interest is so expensive that it is usually beyond most researchers' means. A partial solution to this problem is provided by the existence of large data banks. Certain organizations (e.g., professional organizations, national governments, and such international organizations as the United Nations) regularly collect basic data on their constituencies. These data are made available to researchers as well as to other interested parties.

An example with which you probably already have some familiarity is provided by the U.S. Bureau of the Census. The purpose of the Bureau is to collect data at regular intervals on a wide variety of demographic variables. Large, nationally representative samples are employed.

Particular agencies, including educational agencies, also collect data on variables relevant to their more specialized interests. The International Association for the Evaluation of Educational Achievement, which is headquartered in Stockholm, Sweden, maintains a data bank on the academic performance of large, nationally representative samples of students in 22 countries. Data are available on computer-

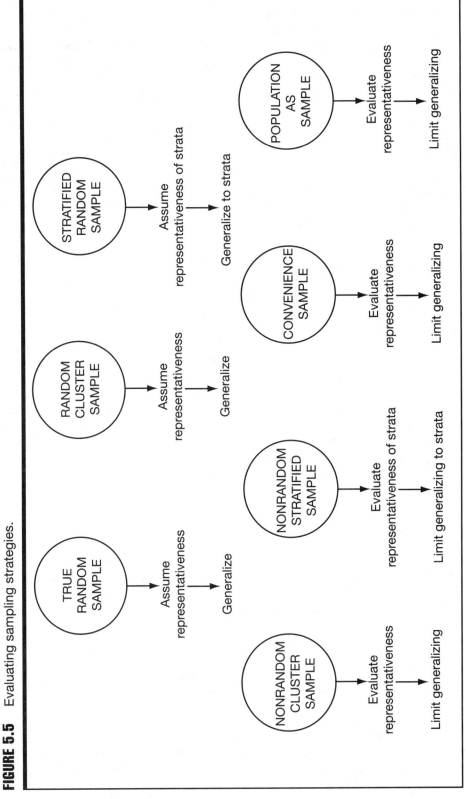

FIGURE 5.5 Evaluating sampling strategies.

readable tape. The National Center for Education Statistics of the U.S. Department of Education also maintains a number of data banks on computer-readable tape. Most of the data banks reflect large, nationally representative samples. The Cooperative Institutional Research Program, for example, maintains data on over four million college students and 900 institutions. The problem with these data banks, of course, is that they contain only the most basic kinds of information. Most variables of interest to educational researchers are not included. If a researcher is lucky enough to be interested in the kinds of variables represented in these data banks, then they are an excellent source of subjects. Such a researcher can claim very wide generalizability of results.

SUBJECT ATTRITION

Ideally, researchers should determine which subjects or cases will be included in their samples, either by randomly selecting subjects or cases or by choosing subjects or cases who represent population characteristics that the researcher considers relevant. Often, however, subjects themselves determine whether or not they will participate, either consciously or unconsciously. This can present serious threats to generalizability.

The use of questionnaires is especially troublesome in this respect. A researcher may select a random sample of parents from a particular school to receive a questionnaire about their children's education. The researcher, however, has little control over who returns the questionnaire; often as many as half or even three-fourths of the intended subjects simply fail to respond. The ultimate research sample is thus not a random sample of all parents from the school; it is, rather, a sample of parents who are willing to return the questionnaire. Often this must be assumed to affect the generalizability of results. Perhaps parents who are willing to return a questionnaire about their children's education are more conscientious about their children's education; their answers cannot, therefore, represent the answers of the less conscientious parents who failed to respond.

Researchers know that response rate tends to be a problem with questionnaires, so they often make one or more follow-up contacts of individuals who failed to respond. In order to do this, the researcher must identify the subjects in some way, so that she knows who has and has not responded. However, one of the important considerations in the validity of questionnaires as operational definitions is often whether the subjects are anonymous. If researchers ask questions about sensitive topics, anonymity increases the probability that subjects will be candid in their responses. But researchers cannot both maintain subjects' anonymity and follow up on nonrespondents. In a given study, a researcher must decide which is more important—a good response rate or protecting subjects' anonymity.

Longitudinal studies are also particularly troublesome in this regard. Some research questions require following subjects for extended periods of time. This is because some effects of interest only manifest themselves after a period of time. Berrueta-Clement et al. (1984), for example, studied the effects of a preschool program on at-risk children. They randomly assigned at-risk children to receive or not receive the program. Then they followed the children into early adulthood. Subjects who received the program benefitted in important ways. They were more successful in school, and their rates of such things as arrest and early pregnancy were lower than the rates for subjects who had not received the program.

Attrition was not a serious problem in this study. However, in many longitudinal studies it is. Subjects change their residences, sometimes without leaving a forwarding address. Even when researchers know where subjects are, they can become so geographically scattered that it is prohibitively expensive to continue studying them. Subjects refuse to continue cooperating in the study. Subjects even die or become incapacitated in ways that prevent them from continuing to participate in the study.

Often these factors must be assumed to affect the generalizability of the study's results. Subjects who have less residential stability, for example, may differ from other subjects in ways that affect the research results. Thus, the research results cannot be considered representative of the kinds of subjects who have been lost.

There is some attrition in most educational research. No matter how carefully researchers choose their subjects, some subjects are lost. Subjects mark their answer sheets wrong, or are absent on the day of test, or refuse to cooperate with the researcher. Because such subjects are often less capable students, the research sample is more capable than the population it was intended to represent.

If the amount of self-selection is small, generalizability is not greatly impaired. Conscientious researchers report on the nature and extent of self-selection so that you may judge for yourself.

Figure 5.6 depicts the effect of subject attrition on generalizability. The figure uses the example of a longitudinal study in which some subjects change residences during the study and are thus unavailable for further study. The principle would be the same, however, for subjects who leave any kind of study (not just a longitudinal study) for any reason (not just change of residence).

The figure shows the relationship between the sample and population at the beginning and end of the study. At the beginning of the study, the sample represents the entire population. By the end of the study, however, subjects who have moved are no longer in the sample. Thus, at the end of the study, the sample represents only those subjects who did not move; it is no longer representative of subjects who did move.

■ EXERCISE 7

What problem do you see with the following sample? A nationally syndicated newspaper columnist reports that she has received 60,000 responses to a question she raised in her column about public schools. She reports that 70% of her respondents indicated that their school experience was negative overall, while 30% indicated that their school experience was positive overall. She concludes that most Americans have a negative school experience.   ■

ETHICS

It probably makes sense to you that we are treating research ethics at this point in the book. The most obvious ethical consideration in research involves the welfare of research subjects, and this chapter has been largely about research subjects. However, there is another reason that we are including this discussion at this point.

Our treatment of ethics will reflect both researchers' and subjects' concerns. Subjects' concerns are more intuitively understandable. But to understand researchers' concerns, you need to understand the basic principles of good research. We are now at the end of the section of the book that deals with quantitative research design.

FIGURE 5.6   The effect of subject attrition on generalizability.

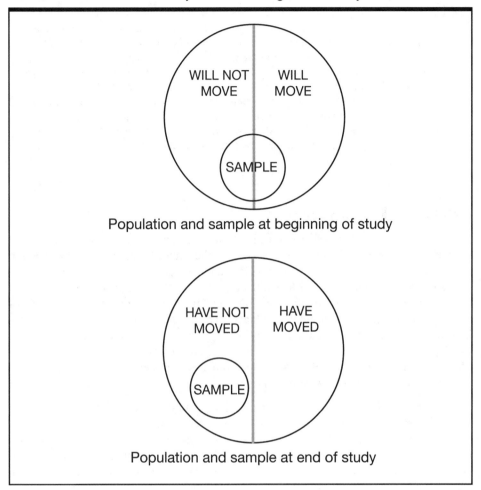

Having read the preceding chapters, you now know something about what constitutes good quantitative research and can better understand quantitative researchers' perspective on ethical issues.

You may wonder why we're not waiting until after the section on qualitative research to take up the issue of research ethics. The fact is that qualitative researchers tend to deal with research ethics differently than quantitative researchers do. In the qualitative chapters, ethical issues will be treated in a way that reflects current qualitative trends.

Most scientists seem to engage in ethical practice. A recent example was provided by a group of medical researchers studying the effects of cholesterol-lowering medication on circulatory disease. The researchers called a halt to the study before it was due to end. The death rate in the control group was obviously higher than that in the experimental group; continuing the study would have been equivalent to a death sentence for some members of the control group.

Scientists, however, as with any group of people, can hardly claim perfection, and unethical scientific practice does occur. In an interesting book on scientific ethics, Diener and Crandall (1978) recall some of the lowest ethical points in modern science.

> In a medical study on the treatment of syphilis, a control group of infected men was left untreated. Even after the experiment was over and remedies for syphilis had been discovered, these men did not receive treatment. They were forgotten by the experimenters and their health deteriorated for many years. In another experiment, during World War II, radioactive plutonium was injected directly into the bloodstream of eighteen men, women, and children without their knowledge. It was believed at the time that even small amounts of plutonium could cause cancer. In a third study, conducted by the CIA and the United States Army, subjects were given the hallucinogen LSD without their knowledge; at least one man subsequently became very disturbed and committed suicide (p. 128).

Institutional Review Boards

In the early 1970s, there was a good bit of publicity about these kinds of unethical treatment of research subjects. The response of the scientific community has been to codify ethical guidelines for human research and to create agencies to oversee compliance with these guidelines. Most universities and other nonprofit employers and funders of researchers now require an ethics review by an independent committee of all proposals for research on human subjects. The generic term for these committees is Institutional Review Boards (IRBs). Within a given organization, such a committee usually has a specific name. In the College of Education at the University of New Mexico, for example, the IRB is called the Human Research Review Committee.

The following criteria for approving proposals are common to most IRBs:

1. Is anonymity, or at least confidentiality, of subjects assured?

Anonymity means that even the researcher cannot associate particular variable values with individual subjects. True anonymity is possible, for example, when a researcher administers an anonymous survey. Typically, each survey that is returned is given an identification number, but even the researcher cannot associate a given subject's name with that ID number.

When the research design does not afford anonymity, then the researcher must carefully preserve the confidentiality of results. A researcher who interviews subjects knows which subject made which responses. It is incumbent on that researcher to use only ID numbers on interview records and to keep information that could link subjects' names with their ID numbers confidential—e.g., in a locked file.

2. Does the research have the potential for impairing either the physical or psychological well-being of the subjects? If so, is the harm justifiable and unavoidable? Will the subjects be informed of this potential? Will the subjects be offered appropriate treatment at no cost to themselves for any harm suffered as a result of participating in the research?

3. Will subjects give informed consent to their participation in the research? Will their consent to participate be obtained without coercion?

Such guidelines are clearly desirable, but they pose threats to both the internal and external validity of research, especially in the areas of self-selection and expectancy.

The first guideline, relating to anonymity/confidentiality, usually causes researchers no problems. It is the second and third guidelines that cause difficulty.

One reason is that potential for impairing either the physical or psychological well-being tends to be interpreted broadly by IRBs. For example, deception of subjects is usually considered by IRBs to have the potential to harm them psychologically. But the internal validity of a great deal of research depends on "deceiving" subjects. As an example, an important part of many research designs is that subjects, and sometimes others, be "blind" to the purpose of the research. This is because subjects who know the purpose of the research may consciously or unconsciously change their behavior.

Threats to both internal and external validity can come from requiring subjects to give informed consent. If subjects are to be deceived, they must give informed consent. But how valid is the researcher's attempt at deception likely to be if subjects are aware that they are being deceived? And subjects who do not give informed consent must be eliminated from the study. This can destroy a researcher's careful representative sampling strategy.

Many researchers feel that some current IRB practices with respect to informed consent are counterproductive. IRBs typically require that research subjects sign detailed consent forms before the research takes place. In addition to describing what is expected of the subject (e.g., filling out a questionnaire) if he or she does consent to participate, such consent forms apprise subjects of their legal rights. For example, subjects are given names and phone numbers of people, often including people in their state's risk-management office, whom they can contact if they feel they have been harmed by the research.

Since most research does not, in fact, have much potential for harming subjects, this kind of statement can unduly alarm subjects. Thus, a procedure that is intended to allay subjects' anxiety may actually increase it. Anxiety generated by this kind of consent form may cause subjects to refuse to participate in a study that would not actually harm them and might even benefit them. For example, experimental subjects often get effective treatments for very real problems at no cost to themselves.

One recent study (Mann, 1994) showed that consent forms can be counterproductive in an unexpected way. Subjects in her study were given identical written information about the study. For one group, the information was presented as an "Information Sheet," which they were not asked to sign. For the other group, the information was presented as a "Consent Form," which they were asked to sign. After the study, Mann asked the subjects questions about the forms, including a question about their legal rights. About two-thirds of the subjects in the Information Sheet group correctly remembered that they had the right to sue if they were harmed by the research. But about two-thirds of the subjects in the Consent Form group believed, incorrectly, that by signing the form they had given up their right to sue.

Recent Trends

Some of the current writers on research ethics (e.g., Rosenthal and Rosnow, 1994) argue that the focus in ethics has gotten too narrow. These writers feel that focusing on such things as longer and longer consent forms obscures the real, and broader, issue. The real issue, they feel, is that a great deal of research is poorly designed and is, therefore, at best useless and at worst harmful. Poorly designed research wastes taxpayers', researchers', and subjects' resources, including time, money, and psychological investment; it keeps those resources from being spent more productively; and it leads to inaccurate information. This is felt to be a much more serious question than whether a small change in a particular practice will add a small increment of protection to the subjects of particular kinds of studies.

Rosenthal and Rosnow (1991) propose a model for IRBs to use in ethical screening of research proposals. Their model weighs the potential utility and costs of doing the research against the potential utility and costs of not doing the research. Research that has the potential to answer a question of little interest would have poor potential utility as would badly designed research. Research that has the potential of harming subjects would have high potential cost (to subjects); well-designed research might also be of high cost (to taxpayers). However, if the answer to the research question is of great interest, the potential cost of not doing the research would be high—perhaps high enough to outweigh potential harm to subjects.

The problem with implementing such a model, of course, is in assigning comparable values to particular utilities and cost so that they may be weighed against each other. How many "units" of harm does a proposed study entail, and how many like units of benefit will the study probably provide? Is the possibility of killing one research subject equal to the potential of saving one other person's life in the future? No? How about 20 other people's lives? Or perhaps it should be 100, or 1,000. How does the equation change if the research subject probably would have died anyway?

Although there seems little chance that IRBs will come up with answers to questions like these in the near future, many researchers applaud the field of research ethics for turning its attention to such broader questions.

■ EXERCISE 8

Imagine an experimental study about the interactive effects of actual test difficulty and perceived test difficulty on test anxiety. This research requires four groups of subjects: those who take an easy test that they perceive to be easy; those who take an easy test that they perceive to be difficult; those who take a difficult test that they perceive to be easy; and those who take a difficult test that they perceive to be difficult. To do this research experimentally requires using two different tests, an easy test and a difficult test, and setting up two different kinds of perceptions, that the test is easy and that the test is difficult. The researcher attempts to create the perceptions by telling subjects in a believable way that the test they are about to take will be easy or difficult. She does this by asking subjects to read a page of instructions before they begin the test. For some subjects, the instructions contain the following sentence: Most students find this test easy, so just relax and enjoy taking the test. For other subjects, the instructions contain a different sentence: Most students find this test very difficult, but do your best. The researcher follows ethical guidelines and obtains informed consent from her subjects. What internal validity problem do you see in this study?   ■

This chapter has focused on sampling of subjects or cases, because most of the strategies available to researchers for enhancing their studies' generalizability involve this kind of sampling. However, it is important that you do not lose sight of the fact that factors other than subject characteristics affect a study's generalizability. Indeed, almost everything about research has the potential to affect its generalizability—the study's location in time and space, as well as everything that happens to the subjects during the study.

Because it is empirical, research has to be done at particular times and places and in particular ways. This is another way of saying that everything about a particular study is a sample—not just the subjects or cases. A study is done at a sample of times, in a sample of places, and in a sample of possible ways. All of these kinds of samples may affect a study's representativeness and thus its generalizability. Researchers sometimes try to enhance the generalizability of their studies by conducting them at several times, in several places, and in several different ways. But no single study can be done at all times and places and in all possible ways. Thus, even when sampling of subjects or cases is very representative, the generalizability of other aspects of any single study is usually very limited.

INTERNAL–EXTERNAL VALIDITY TRADE-OFFS

Chapter 4 presented a fairly traditional view of research design: that experimental is better. With respect to causal argument, this is clearly true. There is, however, an important disadvantage to experimentation: its artificiality. The control exercised by experimental researchers enhances their causal arguments, but it decreases the generalizability of their results. In the real world, the temperature, humidity, and lighting in people's environments are not held constant. Neither are the time of day, the height of their desks, and so forth. The very fact that permission is harder to obtain for experiments must ultimately reflect on their generalizability. Principals who are willing to allow researchers to determine children's classroom assignments randomly may head up schools that differ in important ways from typical schools. Subjects who are told that they may be deceived may behave differently as a result.

In fact, although experimentation is usually superior to nonexperimental research in establishing cause, nonexperimental research is usually superior to experimentation in generalizability. The two research modes should thus be viewed as complementary. It is often desirable to approach the same research question in both ways. If experimentation demonstrates that a causal relationship between two variables is highly likely, then nonexperimental research can establish whether and under what conditions the relationship is found in the real world.

Animal studies provide a good example of the complementarity of experimental and nonexperimental studies. Many people are quick to criticize the use of animal studies in answering research questions with potential applications to people. What such critics do not realize is that animal studies often provide our only possible or ethically acceptable way of doing experimental research and thus establishing causality. Prudent researchers follow up such animal studies with nonexperimental research to check on the generalizability of animal findings to people.

A recent example that has received wide coverage in the media is the relationship between cigarette smoking and health. It would obviously be unethical to study such a relationship experimentally in humans; experimenters would have to randomly assign some people to smoke and others not to smoke. Even if there weren't ethical problems, there would be practical ones: it would take 20 or more years for most of the smokers to begin developing serious health problems.

On the other hand, nonexperimental studies always leave cause in doubt. Even though it is established that heavy smokers are much more likely to suffer from cancer and circulatory disease, it is always possible that a third variable is the cause of the health problems. Perhaps there is some genetic factor that predisposes people both to smoke and to contract cancer. Perhaps smokers tend to have different diets or different exercise patterns, and these are the true causes of their circulatory problems.

However, extensive experimentation has been done on laboratory animals. Such animals, when randomly assigned to breathe tobacco smoke, consistently have more health problems than animals who are randomly assigned not to breathe tobacco smoke. Because a causal relationship between smoking and poor health has been established for animals, we can be more confident that the relationship between smoking and health that has been established for humans in many nonexperimental studies is in fact a causal one.

Field Versus Laboratory Studies

Some educational researchers try to increase the generalizability of their experimental research by conducting it in the real world rather than in a laboratory. Such studies are called *field experiments*. A researcher who randomly assigns children to open and traditional classrooms in a school is conducting a field experiment. Such a decision, of course, represents a trade-off. Although generalizability may be increased, field experimenters give up some of the control of potentially confounding variables that they have in a laboratory situation (e.g., physical environment).

Similarly, some nonexperimental researchers attempt to increase their control of potentially confounding variables by conducting their research in laboratories instead of the field. For example, a researcher might bring young children of various ethnicities into a specially equipped room to observe differences in their modes of play. Again, there is a trade-off; while the researcher's control of confounding variables in the research setting is increased, the generalizability of her results to the real world is decreased. Figure 5.7 summarizes internal-external validity trade-offs and depicts the usual advantages and disadvantages of different research designs.

EVALUATING EXTERNAL VALIDITY

In evaluating the generalizability of research results, you must decide to what extent the study probably represents other situations with respect to the research question. This involves evaluating whether and how aspects of the study are likely to be relevant or irrelevant to the research question. You may, for example, decide that the time of day the research was conducted is not likely to have affected the research results, while the location of the study is likely to have affected the results. You must then consider how the study's location might have limited its generalizability. You may, for example, decide that the results of an urban study probably represent suburban and other urban settings, but not rural settings.

These kinds of evaluations can be very difficult to do. We can never be sure that we have identified all of the characteristics of a study that might have affected the research results, much less what those effects might have been. This is why random sampling is so valuable: It gives us confidence that the characteristics of the subjects or cases in a study represent most characteristics of subjects or cases in the sampled population—even characteristics we know nothing about. But random sampling is not a panacea: We are rarely able to sample true populations of interest, and the populations we do sample may or may not represent larger populations. Even if a sample represents a true population of interest, factors other than sample characteristics affect a study's generalizability.

If the process of evaluating generalizability reminds you of the process of evaluating confounding variable control, you are right. In evaluating confounding variable

FIGURE 5.7   Internal-external validity trade-offs: usual advantages and disadvantages of different research designs.

	LABORATORY RESEARCH	FIELD RESEARCH
EXPERIMENTAL RESEARCH	Causal argument + Generalizability −	Causal argument o Generalizability o
NONEXPERIMENTAL RESEARCH	Causal argument o Generalizability o	Causal argument + Generalizability −

+ better
o fair
− worse

control, first you must decide whether the researcher has identified and controlled all the potentially confounding variables. This is very difficult: We can never be sure that we have identified all of the potentially confounding variables. Random assignment is very valuable: It gives us confidence that potentially confounding subject variables have been controlled—even those we can't identify. But random assignment is not always possible; and even when it is used, it does not control variables in the research situation.

The resemblance between internal and external validity evaluations doesn't stop here. The interesting thing is that potentially confounding variables and characteristics of the study that may affect research results tend to be the same things: potential causes of the dependent variable in the study. Confounding variables undercut causal argument precisely because they may be causes of the dependent variable in the study, and characteristics of the study may affect research results precisely because they may affect the dependent variable in the study. Thus, when we have identified potentially confounding variables, we have also identified many of the characteristics of the study that may affect the research results.

An example is the easiest way to make this point. Imagine that a school district is piloting an inservice program to increase teachers' awareness of sexism in the classroom. The district will evaluate the program by observing incidences of sexism in the classrooms of teachers who did and did not participate in the program. If there is less sexism in the classrooms of teachers who participated in the program, the district would like to be able to conclude that the program was responsible for this result. What potentially confounding variables would, if not controlled, pose a serious threat to the validity of this conclusion?

One obvious answer is teachers' gender. It is possible that female teachers were already less sexist than male teachers before the program began. If more female than male teachers participated in the inservice program, then the fact that there is less sexism in participating than nonparticipating teachers' classrooms after the program may be due to the fact that the participating teachers are predominantly female, not to their having participated in the inservice.

But suppose that this potentially confounding variable is controlled by keeping gender constant, by offering the inservice only to male teachers. If the inservice is successful in the pilot, the district would like to be able to conclude that the program would also be successful for the rest of the teachers in the district. What characteristics of the population may affect the success of the inservice in the population? Does the sample represent the population with respect to these characteristics? One characteristic of the population that may affect the success of the inservice in the population is teachers' gender. It seems possible that there are differences in male and female teachers' responses to an inservice program on sexism. And the sample does not represent the population with respect to this characteristic. Even if the inservice is successful for male teachers, it may not be successful for female teachers. The results of this research cannot safely be generalized to the entire population of interest, because the research sample does not represent the population with respect to a characteristic that may affect the research results. In this example, the same factor—subjects' gender—may affect both internal and external validity, because it may affect the dependent variable in the study: sexism.

Studies cannot be externally valid if they are not internally valid: If research results are not valid for the research situation, there is no point in even asking whether they might be valid for other situations. However, internal validity is rarely the ultimate problem. Even when studies are valid for the situations in which the research was done, an important question remains: Can these results be generalized to other situations?

Single studies rarely afford an opportunity to conduct research on truly representative samples of large populations of interest in a wide variety of contexts. There are thus few single studies with good external validity. This is another reason that replication is such an important part of the research enterprise. If many different researchers, working with many different samples in many different contexts, consistently get similar answers to similar research questions, then our confidence in the generalizability of the findings is enhanced. Each individual study has limitations with respect to generalizability, but these limitations will differ from study to study; one study may thus compensate for the weaknesses of another.

Figure 5.8 summarizes the process of evaluating the external validity of a study.

■ EXERCISE 9

In Summary Exercise 1g, chapter 4, you were asked to identify the potentially confounding variables in a study by Hebbeler. Hebbeler's sample is described below. What characteristics of the sample seem likely to restrict the external validity of her study? Are some of these the same as the potentially confounding variables that you identified in the chapter 4 exercise?

Hebbeler (1985) studied the effects of Head Start on school performance. The treatment group (Head Start graduates) was composed of children who had attended the Head Start program in the Montgomery County (Maryland) public schools for at least eight months in either 1970–71, 1974–75, or 1978–79. The comparison group was comprised of children who had applied to the program in one of those school years but who were not admitted or attended for less than a month. Dependent-variable data were collected from county records during the students' fourth-, eighth-, and twelfth-grade years, respectively. "No attempt was made to collect data on students who had transferred out of the system" (p. 209). "Rates of attrition from year to year were similar for the Head Start and comparison groups. The major difference

FIGURE 5.8   Steps in evaluating external validity.

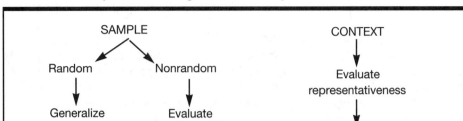

was that a sizable percentage of the comparison group never enrolled in the system at all." In 1983–84, the year data were collected for this study, 1,164 students from the original Head Start group were still enrolled in the county schools; 229 of the original comparison group students were enrolled. ∎

SUMMARY

External validity presents some of the most resistant problems that researchers face. Conducting research on the entire population of interest offers a solution to the problem of subject representativeness, but in practice this solution is usually available only to researchers whose populations of interest are highly local. Most researchers must thus work with samples. However, samples do not necessarily represent populations. If researchers wish to generalize their results, they must try to identify the characteristics of populations that may affect the research results and to select samples that represent the population with respect to these characteristics. This is very difficult to do. We can never be sure that all the relevant characteristics of the population have been identified, because we can never be sure that we know all of the characteristics that may affect the research results. Even if we could identify all of the relevant characteristics, it would be difficult to put together a sample that represents all of these characteristics.

Random sampling provides a solution to this problem. When a sample is random, we assume that the sample represents the population with respect to any characteristic, whether or not it has been identified as relevant. Random sampling maximizes the probability that the sample represents the population, no matter what the research question is. However, random sampling requires that all members of a population be identified and available for the study. Most researchers who publish in national journals are interested in populations of such large size that their individual members cannot be identified. Even when members of a population can be identified, self-selection presents a problem; researchers are usually unable to ensure that all persons selected to be studied will be able or willing to participate in the study.

Thus, bona fide random sampling of populations of interest is rarely an option. Most researchers must work with nonrandom samples, make what arguments they can for the representativeness of their samples, and acknowledge the remaining nonrepresentativeness of their samples as limitations on the generalizability of their studies.

Cluster sampling is often the best alternative to random sampling. In cluster sampling, relevant characteristics of the population are identified and then successively sampled as representatively as possible. Stratified sampling is used when population characteristics are unequally distributed. The use of convenience samples is often the most practical strategy, but convenience samples also typically present the most severe generalizability problems.

Because truly representative sampling is so difficult, few single studies have good generalizability. Only when a study has been replicated many times, on many different kinds of subjects or cases, and in many contexts, do we begin to arrive at an understanding of how the results generalize.

The welfare of research subjects is an important concern. Subjects have a right to confidentiality, to be informed about any aspect of the research that may affect them, and to decline without penalty to participate in research; and researchers have a responsibility to protect subjects' welfare even when informed consent has been obtained. However, the implementation of ethical guidelines often affects both the internal and external validity of research.

Internal and external validity concerns tend to be opposed. Good control of potentially confounding variables tends to decrease generalizability of a study's results. This problem can rarely be solved in a single study. Good causal argument with wide generalizability emerges only after many separate studies have been done on the same research question.

SUMMARY EXERCISES

1. Excerpts from a number of published research reports follow. Assess each study's external validity. What kind of sampling strategy did the researcher(s) employ? How does the sample limit generalizability? Do other characteristics of the research context limit generalizability? Do you see any internal-external validity trade-offs in the study?

a. Thompson and Zerbinos (1995) studied gender roles in animated cartoons (p. 654).

> Results indicated notable discrepancies between prominence and portrayal of male and female characters. Both male and female characters were portrayed stereotypically. Compared to female characters, male characters were given much more prominence, appeared more frequently, engaged in more of almost all of the noted behaviors, and talked significantly more. When male or female behavior and communication variables were divided by number of male or female characters or by total talk time, results indicated consistency with gender role stereotypes. Comparisons of pre- and post-1980 cartoons, however, indicated significant change toward a less stereotypical portrayal of the characters, particularly female characters.

Using a local edition of *TV Guide,* the researchers (who are affiliated with a university in Dayton, Ohio) generated a list of all ongoing children's cartoon series on all network and cable channels during February 1993. There were 92 such channels. Forty-one different cartoon shows were identified, and two hours of each show were taped. Since individual cartoon episodes ranged in length from about 10 minutes to an hour, a total of 175 episodes were taped to yield a total of two hours from each show. The tapes were then coded to provide information on the variables of interest to the researchers.

b. Stockwell and Dye (1980) studied the effects of "counselor touch on client evaluation of counseling and level of self-exploration." Subjects were 56 men and 44 women randomly selected from students "enrolled in an undergraduate education course devoted to personal growth and the building of interpersonal communication" (p. 443).

c. Jayanthi et al. (1994) studied school districts' testing policies, including policies requiring accommodations when testing students with disabilities. About 60 percent of the districts in their study had policies on standardized testing that included accommodating disabled students.

Subjects for the study were 550 school districts nationwide. These school districts were selected in the following manner. First, a listing of all school districts nationwide ($n = 15,713$) was obtained from an index . . . provided by the U. S. Department of Education. Then a stratified random sample was selected from this listing according to three demographic criteria: (a) geographical location within the nine census regions of the country. . . ; (b) location of the school district (. . . urban, suburban, and rural . . .); and (c) type of the school district (e.g., independent or shared superintendent). Using this procedure, a total of 550 school districts (about 3.5% of all school districts nationwide) were selected to participate in the study (p. 696).

A survey was sent to these 550 school districts; 214 (38.9%) of the surveys were returned.

d. In a longitudinal study, Caspi and Silva (1995) found that personality traits of young adults can be predicted from their behavior in early childhood. Early childhood behavior was characterized as undercontrolled, inhibited, confident, reserved, or well-adjusted. Young adults' personality was characterized in terms of such things as impulsivity, danger seeking, aggression, and social potency.

Subjects were adolescents involved in the Dunedin (New Zealand) Multidisciplinary Health and Development Study. . . . Briefly, the study is a longitudinal investigation of the health, development, and behavior of a complete cohort of consecutive births between April 1, 1972, and March 31, 1973, in Dunedin, New Zealand. Perinatal data were obtained, and when the children were traced for follow-up at 3 years of age, 1,139 children were located in the province and asked to participate in the longitudinal study. Of these, 1,037 (91%) were assessed.

The sample has been reassessed with a diverse battery of psychological, medical, and sociological measures every 2 years since the children were age 3. Data were collected for 991 subjects at age 5, 954 at age 7, 925 at age 11, 850 at age 13, 976 at age 15, and 1,008 at age 18. Over the years the sample has remained representative of the full range of the population on important variables such as SES and IQ. . . . Regarding racial distribution, members of the sample are predominantly of European ancestry (less than 7% identify themselves as Maori or Polynesian).

e. Leak (1980) studied "Effects of Highly Structured versus Nondirective Group Counseling Approaches on Personality and Behavioral Measures of Adjustment in Incarcerated Felons" (p. 521).

The initial pool of subjects was a group of 80 inmates at Kansas State Penitentiary who volunteered for a group counseling program at the prison's mental health unit. All volunteers were accepted for the program regardless of prior mental disturbance or criminal background. Volunteers were randomly assigned to one of three experimental conditions: PEER ($n = 27$), traditional ($n = 27$), or no-treatment control ($n = 26$). Within each treatment condition, volunteers were randomly assigned to a specific counseling group. During the course of treatment, several subjects dropped out for numerous reasons (three subjects from PEER, four subjects from the traditional group, and six subjects from the control group).

f. Green and Stager (1986) investigated a question of considerable interest to many researchers: What conditions subjects' responsiveness to mailed questionnaires (pp. 203–204)?

A systematic random sample was chosen from the State Department of Education list of educators in the state of Wyoming. A total of 750 teachers' names was drawn. The sample was composed of elementary (48%), junior high (24%), and senior high teachers (28%). They were located in rural areas (22% in areas of less than 1,000 population), small towns (52% in towns from 1,000–9,999), and larger towns (27% in towns of more than 10,000). Of the sample, 64% were female and 36% were male.

Procedure
Two experimental treatments were employed with subjects randomly assigned to each. First, salutations on the cover letter were varied with one form being "Dear Educator" typed and xeroxed (50%). The more personalized form had the addressee's surname written in by hand (50%). Second, the letter was either signed by hand in blue ink (51%) or had a xeroxed signature (49%).

A three-page (double-sided) survey instrument was sent to all those in the sample with a cover letter and a stamped (metered) return envelope. The survey consisted of 49 questions asking teachers for demographic information, courses taken in tests and measurement, attitudes toward standardized and classroom testing, use of tests for grading, purposes in giving classroom and standardized tests, and interest in topics for inservice training. Responses to attitude items clustered in the 2-, 3-, and 4-categories of a 6-point rating scale, suggesting that most respondents did not have particularly strong attitudes on the subjects. Two weeks later, a follow-up letter was sent; two weeks after this, a second survey form, return envelope, and cover letter were mailed.

Significant effects were found for vicinity population but not for personalization, sex, or grade level taught. Significantly higher response rates were obtained from rural areas in comparison to more urban areas. Differential responses to the first, second, and third mailings by sex, level taught, and area population were also found.[1]

g. Frederick, Howley, and Powers (1986) studied differences in oxygen demand between runners wearing hard- and soft-soled shoes (pp. 174–175).

Measurements of the oxygen cost per kilometer (OCK) while running were made on 10 well-trained male distance runners. The subjects ranged in weight from 59.1 to 81.6 kg and all were healthy and running regularly at the time of the study. Each subject was required to run six trials on the treadmill at his actual or estimated marathon race pace. . . . Three trials were run in each of two pairs of test shoes. . . . All subjects were acquainted with treadmill running and the measurement procedures before the study began, and all had run between 10 and 20 miles during the previous week in the test shoes they would wear during the study.

---

[1]*Journal of Experimental Education*, Vol. 54, pp. 203–206, 1986. Reprinted with permission of the Helen Dwight Reid Educational Foundation. Published by Heldref Publications, 1319 Eighteenth Street, NW, Washington, DC 20036-1802. Copyright ©1986.

h. Travis and Kohli (1995) examined the relationship between birth order and educational attainment.

> The data in this study were collected as part of the Adult Life Cycle Project. The data come from . . . a sample of adults (male and female) from city blocks randomly chosen within census tracts mirroring the actual class and racial percentages in a medium-sized California metropolitan area (population 221,000). The Adult Life Cycle Project was completed over an 11-month period (ending in 1979) with the use of a simple (single-stage) cluster procedure similar to Blalock's cost-sampling error model (Blalock, 1960). A survey technique fostering maximum use of small field staff and administrative staff was used. A "leave behind" strategy was used, similar to that used in the Oakland study, wherein questionnaires designed for self-administration were deposited with the respondent at home and retrieved on a subsequent visit 3 days later. This approach provides personal contact during the initial visit, plus an opportunity to answer any questions that may have arisen by the time of the follow-up call. There was a completion rate of 74% (after considering refusals, ineligibles, and those never at home), which yielded a usable sample of 817 respondents (p. 501).

2. Find three published quantitative research reports in a field of interest to you. Evaluate the external validity of each study. What sampling strategy was employed? How does the sample limit generalizability? Do other characteristics of the research context limit generalizability? Does the study involve ethical issues? If so, how were they handled and how did this affect generalizability? Do you see any internal–external validity trade-offs in the study?

3. Imagine that your classmates are the subjects of a study about the effectiveness of this textbook. How might their characteristics limit generalizing?

6

Descriptive Statistics for Single Variables

When a quantitative researcher has completed the data collection stage of research, the result is data—usually lots of data. If the research has been done properly, the data contain the answer to the research question, but the answer does not leap out of the data. The data are simply variable values. These values must be analyzed to provide the answer the researcher is seeking. The tool that quantitative researchers use to analyze their data is statistics.

There are two basic kinds of statistics: *descriptive* and *inferential*. Descriptive statistics describe variable values in an empirical sample; inferential statistics use known variable values from an empirical sample to make guesses (inferences) about unknown variable values in a population that the sample represents. Inferential statistics are based on descriptive statistics, so we will deal with descriptive statistics first, in this and the next chapter, and with inferential statistics in chapter 8. Descriptive statistics, in turn, come in two basic kinds: those that reduce data on a single variable and those that assess relationships between variables. Relationship-assessing statistics are based in part on data-reducing statistics, so we will deal with data-reducing statistics first, in this chapter. Chapter 7 is about descriptive statistics that assess relationships between variables.

To begin our discussion of data-reducing statistics, imagine that the president of a large university decides that she would like to know the entrance examination scores of this year's entering students. The president telephones the director of testing at the university and asks him to provide her with this information. The university has about 5,000 entering students each year. Entrance examination scores are available on most of these students.

Will the director of testing simply send the president 5,000 test scores? Of course not. No one (not even a university president) can look at 5,000 numbers and make sense of them. The director of testing will need to reduce these data to some manageable size. The trick is to do this without losing information or misrepresenting the original data set.

The director of testing can choose from a number of statistical techniques for reducing data. He will want to choose the technique (or techniques) that provides adequate reduction while preserving the most information possible and not misrepresenting the original data set. Guidelines are available to help the director of testing to do this.

FREQUENCY DISTRIBUTIONS

Frequency distributions are among the simplest data-reduction statistics. A frequency distribution shows the number or percent of subjects or cases having particular values of a variable. Here is the result of a (very small) study.

Subject	Sex
a	Female
b	Male
c	Male
d	Female

The frequency distribution on this variable for this sample would look like this.

	n	%
Female	2	50
Male	2	50

Frequency distributions provide perfect data reduction: They retain all the information that was in the original data set and they do not misrepresent the original data set in any way. The proof of this is that we can recreate the original data set perfectly from a frequency distribution.

Imagine that we are given the following frequency distribution:

	n
Anglo	4
Hispanic	2

From this, we know that the original data set must have looked exactly like this.

Ethnicity

Anglo
Anglo
Anglo
Anglo
Hispanic
Hispanic

We cannot, of course, attach names to the subjects or put them in their original order, but that is irrelevant. Researchers don't use that kind of information anyway.

■ EXERCISE 1

Create a frequency distribution showing both number and percent for each of the following data sets. (Because identification of subjects (as *a, b, c,* etc.) is irrelevant to data analysis, that information has been omitted from the data sets.)

a. *Type of Counseling*	b. *Test Score*	c. *Rating*
Directive	57	3
Nondirective	51	4
Nondirective	55	4
Directive	55	1
	54	2
	53	5
	55	5
	56	
	56	■

■ EXERCISE 2

Recreate the original data sets from each of the following frequency distributions.

a.
Type of Counseling	*n*
Directive	3
Nondirective	4

b.
Rating	*% (n = 20)*
Low	30
Average	40
High	30

c.
Score	*n*
50	1
51	1
52	3
53	5
54	4
55	2 ■

The trouble with frequency distributions is that, although they provide perfect data reduction, they sometimes do not provide enough data reduction. This is because there are as many data points in a frequency distribution as there are values of the variable being reduced. If the variable has many values, the amount of reduction is simply not adequate.

To return to the example of the entrance examination scores of entering students, suppose these students' scores range from 51 to 100. A frequency distribution of their scores would contain 50 data points: the number of students having each score from 51 to 100. This would be an improvement over the original 5,000 scores, to be sure, but the president is going to have trouble looking at 50 numbers and making any sense of them, as well.

Frequency distributions are therefore useful only when the number of variable values is small. This is usually true of categorical variables and usually not true of continuous variables, so frequency distribution is the data-reduction statistic of choice for categorical variables. Frequency distribution always provides perfect data reduction, and with categorical variables it usually provides adequate reduction. Frequency distribution is also sometimes used for semicontinuous variables with a small number of values.

Graphic Frequency Distributions

Frequency distributions can also be put into graphic form. If you're like many people, graphs probably have been the things you skipped when reading, but in order to understand something about statistics, you're going to have to learn something about graphs. Graphs have two axes (lines): a horizontal axis and a vertical axis (Figure 6.1). Each axis is marked off in equal intervals representing some unit of measure. One kind of graph, called a *frequency polygon,* has a horizontal axis representing a variable; the axis is marked off in equal units representing values of the variable. If the variable to be graphed is students' scores on a test, for example, the axis is marked off in equal units representing the test scores.

On a frequency polygon, the vertical axis represents numbers (frequencies) of subjects or cases. The graph shows how many subjects had what test score. A simple frequency polygon can be constructed from the following frequency distribution for an imaginary data set, showing the number of subjects who had each possible test score from 50 to 59.

Test Score	n
50	1
51	2
52	4
53	6
54	9
55	8
56	7
57	4
58	2
59	1

FIGURE 6.1 Frequency polygon.

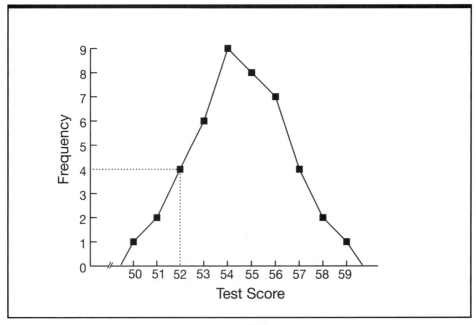

To construct a frequency polygon from the data given, we locate a test score on the horizontal axis—for example, 52 (see Figure 6.1). Next we locate on the vertical axis the number of subjects who had this test score—in this example, 4. We then draw two imaginary lines, one to the right of the 4 on the vertical axis and one up from the 52 on the horizontal axis. Where these two lines meet, we place a point. This point represents the number of people (4) who had the given score (52). We repeat this process for all scores and then connect the dots.

For people used to dealing with graphs, a great deal of information is conveyed by a glance at this frequency polygon. The shape, rising as we look from left to right and then falling again, tells us that relatively few people scored in the low 50s, more people in the mid 50s, and few in the high 50s.

■ EXERCISE 3

Create a frequency polygon for the following data set.

Attitude Score	n
4	1
7	3
8	3
9	4
10	6
11	7
12	5
13	3
15	1

■

The Normal Curve

The famous *normal curve* is a frequency polygon. The normal curve is depicted in Figure 6.2. What the normal curve tells us is much the same thing that the frequency polygon of test scores above told us: that few people have very low values of the variable being graphed, more people have medium values, and few have high values. The normal curve figures prominently in statistics, so you will be hearing about it again.

However, not all variables have frequency polygons that look like this; that is, not all variables curve normally. If we were to graph a frequency distribution of the ages of people in the United States, for example, the graph would not be normal in shape. If it were, that would mean that there are about as many very young people as very old ones. This is, of course, not true; there are many more very young people than very old ones.

MEASURES OF CENTRAL TENDENCY

What do we do to reduce data on continuous variables when frequency distribution doesn't provide enough reduction? For this problem we can choose from a family of statistics called *measures of central tendency*. These are statistics that indicate the

FIGURE 6.2   The normal curve.

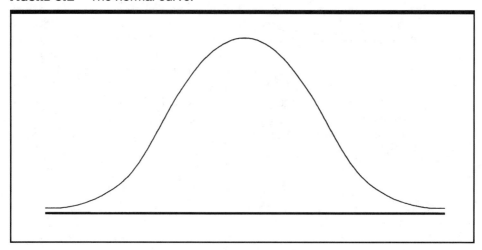

center or midpoint of a set of variable values. Two measures of central tendency are commonly used: the mean and median.

The Mean

The *mean* is a statistic with which you are already very familiar. You may know it better by the name average. If your professor tells you that you have scores of 80, 90, and 100 on three exams, you know that your average score on the exams is 90. Technically, 90 in this case isn't called an average; it's called the mean.

As you already know, the mean is calculated by adding all of the scores and then dividing the total by the number of scores. Statisticians have a formula to express this. The formula is:

$$\bar{X} = \frac{\Sigma X}{n}.$$

$\bar{X}$ is the symbol for the mean. Σ is what is called the summation sign. It is read "sum of" and means "add 'em up." X represents the values of a variable, as you already have learned. The letter n stands for the number of variable values in the sample—that is, the number of variable values that were added. And the line between ΣX and n means divide. The formula is read "the sum of X divided by n." To substitute the test scores 80, 90, and 100 in the formula for the mean, we would say "the sum of 80, 90, and 100 divided by 3."

The mean is a good data-reduction statistic for these test scores. It tells us where the midpoint of the scores is, and in so doing it does not misrepresent the original data. However, the mean isn't always the best measure of central tendency to use. Consider the following problem.

Imagine that you are an employee of the federal government. It is your job to collect data on neighborhood incomes so that your boss in Washington can decide which neighborhoods are eligible for urban renewal funds. For a particular neighborhood (again unrealistically small), you have collected the following data on the annual incomes of five households.

Household	Income
a	$2,000
b	4,000
c	6,000
d	8,000
e	100,000

Your boss, like the university president, doesn't want to see the raw data; he wants you to reduce the data before you send them on to him. If you calculate the mean of these incomes, the result will be $24,000. That does not make this neighborhood a very likely candidate for urban renewal funds, but most of the families in this neighborhood obviously deserve assistance. The mean is not a very good data-reduction statistic in this case. It misrepresents the original data. This is because the data set has what is called an *outlier:* the value of $100,000. An outlier is a variable value that "lies out" from other values in the data set; it is noticeably higher or lower than other values in the data set. Outliers pull the mean in their direction. In the example above, the outlier is high and pulls the mean in a high direction, away from more typical values in the data set. The mean thus misrepresents the data set by suggesting that typical values are higher than they in fact are.

The Median

For this kind of problem, we use a statistic called the *median.* The median is determined by arranging the variable values in order and finding the middle value. For the income data above, which are already arranged in ascending order, the median is $6,000. This reflects typical values in the data set much more accurately than does the mean of $24,000.

But how do we find the median when there is an even number of variable values in the data set, as there is in the income data above if we remove household *a?* Now there is no middle value.

Household	Income
b	$4,000
c	6,000
d	8,000
e	100,000

In this case, the median is the mean of the middle two values: $7,000. (There is a more complicated way to figure the median, but this definition will suffice.)

When to Use the Mean Versus the Median

How do we decide when to use the median and when to use the mean? A very general answer to this question is that we use the mean whenever we can, because the mean contains more information than does the median. This is because the mean reflects every variable value in the data set; every value is used in calculating the mean. Consider the two data sets that follow.

X	X
2	4
4	4
6	6
8	8

The data sets are not the same, but their medians are the same: 5. The mean, which is 5 for the first data set and 5.5 for the second data set, thus gives us more information about these data sets than does the median. It tells us, as it should, that although both have midpoints near 5, the second contains scores that are a bit higher overall than those in the first. At this point, then, the rule is to use the mean whenever we are reducing data on a continuous variable, unless the data set has an outlier (or outliers) in one direction. In that case, the median is a better choice. As you learn more about statistics, it will be possible to introduce a more sophisticated basis for choosing between the mean and the median.

■ Exercise 4

Arrange each of the following data sets in ascending or descending order. Calculate the mean and median for each data set. Notice what causes differences between the mean and median. Notice how the median is not affected by the outliers, while the outliers pull the mean in their direction. Decide which statistic seems more appropriate for each data set and why.

a. X	b. X	c. X
3	54	1
5	52	4
6	53	2
5	30	5
4	50	1
8	51	3
6	55	
5	54	
4	53	

■

MEASURES OF DISPERSION

Measures of central tendency alone do not adequately describe data. Remember that in reducing data our goal is to get a large number of data points down to manageable size while losing the least information possible. It is clear from the following examples that measures of central tendency alone cannot do the job.

X	X
1	2
2	2
3	3
4	4
5	4

The mean of both of these data sets is 3; so is the median. However, the data sets are clearly not the same. How would you describe the difference? Would you say that variable values in the first data set spread out more while values in the second cluster more closely together? Statisticians refer to this as the dispersion of a data set. Dispersion is used with reference to the center of the data set; and the center of a data set is the median or the mean. Statisticians would say that values of the variable in the first data set are more disperse from the mean, while values in the second data set are less disperse from the mean.

One way to indicate dispersion is to state the median or mean and then the minimum and maximum values. The first data set can be described as having a mean of 3, a minimum of 1, and a maximum of 5; the second data set can be described as having a mean of 3, a minimum of 2, and a maximum of 4. For such simple data sets, this adequately describes the differences. However, this is too simple a treatment for the following data sets.

X	X
1	1
2	1
3	3
4	5
5	5

These data sets have identical means, minima, and maxima, but the data sets are not the same.

What is needed is a statistic that measures dispersion in as sophisticated a way as the mean measures central tendency—that is, a statistic that takes every variable value into account. What is needed is a measure of average dispersion.

Why not calculate every subject's dispersion from the mean and then average the results? In fact, we can and do calculate every subject's dispersion from the mean; this yields what is called a *deviation score*. The formula for deviation score is as follows:

$$x = X - \overline{X}$$

In this formula, x is the symbol for deviation score. The other symbols you already know: X for the values of a variable and $\overline{X}$ for the mean. In a data set with a mean of 3, the deviation score for a variable value of 4 is 1 (because $4 - 3 = 1$).

The example below shows deviation scores for two data sets, each having a mean of 3.

X	x	X	x
1	-2	2	-1
2	-1	2	-1
3	0	3	0
4	1	4	1
5	2	4	1

The deviation score for an individual with a variable value below the mean is a negative number, and the deviation score for an individual with a variable value above the mean is a positive number. Remember, what we're trying to do is get a measure of how far people are from the mean. An individual with a variable value of

1 is 2 points *below* the mean, so his or her deviation score is −2; an individual with a variable value of 5 is 2 points *above* the mean, so his or her deviation score is 2. Dealing with negative numbers is necessary in statistics, but fortunately it's easy. To subtract 3 from 1, you just turn the problem around and subtract 1 from 3; then you put a minus sign in front of the answer. So $1 − 3 = −2$ and $2 − 3 = −1$. (We don't usually show the plus sign in front of positive numbers; we just assume that if there's no sign the number is positive.) But wait—aren't we trying to reduce data? So far we've only increased it. We started out with five data points in each data set, and now we have 10. Oh yes, we were going to calculate these deviation scores so we could average them—add them all up and then divide by the number of them that we had. But what happens if we try to average our deviation scores? We come up with zero. For the first data set, $(−1) + (−2) + 0 + 1 + 2 = 0$. And zero divided by anything is zero. Try averaging the deviation scores in the second data set. That should come out to be zero also. The positive and negative deviation scores cancel each other out. This is always true of deviation scores, by definition, and it is such a common problem in statistics that it has a name: the *zero-sum problem.*

We need to get rid of the negative and positive signs that cause the zero-sum problem. We can't just ignore them, but we can get rid of them by squaring the numbers. Squaring means multiplying a number by itself, and a negative number multiplied by a negative number is positive: −1 times −1 is 1. So what we do looks like this.

X	x	x^2	X	x	x^2
1	−2	4	2	−1	1
2	−1	1	2	−1	1
3	0	0	3	0	0
4	1	1	4	1	1
5	2	4	4	1	1

Now we average the squared deviation scores. For the first data set, the result is 2 ($4 + 1 + 0 + 1 + 4$, divided by 5). For the second data set, the result is 0.8 ($1 + 1 + 0 + 1 + 1$, divided by 5). The trouble is, we were trying to come up with an average deviation score, and 2 is clearly too high for the first data set: 2 is the largest deviation score in the data set, not the average. When we squared to get rid of the negative signs, we also increased the size of the numbers, so now to get things back in proportion we have to take the square roots of our results.

Here's where a calculator comes in handy: The square root of 2 is 1.4, and the square root of 0.8 is 0.9. (Surprised at that last one? Well, remember that a decimal is another way to represent a fraction. When we square a number, we multiply it by itself; thus, when we square a decimal, we're multiplying a fraction by a fraction—e.g., one-half of one-half is one-fourth. Multiplying a decimal by itself yields an even smaller decimal. Conversely, taking the square root of a decimal yields a larger decimal.)

So we finally have what we set out to get: a measure of average dispersion. The average dispersion in the first data set is 1.4 and in the second 0.9. If you look back at the data sets, this solution should seem satisfactory. The first data set is more disperse from the mean and the second less disperse, and this is just what our averages tell us. (Besides, if we calculate the average dispersion this way instead of some other way, we'll be able to do very useful things with it later.)

THE STANDARD DEVIATION

Perhaps without knowing it, you have just come to understand something you probably have heard about for a long time without really understanding: the *standard deviation*. The symbol for the standard deviation of a variable in a sample is *S*, and the formula for this standard deviation is:

$$S = \sqrt{\frac{\Sigma x^2}{n}}$$

This formula describes what you have just seen: The square root of the sum of the squared deviation scores divided by the number of scores.

■ EXERCISE 5

Calculate the standard deviation for the following data set. Save your answer to use in a later exercise.

X
2
4
6
8
10

■

THE RELATIONSHIP BETWEEN THE STANDARD DEVIATION AND THE NORMAL CURVE

The standard deviation is so well known because it has a very special relationship with a certain kind of frequency distribution: the normal curve.

As noted earlier, many, although not all, variables tend to distribute normally (for example, height, intelligence, and manual dexterity). The *normal curve* is a frequency polygon: a frequency distribution in graphic form. The normal curve tells us, among other things, that few people have very low or very high values of the variable—that most people have middle-range values. For example, few adult men in the United States have heights of five feet or seven feet; most are within a few inches of six feet in height. Similarly, few people are either profoundly retarded or geniuses; most people are in the middle range of intelligence.

However, when a variable distributes perfectly normally, the normal curve tells us something more precise than this. (Perfectly normal distributions happen only in theory; however, variables that closely approach a perfectly normal distribution when samples are random and sample sizes large enough are considered to distribute normally.) For example, it tells us that about two-thirds of the people (or things) in the distribution have variable values that fall between the mean and one standard deviation above or below the mean.

Most tests of cognitive ability and achievement distribute normally. If such a test has a mean of 50 and a standard deviation of 10, we know that about two-thirds of the people in a large, random sample will score between 40 and 60 on this test, 40 being one standard deviation (10 points) below the mean of 50, and 60 being one standard deviation above the mean. Not only that, but the normal curve tells us the percents of people who will be at various score ranges, all expressed in standard deviation units. Figure 6.3 depicts the relationship between the standard deviation and the normal curve.

What the figure tells us is that 34.1% of the people will score between the mean and one standard deviation above the mean ($+1S$); and, since the curve is symmetrical, 34.1% of the people will score between the mean and one standard deviation below the mean ($-1S$). 13.6% of the people will score between one and two standard deviations above the mean—that is, between $+1S$ and $+2S$; and 13.6% will score between one and two standard deviations below the mean—that is, between $-1S$ and $-2S$. 2.2% will score between two and three standard deviations above the mean—that is, between $+2S$ and $+3S$; and 2.2% will score between two and three standard deviations below the mean—that is, between $-2S$ and $-3S$. That leaves less than one percent—0.1%, to be more exact—who will score more than three standard deviations above the mean, and 0.1% who will score more than three standard deviations below the mean.

To use this information for a normally distributed variable that we have measured, we first calculate the mean and standard deviation of the variable for our subjects, using the formulas that we gave earlier in this chapter. To continue with the example we began above, suppose that the variable is a test, which we find has a mean of 50 and a standard deviation of 10 in our sample. We then superimpose values of our variable for the standard deviation units on the horizontal axis of the normal curve. Figure 6.4 shows this.

In Figure 6.4, the value 60 appears on the horizontal axis below $+1S$. This is because in our sample, which has a mean of 50 and a standard deviation of 10, the value 60 is one standard deviation above the mean: $X + 1S = 50 + 10 = 60$. The value 30 appears below $-2S$, because in our sample the value 30 is two standard deviations below the mean: $X - 2S = 50 - 20 = 30$.

FIGURE 6.3   The relationship between the standard deviation and the normal curve.

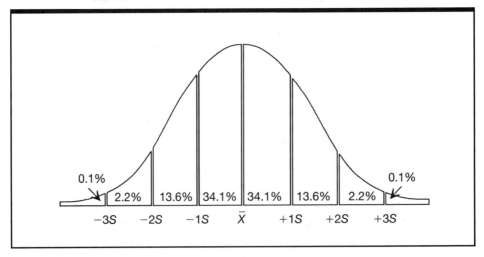

FIGURE 6.4   The normal curve, showing values for a variable with a mean of 50 and a standard deviation of 10.

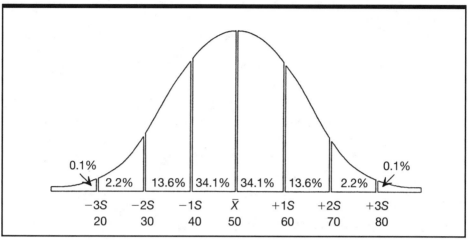

As we will soon see, there are many things we can do with the information that the normal curve provides. For now, let's take a look at what Figure 6.4 tells us about an individual whose score on the test is 20. This score is three standard deviations below the mean. Only 0.1% of the people who took the test scored lower. This individual's score is thus very low compared to the rest of the group.

At this point you may want to reread the last few paragraphs and look carefully at the figures to be sure you understand this important concept. If you don't understand, it will be difficult for you to follow the next few pages of text.

■ Exercise 6

A test has a mean of 100 and a standard deviation of 10. Superimpose this information on the horizontal axis of the curve in Figure 6.4. What percents of people fall within what score ranges on the test? If you are told that your score on this test is 122, what do you know about yourself?   ■

Not only does the normal curve permit us to make these kinds of statements about what people's variable values will be; it also permits us to make more specific statements. If a variable has a mean of 50 and a standard deviation of 10, not only do we know that about 34% of the people score between 50 and 60; we also know what percent score between any two values—for example, 42 and 43, or 58 and 59.

Statisticians have drawn up a table showing the percent of a group that will have each value of a variable that is normally distributed. To make the table useful for all variables that distribute normally, the table expresses variable values in standard deviation units.

Z-Scores

The vehicle for doing this is called a *z-score*; *z*-scores express variable values in standard deviation units. There is a different *z*-score for every possible variable value.

Let's return to the example of a test with a mean of 50 and a standard deviation of 10. A test score of 40 would correspond to a z-score of -1 (that is, one standard deviation below the mean); a test score of 60 would correspond to a z-score of 1 (one standard deviation above the mean).

There is a formula for converting any variable value to a z- score. The formula is:

$$z = \frac{X - \bar{X}}{S}$$

You already know the symbols in this formula. X is the symbol for an individual's raw score; $\bar{X}$ is the symbol for the mean; and S is the symbol for the standard deviation.

To convert the test score of 40 to a z-score, we do this:

$$z = \frac{X - \bar{X}}{S} = \frac{40 - 50}{10} = \frac{-10}{10} = -1$$

To convert the test score of 60 to a z-score, we do this:

$$z = \frac{X - \bar{X}}{S} = \frac{60 - 50}{10} = \frac{10}{10} = 1$$

But what about a test score of 55? Well,

$$z = \frac{X - \bar{X}}{S} = \frac{55 - 50}{10} = \frac{5}{10} = 0.5$$

This tells us that a test score of 55 is 0.5 standard deviation units (one-half of 10, or 5 points) above the mean.

Once statisticians have variable values converted to z- scores, they simply look them up in a table to find what percents of the values fall between particular z-scores.

■ EXERCISE 7

Using the data set from Exercise 5, calculate the z- scores for raw scores of 2 and 8. You'll need the mean and standard deviation of the data set, which you calculated for Exercise 5. ■

Perfect Data Reduction Again

This relationship between the standard deviation and the normal curve is important for the following reason. If a variable distributes perfectly normally, a statistician needs only three numbers—the mean, the standard deviation, and the n—to reconstruct the original data set perfectly. By using z-scores and the z table, the statistician can tell exactly what percents of the scores were 0, 1, 2, and so forth. This is a powerful tool. If a variable is perfectly normally distributed, we can reduce even a large data set to just three numbers with no loss of information, because we can perfectly reconstruct the original data set from those three numbers.

Of course, in the real world, variables never distribute perfectly normally. However, if a distribution is very nearly normal (which almost always happens with large random samples—that is, unless the variable is one of those that just plain does not distribute normally), we can still reduce many data points to just three with almost no distortion or misrepresentation of the original data set.

Knowing this permits you to understand the real rule about when to use the mean and when to use the median to reduce data on a variable. If the variable distributes very nearly normally, the mean and standard deviation are obviously the data-reduction statistics of choice because they provide such effective reduction while preserving so much information. If the distribution departs substantially from normal, however, the median is a better choice; with non-normal distributions, the standard deviation loses its power. There are rules for judging how nearly normal is near enough to use the mean. They are beyond the scope of this book, but if you're interested, you can consult any comprehensive statistics text (e.g., Hildebrand, 1986).

Other Kinds of Transformed Scores

Understanding z-scores permits you to understand a basic practice in testing: transforming test scores. Such transformations are necessary because raw scores, the number of items an individual got right, have little meaning. Suppose you meet with your child's teacher to discuss his achievement test scores. The teacher tells you that your child's raw score in reading was 60 and in math 40. How much information do you now have about his reading and math performance? Do these raw scores mean that your child is doing better in reading than in math? Not necessarily.

The reading test might have had 100 items and the math test only 50 items, in which case the child got a higher percent of items right on the math test than on the reading test. Even if both tests had 100 items, the child might still be doing as well in math as in reading. Perhaps the math test is more difficult for the child's grade level than is the reading test. Which is better: getting 40% of the questions right on a hard test or 60% right on an easy test?

Psychometrists solve this problem by transforming raw scores to scores that do have meaning. They do this by comparing individuals' scores with those of other individuals. The most basic kind of transformed score is a *percentile score*. Essentially, a percentile score indicates the percent of people taking the test whose raw score is the same as or lower than a given individual's. A percentile score of 50 for an individual means that the individual's raw score is the same as or higher than the raw scores of 50 percent of the people who took the test.

If we know who these other people are, percentile scores have meaning. Commercial test publishers stay in business primarily because they provide percentile scores on useful groups of people. If your child took a nationally standardized achievement test, his score can be transformed to a percentile score. These percentiles are based on large, representative samples of children in your child's grade in school from all over the United States.

If your child's teacher tells you that his raw score of 60 in reading transforms to a percentile score of 84, while his raw score of 40 in math transforms to a percentile score of 67, you suddenly have a lot of information about how your child is doing. He is doing well in both reading and math compared with children of his grade in the United States. However, he is doing better in reading than in math, so if you want to give your child special help, you should probably focus on math rather than reading.

The trouble with percentile scores is that, although they are meaningful, they are not mathematically manipulable. For reasons that are beyond the scope of this book, the way percentile scores are obtained means that they cannot legitimately be added, subtracted, multiplied, and divided. For statisticians, who need to calculate things like means and standard deviations to stay in business, this is bad news. But there is a way to solve this problem: z-scores. It is permissible to manipulate z-scores mathematically. And because of the relationship between the standard deviation and the normal curve, z-scores on variables that distribute normally correspond to percentiles.

If the mean and standard deviation of the reading test in the national sample are 50 and 10, your child's reading score of 60 can be converted to a z-score of 1, one standard deviation above the mean. And, as you will see if you refer to Figure 6.3, when a variable distributes normally, a z-score of 1 corresponds to a percentile score of 84, because 84% of the people are at or below one standard deviation above the mean. The trouble with z-scores is that they are hard to understand intuitively. They come in negative numbers and decimals. How do you think most parents would react to being told that their child's science score was 1.2 and his social studies score -0.11? So statisticians transform z-scores, in turn, to other kinds of standard scores just to make them look more like what test scores are supposed to look like.

You probably know that most IQ tests have a mean of 100 and a standard deviation of 15. Is this because psychometrists are clever enough to design a test on which the "average" person gets 100 items right and on which 34% of the people get between 85 and 100 of the questions right? Of course not. IQ scores are transformed by the following formula:

$$IQ = 100 + 15z$$

To find out your IQ score, psychometrists convert your raw score on the test to a z-score and then convert the z-score to an IQ score. If your z-score on the test is 1, then your IQ score will be 115, one standard deviation above the mean.

Using this kind of formula we can transform raw scores to look like anything we want. If we want a test to have a mean of 50 and a standard deviation of 10, we first transform each individual's raw score on the test to a z-score; then we transform each z-score as follows:

$$50 + 10z$$

This particular transformation is used so commonly that it has a name. Raw scores that have been transformed to have a mean of 50 and a standard deviation of 10 are called *T-scores*. Figure 6.5 shows the normal curve with a variety of different values on the horizontal axis. First the axis has been labeled in terms of the mean and standard deviations. Then an imaginary set of raw scores has been provided, followed by z-scores, which are in standard deviation units, and *T*-scores, which have a mean of 50 and a standard deviation of 10.

■ EXERCISE 8

A test that distributes normally has a raw-score mean of 32 and standard deviation of 4. Your raw score on the test is 34. Convert your raw score to a z-score. Now convert

FIGURE 6.5 The normal curve, showing values for a variable as raw scores, z-scores, and T-scores.

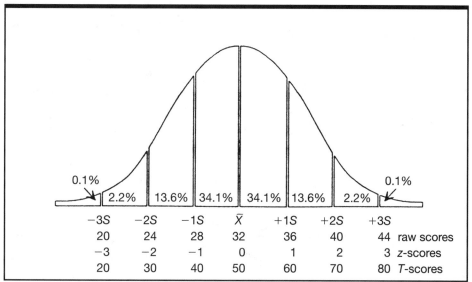

your z-score to conform to a mean of 50 and a standard deviation of 10. What information do these transformations give you about how you did on the test?

■

SUMMARY OF DATA-REDUCTION STATISTICS

It took a long time, but we now have a data-reduction statistic for every possible problem. The choice of a statistic for a particular problem depends on two things: whether the variable is categorical or continuous and, if the variable is continuous, whether it is normally (or, in practice, nearly normally) distributed.

If a variable is categorical (or, sometimes, semicontinuous with few values), the appropriate data-reduction statistic is frequency distribution. If a variable is continuous but not normally distributed (this includes semicontinuous variables), we use the median, often accompanied by the minimum and maximum to show the dispersion. If a variable is nearly normally distributed, which is true of many variables in educational research, we use the mean and standard deviation. Figure 6.6 summarizes these rules.

Having learned these rules and the reasons for them, you will be indignant to see in the educational research literature the routine use of the mean and standard deviation with variables that patently are not normally distributed. The mean and standard deviation contain so much information as compared with the median, minimum, and maximum that it is tempting to use them even when they're not appropriate. Conscientious researchers often compromise by reporting the median along with the mean and standard deviation. However, you need to be aware that, although the standard deviation and z-scores can be calculated on any continuous data, they lose their special meaning if the variable is not at least nearly normal in distribution.

FIGURE 6.6   Reducing data on a single variable.

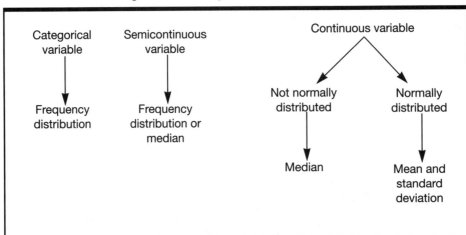

SUMMARY

Descriptive statistics describe variable values in an empirical sample. Some descriptive statistics reduce data on a single variable. Frequency distribution is the appropriate data-reduction statistic for categorical variables and for some semicontinuous variables. The mean and median describe the central tendency of a set of continuous or, sometimes, semicontinuous variable values. The mean is appropriate for normally distributed sets of values; the median is appropriate for non-normally distributed sets, including those with outliers. The standard deviation indicates the average dispersion of a set of variable values from its mean.

The relationship between the standard deviation and the normal curve permits us to make predictions about the percent of individuals who will have particular scores. z-scores express variable values in standard deviation units; z-scores thus facilitate this kind of prediction. There are other kinds of transformed scores, as well, most based on z-scores.

SUMMARY EXERCISES

1.   What would be the appropriate data-reduction statistic or statistics for each of the following variables? Why?

a.   Locus of control, with the values *internal* and *external*

b.   Course grade, with the values *A, B, C, D,* and *F*

c.   Reading ability test score

d.   Student's rating of teacher, from 1 (poor) to 5 (excellent)

e.   Gender-role identity, with the values feminine, masculine, undifferentiated, and androgynous

f.   The height of a group of seventh-graders

2. Below are the results of descriptive statistical analyses from several published research reports. What statistical techniques were used? What information do the statistics provide? Does any of the excerpts report transformed variable values?

a. Givon and Goldman (1987) studied subjects' ability to discriminate tastes and their taste preferences. They developed a measure of preferential discrimination with possible scores ranging from 0 (no discrimination) to 1 (perfect discrimination). "Respondents' scores of preferential discrimination ranged from 0 to 1, with a mean of .67 and a median at .70" (p. 304).

b. Weisner and Gallimore (1977) did a cross-cultural study of who caretakes young children. They reported their data (p. 170) as shown in Table 6.1.

c. Senechal, Thomas, and Monker (1995) studied individual differences in four-year-olds' acquisition of vocabulary during storybook reading. "Children were classified as either high in word knowledge . . . or low in word knowledge . . . on the basis of a median split of their PPVT-R standard scores (Mdn = 101)" (p. 220).

d. Subrahmanyam and Greenfield (1994) studied the effect of video-game practice on spatial skills in girls and boys. Their sample of 61 fifth-graders included 28 boys and 33 girls. The age of the subjects was reported as following: "M = 11 years, 1 month; SD = 3.5 months" (p. 18).

e. Wentzel (1993) investigated the relationship between social behavior and academic competence in middle school. The average student age was 11.87 years for sixth graders and 13.08 years for seventh graders. The sample was equally representative of boys (52%) and girls (48%), with 68% of the sample being White, 23% Black, 5% Hispanic, and 7% of other minority status (p. 358).

TABLE 6.1 Principal companions and caretakers during early childhood as rated from ethnographic sources on 186 sampled societies.*

	Summary Rating	
	N	Percentage
Peer group (single sex)	10	5.4
Peer group (sex unspecified)	1	.5
Peer group (both sexes)	43	23.1
Older children (single sex)	22	11.8
Older children (sex unspecified)	8	4.3
Older children (both sexes)	22	11.8
Adults (single sex)	14	7.5
Adults (sex unspecified)	—	—
Adults (both sexes)	21	11.3
Could not be coded	45	24.2
TOTAL	186	100.0

*Tabulated from Barry and Paxson (1971: table 1, column 15(b1), combining all coding confidence levels and sex designations, if any).

3. Levitt, Guacci-Franco, and Levitt (1994) investigated the relationship between social support and achievement in childhood and early adolescence. Measures of support and loneliness operationally defined two of their independent variables. Due to age differences in children's ability to read, children in grades 1 and 2 were given different forms of the instruments from older children. The authors transformed the children's scores on the support instrument, but they did not transform their scores on the loneliness instrument. They give the following information about means and standard deviations on the two instruments at various grade levels (p. 214).[1]

	Grade Level					
	1–2		4–5		8–9	
	M	(SD)	M	(SD)	M	(SD)
support	3.81	(1.28)	4.44	(1.28)	4.57	(1.39)
loneliness	1.44	(0.32)	1.98	(0.65)	2.02	(0.61)

What can you conclude about the relative support and loneliness of children in the three grade groups? For example, are children in grades 1 and 2 more or less lonely than children in grades 4 and 5?

---

[1]From Levitt, Guacci-Franco, and Levitt, "Social Support and Achievement in Childhood and Early Adolescence." *Journal of Applied Developmental Psychology*, Vol. 15, p. 214, 1994. Copyright ©1994 by Ablex Publishing Corp.

7

Descriptive Statistics for Assessing Relationships Between Variables

Chapter 6 presented descriptive statistical techniques for single variables. These techniques are useful when research focuses on a single variable, but, as we pointed out in Chapter 2, most quantitative research focuses on the relationships between variables. This chapter will present descriptive statistical techniques that help researchers analyze such relationships. The good news is that many of them are based on single-variable techniques.

HYPOTHESIS FORMULATION

In order to understand statistics for assessing relationships between variables in a sample, you need to understand something more about how researchers formulate hypotheses. There are two kinds of hypotheses: *association hypotheses* and *difference hypotheses*. Whether a researcher formulates her research question as an association or difference hypothesis depends on whether the variables involved are categorical or continuous.

Association Hypotheses

When both the independent and dependent variables are continuous, hypotheses can be expressed in the following form or some variation of it:

As *X* increases, *Y* increases.

What this means is that as the values of the independent/predictor variable increase across a group of subjects or cases, the values of the dependent/criterion variable also increase. Substituting names for *X* and *Y,* the following is a real world example of a hypothesis in this form: As IQ score increases, grade-point average (GPA) increases. What this hypothesis says is that for a group of subjects, IQ and GPA are positively related: Their values go up and down together. It predicts that subjects with lower IQ scores will have lower GPAs, and subjects with higher IQ scores will have higher GPAs. If research to test this hypothesis were conducted, results might look something like this:

Subject	IQ Score	GPA
a	90	2.0
b	95	2.5
c	100	3.0
d	105	3.2

With such results for a larger group, a researcher would be in a position to conclude that IQ and GPA are positively related: that as the values of IQ increase over this group of subjects, the values of GPA also increase.

A variation of this hypothesis form is:

As X increases, Y decreases.

The following is an example of a hypothesis in this form: As anxiety increases, test score decreases. This hypothesis predicts what is called a negative relationship: As the values of one of the variables go up, the values of the other go down. Research results confirming this hypothesis might look like the following.

Subject	Anxiety Score	Test Score
a	2	27
b	5	23
c	7	22
d	9	18

In this book hypotheses in this form, whether positive or negative, are called *association hypotheses*. When you see a research question or hypothesis that contains one continuous independent variable and one continuous dependent variable, you should be able to express it in this form, even if the researcher has expressed it somewhat differently. Imagine that you encounter the following research question in the literature:

Does increasing a child's speaking vocabulary also increase the child's reading comprehension? You should be able to translate the question to this hypothesis:

■ As speaking vocabulary increases, reading comprehension increases.

Difference Hypotheses

The second form in which hypotheses can be stated applies to hypotheses in which at least one of the variables (usually the independent variable) is categorical. The other variable (usually the dependent variable) may be either categorical or continuous. In this form, the name of the categorical variable is not directly mentioned. Only the values of the categorical variable are mentioned; its name must be inferred. This hypothesis form can be represented as follows: There will be a difference in the Y values of persons in X_1 and X_2 groups. As usual, Y symbolizes the dependent/criterion variable. X_1 and X_2 represent values of the categorical variable X, not the variable itself. Here is an example of a hypothesis stated in this form:

There will be a difference in the math test scores of boys and girls.

Gender is the independent variable, but the name of this variable is not mentioned in the hypothesis statement. Only its values are mentioned: boys (X_1) and girls (X_2). The name of the variable must be inferred. If research were conducted to test this hypothesis, results might look something like the following:

Subject	Gender	Score
a	Female	45
b	Female	47
c	Male	52
d	Male	53

When you see a research question or hypothesis in the literature with at least one categorical variable, you should be able to translate it to this form, even if the researcher has stated it somewhat differently. Here is a research question containing one categorical variable:

- Do Anglo children learn more in open classrooms than ethnic-minority children do?

In this question the categorical variable is ethnicity. However, only the variable values are mentioned in the question; its name must be inferred. The variable values are Anglo and ethnic-minority. The dependent variable is learning. This research question can be translated to the following hypothesis form:

- There will be a difference in the open-classroom learning of Anglo and ethnic-minority children.

As a second example, here is a hypothesis as a researcher might state it:

- Secondary students who are permitted to choose their courses will report more satisfaction with school than secondary students who are not allowed to choose their courses.

The hypothesis can be rephrased as follows:

- There will be a difference in the reported satisfaction with school of secondary students who are and are not allowed to choose their courses.

In this book hypotheses in this form are referred to as *difference hypotheses*.

■ EXERCISE 1

State each research question below in association hypothesis form or difference hypothesis form by making the appropriate substitutions in the following sentences.

- Association form: As X increases, Y increases (or decreases).
  Example: As typing practice increases, typing errors decrease.
- Difference form: There will be a difference in Y of X_1 and X_2.
  Example: There will be a difference in the reading readiness of Head Start and non–Head Start children.

In order to do this problem, you will need to decide which is the X (independent/predictor) and which is the Y (dependent/criterion) variable in each question. You will also need to decide whether X and Y are continuous or categorical, and if X is categorical what its values are (X_1, X_2, X_3, etc.–categorical variables can have more than two values).

a. Are the grade-point averages of people with an internal locus of control orientation higher than the grade-point averages of people with an external locus of control orientation?

b. Is gender related to locus of control orientation?

c. Do people who had higher college grade-point averages receive higher starting salaries in their first jobs?

d. Are IQ test scores and achievement test scores related?

e. Who spends more time on task: students who are rewarded for being on task, students who are punished for being off task, or students who are ignored when they are off task? ■

DESCRIPTIVE STATISTICS
FOR DIFFERENCE HYPOTHESES

If the relationship to be assessed involves a difference hypothesis, you already know almost all you need to know about the descriptive statistics that are used. For difference hypotheses, the rule is to calculate the appropriate data-reduction statistic on Y separately for each X group. For example, if the hypothesis is that there will be a difference between men's and women's math test scores, the dependent variable (Y) is math test score. The appropriate data-reduction statistics for this variable are the mean and standard deviation, because math test scores (usually) distribute nearly normally. To analyze these data, we calculate mean math test scores for both X groups: men and women. If there is a difference between men's and women's mean math test scores, then we say that there is a relationship between the variables in the sample. (Relationships in samples may be due to sampling error, but that is a point we will take up in chapter 8.) Results of this kind of analysis are usually presented in a table that looks something like the following.

Mean Math Test Score

Men	Women
97.28	95.86

Similarly, if the hypothesis is that there will be a difference between men's and women's incomes, the dependent variable is income. Income does not distribute normally. (If it did, there would be as many very rich people as there are very poor ones. Unfortunately, there are many more very poor people than very rich ones.) The appropriate data-reduction statistic for income is thus the median. To analyze these data, we calculate median incomes for men and women and compare them. If there is a difference, then there is a relationship between the variables in the sample. Such results are usually presented in a table that looks something like the following.

Median Income

Men	Women
$28,000	$26,000

Finally, if the hypothesis is that there will be a difference between men and women with respect to locus of control orientation, the dependent variable is locus of control orientation. This variable is categorical: Its values are internal and external. A researcher would analyze the relationship of this variable with gender by computing the frequency distributions of locus of control orientation for men and women. If there were a difference between the percents of men and women who have internal and external locus of control orientations, the researcher would conclude that there is a relationship between the variables in the sample. The results would be presented as follows.

	Women	Men
Internal Locus of Control	20%	40%
External Locus of Control	80%	60%

■ EXERCISE 2

What would be the appropriate relationship-assessing statistics for the following hypotheses? Why?

a. Rural, urban, and suburban children's reading ability test scores

b. Older and younger women's gender-role identities (feminine, masculine, undifferentiated, or androgynous)

c. Students' ratings of tenured versus untenured professors on a scale of 1 to 10

d. Attitude toward computers (positive or negative) of subjects who have and have not taken a computer course ■

Effect Sizes

The problem with these descriptive statistics for difference hypotheses is that they tell us nothing about the strength of the relationship between variables. Imagine research on the effectiveness of a new program for raising children's math performance. The mean math posttest score of children in the new program is two points higher than that of children in the traditional program. Thus there is a relationship between type of program and performance, in favor of the new program. But is that relationship strong, moderate, or weak? Does two points on a math test represent a lot of difference or relatively little difference? Put in the most concrete terms, does the new program help enough that school districts should consider using it?

This is similar to the problem we encountered in chapter 6 with interpreting individuals' variable values. Sometimes variable values have no intrinsic meaning. This is often the case with test scores. An individual who gets a raw score of 52 on a test might have done well or poorly. The solution to the problem with individuals' variable values is to transform them to z-scores—that is, to express them in standard-deviation units. Because of the relationship between the standard deviation and the normal curve, z-scores make raw scores meaningful. A z-score of -1 is low; only about 16% of the group scored below this. A z-score of +1 is high; only about 16% of the group scored above this.

The solution to this new problem is similar. We can tell whether a relationship between variables is strong or weak by expressing the relationship in standard-deviation units. This assesses what is called the *effect size*. The formula for calculating effect size is as follows:

$$ES = \frac{\overline{X}_1 - \overline{X}_2}{S}$$

In this formula, the means in the numerator are the means of the two groups being compared. If we are comparing experimental and traditional groups' math test scores, then $\overline{X}_1$ is the experimental group's mean, and $\overline{X}_2$ is the traditional group's mean. The S in the denominator is a standard deviation. Which standard deviation is used depends on the researcher's purpose. In this example, it would probably be the standard deviation of the math test for the traditional group. This formula would then express the difference between the two groups in terms of the standard deviation of the traditional group. It would tell us how many standard deviations of improvement the new method caused.

This formula should look familiar; it is similar to the formula for z-scores that was given in chapter 6. An effect size calculated in this way is a kind of z-value. For this example, suppose that $\overline{X}_1 = 52$, $\overline{X}_2 = 50$, and $S = 2$.

$$ES = \frac{52 - 50}{2}$$
$$= \frac{2}{2}$$
$$= 1$$

The effect size is 1. The mean math score in the new program is one standard deviation higher than the mean math score in the old program. Because of the relationship between z-values and the normal curve, another way of saying this is that the mean math score for the new math group is at the 84th percentile for the traditional math group. The new program caused 34 percentile points of gain. This is a large effect and reflects a strong relationship between the variables. If this research were well-done and replicated, school districts would certainly want to consider adopting the new program.

But suppose that $S = 25$.

$$ES = \frac{52 - 50}{2}$$
$$= \frac{2}{25}$$
$$= .08$$

The effect size is .08. The new program raised children's mean math score by .08 of a standard deviation. A z-table indicates that the mean for the new math group is now at the 53rd percentile for the traditional group. Now the new program caused only three percentile points of gain. This is a smaller effect and reflects a weaker relationship between the variables. School districts would have to consider whether the cost of changing programs would be justified for three percentile points of gain.

Knowing effect sizes is clearly helpful, but their use is relatively new. In much of the research you read, researchers may not report effect sizes. The good thing is that you can usually calculate them yourself, since researchers do tend to report means and standard deviations.

■ EXERCISE 3

Locate a research report that compares two groups on some variable by presenting the groups' means and standard deviations for that variable. Name the categorical variable and its values. Name the continuous variable. Calculate the effect size for the relationship. What standard deviation did you use in the denominator of the effect-size formula? Why did you choose this standard deviation? Does this effect size seem to you to reflect a strong, moderate, or weak relationship between the two variables? Why?   ■

Multiple Independent Variables

So far we have dealt with hypotheses involving relationships between only two variables. However, as we pointed out in chapter 2, single studies often involve relationships between more than two variables, almost always one dependent variable and two or more independent variables. This is because researchers are ultimately interested in understanding cause and effect, and most effects have more than one cause.

A researcher might, for example, be interested in the relationship between the independent variables *ethnicity* and *socioeconomic status (SES)* and the dependent variable *IQ*. Such a researcher would collect data on all three variables for the same subjects so he could study the interaction effect (whether ethnicity and SES affect IQ differently when they operate together), as well as the main effects (the effect of each of the independent variables alone on the dependent variable). This is because independent variables often have effects when they are in the company of other independent variables that are different from the effects that they have when they are alone. Researchers testing difference hypotheses with multiple categorical independent variables usually present their results in a table that looks something like the following. This table is based on the example of ethnicity, SES, and IQ; numbers in the table represent mean IQ scores.

	Mean IQ Test Score		
	Anglo	*Hispanic*	*All*
Not Poor	100	100	100
Poor	100	80	90
All	100	90	95

This table contains a great deal of information. First, in the center of the table are the IQ means for the subgroups created by combining the independent variables: 100 for non-poor Anglos, 100 for non-poor Hispanics, 100 for poor Anglos, and 80 for poor Hispanics. This information is relevant to the interaction analysis. Second, in the margins are the mean IQs for the main effects analyses: 100 for all Anglos and 90 for all Hispanics, and 100 for all non-poor children and 90 for all poor children. Finally, in the lower-right corner is the mean IQ score for all children in the study: 95. (It should be noted that with the four subgroup means given, the marginal and total means would be as given only if there were equal numbers of children in each of the four subgroups.) The marginal means tell us that both main effects are present; that is, there is a relationship between ethnicity and IQ, such that Anglo children have higher IQs than do Hispanic children; and there is a relationship between SES and IQ, such that non-poor children have higher IQs than do poor children. It thus seems that both minority ethnicity and poverty operate to lower IQ. However, the means in the center of the table, representing the interaction analysis, tell us that minority ethnicity and poverty have these effects only when they are combined; alone they do not lower IQ. Hispanic children's IQ scores are not lower if the children are not poor; and poor children's scores are not lower if the children are not Hispanic.

This example, which is a simplified version of real-world findings, dramatically illustrates the importance of interaction analyses. If we were to attend only to main effects and base educational policy on them, we would waste resources. In this example, basing policy on main effects only would cause us to implement IQ-raising programs for all poor children and all Hispanic children, when it is only children who are both poor and Hispanic who really need the help.

Sometimes, however, main effects do operate independently of one another, instead of interacting. The following version of the above study illustrates this possibility.

Mean IQ Test Score

	Anglo	*Hispanic*	*All*
Not Poor	100	90	95
Poor	90	80	85
All	95	85	90

In this version, the marginal data on main effects tell us that both main effects are present: Minority ethnicity and poverty are both associated with lower IQ. However, unlike the previous example, the center of the table tells us that the interaction is not present; that is, in this case, ethnicity and SES do operate independently of one another.

The mean of 100 for non-poor Anglo children reflects the absence of either minority ethnicity or poverty; the mean of 90 for non-poor Hispanic children reflects the presence of minority ethnicity and the absence of poverty; the mean of 90 for poor Anglo children reflects the absence of minority ethnicity and the presence of poverty; and the mean of 80 for poor Hispanic children reflects the presence of both poverty and minority ethnicity. When poverty is present alone, it is effective; when minority ethnicity is present alone, it is effective; and when both minority ethnicity and poverty are present together, they are both effective. However, their combined effect is simply additive; the two variables in company do not do anything more than the sum of what each of them does alone.

When you read research reports involving difference hypotheses with more than one categorical independent variable, you need to remember the lesson you have learned in this section. When there is no interaction effect, main effects may be interpreted directly; but when an interaction effect exists, main effects can be interpreted only in light of the interaction.

■ EXERCISE 4

A researcher studies the relationship between teacher gender, student gender, and student performance. The researcher finds similar performance levels for boys with male teachers and girls with either male or female teachers. However, the performance level of boys with female teachers is lower than that of the other three groups of children. What main and interaction effects are present? If main effects are present, can they be interpreted directly? What explanation can you offer of this result; that is, why do you think this result was obtained? ■

DESCRIPTIVE STATISTICS
FOR ASSOCIATION HYPOTHESES

For association hypotheses, as opposed to difference hypotheses, we are not interested in difference; we are interested in how closely the values of X and Y follow each other. To understand the statistics used to test association hypotheses in a sample, you need to understand another kind of graph.

Scattergrams

In frequency polygons, which are used to show the frequency distribution of a single variable, the horizontal axis represents the variable and the vertical axis represents the number of subjects or cases. With scattergrams, which are used to show the relationship between two variables, the horizontal axis still represents a variable: X, the independent variable in the analysis. However, the vertical axis now also represents a variable: the dependent variable, Y. In fact, the horizontal axis in a scattergram is usually called the X axis, and the vertical axis is usually called the Y axis (Figure 7.1).

To construct a scattergram, we mark off the X axis with values of the independent variable and the Y axis with values of the dependent variable. We then place a point on the graph for every subject. The point is located where the subject's X and Y values intersect. The data set and scattergram in Figure 7.1 illustrate the principle.

The first question with association hypotheses is whether X and Y are related. If the answer is yes, then we ask two more questions: how they're related and how strong the relationship is. If X and Y are related, the relationship may be positive or negative. In a positive relationship, high values of X and Y are found together (i.e., for the same subjects), and so are low values. The data in Figure 7.1 depict this: subject a, who has a low value of X, also has a low value of Y; and subject d, who has a high value of X, also has a high value of Y.

In a negative relationship, the reverse is true: High values of X are found with low values of Y, and low values of X are found with high values of Y. The data and scattergram in Figure 7.2 depict this possibility.

Notice that the direction of slope of the scattergram reflects the direction of the relationship: When the relationship is positive, the slope is positive—that is, up from left to right; when the relationship is negative, the slope is negative—that is, down from left to right.

The strength of a relationship has nothing to do with its direction. Strength is a matter of how closely the Y variable follows the X variable. In both of the data sets and scattergrams above, X and Y are perfectly related. In the first data set, for every unit of increase in X across the group of subjects, there is exactly one unit of increase in Y. The scattergram reflects this in the following way: We can connect all the points in the scatter with a perfectly straight line. In the second data set, for every unit of increase in X, there is exactly one unit of decrease in Y, and we can again connect all the points in the scatter with a perfectly straight line. It is important to realize that the strength of a relationship doesn't depend on matching units of increase in X and Y but on matching proportions of units. For example, the relationship which is depicted in Figure 7.3, is also perfect. For every two units of increase in X, there is exactly one unit of increase in Y, so we can again connect all the points in the scatter with a perfectly straight line.

What two-dimensional shape is most different from a straight line? How about a perfect circle? When there is no relationship between X and Y—when, as X increases

FIGURE 7.1   Scattergram showing perfect positive relationship.

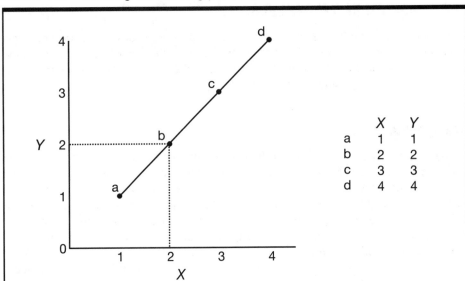

across a group of subjects, *Y* neither increases nor decreases but "does its own thing"—the points on the scattergram can be enclosed only by a perfect circle. The data set and scattergram in Figure 7.4 demonstrate this.

Figure 7.5 shows a data set and scattergram in which *X* and *Y* are related, but not perfectly. As the values of *X* increase across this group of subjects, the values of *Y* also tend to increase, but not in perfect proportion. The scattergram reflects this. The scatter of points does not lie on a straight line, but neither can it be enclosed only by a perfect circle. This scatter of points can be enclosed by an oval, and the oval has a

FIGURE 7.2   Scattergram showing perfect negative relationship.

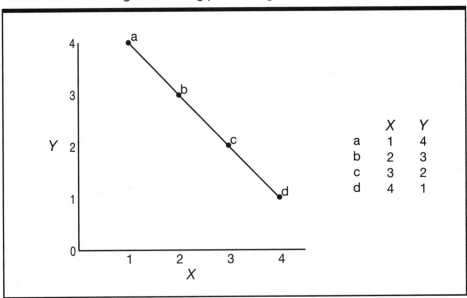

FIGURE 7.3 Scattergram showing perfectly proportional increase in *X* and *Y*.

	X	Y
a	2	1
b	4	2
c	6	3
d	8	4

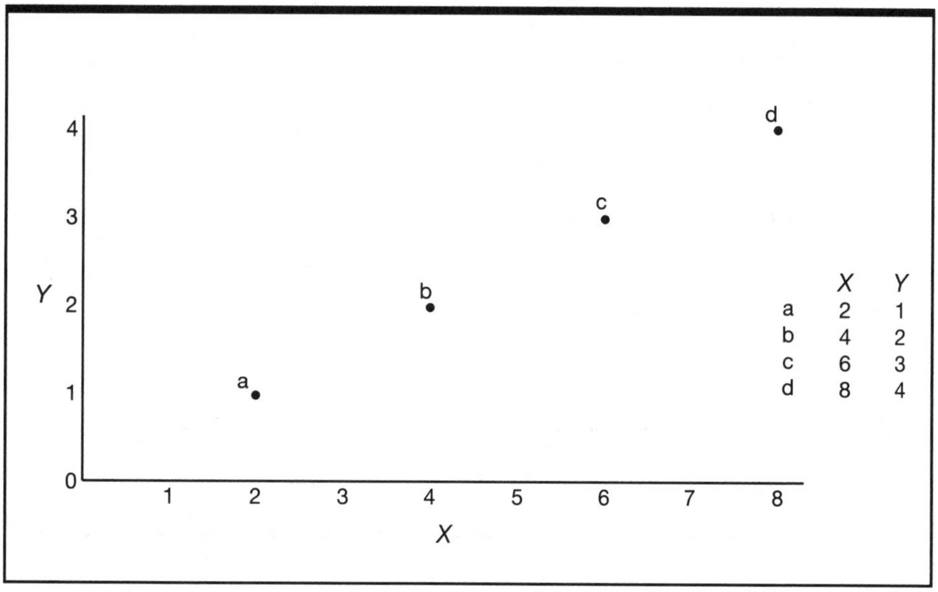

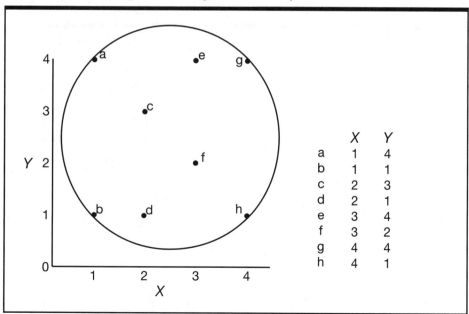

positive slope. This tells us that there is a positive, although not perfect, relationship between *X* and *Y*: that as *X* increases across this group of subjects, *Y* tends to increase, although not in perfect proportion.

Figure 7.6 is another example of an imperfect relationship. The scatter of points in the figure can be enclosed by an oval, and the oval has a positive slope. The oval in this scattergram, however, is wider than the oval in the scattergram in Figure 7.5. That is because the relationship in Figure 7.5, although not perfect, is stronger than

FIGURE 7.4 Scattergram showing no relationship between *X* and *Y*.

	X	Y
a	1	4
b	1	1
c	2	3
d	2	1
e	3	4
f	3	2
g	4	4
h	4	1

FIGURE 7.5 Scattergram showing strong but imperfect positive relationship.

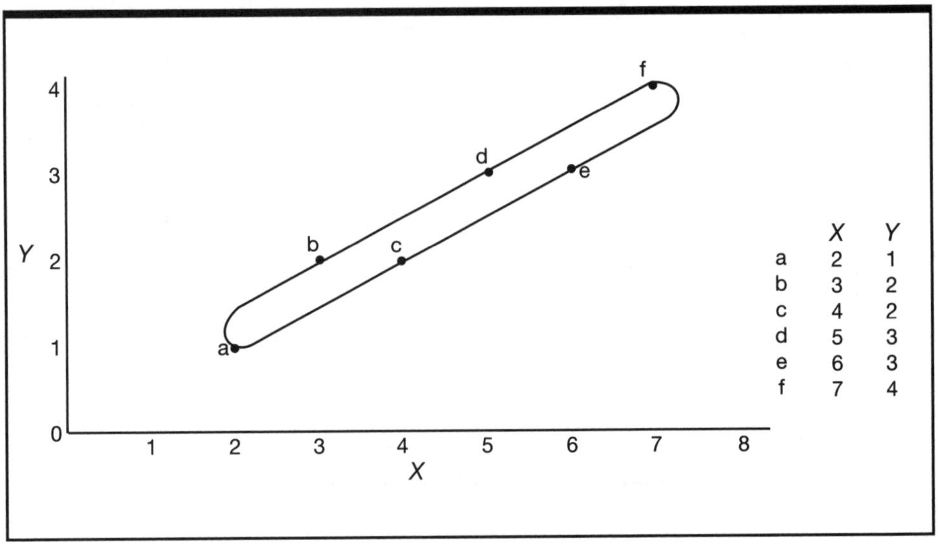

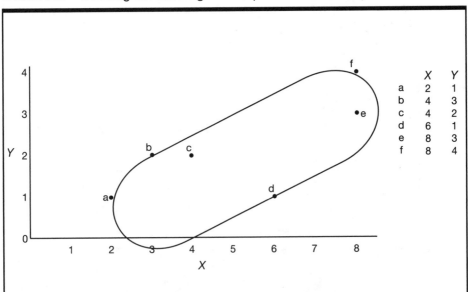

the one in Figure 7.6. In Figure 7.5, Y increases with X in more nearly perfect proportion than it does in Figure 7.6.

Thus scattergrams tell us what we want to know about association hypotheses. First, they tell us whether there is a relationship: If the scatter of points can be enclosed by something other than a circle, there is a relationship. Second, they tell us whether the relationship is negative or positive: If the scatter slopes up from left to right, then X and Y are positively related; if the scatter slopes down, the relationship is negative. Third, they tell us how strong the relationship is: If the oval that encloses the scatter is narrow, the relationship is strong; if the oval is wide, the relationship is weak.

FIGURE 7.6 Scattergram showing weaker positive relationship.

■ EXERCISE 5

For each of the data sets below, draw a scattergram. Indicate whether there is a relationship between the variables and, if so, whether the relationship is positive or negative and weak or strong.

a.	X	Y	b.	X	Y	c.	X	Y
	40	4		1	1		3	5
	38	8		1	4		4	10
	32	8		4	4		5	7
	24	12		4	1		6	9
	20	14					8	7
	20	16					8	12

■

■ EXERCISE 6

Decide whether the relationships between the following pairs of variables would be positive or negative.

a.   Alcohol consumption and clarity of speech
b.   Time spent studying and exam grade
c.   Children's age and height

■

Correlation Coefficients

Visually judging the width of an oval is not very precise. We need a better way to assess the strength of a relationship, and we have a way. In fact, we have a whole family of ways: *correlation coefficients*. There are formulas for calculating various correlation coefficients. Which formula a researcher uses depends on certain characteristics of the data. A discussion of these characteristics is beyond the scope of this book, but any standard statistics text discusses this in more detail.

When a researcher has decided which formula is appropriate for the data, he plugs the values of the X and Y variables for the subjects into the formula and comes up with a correlation coefficient for the data. (Actually, researchers don't usually do the calculations themselves—they have computers do them.) The coefficient shows both the strength and the direction of the relationship between the variables. The value of the coefficient shows the strength of the relationship. The value of correlation coefficients is always between 0 and 1. A coefficient of 0 means that there is absolutely no relationship between the variables, while a coefficient of 1 means that there is a perfect relationship between the variables. Because we rarely find either absolutely no relationship or a perfect relationship, our calculated coefficients are usually decimals, such as .32 or .58 or .84. The lower the coefficient—that is, the closer to 0—the weaker the relationship; the higher the coefficient—that is, the closer to 1—the stronger the relationship.

The sign of the coefficient shows the direction of the relationship. If the relationship is negative, the coefficient has a negative sign. A coefficient of −.91 thus indicates a strong negative relationship. It tells us that, as the values of X increase across the subjects in the study, the values of Y decrease in almost perfect proportion—that subjects in the study who have higher values of X have lower values of Y and vice versa. A coefficient of .27 means a weak positive relationship—as the values of X increase across the subjects, the values of Y tend also to increase, although in very imperfect proportion.

Interestingly, when we use a correlation coefficient to assess the strength of a relationship, we do not actually interpret the coefficient directly. What we interpret is something called the *coefficient of determination,* which is the squared correlation coefficient. For a correlation coefficient of .90, the coefficient of determination is .90^2, or .81; for a correlation coefficient of $-.80$, the coefficient of determination is $-.80^2$, or .64. You need to know this to understand how researchers interpret correlation coefficients. If a researcher calculates a correlation coefficient of .40, she is apt to say that the relationship is weak. This is because she is really interpreting the coefficient of determination, which is .16. When correlation coefficients drop below .40, they are fairly weak; $.30^2 = .09$; $.20^2 = .04$.

The most well-known correlation coefficient is Pearson's r. Pearson's r is symbolized r; if you read a research report, and the researcher says that $r = .60$, you will know that, in the researcher's sample, there is a moderate ($.60^2 = .36$) positive relationship between the two variables. Other coefficients are interpreted similarly, whatever they are called. If you read, for example, that tau $= -.20$, you will know that, in the researcher's sample, there is a very weak ($-.20^2 = .04$) negative relationship between the two variables.

■ Exercise 7

For the following correlation coefficients, calculate r^2 and interpret the relationship; that is, indicate whether it is strong and positive, weak and negative, etc.

a. $r = .60$
b. $r = -.30$
c. $r = .90$ ■

■ Exercise 8

In a study of the relationship between intelligence and academic achievement among hearing-impaired children, Phelps and Branyan (1990) found correlations of the K-ABC Nonverbal IQ test with the WRAT-R (an achievement test) and the K-ABC Achievement subtests ranging from .51 to .65. Interpret this result.   ■

Multiple Correlation

Partial Correlation

Just as researchers with difference hypotheses may need to do analyses on more than one independent variable, so may researchers with association hypotheses. There are two correlational techniques for such analyses. The first is called *partial correlation.* Partial correlation permits a researcher to assess the degree and direction of relationship between two variables when one or more additional variables is controlled for.

These controlled variables are usually conceptualized as confounding variables. Thus, partial correlation is one of the statistical ways to control confounding variables that we promised in chapter 4 to tell you about.

Suppose that a researcher is interested in the relationship between study time and exam grade and has obtained the following data.

Study Hours	Exam Grade
1	50
2	50
3	50

These results seem to indicate that there is no relationship between the two variables: the correlation coefficient for these data would be 0.

It may be, however, that these students' intelligence differs in a way that accounts for these results. For example, the following may be true.

Study Hours	Exam Grade	IQ
1	50	115
2	50	100
3	50	85

Now the results make sense. The student who spent only an hour studying was probably able to get a grade of 50 because she is very bright. The student with an IQ of 85, however, had to study for three hours to obtain this score.

This kind of eye-balling of data is all well and good, but researchers need a more precise way to analyze data like these. Partial correlation provides a solution. A good (although oversimplified) way to conceptualize what partial correlation does is as follows. Imagine that we have a technique for adjusting each student's exam grade to be what it would have been if all students had had the same IQ: for example, 100. Then the results of the study time research might look like the following.

Study Hours	Adjusted Exam Grade
1	45
2	50
3	55

Now if the researcher correlates study time and exam grade, the coefficient will be 1.0.

Multiple Regression

More often, however, researchers are not as interested in controlling for the effects of additional variables as in knowing just how additional variables combine to affect the dependent variable. Thus, researchers will more often go ahead and build these additional variables into the analysis as bona fide independent variables rather than control them out of the analysis with partial correlation.

The technique for doing this with association hypotheses is called *multiple regression*. Multiple regression does for association hypotheses what interaction analysis does for difference hypotheses. Multiple regression analyzes the relationship between one dependent variable and more than one independent variable. It yields a single correlation coefficient that represents the degree of relationship between multiple continuous independent variables and a continuous dependent variable.

Imagine that a researcher is interested in the combined effects of study time, intelligence, motivation (operationally defined by some kind of test of motivation), and prior knowledge (operationally defined by a pretest) on the dependent variable *exam score*. The multiple regression coefficient (symbolized R) is as follows: $R =$ .87. This means that the correlation coefficient between all four independent variables and the dependent variable is .87. This coefficient is interpreted much as are simpler coefficients: the nearer the value to 1.0, the stronger the relationship; and the R is squared to yield a coefficient of determination. Multiple Rs, however, do not have signs, because the individual independent variables may relate positively or negatively to the dependent variable.

The trouble with multiple Rs is that they do not tell us how much each variable contributes to the total relationship. This problem can be solved by using what is called *stepwise multiple regression*. This technique tells us how much each independent variable adds to the multiple R as it is entered into the equation. The results of a stepwise multiple regression for the problem above might look something like this.

Independent Variable	R
IQ	.70
Pretest	.80
Study hours	.85
Motivation	.87

You may be surprised that variables added later seem to contribute so little to the analysis. This is typical of multiple regression analyses and is due to the fact that the independent variables are related to each other as well as to the dependent variable. Motivation, for example, is partly a function of intelligence; brighter students tend to have higher motivation. The portion of motivation that overlaps with intelligence is entered into the analysis when intelligence is entered. Motivation is also related to pretest and time spent studying. By the time motivation is entered into the analysis, so much of its relationship with the dependent variable has already been accounted for by the other independent variables that there is little left for it to contribute uniquely.

■ EXERCISE 9

Interpret the following findings.

a. A researcher reports that the partial correlation coefficient between grade-point average and income, controlling for years of education completed, is .15.

b. A researcher reports that the multiple correlation coefficient between years of education completed, grade-point average, and income is .30.

c. Wilson, Mundy-Castle, and Sibanda (1990) studied the relationship between field independence and computer competence in a sample of Black and White girls in Zimbabwe. Field independence characterizes individuals "who are analytical, able to differentiate discrete parts of a situation. . . , and able to restructure problems" (p. 277). Correlation coefficients between their measures of field independence and computer competence were .47 for Blacks and .33 for Whites. "When the influence of intelligence was eliminated" (p. 278), the correlations were .29 for Blacks and .27 for Whites.   ■

This concludes your introduction to relationship-assessing statistics. The statistic used depends on several things: e.g., whether the researcher is testing a difference hypothesis or an association hypothesis, whether the dependent variable is categorical or continuous, and whether the hypothesis to be analyzed contains one or more than one independent variable. Then there are special considerations. For example, if a variable is continuous, what we do with it depends on whether it is normally distributed. If the hypothesis is an association hypothesis with more than one independent variable, what we do with it depends on whether we want to treat the additional variables as confounding variables and control them out of the analysis or build them in. Figure 7.7 summarizes these rules.

FIGURE 7.7   Assessing relationships between variables in a sample.

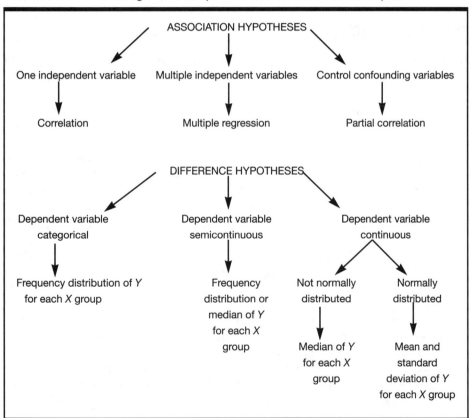

SUMMARY

There are descriptive statistics for assessing relationships between variables. For difference hypotheses, the appropriate relationship-assessing statistic depends on the dependent variable: We calculate the appropriate data-reduction statistic on the dependent variable separately for each independent-variable group. If there is a difference between these statistics, then there is a relationship between the variables. For association hypotheses, the appropriate relationship-assessing statistic is some kind of correlation coefficient. Correlation coefficients indicate the strength and direction of relationships.

When more than one independent variable is being analyzed, difference hypotheses require interaction analyses. When interaction effects are present, main effects should not be interpreted directly. With association hypotheses, multiple independent variables either may be treated as confounding variables and statistically controlled out of the analysis using partial correlation or may be built into the analysis using multiple regression.

SUMMARY EXERCISES

1. Below are the results of descriptive statistical analyses from several published research reports. What statistics were used? What information do the statistics provide?

a. Ryska (1993) studied the relationships in a group of high-school tennis players between an independent variable, anxiety, and five dependent variables, involving perceived amount of coach support. The anxiety variable had four values: low anxious, high anxious, defensive high anxious, and repressive. The dependent variables represented five dimensions of perceived coach support: emotional, informational, companion, nurturance, and a composite score. His descriptive statistical results are presented in [Table 7.1].[1]

b. Pianta and Ball (1993) studied the relationships between two independent variables and two dependent variables in a group of kindergarten children. One of the independent variables was maternal support; this involved the degree to which the mother reported having a supportive social network, including the father. The second independent variable was the child's risk level based on early medical and/or developmental difficulties.

   The dependent variables were the teacher's ratings of the child on two subscales involving behavioral problems and competence in the kindergarten classroom. The researchers reported the following results: The r^2 between maternal support and behavior problems was .09 for the low risk children and .24 for the high risk children. The r^2 between maternal support and competence was .20 for the low risk children and .30 for the high risk children.

c. Vierra (1984) studied the relationship between Chicano children's scores on the reading portion of the Stanford Achievement Test and their teachers' ethnicity. "For the third graders, the pre-test level was Primary 1 and the post-test level

---

[1]*Journal of Psychology*, Vol. 127, pp. 409–418, 1993. Reprinted with permission of the Helen Dwight Reid Educational Foundation. Published by Heldref Publications, 1319 Eighteenth Street, NW, Washington, DC 20036-1802. Copyright ©1993.

TABLE 7.1 Differences in perceived coach support for social desirability groups.

Support	Low anxious (n = 69)	High anxious (n = 80)	Defensive high anxious (n = 53)	Repressive (n = 68)
Emotional				
M	14.19	14.50	15.36	15.71
SD	3.69	3.79	3.69	3.63
Informational				
M	9.61	9.48	9.66	10.28
SD	2.34	2.17	2.24	1.82
Companion				
M	11.03	10.99	11.04	11.66
SD	2.08	2.47	2.19	2.33
Nurturance				
M	5.06	5.33	5.69	5.34
SD	1.76	1.64	1.55	1.64
Composite Coach				
M	39.88	40.29	41.75	42.99
SD	7.24	7.55	7.63	7.32

Primary 2; for the fourth-graders, the pre-test level was Primary 2 and the post-test level Primary 3" (p. 286). She reported data as both raw scores and transformed (scale) scores. Transformed scores are on the same scale for each level of the test, which facilitates comparison between the two different levels (p. 286).

. . . tabled raw-score gains from pre- to post-test are negative. This does not mean that the children's reading ability decreased over the year. It simply reflects the fact that each grade level was pretested with a lower level of the SAT and post-tested with a higher and therefore more difficult level. Scale-score gains are positive, indicating that the children's reading ability in fact increased over the year.

The table also shows a large difference between third and fourth-graders' raw-score gains. This does not mean that third-graders' reading improved much more than that of fourth graders. Scale-score gains show a much more modest difference between the two grade levels.

Vierra's descriptive statistical analyses (p. 287) are presented in Table 7.2.

d. Lanis and Covell (1995) studied the effects that images of women in advertisements have on attitudes related to sexual aggression. Subjects were randomly assigned to view one of three kinds of advertisements: those in which females were portrayed as sex objects, those in which females were portrayed in "progressive" roles, and control advertisements. In the control advertisements, no human figures appeared; these advertisements should have had no effect on subjects' attitudes toward women. Subjects were then administered a Sexual Attitude

TABLE 7.2   Chicano children's pre- and post-test scores and gains, by grade level and teacher ethnicity.

	Pre-test		Post-test		Gain		N
	Mean raw score	*Mean scale score**	*Mean raw score*	*Mean scale score**	*Mean raw score*	*Mean scale score*	
3rd grade							
Anglo teachers	129.40	125	126.42	137	−2.98	12	570
Hispanic teachers	130.04	125	126.77	137	−3.27	12	471
TOTAL	129.69	125	126.58	137	−3.11	12	1,041
4th grade							
Anglo teachers	129.55	138	90.93	146	−38.62	8	623
Hispanic teachers	129.22	138	90.32	146	−38.90	8	465
TOTAL	129.40	138	90.67	146	−38.73	8	1,088

*Raw score mean converted to scale score

Survey. Higher scores on the survey were considered to reflect more "rape-supportive" beliefs. Mean scores on the survey were as follows:[2]

	Sex-object	*Progressive*	*Control*
Females	70.53	59.73	85.20
Males	102.73	88.80	78.07

2.   Locate at least three relational, quantitative research reports on topics of professional interest to you in research journals. Select reports which, taken together, use all of the basic descriptive statistical techniques (i.e., correlation coefficients, frequency distributions, and measures of central tendency). You may find that some articles are complex, involving many different kinds of analyses among many different variables. Nevertheless, try to identify at least one correlational analysis, one frequency distribution, and one measure of central tendency to focus on. For each analysis, answer the following questions: What variable or variables are being analyzed? What descriptive statistical technique was used (e.g., Pearson's *r* or the mean and standard deviation)? What information does the statistical technique provide about the variable or about the relationships between variables?

_____

[2]From K. Lanis and K. Covell, "Images of Women in Advertisements: Effects on Attitudes Related to Sexual Agression." *Sex Roles*, Vol. 32, p. 6. Copyright ©1995 by Plenum Publishing Corp. Used with Permission.

8

Inferential Statistics

Suppose I offer to bet you five dollars that when I toss a coin three times it will come up heads each time. Will you take the bet? If you do, you have only one chance in eight of losing.

If I toss a fair coin three times in a row, the probability that I will get heads all three times is one in eight. The following series of diagrams shows why this is true.

On the first toss, it is equally probable that the coin will come up heads or tails. This can be represented as follows:

First toss   *H*   *T*

On the second toss, it is again equally probable that the coin will come up heads or tails, regardless of what happened the first time. Thus, we need to add the probabilities for the second toss to the probabilities for the first toss, as follows:

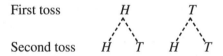

By the end of the second toss, there are thus four equally probable outcomes: If the first toss was heads, the second toss may be either heads or tails; if the first toss was tails, the second toss may be either heads or tails. The lines in the diagram above represent these four equally probable possibilities.

On the third toss, it is equally probable that the coin will come up heads or tails, regardless of what happened on the first two tosses. So we need to add the probabilities for the third toss to the probabilities for the second toss, as follows.

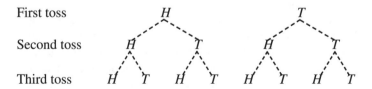

By the end of the third toss, there are thus eight equally probable outcomes: If the first two tosses were heads, the third may be either heads or tails; if the first toss was heads and the second tails, the third may be either heads or tails; and so forth. The lines in the diagram above represent these eight equally probable possibilities. There is thus one chance in eight of throwing heads three times in a row.

Knowing this, will you take the bet I offered you? That depends on whether you are willing to take one chance in eight of losing five dollars in order to have seven chances in eight of winning five dollars. Most people would take such a bet. Now suppose I offer to bet you $5,000. Are you willing to take one chance in eight of losing $5,000, to have seven chances in eight of winning $5,000? Most people would not take this bet. Even though it is very probable (seven chances in eight) that they would win, they cannot afford the one chance in eight of losing.

But suppose you take the $5,000 bet and lose. At this point you have two choices. You can either conclude that something that only happens one time in eight has in fact happened (after all, one time in eight is a lot more than never), in which case you will pay me my money. Or you can conclude that there are seven chances in eight that I cheated, in which case you will ask to see my coin.

This little example constitutes your introduction to inferential statistics. Inferential statistics, like the coin-toss example, are based on the mathematics of probability. A researcher uses inferential statistics when she needs to guess about something she doesn't know. The statistic is useful to her in deciding which guess to make because it tells her the probabilities that various guesses will be correct.

In deciding whether to take my coin-toss bet, you need to make a guess about something you don't know: whether you will win or lose. The mathematics of probability tell you that the guess that you will win has seven chances in eight of being correct, whereas the guess that you will lose has only one chance in eight of being correct. This information doesn't tell you which guess to make; that depends on how much you are being asked to risk and how willing you are to take the risk. However, it's better than no information at all. You can use this information in deciding which guess to make.

Inferential statistics are based on descriptive statistics, but they are also very different from descriptive statistics. With descriptive statistics, the problem is to make sense of what we know—to draw conclusions about the sample on which we have empirical data. With inferential statistics, the problem is to make informed guesses about what we don't know—to make guesses about unknown populations.

At this point, you need to refresh your mind about some of the concepts from chapter 5. Remember that although researchers are interested in populations they usually do their research on samples. This is because doing research on entire populations is often impossible, more often impractical, and, in any case, usually unnecessary. If a sample is representative, we can learn what we need to know about the population from the sample. However, even random samples don't perfectly represent populations; the best sample is likely to contain some sampling error. This is where inferential statistics come in.

Inferential statistics provide an estimate of how much error is likely in a given random sample: of how much difference is probable between a random sample and the population from which it was drawn. Inferential statistics thus permit us to make the most informed guesses we can about populations. Random sample data often show a relationship between variables. The question is whether this relationship also exists in the population from which the sample was drawn. Because even random samples don't exactly represent populations, it is possible that it does not—that the relationship in the sample is instead due to sampling error. Some inferential statistics are designed to tell us how likely this is. They tell us the probability that a relationship found in a random sample is due to sampling error, in which case there is no relationship between these variables in the population from which the sample was drawn.

Imagine a study of the relationship between sex education and teenage pregnancy. A stratified random sample of 100 twenty-year-old women is drawn, containing 50 women who had a sex education course when they were sophomores in high school and 50 women who have never had a sex education course. Twenty of the women who had no formal sex education had teenage pregnancies, while only 10 of the women who had sex education classes as sophomores had teenage pregnancies. In the sample, then, women who did not receive formal sex education had more frequent teenage pregnancy. The question is whether this is also true in the population from which the sample was drawn. It is possible that the difference between the two groups of women in the sample is due to sampling error: that in the population teenagers who do and do not receive formal sex education are equally likely to undergo teenage pregnancy. Inferential statistics tell us how probable this is.

Inferential statistics are based on two things: how strong the relationship is in the sample, and how large the sample is. When there is a strong relationship between variables in a large random sample, it is very unlikely that the relationship is due to sampling error. Even when there is a somewhat weak relationship between variables, if the sample size is very large it is not very likely that the relationship is due to sampling error, because larger samples tend to be more representative. And even when the sample size is fairly small, if the relationship is very strong it is not very likely that the relationship is due to sampling error.

p VALUES

Most inferential statistical techniques yield what is called a *p* value. The *p* stands for probability—the probability that there is no relationship between the variables in the population, that the relationship in the sample is due to sampling error. If the researcher in the study of sex education and teenage pregnancy uses an inferential statistic to analyze the data, the statistic will result in a *p* value. Suppose the *p* value is .10. This means that there is a 10% chance that there is no relationship between the variables in the population—that the relationship in the sample is due to sampling error. The *p* value says that only 10% of the time will random samples of this size contain this much or more difference between two groups when there is no difference between the groups in the population.

Null and Alternative Hypotheses

Researchers often phrase their hypotheses in what is called *null* form. A *null hypothesis* says that there is no relationship between the variables of interest. Researchers do this because the most widely used inferential statistics test null hypotheses for populations; they test the probability that, given a certain set of random sample data, the null hypothesis is true in the population from which the sample was drawn. For every null hypothesis, there is what is called an *alternative hypothesis*. The alternative hypothesis is that there *is* a relationship between the variables in the population. Usually researchers believe that the alternative hypothesis is true. However, the most widely used inferential techniques do not directly test alternative hypotheses; alternative hypotheses are tested indirectly.

A researcher who believes that the alternative hypothesis is true in the population hopes that the inferential statistical analysis will result in a low *p* value. The *p* value is the probability that the null hypothesis is true in the population. If this probability is low, the researcher can reject the null hypothesis and accept the alternative hypothesis. If the probability is low that the null hypothesis is true, then the probability is high that the alternative hypothesis is true. A null hypothesis says that there is no relationship between the variables in the population—for example, that teenagers in the population who do and do not have formal sex education are equally likely to become pregnant. In inferential statistical analyses, a null hypothesis always refers to the population, not the sample.

■ Exercise 1

A researcher tests the null hypothesis that there is no relationship in the population from which her sample was drawn between preschool attendance and first-grade reading readiness. What is the alternative hypothesis? The researcher calculates an inferential statistic; $p = .13$. What conclusions does the p value permit about the null and alternative hypotheses? ■

p Values and Decision Making

The question we can ask of inferential statistics is the probability that the null hypothesis is true in the population. The answer we get is based on our sample data; it is the probability that a relationship as strong (or weak) as the one in our sample, found in a sample as large (or small) as the one we have, is due to sampling error. If the relationship in the sample is probably due to sampling error, then the null hypothesis is probably true in the population.

Once a p value has been obtained, we have to decide what to do with it. If $p = .10$, we know that there is a 10% chance that the relationship between the variables that was found in the sample is due to sampling error—that there is no relationship between these variables in the population. Conversely, there is a 90% chance that the relationship between the variables that was found in the sample is not due to sampling error—that there is a relationship between these variables in the population. What we do with this information depends entirely on the research question and its practical implications, much as, in the coin-toss example, the decision we make about whether to take the bet depends not just on our probability of losing but on how much money we are risking.

Error Types

With inferential statistics, we use what we do know—what happened in a sample—to make an informed guess about what we don't know—what's going on in the population. Most inferential statistics permit us only two guesses: either that the null hypothesis is true and there is no relationship between the variables in the population, or that the null hypothesis is false and there is a relationship between the variables in the population. However well informed, a guess is a guess, and guesses may be wrong. The decision we make about the population may be wrong. Because we have two possible guesses and either may be wrong, we have two possible ways to be wrong. We can either reject a null hypothesis that is in fact true or retain a null hypothesis that is in fact false. The first is called a *Type I error;* the second is called a *Type II error.*

Figure 8.1 depicts the two error types in terms of the two considerations: the actual truth or falsity of the null hypothesis, and the decision we make about the null hypothesis. The null hypothesis refers to the population. In the population, the null hypothesis is either true or false. We haven't studied the population, so we don't know whether the null hypothesis is true or false in the population. But it has to be either true or false. In the population, either sex education prevents teenage pregnancy or it doesn't.

What we do know is what happened in our sample. We will use this information to make a guess about the population. The guess we make will be either to retain the null hypothesis (to behave as if the null hypothesis is true in the population) or to reject the null hypothesis (to behave as if the null hypothesis is false in the population).

In Figure 8.1, the symbol H_0 refers to the null hypothesis. The columns of Figure 8.1 refer to the actual truth or falsity of the null hypothesis in the population. The rows of Figure 8.1 refer to the decision we will make about the null hypothesis in the population.

As the figure shows, there are four possible outcomes of this situation, two of them correct and two incorrect. If we decide to retain a null hypothesis which is in fact true, our decision will be correct. If we decide to retain a null hypothesis which is in fact false, we will have made a Type II error. If we decide to reject a null hypothesis which is in fact true, we will have made a Type I error. If we decide to reject a null hypothesis which is in fact false, we will be correct.

In deciding which guess to make, we need to consider the consequences of being wrong, and the consequences depend on the practical implications of the guesses. To continue with the sex education example, what are the practical implications of the two possible guesses about the null hypothesis? To guess that the null hypothesis is false and the alternative hypothesis is true means to believe that there is a relationship between sex education and teenage pregnancy in the population—that sex education lowers the rate of teenage pregnancy. If the educational community makes this guess, the policy implication will be to require sex education classes in middle or high school. If this guess is wrong, then resources spent for this purpose will be wasted.

On the other hand, to guess that the null hypothesis is true means to believe there is not a relationship between sex education and teenage pregnancy in the population—that sex education does not lower the rate of teenage pregnancy. If the educational community makes this guess, the policy implication will be not to offer sex education classes. If this guess is wrong, then preventable teenage pregnancy will occur.

We have two possible guesses and two possible kinds of error. We can reject the null hypothesis, in which case we will require sex education. If this guess is wrong—

FIGURE 8.1   Type I and II errors.

	H_0 true	H_0 false
Retain H_0	Correct Decision	Type II error
Reject H_0	Type I error	Correct Decision

that is, if we make a Type I error—we will waste resources. Or we can retain the null hypothesis, in which case we will not offer sex education. If this guess is wrong— that is, if we make a Type II error—we will permit preventable teenage pregnancy. In deciding which guess to make, we need to know which kind of mistake worries us more. In this example, let's hope that educators would be more worried about a Type II error than a Type I error; that is, they would be more worried about permitting preventable teenage pregnancy than about wasting resources. This is the same thing as saying they would be more worried about retaining a false null hypothesis than about rejecting a true null hypothesis.

■ Exercise 2

Here is a null hypothesis: There is no relationship between teachers' salaries and teacher quality. What would be the policy implications of rejecting the null? Retaining the null?

What would be the consequences of a Type I error (deciding to reject a null that is in fact true)? A Type II error (deciding to retain a null that is in fact false)?   ■

The Probability of Error Types

The p value is the probability of a Type I error. Because p is the probability that the null hypothesis is true, then p is the probability that we will be wrong if we reject the null hypothesis, and wrongly rejecting the null hypothesis is a Type I error. The p value in the sex education study is .10. If we decide to reject the null hypothesis, we have a 10% chance of making a Type I error—that is, a 10% chance of wasting resources.

The probability of making a Type II error involves what is called the power of an inferential statistical analysis. The power of a statistical test refers to the probability of correctly rejecting a null hypothesis that is indeed false. Thus, the probability of making a Type II error is 1 - the power value for the statistical test. For example, if the power of the statistical test is .80, then the probability of making a Type II error is 20% (1 - .80 = .20). If the power of the statistical test used in the sex education study is .80 and we decide to retain the null hypothesis, then we have a 20% chance of making a Type II error—that is, a 20% chance of permitting preventable teenage pregnancy.

Most published research reports in education and other human behavior fields provide information about p values for hypothesis tests, or the probability of a Type I error. Thus, if a researcher rejects the null hypothesis, a reader knows the probability that a Type I error has been made. However, few published research reports provide information about statistical power. Thus, if a researcher retains the null hypothesis, a reader typically has no information about the probability that a Type II error has been made.

The p value that often is used as the criterion for rejecting the null is .05. If an inferential statistic yields a p value of .05 or less, researchers usually decide to reject the null hypothesis and accept the alternative hypothesis that there is a relationship between the variables in the population. This means that a Type I error is possible; the p value tells us how possible. If $p = .04$, then there is a 4% chance of a Type I error. If the p value is greater than .05, researchers usually decide to retain the null—that there is no relationship between the variables in the population. This means that a Type II error is possible, although we usually don't know how possible.

Interestingly, when statistical power is calculated for representative samples of published research, the average power is often something like .80, which gives a 20% chance of Type II error. This is much higher than the .05, or 5%, standard researchers typically use for a Type I error. This might make sense if Type I errors were always more serious than Type II errors, but this is not necessarily the case; whether a Type I or II error is more serious depends entirely on the practical consequences of our decisions about the population. In the sex education example, we might argue that a Type II error would be more serious; a Type II error would mean we forego an opportunity to prevent teenage pregnancy, whereas a Type I error would result in our spending money in a fruitless effort.

This tendency of researchers to "favor" Type I error protection is a problem, to which many methodologists (e.g., Cohen, 1990) have called attention. Researchers' practices in this regard seem to be changing, but slowly, so you are unlikely to encounter much information about power analyses in the research reports you read in the near future.

Statistical Significance

p values that fall at or below the criterion (e.g., .05) that the researcher has set for rejecting the null hypothesis are described as statistically significant; p values that fall above this criterion are described as statistically nonsignificant. In discussing the results of their inferential statistical analyses, researchers often report the p values that they obtained in their analyses only in terms of their significance. For example, an obtained p value of .02 will be reported only as $< .05$, and an obtained p value of .07 or .84 will be reported only as $> .05$.

■ EXERCISE 3

In the following examples, if the researcher uses the conventional criterion ($p < .05$), will he or she reject or retain the null? What error type will thus be possible? What is the probability of this error?

a. A researcher tests the null hypothesis that there is no relationship between principals' training and effectiveness in the population from which his sample was drawn; $p = .03$.

b. A researcher tests the null hypothesis that there is no relationship in the population from which her sample was drawn between the number of social studies courses that secondary students have had and their scores on a dogmatism scale; $p = .08$. ■

CHOOSING AN INFERENTIAL TECHNIQUE

There are many different, named inferential statistical techniques. Most inferential statistics about the relationship between variables in a population are based on the kind of reasoning to which you have just been exposed. But the particular statistic that is used for a given problem depends on the peculiarities of that problem.

This is also true of descriptive statistics, as you saw in chapters 6 and 7. Descriptive statistics for reducing data on a single variable all have the same goal, but the particular statistic that is used for a given problem depends on the peculiarities of that problem, such as whether the variable is categorical or continuous and, if it is continuous, whether it distributes normally. Similarly, the descriptive statistic that is used for analyzing relationships between variables in a sample depends on the peculiarities of the problem, such as whether the relationship is expressed as a difference hypothesis or an association hypothesis, whether the hypothesis involves one or more independent variables, and whether the researcher wishes to control potentially confounding variables out of the analysis or build them into the analysis as bona fide independent variables.

The choice of an inferential statistic depends on these same kinds of considerations. We will briefly discuss a few of the most commonly encountered inferential statistics. If you encounter a statistic that we do not discuss, you should remember the following: Any inferential statistic used to test a hypothesis about the relationship between variables in a population will yield a p value, and p values are interpreted as you have learned. They are the probability that the null hypothesis is true in the population from which the research sample was drawn. And the null hypothesis is always that there is no relationship between the variables in the analysis.

Chi Square

Chi square is an inferential statistic that is appropriate to use when a researcher wants to test a difference hypothesis involving a categorical dependent variable. Suppose that a researcher is interested in the relationship between gender and political party affiliation. There is one independent variable, gender, and it is categorical. The hypothesis is therefore a difference hypothesis: that there is a difference between men and women with respect to political party affiliation. The dependent variable, political party affiliation, is also categorical.

Imagine that the research sample yields the following data:

	Women	*Men*
Democrats	70%	60%
Republicans	30%	40%

In the sample, there is a relationship between these variables; there is a difference between men's and women's political party affiliations. However, this sample difference may be due to sampling error; the null hypothesis may be true. There may be no difference between men's and women's political party affiliations in the population from which this sample was drawn. The researcher will perform a chi square analysis to determine the probability that the sample results are due to sampling error and that the null hypothesis is therefore true; the analysis will yield a p value. Suppose the researcher reports that $p < .05$. He can then conclude that only five times in 100 will a sample of this size yield a difference of this magnitude when there is no difference in the population—that there is less than a 5% chance that the null hypothesis is true. Unless the researcher is very worried about a Type I error, he will probably decide on the basis of the chi square analysis to reject the null hypothesis. He will thus conclude that the relationship found in his sample is not due to sampling error—that in the population from which this sample was drawn, men's and women's political party affiliations differ. But the chi square analysis provides no information about how great that difference is.

Analysis of Variance

Perhaps the most commonly encountered family of inferential statistics is *analysis of variance,* which is abbreviated ANOVA (pronounced a-nó-va). There are many different varieties of ANOVA. The simplest kind is what is called *oneway ANOVA.* This statistic is appropriate for testing difference hypotheses with one dependent variable that is normally distributed and one categorical independent variable. A researcher interested in differences between men's and women's math test scores would use oneway ANOVA.

Suppose this researcher found the following sample results for mean math test score:

> *Mean math test score*
> *Men*   *Women*
> 94.28   92.81

Again, there is a relationship between the variables in the sample: There is a difference between the mean math test scores of men and women in the sample. And again, the question is whether this relationship is due to sampling error—whether the null hypothesis is true.

A oneway ANOVA on the researcher's sample data would yield a *p* value. This *p* value would be the probability that a difference this great in a sample of this size will be found when the null hypothesis is true—that is, when there is no difference in the population from which the sample was drawn. Suppose the researcher reports that *p* > .05. Unless the researcher is very worried about a Type II error, she will probably retain the null. She will conclude that there is not enough evidence to reject the null.

When researchers do oneway ANOVAs on independent variables having more than two values (for example, ethnicity, having the values *Anglo, Black,* and *Hispanic*), the analysis yields only one *p* value. This *p* value is the probability that the null hypothesis is true in the population: that the mean dependent variable values are the same for all independent variable groups in the population. If the *p* value is low enough to warrant rejecting the null, then the researcher will conclude that the mean dependent variable values for all independent variable groups in the population are not the same. The trouble is, the researcher still doesn't know which groups in the population differ. In the population, do all three groups have mean dependent variable values that differ, or do two of the groups have the same mean, which differs from that of the third group? When the independent variable has more than two values, oneway ANOVA must be followed by other tests to determine exactly which groups differ in the population. These other tests are called *multiple-comparison tests.* There are a number of multiple-comparison tests—for example, the Scheffé test, named, as are many statistical techniques, for the statistician who invented it. Multiple-comparison tests yield *p* values for any group comparison the researcher wants. In the ethnicity example, the researcher would probably do three multiple-comparison tests, each one yielding a *p* value: one for Anglos and Blacks, one for Anglos and Hispanics, and one for Blacks and Hispanics. Imagine that the first and second *p* values were less than .05, but the third was more than .05. The researcher would conclude that in the population, Anglos differ from Blacks and Hispanics on the dependent variable, but Blacks and Hispanics do not differ from one another.

Factorial Analysis of Variance

There are inferential statistics for testing hypotheses involving multiple independent variables, too. The most commonly encountered ones belong to the family of *factorial analysis of variance.* Factorial ANOVA is used when researchers wish to make inferences about the relationships in populations between two or more categorical independent variables and a normally distributed dependent variable. In describing factorial analyses of variance, researchers use such designations as 2 × 3 factorial ANOVA, or 2 × 3 × 2 factorial ANOVA. The numbers refer to the independent variables—specifically, to the number of values that each independent variable has. A 2 × 3 factorial ANOVA involves two independent variables, one having two values and one having three values—e.g., gender (male and female) and ethnicity (Anglo, Black, and Hispanic). A 2 × 3 × 2 ANOVA involves three independent variables, the first having two values, the second having three values, and the third having two values—e.g., gender (male and female), religious affiliation (Catholic, Jewish, Protestant), and ethnicity (Anglo and Black).

If you think back to descriptive statistics you will remember that difference hypotheses with more than one independent variable involve both main effects and interaction effects. *Main effects* refer to the relationship between one independent variable at a time and the dependent variable. *Interaction effects* refer to the relationship that two or more independent variables, taken together, have with the dependent variable.

Factorial ANOVA yields *p* values for all possible main and interaction effects in a given set of variables. Imagine a study in which the researcher wishes to know the relationship between two independent variables, ethnicity and socioeconomic status (SES), and the dependent variable, IQ test score. Suppose that the mean IQ test scores for the sample were as follows.

	Mean IQ Test Score		
	Anglo	*Hispanic*	*All*
Poor	97.82	81.64	89.73
Not poor	100.15	98.37	99.26
All	98.99	90.01	94.50

There are relationships between the variables in the sample; that is, there are differences between the means of the various groups in the sample. The question is whether these differences are merely due to sampling error. A 2 × 2 factorial ANOVA on these data would yield three *p* values: one for the ethnicity main effect, one for the SES main effect, and one for the interaction between ethnicity and SES. The *p* value for the ethnicity main effect would be the probability that the null hypothesis is true in the population—the null hypothesis being that there is no difference in the population between the mean IQ test scores of Anglos and Hispanics. If the *p* value for this main effect were less than .05, the researcher would probably reject the null hypothesis and conclude that there is a relationship between ethnicity and IQ in the population. Similarly, the *p* value for the SES main effect would be the probability that there is no relationship between SES and IQ test score in the population: that mean IQ test scores of poor and middle-income children in the population are the same. If the p value for this main effect were less than .05, the researcher would probably conclude that there is a relationship between SES and IQ in the population. The p value for the interaction would be the probability that there is no interaction in the population between the variables ethnicity and SES as they affect IQ. If the p value for this interaction effect were greater than .05, the researcher would probably conclude that these two independent variables do not interact in the population to affect the dependent variable.

The same caution applies here that was given when interaction analyses were discussed as descriptive statistics. When an interaction effect is statistically significant, the independent variables in the population probably have different effects in combination from the effects they have alone. The p values for main effects—that is, population main effects—then should not be interpreted directly; only when an interaction effect is not statistically significant should main effects be interpreted directly for the population.

Analysis of Covariance

One technique in the ANOVA family is designed to statistically control potentially confounding variables: *analysis of covariance* (ANCOVA). ANCOVAs involve one or more categorical independent variables, a normally distributed dependent variable, and one or more *covariates;* the covariates are the potentially confounding variables.

A researcher interested in the relationship between science program and children's science learning may not be able to assign children randomly to the different programs. If children in the various programs have different levels of science knowledge when they begin the programs, this could be a very serious confounding variable. If, at the end of the study, children in one of the programs have higher science knowledge scores, but these children also had higher scores when the programs began, it will be impossible to know whether the higher end-of-program scores resulted from the program or just from the fact that these children were already ahead when the programs started. This researcher could solve the problem by keeping pretest scores constant or by matching children in the various treatment groups on pretest score. However, either of these solutions would affect the generalizability of the researcher's results. Often a better solution is to do an ANCOVA. Science program would be the independent variable, post-test score the dependent variable, and pre-test score the covariate. The analysis would test the null hypothesis that there is no relationship in the population between science program and post-test score when the effect of pre-test score on post-test score is statistically controlled.

Again, it is important for you to understand that none of these analysis of variance techniques can provide information about the strength of relationships in the population that was sampled. When researchers do ANOVAs and reject null hypotheses, they conclude that the dependent variable means of the independent variable groups in the population differ; but ANOVA provides no information about how much they differ.

Significance of Correlation

Another family of inferential statistics that is frequently encountered is *significance of correlation*. When researchers calculate correlation coefficients on sample data, they need to know how likely it is that relationships found in samples would also be found in the populations that the samples represent. Significance of correlation, like other inferential statistics, yields a *p* value. The *p* value is the probability that the sample was drawn from a population in which there is no relationship between the variables—that is, in which the correlation coefficient, if calculated, would be zero. A researcher might, for example, calculate a correlation coefficient on the variables IQ score and grade-point average in a sample of 80 people. Imagine that the coefficient is .50. The researcher would also calculate the significance of this coefficient. Imagine that the *p* value is .01. This means that only one time in 100 would a sample of 80 people produce a correlation coefficient of .50 or higher when there is no relationship between the variables in the population from which the sample was randomly drawn.

The *p* value does not mean that the coefficient in the population, if calculated, would be the same as that in the sample—.50. Significance of correlation cannot tell us what the coefficient in the population is—just the probability that it is zero. Of course, if there is a low probability that the coefficient in the population is zero, the researcher will probably conclude that it is not zero—that there is a relationship between the variables in the population. But significance of correlation does not provide information on how strong this relationship is.

Figure 8.2 summarizes the information we have presented on inferential statistical techniques for testing null hypotheses.

FIGURE 8.2   Inferential statistical techniques for testing null hypotheses.

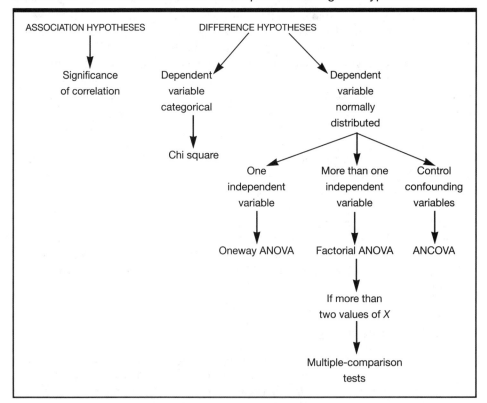

■ Exercise 4

Several examples of inferential statistical usage follow. For each example, interpret the result.

a. A researcher studies the relationship between the basis on which school boards are elected and constituents' satisfaction with school boards' performance. She finds that, in her sample, a lower percent of constituents in districts with at-large elections are satisfied than in districts with elections by precinct. Her chi square analysis results in a p value of .48.

b. A researcher studies the relationship between the per-student expenditure of school districts and student's achievement test score. For her sample, the correlation coefficient is .32; $p = .01$.

c. A researcher studies the relationship between student's ethnicity (White or Black), neighborhood type (integrated or segregated), and achievement test score. In the sample, White students' scores in integrated and segregated neighborhoods are similar; Black students' scores in integrated neighborhoods are higher than those of Black students in segregated neighborhoods, but not as high as those of White students. The researcher subjects his sample data to a 2 x 2 factorial ANOVA, which yields the following results:

	p
Main Effects	
Ethnicity	.02
Neighborhood	.03
Interaction Effect	
Ethnicity X Neighborhood	.02

d. A researcher studies the relationship between the type of introduction students have to the school library and the number of books they check out during the school year. There are three treatment groups: introduced by the librarian, introduced by their teacher, and no introduction. In the sample, students introduced by the librarian check out more books than do students introduced by their teacher, who in turn check out more books than do students who receive no introduction. The researcher subjects his sample data to a oneway ANOVA; $p = .02$. Multiple-comparison tests yield the following results:

	p
Librarian versus Teacher	>.05
Librarian versus Control	<.05
Teacher versus Control	<.05

e. A researcher performs an ANCOVA. The independent variable is cognitive style (field independent or field dependent); the dependent variable is a test score; the covariate is IQ; $p < .05$.   ■

LIMITATIONS OF NULL HYPOTHESIS TESTING

As we have pointed out, the kinds of inferential statistics we have described provide very limited information. They tell us only the probability that the null hypothesis is true for the population that was sampled. We are often able to reject this hypothesis, but we still have little information about the variables in the population. Significance of correlation, for example, tells us only the probability that the coefficient in the population is zero. If we reject this null hypothesis, we conclude that the coefficient in the population is probably not zero; but not zero means anything from .01 to 1.0.

In practice, researchers make heavy use of descriptive statistics—that is, of sample results—to interpret inferential results. Suppose that, in a sample, $r = .90$ and that the coefficient is statistically significant. Although the inferential test tells us only that the coefficient in the population is probably not zero, we use the descriptive statistic of .90 to guess that the coefficient in the population is probably fairly high and positive. If, on the other hand, a sample r is $-.20$ and that coefficient is statistically significant, we will guess that the coefficient in the population is probably fairly low and negative.

Similarly, ANOVA tells us only the probability that there is no relationship between the variables in the population. Imagine a study of the relationship between type of high school attended (public or private) and SAT score; $p = .02$. The p value tells us only that it is not likely that the SAT scores of public- and private-school graduates in the population are the same. It does not tell us which group scores higher, much less how much higher they score. If, in the sample, the mean SAT score of private-school graduates is higher than the mean score of public-school graduates, we use the sample results to guess that this is probably true in the population as well.

Statistical Conclusion Validity

In discussing research design in chapters 2–4, we stressed that the answer to the research question is only as valid as the research process. Research designers must attend to several different named kinds of research validity issues: those involving measurement validity, internal validity, and external validity.

There are validity issues in the analysis of research results as well; in quantitative research, the relevant term is *statistical conclusion validity*. Even if research data are validly collected, invalid methods of analyzing the data will result in invalid conclusions.

Quantitative methodologists are increasingly critical of what they see as the overuse, as well as misuse, of null-hypothesis tests in human behavioral research. This misuse and overuse create a number of different kinds of problems with the statistical-conclusion validity of much of the human behavioral research that is reported in professional journals, even well-respected ones.

That these problems exist on such a wide scale is unfortunate, especially since we have relatively simple techniques for solving at least some of them. In this chapter, we mentioned one such technique: power analyses. But until a new generation of researchers is trained in the use of these techniques, they are not likely to be widely used. In at least the near future, you will probably continue to see an over-reliance on null-hypothesis testing and p values in the quantitative research reports you read.

LIMITATIONS OF INFERENTIAL STATISTICS

Once you grasp the concept of p values—that they test the null hypothesis for the population—interpreting most published inferential statistical results is, on one level, easy. No matter what the name of the test is, if it tests a null hypothesis it yields a *p* value. And these *p* values are interpreted as you have learned: They are the probability that the null hypothesis is true in the population from which the sample was randomly drawn. Imagine that you read a research report about the relationship between learning disability and self-esteem. The researcher uses an inferential technique that you have never heard of before: the Mann-Whitney *U* Test. The researcher reports that *p* = .17. Even though you have no familiarity with the test, you can interpret the *p* value; it is the probability that the null hypothesis is true in the population from which the researcher's sample was randomly drawn. Thus you conclude that there is a 17% chance that there is no relationship between learning disability and self-esteem in the identified population.

However, as is often true, a little knowledge can be a dangerous thing. Inferential statistical theory and practice are complex; this chapter has given you only an introduction. We would thus like to leave you with a number of cautions to remember when you read inferential statistical analyses. First, inferential statistical theory is based on true random sampling. To refer back to the coin-toss example, will you bet even five dollars that I can throw heads three times in a row in a nonrandom sample of tosses? If you do, you'll lose your money. I'll simply toss the coin until it does come up heads three times in a row. The one-in-eight probability of three heads is based on a random sample of tosses. Whether I get heads three times in a nonrandom sample of three tosses depends on the pattern that is used in selecting the sample, not on chance.

Similarly, the *p* values that inferential techniques yield are theoretically valid only if the techniques were applied to true random samples. Add this to what you learned in chapter 5 about the rarity in educational research of true random samples, and you will understand why we want to warn you to apply your knowledge of inferential statistics with caution.

In practice, inferential techniques turn out to be valid when applied to very representative samples, even when the samples are not truly random. An excellent example of this is provided by political polls. When you read in the newspaper that a given candidate is predicted to win an election, that prediction results from the application of inferential statistical techniques to sample data. Pollsters ask a sample of people for whom they plan to vote; they then analyze the sample data with an appropriate inferential statistic to determine how probable it is that the sample results represent the population. If the probability is high enough, they make a prediction about what the population will do based on what the sample said it would do.

These samples cannot be truly random; it is impossible for the pollsters to identify all persons who will vote, much less randomly sample them. But for major polls, the samples are carefully drawn to be highly representative. The effectiveness of the sampling techniques used is dramatically illustrated by the fact that such polls are rarely wrong; serious pollsters have an enormously high success rate in predicting the outcomes of major elections.

But major pollsters in national elections have financial resources that are beyond the reach of most educational researchers; a number of people are willing and able to pay the price of knowing how such an election will turn out. Educational researchers rarely have the resources to assure that their samples are as representative as these.

There are exceptions. Nationally standardized achievement testing, for example, is big and competitive business. Most school districts in the United States administer such tests to at least a substantial portion of their students every year. The major purpose for this testing is to know how the district is doing relative to other districts in the country. Thus, the publishers could not sell their tests if they did not go to the expense of selecting representative samples. But for most educational research purposes, it would be difficult to justify the expense of such representative sampling.

How, then, should you interpret the inferential statistical results that are most often seen in the educational research literature? If, in a given study, a researcher uses a sample (e.g., a convenience sample) that is patently not representative of any population, what does this say about the researcher's inferential statistical results? The strictest interpretation would be that the results are invalid.

Even without extreme strictness, a good argument can be made that inferential statistics are over-used and over-interpreted in many fields—not just education—in which highly representative sampling is fairly rare. Our advice to you is to interpret inferential statistical results very cautiously when samples are not very representative. Unless samples are obviously severely flawed, it is probably safe to consider the inferential results to be indicative. However, p values are so precise that it is tempting to consider them as more than indicative.

The second major caution we would like to leave you with involves statistical versus practical significance. Suppose that a researcher tests whether a new method of teaching spelling is more effective than the traditional method. The p value is low enough that the researcher rejects the null hypothesis and concludes that the new method would be more effective in the population than the old method is. Does this mean that schools should adopt the new method? Not necessarily.

First, the inferential statistic says nothing about how much more effective the new method will be. An effect-size estimate would predict this, but effect-size estimates are not often used. This is unfortunate. What if the new method teaches children to spell an average of one more word correctly per year in school than the old method does? If the sample is large enough, this will be statistically significant, but it certainly has little practical significance.

Second, there are considerations other than effectiveness. Even if the new method is considerably more effective than the old one, policymakers have to consider how practical it will be to replace the old method with the new one. Even in medicine, where lives are at stake, statistically significant research findings are not always widely implemented because they are too expensive.

Our final word of caution involves the fact that statistical analyses are the final stage in the quantitative research process. Statistical analyses are done after data are collected. There is a saying in the research world that is appropriate here: garbage in, garbage out. Statistical analysis cannot make bad research designs good. If independent and dependent variables were not validly measured or potentially confounding variables were not controlled, the lowest p value on record cannot tell us what we want to know.

SUMMARY

Inferential statistics use data from an empirical sample to make inferences about the population from which the sample was drawn. The inferential statistics that are widely used test null hypotheses; they result in p values, which are the probability that the null hypothesis is true in the population. If this probability is low, then we reject the null and accept the alternative hypothesis, that there is a relationship. In using inferential statistics in this way, we can make either a Type I error—rejecting a true null—or a Type II error—retaining a false null. Which error type is more serious depends on the practical consequences of our decisions about null hypotheses and varies from research question to research question. If we are more worried about making a Type I error we should require a low p value for rejecting the null. The probability of a Type II error is not usually ascertained; however, if we require a fairly high p value for rejecting the null, we are more likely to reject and less likely to retain the null. Because we can make a Type II error only if we do retain the null, raising the p value for rejecting the null will decrease the probability of a Type II error.

Statistical significance refers to whether the obtained p value was above or below the value that the researcher decided to require for rejecting the null; .05 is conventional. Often researchers do not report obtained p values but only whether the obtained p value was significant.

The choice of an inferential statistic depends on the kinds of variables being analyzed. The most frequently encountered inferential statistics are chi square, which is appropriate for categorical independent and dependent variables; analysis of variance, which is appropriate for categorical independent and normally distributed dependent variables; and significance of correlation. Oneway ANOVA involves one independent and one dependent variable; if the independent variable has more than two values, multiple-comparison tests are required to know just what groups probably differ in the population. Factorial ANOVA is used when there are multiple independent variables and results in p values for main and interaction effects. Analysis of covariance is used to control potentially confounding variables, which are called covariates.

Inferential results should be interpreted with caution. Inferential statistical theory is based on truly random sampling, which is rare in educational research; statistical significance may not mean practical significance; and statistics cannot compensate for bad research design.

SUMMARY EXERCISES

1. Excerpts from a number of published research reports are provided below. Each excerpt consists of the results of some or all of the statistical analyses that the researcher(s) performed. For each excerpt, interpret the statistical analyses.

a. Turnbull and Bronicki (1986) studied the effect of instruction about mental retardation on second-graders' attitudes toward retarded persons (p. 45). (Turnbull was 10 years old at the time the study was conducted and did the study as a science project; Bronicki served as statistical and design consultant.)

   I compared pre-test and post-test scores for each group using the Wilcoxon Sign Test for Related Samples. There were no significant differences between the control group's pre- and post- test scores. I found a significant difference between the experimental group's pre- and post-test scores, $p < .01$. The posttest scores of the kids in this group very clearly changed in a positive direction following my lesson about mental retardation. This is a real difference rather than a chance one.

b. Rothschild et al. (1986) studied subjects' physical, cognitive, and affective responses to viewing television commercials. Among their interests were the relationships between a physical response variable, electroencephalogram recording (EEG, a measure of electric activity in the brain), and a number of cognitive and affective variables, which were measured both immediately after the

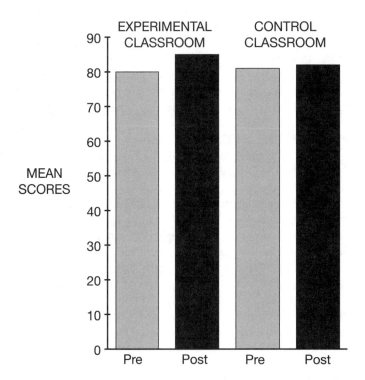

subjects viewed the commercials and two weeks later. The cognitive and affective variables were such things as the subjects' recall of the advertised brand name and how entertaining the subjects thought the commercials were. Their results (p. 203) were as presented in Table 8.1.[1]

c. For this exercise, refer back to Summary Exercise 1a (Ryska, 1993) in chapter 7. In this exercise, a table was presented showing descriptive data for a study of high-school athletes' anxiety and perceptions of coach support. The descriptive data showed differences between the independent-variable (anxiety) groups on all five of the dependent (coach-support) variables, and most of these differences were in similar directions—i.e., low anxiety students perceived less support on all five coach variables, and repressive students perceived more.

Differences between the two high anxious groups and the two extreme groups existed but were not as clearcut. The question that can be answered by inferential statistics is whether any of these sample differences is statistically significant. Table 8.2 shows the same table that was presented in the exercise in chapter 7; now, however, the author's inferential statistical results have been added, just as he reported them (p. 415).[2]

---

[1]From M. Rothchild, E. Thorson, B. Reeves, J. Hirsch, and R. Goldstein, "EEG Activity and the Processing of Television Commercials." *Communication Research*, Vol. 13, pp. 182–220. Copyright © by Sage Publications. Reprinted by Permission of Sage Publications, Inc.

[2]*Journal of Psychology*, Vol. 127, pp. 409–418, 1993. Reprinted with permission of the Helen Dwight Reid Educational Foundation. Published by Heldref Publications, 1319 Eighteenth Street, NW, Washington, DC 20036-1802. Copyright ©1993.

TABLE 8.1   Correlation of EEG data with recall, recognition, and adjective factors.

CORRELATION[1] OF AGGREGATE EEG WITH:

Aggregate immediate recall	$-.783^{**}$
Immediate Product Recall	$-.771^{*}$
Immediate Brand Recall	$-.317$
Immediate Claim Recall	$-.652^{*}$
Immediate Scene Recall	$-.713^{*}$
Aggregate immediate recognition	$-.754^{*}$
Immediate Product Recognition	$-.748^{*}$
Immediate Brand Recognition	$-.325$
Immediate Claim Recognition	$+.121$
Immediate Package Recognition	$-.638^{*}$
Aggregate delayed recall	_____ [2]
Delayed Product Recall	$-.656^{*}$
Delayed Brand Recall	_____ [2]
Delayed Claim Recall	_____ [2]
Delayed Scene Recall	_____ [2]
Aggregate delayed recognition	$-.388$
Delayed Product Recognition	$-.483$
Delayed Brand Recognition	$+.035$
Delayed Claim Recognition	$+.135$
Delayed Package Recognition	$-.050$
Immediate entertaining adjective factor	$-.750^{*}$
Immediate personal relevance adjective factor	$-.438$
Immediate warm adjective factor	$-.708^{*}$
Immediate dislike adjective factor	$+.750^{*}$
Delayed entertaining adjective factor	$-.888^{**}$
Delayed personal relevance adjective factor	$-.683^{*}$
Delayed warm adjective factor	$-.238$
Delayed dislike adjective factor	$+.450$

1. Correlations are Spearman rank order; $n = 9$; unit of analysis is the commercial.
2. The absence of a correlation is due to a lack of any recall for over half the brands in the delayed condition.

$^{*}p < .05;\ ^{**}p < .01.$

TABLE 8.2 Differences in perceived coach support for social desirability groups.

Support	Low anxious ($n = 69$)	High anxious ($n = 80$)	Defensive high anxious ($n = 53$)	Repressive ($n = 68$)
Emotional				
M	14.19	14.50	15.36	15.71
SD	3.69	3.79	3.69	3.63
Informational				
M	9.61	9.48	9.66	10.28
SD	2.34	2.17	2.24	1.82
Companion				
M	11.03	10.99	11.04	11.66
SD	2.08	2.47	2.19	2.33
Nurturance				
M	5.06	5.33	5.69	5.34
SD	1.76	1.64	1.55	1.64
Composite Coach				
M	39.88	40.29	41.75*	42.99*
SD	7.24	7.55	7.63	7.32

* Denotes significant difference from nonasterisk groups at $p < .05$ level.

d. Stephen and Zweigenhaft (1986) studied "The Effect on Tipping of a Waitress Touching Male and Female Customers" (p. 142).

The average tip in the Female-Touch condition was 15%; the average tip in the Male-Touch condition was 13%; the average tip in the No-Touch condition was 11%. A one-way analysis of variance comparing the three conditions was significant. $F(2.109) = 13.79$, $p < .01$. Tukey's Honestly Significant Difference Test revealed that the difference between the Female Touch and the No-Touch condition was significant, but that the differences between Male Touch and Female Touch and between Male Touch and No Touch were not significant.

The main effect for touch, then, in this study, was based on the touching of the female customer rather than the touching of the male customer. This finding provides support for the view that waitresses in the United States may enhance their incomes when they touch the female rather than the male in serving male-female couples.

e. Mayer and Anderson (1992) conducted a number of experiments investigating how best to help students build connections between words and pictures in multi-media learning. They reported the results of one of their experiments as follows (p. 450).

All [seven of] the treatment groups generated approximately equivalent numbers of idea units, approximately 5 out of 8, whereas the control group generated considerably fewer, approximately 3 out of 8. An analysis of variance performed on these data confirmed that the groups differed significantly from one another, $F(7,136) = 6.68$, $p < .001$, $MSe = 1.63$; subsequent Tukey tests (based on an alpha of .05) revealed that each of the treatment groups except the AAA-only group scored significantly higher than the control group and none of the treatment groups differed significantly from one another.

f. Nicholls and Nelson (1992) studied "Students' Conceptions of Controversial Knowledge." "Elementary school students were interviewed [and asked 12 questions about] the existence of intelligent life in space and of whether more money should be invested in space exploration than health care on earth" (p. 224). Descriptive statistical analysis of question 11, which involved whether the student thought a teacher should teach a position opposing that of the student, showed grade and topic differences: For noncontroversial topics, there was a tendency for a student to feel that teachers should teach the position the student held; for controversial topics, there was a tendency for a student to feel that teachers should not teach the position the student held. Older students were more likely to make this distinction than were younger students.

Inferential statistical analysis of question 11 yielded the following results:

We conducted post hoc tests of the effect of grade for each of the five topics. These were not significant for the convention, $F(5, 54) < 1$, the noncontroversial scientific topic, $F(5, 54) = 1.12$, or the noncontroversial ethical topic, $F(5, 54) < 1$. Grade effects were significant for the controversial scientific topic $F(5, 44) = 4.65$, $p < .01$, and the controversial ethical topic, $F(5, 54) = 4.35$, $p < .01$. (p. 228).

2. Find three quantitative research reports in your field in education that have been published in journals. What descriptive and inferential statistics did the researchers use to analyze their data? What were the results of their analyses? What do these results mean?

SUGGESTED READINGS

Hays, W. (1994). *Statistics* (5th ed.). Fort Worth: Harcourt Brace.

Runyon, R., and Haber, A. (1991). *Fundamentals of Behavioral Statistics* (7th ed.). New York: McGraw-Hill.

Spatz, C., and Johnston, J. (1989). *Basic Statistics: Tales of Distributions.* Belmont, CA: Brooks-Cole.

Part III
Qualitative Research

To introduce you to qualitative research and to point up the differences between qualitative and quantitative research, we are going to present a mini-example involving the same research question as it might be pursued first by a quantitative and then a qualitative researcher.

The research question is whether children in Mr. Jackson's seventh-grade class like school. Based on the quantitative chapters of this book, you can pretty much predict what a quantitative researcher would do with this question. The researcher would identify the variable to be studied, liking school, and then operationally define the variable. Perhaps the operational definition would be the children's answer to a questionnaire item asking them to indicate whether they like school usually, sometimes, or rarely. The researcher would administer the questionnaire to the children and then tally their responses. The results would be analyzed and reported statistically—the researcher might, for example, say that 4 of the 20 children, or 20%, said they usually like school; 14 of the children, or 70%, said they sometimes like school; and 2 of the children, or 10%, said they rarely like school. The answer to the research question would be that, when asked in this context, most of the children say they sometimes like school, some of the children say they usually like school, and a few of the children say they rarely like school.

A qualitative researcher would go about investigating this research question very differently. She might, for example, talk with the children at length, both individually and in small groups, in some informal setting—perhaps on the playground at recess. She might not pose the question of liking school to the children directly but instead use some strategy to get them talking about how they feel about school. After each talk she would make several pages of notes about what the children said and how they said it. She would think about the information contained in the notes and would use this information to guide her next talk with the children. She might, for example, notice that boys seem to talk more freely when they cannot be overheard and resolve to try to talk with each boy alone. When she felt she had talked with the children enough to answer her research question, she would analyze her notes, perhaps by classifying the children's responses in some way that made sense to her. This researcher's results would probably require several pages to report, and the flavor of the report might be something like the following.

On balance, most of the children seemed more positive than negative in their feelings about school. Boys seemed a bit more negative than girls overall, though there were boys who were very positive and girls who were very negative.

None of the children hated or loved everything about school. Most of their comments focused on one of three things: teachers, work, and peers.

For most of the children, teachers were a very central focus in their talk about school. The important thing seemed to be whether or not a teacher was "mean." The children talked a great deal about liking or not liking teachers, past, present, and future. Most of the children liked the teachers they had had but were worried that next year they would have a teacher who had a bad reputation among students—which usually meant a "mean" teacher. One of Laurie's comments typifies what many of the children said: "My sister had Ms. Frank for math last year. She was mean. I hope I get Mr. Lawrence. He's really nice." Several of the children, most of them boys, complained that school involved too much work. Social interactions were a focus of many of the children's reflections and were usually seen as a positive feature of coming to school. Many of the children mentioned liking school because they get to see their friends at school.

The basic similarity between qualitative and quantitative approaches is that both meet the definition of research that was given in chapter 1—that is, both represent empirical processes for answering questions: In the examples just given, both researchers answered the research question by observing real world events that bore on the question. In most other respects, however, the two approaches are very different.

Quantitative researchers study variables. Quantitative research is usually relational—that is, its goal is to investigate relationships between variables. Nonrelational quantitative research, in which the goal is simply to describe the state of some variable, is rare.

Qualitative researchers do not study variables, and often their goal *is* "simply" to describe some empirical situation (we put quotes around the word *simply* here to acknowledge that qualitative research is rarely simple to do—more on that soon). However, qualitative researchers often look for patterns in empirical situations, a search which parallels quantitative researchers' focus on relationships between variables.

The results of quantitative research involve statistical analyses of variable values. In nonrelational quantitative research, statistics are used to describe the state of the variable that was studied; in relational quantitative research, statistics are used to assess the relationship between variables. Analysis of quantitative data usually signals the end of the study.

Since qualitative researchers do not study variables, they cannot use statistical techniques to analyze their research results. How qualitative researchers do collect and analyze empirical data is the subject of the next two chapters in this book. For now, suffice it to say that qualitative researchers collect data on empirical events, record these data in some way, and analyze this record in some way. In most qualitative research, there is an ongoing process of alternating data collection and analysis: A small set of data is collected, recorded, and analyzed in a preliminary way; results of this analysis shape a new round of data collection, recording, and, analysis. This process is repeated, ideally until the researchers feel they have adequate data to meet the objectives of their project. All data are then subjected to a final analysis.

Results of this analysis are reported in narrative-expository style. Narrative-expository style is the style you are reading right now—the style in which this book is written. The reporting of qualitative research results, in narrative-expository style, is very different from the statistical tables in which quantitative results are reported.

LeCompte and Preissle (1993) discuss the differences between qualitative and quantitative research in terms of what they call assumptive modes. Assumptive modes are continuums of possibilities for approaching a research study.

The first continuum they discuss is from enumerative to constructive modes. Quantitative research is strongly enumerative; as you learned in previous chapters, quantitative data are enumerated as variable values and then statistically tested. In contrast, qualitative researchers rarely represent their data numerically; rather, they try to identify constructs or clusters of interactions. There is a tendency in qualitative research to include data about the context surrounding these interactive constructs rather than to isolate individual variables for analysis.

The second continuum is from objectivity to subjectivity. Quantitative researchers lean heavily toward objectivity and the elimination of researcher bias or influence. Qualitative researchers tend toward subjectivity. The research instrument in qualitative research is often the researcher; what he experiences is part of the data. Rather than trying to eliminate the researcher's influence, qualitative researchers often examine the researcher's role in generating the study's data and incorporate data about the researcher's role into the study's findings. This is referred to as a reflexive component of the study.

The third continuum is from verificative to generative modes. Quantitative research tends toward the verificative; the usual purpose of quantitative research is to verify a hypothesis about the relationship between operationally defined variables. Qualitative researchers tend to have greater interest in generating theories or hypotheses. In the terms we used in chapter 1, this is essentially the difference between deductive and inductive reasoning.

Most educational researchers, as well as students of educational research methods, have a predilection, often a strong predilection, for one of the approaches and are suspicious, often very suspicious, of the other. As you read the two different treatments of the imaginary research on Mr. Jackson's class that we presented above, how did you feel? Although you probably do not yet know much about qualitative research, if you are typical you found yourself favoring one of the approaches and criticizing the other.

As you read chapters 2–8, the quantitative chapters, did you feel that quantitative methods are much ado about nothing—that operational definitions, control of confounding variables, random sampling, and statistics take the life out of research? And as you read the example we just provided of qualitative research, did you breathe an internal sigh of relief because we're finally getting to something in educational research that you can identify with?

Or have you felt at home with the quantitative chapters? And do you find yourself thinking now that this qualitative stuff seems too subjective, too fuzzy? Did you want more evidence for the qualitative researcher's conclusions? Did you find yourself objecting that, with the qualitative approach, different researchers in the same situation might have seen different things?

Most educational researchers do either qualitative or quantitative research; few do both. In fact, until relatively recent times, little qualitative research was done in education; many educational researchers had little or no awareness of qualitative methods, and those who did tended to be critical of the approach.

Increasingly, however, educational researchers are acknowledging that qualitative methods have a place in the education research process. A substantial portion of the literature on educational research methods is beginning to be devoted to formalizing the similarities and differences between the two approaches.

Our own strongly held position is that there is room, indeed need, in educational research for both approaches. Each approach has strengths and weaknesses, and the strengths of one tend to compensate for the weaknesses of the other. We will return in chapter 11 to this issue of the complementarity of the two approaches. In the meantime, the next two chapters will introduce you to qualitative research in education.

Chapter 9 discusses collecting qualitative data. It is primarily concerned with the methods most often used by qualitative researchers to collect data: observation and interviewing. In addition, archival and self-report data-generation methods are discussed. This chapter will also revisit the differences between qualitative and quantitative methods with an examination of the issues and concerns that impact how one approaches a qualitative research project. Chapter 10 deals with analyzing qualitative data and the researcher's considerations in the process of formulating research findings. In these chapters, as in the quantitative chapters, we have incorporated excerpts from published research. These excerpts will provide you with an introductory understanding of the nature of qualitative research. However, reading several qualitative research reports in full will greatly help your understanding of what qualitative researchers do and why. You may want to try to obtain some of the reports that we have excerpted in the next two chapters. Be forewarned that qualitative research reports tend to come in varying lengths, from journal articles summarizing a qualitative study and its findings to book-length descriptive ethnographic texts.

There has been a great deal of confusion in the educational research community about what to call qualitative research. In addition to the term we are using, a number of other terms are in use: naturalistic inquiry, case study, ethnography, historical narrative, action research, collaborative research, and field study. Some of these terms are more and some less inclusive. For information about specific types of qualitative research, see the following suggested readings.

SUGGESTED READINGS

Denzin, N., and Lincoln, Y. (1994). *Handbook of Qualitative Research.* Thousand Oaks, CA: Sage Publications.

LeCompte, M., Millroy, W., and Preissle, J. (1992). *The Handbook of Qualitative Research in Education.* San Diego: Academic Press.

LeCompte, M., and Preissle, J. (1993). *Ethnography and Qualitative Design in Educational Research* (2nd ed.). San Diego: Academic Press.

9

Collecting Qualitative Data

Qualitative research questions tend to be broader and more open-ended than quantitative questions. Here are some of the educational issues that have been studied recently by qualitative researchers:

- How immigrant West Indian students use sports as a vehicle for expressions of resistance and ethnic identity in an inner-city Canadian school (Solomon, 1992).
- How a progressive, freedom-enhancing curriculum is introduced in a freshman-level college course (Spatig and Bickel, 1993).
- How students' and teachers' monologue patterns are often conflicting expressions of power (Gutierrez, Rymes, and Larson (1995).
- How students' ethnic identity is a negotiated process across time and social situations, rather than being dictated by group membership (Davidson, Yu, and Phelan, 1993).
- How a writing and literacy program provides a vehicle for a prison inmate and his tutor to analyze critically the dynamics of power in prison (Shethar, 1993).
- Learning-disabled students' strategies for appearing competent and for monitoring and evaluating their own actions (Rueda and Mehan, 1986).

Qualitative researchers have multiple methods for collecting empirical data to answer their research questions—including participant self-report, video/audio taping, observation, interviewing, and archives. Which of the sources is used in a particular study depends on the nature of the research question and on practical considerations. In some studies, only one method is employed; in other studies, a combination of methods is appropriate.

As you learned in chapter 3, quantitative researchers also use a variety of data sources to define variables operationally; however, there are great differences in the ways that qualitative and quantitative researchers obtain data and in the kinds of data that are obtained. Remember that qualitative research does not focus on variables and operational definitions. So how do qualitative researchers employ multiple research methods to collect data? The bulk of this chapter will address that question.

■ EXERCISE 1

What data source or combination of sources (participant self-report, video/audio taping, observation, interview, and archives) would probably be employed by qualitative researchers in pursuing each of the following research questions?

a. What are the effects on schools of economic decline in a midwestern farm community?

b.   What is a typical workday like for an elementary-school librarian?

c.   What problems do students who are physically disabled encounter in dealing with the physical environment at a university?

d.   How do third-graders get acquainted during the first week of the new school year?   ■

OBSERVATION

Both quantitative and qualitative researchers use observation. To the novice, the conduct of quantitative observation may seem esoteric. Its rigor and formality, along with the presence of numerous statistical tables of research results, can be intimidating to the uninitiated. Understanding quantitative observation requires knowledge of a technical language and technical concepts. In contrast, one of the most engaging aspects of qualitative observation is that it is based primarily on something we all do every day: watching what people do and listening to what they say.

We all are active observers. As we grow up, we watch and imitate parents, siblings, and other significant people. When we go to school we observe teachers and peers. Sometimes we have to adjust the behavior we learned at home to the expectations of the school setting. As our social world widens and becomes more complex we are continually observing others, questioning former beliefs and expectations, and trying out new behavior. Our capacity to observe is crucial to social learning.

This same kind of observation is the basic research strategy for qualitative researchers and comprises the majority of their research activity. In the normal course of their data collection, researchers watch how people behave, listen to their conversations, and interact with them in the context of the research setting.

Focus and Setting

In attempting to answer their research questions, qualitative observers choose a focus for observation and a setting in which to observe. They then position themselves in that setting and observe that focus in all its complexity, screening out as little of what's happening as is possible within the limits of humans' perceptual and cognitive processes. Examples of foci and settings for qualitative observation include:

- Test-taking behavior during a college entrance exam
- Social interactions in a teachers' lounge
- Professor-student interactions in a community college class
- Classroom behavior of tenth-grade students
- Interactions between mothers and their preschool children at a playground
- The work of a rural elementary-school principal
- Child-rearing practices of Navajo families in Ramah, New Mexico

Qualitative observation is often fairly extended—that is, researchers observe a setting on many different occasions over an extended period of time. In fact, qualitative observation can be almost continuous over a period lasting as long as a year or more. In the last example given above, of child-rearing practices in a reservation Navajo community, the researcher or research team might well live in the community for a year doing almost continual observation of things having to do with child rearing, including the encompassing context—i.e., the entire community.

Focus

All observations have a focus. Basically, *focus* is what the observer pays attention to within the range of events available for observation. In qualitative research the questions and objectives of the project direct the focus of observation. Depending on the project, observational focus can be a kind of panorama, encompassing a wide range of events, or it can be a close-up, confined to specific events.

In the examples given above, a study of child-rearing practices in an ethnic community suggests a more panoramic focus; everything that happens in the community that involves or might affect children—which would, of course, be almost everything that happens in the community—would be a legitimate focus for the observer. The example of interactions between mothers and children on a playground suggests a more limited focus; researchers would observe and record everything they could that went on between mothers and their children, but they would largely deemphasize many events in the setting because they were unrelated to the research question. Events that they would deemphasize might include such things as a woman walking her dog, a girl with her father, two boys who came to the park together, an adult couple curled up on a blanket under a tree, or a park maintenance worker.

The characteristics of qualitative research also affect focus, especially in extended projects with broad goals. When qualitative researchers first enter an unfamiliar research setting, they observe to get an initial "lay of the land," to begin getting a "handle" on the variety of activities and participants they find there. Then, if the setting is a classroom, someone might suddenly drop a book on the floor, speak loudly, or walk into the room. Whatever catches the observer's attention becomes the focus of observation. This is much the same thing that you do when you enter a new social scene, such as a large social gathering. You look around the room and get a broad picture of what is going on. Later, as you move about the room, you might see someone you want to talk to, or you might spy the buffet table or bar and head over in that direction.

Focus shifts as the researcher's interests become increasingly specific during the course of the study. As data accumulate, focus tends to narrow. For example, Golez (1995) did a qualitative observation study of a site-based teacher education program. After several months, he began to notice that program participants seemed tense about sharing responsibility for determining the program's curriculum. Focusing on this specific issue resulted in the identification of a pattern: Participants were having difficulty making a paradigmatic shift from a traditional to a progressive educational model. This led to a narrowed research focus on the difficulty encountered in implementing a mainstream reform agenda in an established school environment.

Focus also tends to shift when events or behavior in one area of observation become repetitive and predictable to the researcher. When no new information emerges from observation, that focus is said to be saturated. If the same parents invariably show up for conferences with the teacher, or if the same eighth-grade helpers always take the children to the gym at 1:30, it is time for the researcher to shift focus. This continual shift of focus prevents the work from becoming boring to the researcher, an important consideration in long-term projects.

The initial focus of qualitative observation is thus determined by the research objectives and often involves an initial "grand tour" observation to get an overview of the setting and participants. As the research progresses focus changes, in response to new opportunities for data collection that are discovered in the setting and as earlier foci become saturated. In qualitative research, though the objectives of the project direct the initial focus of observation, the objectives as well as the foci are often in a state of evolution, emerging as the research progresses. Figure 9.1 depicts the foci of observation in an observational setting.

■ **EXERCISE 2**

What different activities might be taking place simultaneously in each of the following settings? What might be some of the different foci for observation in each setting? How would a qualitative observer decide what to attend to in each of the settings?

a.   a high-school cafeteria at lunch time
b.   a pediatrician's waiting room
c.   a seventh-grade art class
d.   a board of education meeting
e.   a first-grade class on the playground during recess   ■

Selecting the Setting and Participants

Two of the issues that guide the selection of research settings and participants are *heuristic potential* and *accessibility*. A setting has heuristic potential for pursuing a given research question when it has the potential to provide information of use in answering the question. To give a simple example, a school without a girls' athletic program would have little heuristic potential as a setting for a study of academic achievement among female athletes.

But many settings have heuristic potential for a given research topic. Researchers need to assess the advantages of conducting research in one setting instead of another. For example, would a multicultural school or an all-Native American school be a better setting for a study of the acquisition of mathematical concepts among Native American children? The answer to that question depends on the research objective.

FIGURE 9.1   Setting and observational focus.

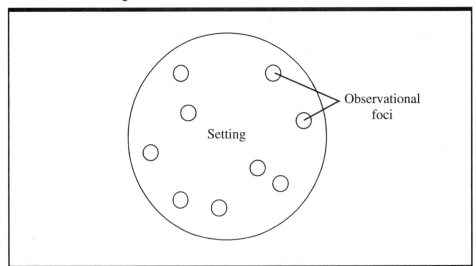

If the researchers are interested in finding out whether Native Americans differ from other groups in how they acquire mathematical concepts, then a multicultural school would be more appropriate. If, however, the researchers are only interested in Native American children, an all-Native American school might have more heuristic potential. Based on what they already know about cultural differences in communication styles, the researchers might predict that in a multicultural setting Native American students would tend to be less expressive, giving the researchers less opportunity to find out what they want to know. Qualitative researchers sometimes do a preliminary sampling of possible settings to help determine which setting to choose.

When researchers have identified a setting with good heuristic potential for their research project, they must gain entry to the setting. A setting's accessibility involves very practical considerations. Will people in the setting accept researchers there? Will they permit access to the kinds of data that need to be collected? What types of constraints will be imposed on publication of results? How far will researchers have to travel to and from the site? How much red tape is involved in getting access to the place? Does the setting have ethical limitations due to a possible negative impact of the study on the participants?

Quantitative researchers have these kinds of problems too, but for qualitative researchers they loom especially large. One reason is that qualitative researchers typically spend more time in research settings than quantitative researchers do, and it's usually more difficult to gain cooperation from people for longer projects. Perhaps more important, however, is that the focus of qualitative research is usually more open-ended, which can be very threatening for people in the research setting. As a dramatic example, would you be more likely to cooperate with a quantitative researcher who wanted you to be one of many subjects filling out an anonymous questionnaire, or with a qualitative researcher who wanted to live with you for a year? Gaining entry to a desirable setting can be a serious problem for qualitative researchers, at times so serious that it severely limits the research enterprise.

Qualitative researchers try to choose settings and participants that will best serve the purposes of the research. If one of the important goals of the research is generalizability, then qualitative researchers employ selection processes that will further that goal. One such process might be random sampling. If random sampling of settings and/or participants is feasible, it might well be employed in qualitative research in much the same way as it is in quantitative research.

If, on the other hand, the goal of the research is to provide in-depth information about particular kinds of settings or participants, random sampling would not be helpful. A purposeful sampling method that targets particular settings or participants would. Romero and Schultz (1992) wanted to study giftedness in a Native American pueblo community. Randomly sampling community members would not have worked for them. Instead, they used a purposeful sampling technique. The pueblo governors identified gifted individuals, whom the researchers then contacted for study. These initial contacts led to more contacts. Ultimately, a sample of participants was obtained that met the goals of the research.

■ EXERCISE 3

What would be some of the appropriate settings for studying the following issues?

a. spontaneous play of seven- to nine-year-olds

b. gender differences in teaching style

c. attachment behavior of fathers and their toddlers

d. how staff members of a local teachers' union help teachers with job-related problems ■

The Researcher's Role

Role is probably a familiar concept to you. It means the behaviors, interactions, and tasks that are associated with a person or function within a social situation. Some qualitative researchers have expanded the concept of the researcher's role to include something they call *positionality*. Positionality refers to a researcher's philosophical position, particularly when this position has the potential to influence the research. Imagine a researcher who defines himself as Chicano, rather than Hispanic American, undertaking a study of school outcomes for Mexican immigrant children. This researcher's positionality will affect his approach to the study. This topic will be further explored later in this chapter.

Doing research requires negotiating an appropriate role for the researcher in the research setting. For quantitative researchers, the appropriate role is usually fairly obvious and limited. But for qualitative observers, the situation can be much more complex.

When qualitative researchers first enter a setting, especially a setting in which they will be doing extended observation, they often assume the role of naive stranger. As the fieldwork progresses during weeks, months, or years of observation, researchers tend to become increasingly immersed in the setting and to establish personal relationships with the people there. Their role evolves into friend. This often carries an ethical consideration, such as how the researcher's departure from the setting will affect participants emotionally. Sometimes a change in role occurs right away; for instance, children in a first-grade class would probably ask an observer for various kinds of help. Becoming a teacher's assistant is an example of how educational researchers commonly adapt their conduct to the context they are observing. Researchers have also functioned as consultants, students, tutors, and community members. There are many ways for a particular researcher to work things out, but it is always necessary for qualitative observers to find some way to fit into the setting they are studying. In addition, the dynamic and complex realities of real life require that researchers renegotiate their roles from time to time in order to maintain a presence in the setting and continue data collection.

Qualitative field researchers are often classified as either *participant observers* or *nonparticipant observers*. Discussing the two roles separately here may clarify their characteristics and their perspectives. In the actual conduct of field research, however, the distinction between the two is seldom exact, and researchers often use a combination of the two approaches, especially during long-term fieldwork.

Participant Observation

Participant observers are actively engaged in the life of the setting they study. In addition to observing, they perform functions and enact roles that are meaningful to the people in the setting. As participant observers, researchers are not only researchers but also actors in the social scene they study. Their experiences become part of the data they collect. They participate for the purpose of developing rapport with the people in the setting and learning what the world looks like from their point of view. The degree to which they participate varies among qualitative researchers and is often linked to their positionality regarding researcher subjectivity.

There are advantages to becoming a participant observer. For one thing, the potential for being intrusive and inhibiting ordinary behavior is minimized when the researcher is perceived as an insider. Most ongoing social organizations, such as schools and classrooms, do not incorporate the role of observer into their design. Many places will try to find something useful for the observer to do in order to make sense of a stranger continuously in their midst.

Another advantage of participant observation is that it affords opportunities for interactions with members of the setting that are not available to someone who is just observing. A participant observer is able to learn the routines and norms of the place firsthand, by experience, and is able to find out what daily life is like for people in that setting. The account a participant observer provides, then, is the perspective of someone within the organization. As a result, researchers who are participant observers develop a great deal of confidence in the truthfulness, or credibility, of their data. A researcher who conducts a reading group probably has understandings about that experience that are beyond the direct experience of an observer who watches a teacher do it. Similarly, a researcher who eats lunch with the students in the school cafeteria is going to learn something about their attitudes and behavior that may not be apparent in a classroom.

The possibility of becoming identified with factions within a research setting is one potential limitation of participant observation; for example, becoming one of the teachers may inhibit interactions with some students. Spending time with union activists could limit access to administrative personnel. Following the principal around for several weeks could create suspicion on the part of some teachers. The potential for jeopardizing an entire project exists when a researcher is perceived to be taking sides. To avoid this problem researchers need to become aware of political realities in their research sites. Often that knowledge develops as the fieldwork progresses.

Many participant observers experience the problem of role conflict, which means that tensions and confusions exist in their respective roles of researcher and participant. Role conflict is described from firsthand experience in the following excerpt from a study by an American researcher of a German school (Warren, 1974, p. 431):

> I had originally anticipated the possibility and value of participating actively in the life of the school as, for example, a teacher of English. In the early months of the study I mentioned this interest in ways I hoped were gentle but persuasive. These attempts failed—a failure which I came to count as a blessing after several experiences of supervising classes in the school.
>
> It was not simply that a teaching responsibility would limit the time available for observation; there was also a question of creating an unnecessary ambivalence, personal and social, with respect to my identity as a researcher and a teacher. I started out as the father of that American boy in the seventh grade. For some first-graders I was simply the man who was always sitting in the back; for some third-graders I was a county school inspector. For most of the pupils (and adults) I was an American who came to learn about German schools. When, however, classes were turned over to me so that I could administer a questionnaire to the fifth grade (it required three periods over as many different days), I quickly became just another teacher. The behavior of the students structured the kind of authority relationship to which they were accustomed, but not to which I was inclined. When the questionnaire was completed, I was glad to return to the sanctity of the observer role.

Role conflict was also experienced by Golez (1995) in his study of a teacher training program undergoing mainstream reform.

> Throughout the preservice teacher education program I was continuously adjusting and adapting to my assorted program duties. I felt, at first, that I wasn't an authority figure or a preservice teacher. Thus, in the weekly seminars I assumed the role of an interactive researcher, occasionally looking up from my laptop and interjecting a perspective. In one such circumstance I was made aware of the distinction attributed to my position. A discussion had ensued surrounding issues of multicultural education in schools. Having considerable experience and opinions surrounding sociocultural issues in schools, I adamantly interjected. I made my point forcibly, as I was accustomed to in graduate seminars. I could, however, feel the tension building especially from the preservice teacher whose opinion was contradicted. Finally the intern with an opposing opinion asked that I not use his dialogue in my research. I immediately deleted the dialogue from my field notes. Reflecting on this incident I re-evaluated my role as a facilitator/researcher in the preservice teacher seminars. From that point on I often suppressed an inclination to interject and assumed a more passive role as a "fly on the wall" researcher (p. 62).

Some qualitative methodologists have expressed concern about participant observers "going native." This phenomenon has also been defined as "over-rapport." It means that the researcher's involvement has gone beyond performing circumscribed tasks and activities to actually living the research. Going native may occur when researchers can no longer maintain the degree of detachment that is requisite to dispassionate, impartial observation. Ironically, rapport and empathy, which are assets in qualitative research, become liabilities to the researcher if the research becomes secondary to issues within the organizations he or she is studying. Sometimes this problem occurs because the setting is engaging and the people are likable. In these circumstances sentiment can undermine detachment. Other qualitative methodologists, however, suggest that the only way to conduct a qualitative study is to go native. There are also researchers who encourage influencing the setting for what is called emancipatory social reconstruction.

Qualitative research projects can require years of fieldwork. Over this period of time, close relationships between the researcher and participants are inevitable as people confide in the observer, relate intimate details of their lives, and simply interact from day to day. Of course, a field setting may not be attractive and pleasing to researchers. In fact, what one observes and experiences may be distasteful or offensive. For instance, the researcher may observe brutal treatment of children by parents or school personnel. The researcher may find particular rules and regulations unjust. Under such conditions the potential for extremely negative bias is present, and there are ethical and methodological decisions to be made that depend in part on the theoretical perspective and positionality of the researcher.

Traditionally, researchers try to overcome bias by leaving the setting temporarily for debriefings with project supervisors or colleagues. Periodic "time outs" can help researchers to reestablish the perspective that is required for collecting reliable data. These respites from observation also provide opportunities for self-reflection and preliminary analysis, which can inform subsequent data collection: "What is there about that place which makes it so easy for me to get emotionally involved with the kids?" Or, "I wonder why those kids don't stage a mass rebellion against that teacher?" In spite of the potential threats to the research enterprise that inhere in participant observation, a manageable degree of emotional involvement can yield knowledge and data that are unavailable to the nonparticipant observer. Very often the relationships with people in the setting make observation personally meaningful and professionally compelling for the researcher. These experiences are among the most distinctive features of qualitative observation.

The following excerpt (Moore, 1976a, p. 71) is an example of participant observation; the researcher is an active participant in the setting.

> I present an afternoon class in mid-June, two weeks before the Day of San Juan. This, however, is shortly after the celebration at the end of the Month of Mary, when children from this particular chantry class have already taken their first communion and thus graduated from it. . . .

> I go to the compound of the foremost doctrine master in the town, José Tsin. He had told me that his classes generally begin every afternoon around 4:00. I arrive almost exactly at this hour, under a light drizzle. . . .

> I call out "Ave María," the proper greeting when a stranger enters a household in Guatemala. A man's voice tells me to come forward. Over to the right, José can be seen standing on the porch of his large ranch shaded in the trees.

Foley (1990) provides another example of participant observation.

> As people got progressively drunker, I discovered one reason I may have been invited. The daughter of a prominent BGL leader came at me in a drunken rage: What the hell are you doin' here? Are you gonna write a book about how Anglos discriminate against Meskins? Why were you in Crystal City last year? Are you a friend of Ramirez's, that son of a bitch? I want to tell you something to put in your damn book. We are the ones who are getting discriminated against. . . .

> I had drifted away from the confrontation toward a conversation among several senior girls. They were talking about going to college, a topic I assumed was quite safe. I sat up on the car fender near one of them to chip in a comment or two, and suddenly she draped her leg over mine. She looked at me in an amused, somewhat defiant way. . . . I quickly removed her leg and continued talking about the virtues of going to the University of Texas. In response, she put her leg back over mine again, so I asked her not to get me in trouble with her boyfriend. She threw back her hair victoriously, smiled, and tossed me an "Okay, Doc."[1]

Nonparticipant Observation

The role of nonparticipant observer has certain advantages over that of participant observer. For one thing, the researcher's responsibilities are limited to one primary activity: observation. The potential for role conflict is greatly reduced in that case. Another advantage is that the circumscribed role of observer tends to decrease the kinds of demands on researchers' time that are predictable when they are active participants in the setting.

The role of nonparticipant observer is advantageous for maintaining social distance from those being observed. A distant, monological, data-gathering approach often provides a different research perspective from the one that would be fostered by a more participatory, dialogical, role. Sometimes, in fact, being an outsider facilitates data collection. An impartial observer can be a nonthreatening presence for people to talk to. There are times, for instance, when it seems safer to tell your troubles to a stranger than to a friend. On the other hand, a researcher's maintaining distance can also limit participants' disclosure.

---

[1]From D. Foley, *Learning Capitalist Culture: Deep in the Heart of Tejas.* © Copyright 1990 by University of Philadelphia Press, Philadelphia. Reprinted with permission of the publisher.

The excerpt that follows is an example of nonparticipant observation. The authors annotated the observation for data analysis at another stage of the project (Goetz and LeCompte, 1984, pp. 148–149):

VALLEY SCHOOL:
(Pat, the teacher, is sitting on a student's desk at the front of the room. The students' desks are haphazardly scattered throughout the room; four girls have pushed theirs together in a row diagonally across the room; some are clustered in twos and others are by themselves. There is no teacher desk immediately visible; it is obscured in the corner behind boxes of materials and a motorcycle engine.)

9:06 discussion	T2A	(T2A) "OK, now let's start." (Todd comes up and gives her a nickel). "OK, now here's our new word for the day. What is it?" (She writes it on the board.) "Bazaar." (She writes *bizarre* and *bazaar* on the board, explains the differences. Goes through sentences using *bizarre* to illustrate bizarre things (italics added).)
9:10	T2A	(T2A) "OK, I would like you to pay attention. We've had some problems with money. What's a dollar sign?" (Children shout the answer. She explains how to read numbers as money.) "Now I want you to pretend you just bought a house. Now, you gotta be careful because houses cost lots of money." (Writes $2856000 on the board. Larry volunteers the decimal placement.) "Darn, I couldn't fool you. Let's see if I can fool this young man." (Does another. He gets it right.) "Who wants a more expensive house—Bernie?" (Does another.) "Let's see, I haven't heard from some of these girls. Aila, that's what I spent at the grocery store." (Does another.)
9:15		"Decimal points are very important when we are writing money numbers." (She demonstrates how to add with decimals by using money numbers. She adds them wrong so that the children can correct them—calling out corrections from the classroom.) "One way to help yourself, people, is to make sure all your dots line up. (R1A) All right, boys and girls, when you
9:30	R1A	get your answers, be sure to put decimal points in."
getting organized	T2A	(T2A) "OK, everybody, a pencil and paper. We're going to do some problems." (Comes over to me and tells me that it is not what she had planned but that it was a good introduction to decimals and that they needed the practice in this.)

The objectives of the research project guide decisions that researchers make regarding their roles in the setting. Sometimes it is appropriate to remain a nonparticipant observer during data collection. Sometimes it is better to be "one of the gang" in order to gather information. During long-term assignments it is difficult to maintain the role of nonparticipant observer continuously. It can be frustrating not to take part in activities that are part of everyday life there. Most researchers, as a result, are likely to use a combination of both roles during the course of their work. They might participate in some aspects of the organization and remain an observer in others.

Figure 9.2 depicts both participant and nonparticipant observers in relation to the observational setting.

■ EXERCISE 4

Would participant or nonparticipant observation probably be used to collect data bearing on each of the following topics? Why?

a.   The first experiences of a southeast-Asian immigrant child in the United States
b.   Inservice training programs in a school district
c.   The professional life of a school superintendent
d.   Social distance between teachers and students in an Israeli school
e.   Personal interactions in a therapy group   ■

Immersion

An issue related to the role of qualitative observers in the research setting is the observer's degree of *immersion* in the setting. The concept of *immersion* refers to the researcher's breadth and depth of involvement with the setting. Both research objectives and practical considerations influence an observer's level of immersion.

Different research objectives require different levels of observer involvement in the setting. Ideally, in research about the lifeways of a community of people, the observer should be present over an extended period of time for the entire range of activities of those people—that is, the researcher should be immersed in the setting. On the other hand, research about children's test-taking behavior might require that the researcher be in the children's classroom for a few days before and after testing, as well as during testing, but it would not require that the researcher be in various settings throughout the school, whenever the school was open, for the entire school year.

Practical considerations also affect the observer's degree of involvement in the setting. While full immersion might be desirable in a given project, time and money resources may limit the project's scope. Characteristics of the setting determine the degree to which an observer can participate, as well. Some settings afford easy access to observers and accommodate researchers with little or no resistance. A researcher who is interested in adolescents' social behavior in shopping malls could spend as much time as he wanted in a mall—sitting on benches, strolling through shops, riding escalators, having a cup of coffee—observing all aspects of adolescents' social behavior there. Other settings impose limits. A researcher who is interested in what

FIGURE 9.2   The relationship between the observer and the setting in participant and nonparticipant observation.

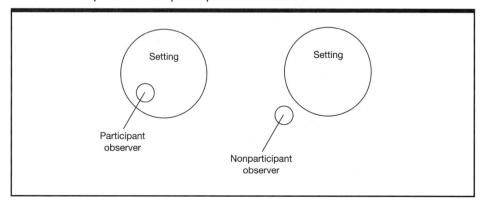

elementary school principals do in the course of their work may be allowed to observe the principal leading a faculty meeting but may not be allowed to observe a conference that the principal has with one of her teachers who has been accused of sexually exploiting a child in the school.

Levels of Immersion

Immersion is usually described in terms of three levels. In practice, however, especially in an extended study, researchers often move back and forth among levels.

The first level is *total immersion*. This level of involvement requires what is called "living the research." To the extent possible, the researcher is continually present in the setting for extended periods of time and observes all aspects of the setting that the participants will allow. Carol Stack (1974), in her study of family life in a poor, urban Black community, lived her research. For several years she spent most of her time in the community; she participated in the life of the community as much as possible, often staying with her young son in the home of one of the families she studied. Douglas Foley (1990) moved into a West Texas community for his study of the social and political relationships between Chicanos and Anglos.

The second level is *partial immersion*. While the researcher does not try to be present at all times or in all places, partial immersion usually involves an effort to obtain fairly broad and deep coverage. Partial immersion is appropriate when adequate knowledge can be achieved without total immersion. For example, good data could be collected without "living the research" in studying these topics: community participation at Board of Education meetings, student behavior in classrooms, and sexism in student-teacher interactions.

Spot observations comprise the third level of immersion in qualitative research. These are typically brief visits to a setting on one or a few occasions. As a student in education, you have probably been required to conduct spot observations as part of your training—perhaps observing in one or a few classrooms for an hour or so.

Spot observations tend to be limited in purpose as well as in nature. Qualitative researchers tend to do spot observations for one of two reasons. First, they can be useful in the early stages of research in establishing productive directions for the research; this is often called *sampling* in qualitative research. Imagine a researcher who wants to do an extended observational study of the problems that teachers encounter in managing multicultural classrooms. A few spot observations of several multicultural classrooms before beginning the research might suggest productive foci for the extended observation and might provide information of use in selecting one classroom to be studied in depth.

Second, spot observations can function to verify and extend the findings of longer-term observation. Qualitative researchers call this *triangulating*—verifying the validity of previous observations with spot observations. A researcher who had observed in one multicultural classroom over a period of weeks or months, for example, might want to make spot observations in several other multicultural classrooms. Comparing the primary setting with other similar settings would help the researcher with such tasks as understanding which aspects of the primary setting were idiosyncratic and which were intrinsic to the multicultural situation. This kind of understanding is of great help in analyzing and interpreting qualitative data.

Figure 9.3 depicts the researcher's presence in the setting at the three levels of immersion we have discussed.

■ EXERCISE 5

Which of the following examples suggest total immersion (living the research) on the part of the researcher? Why? Which suggest partial immersion? Why? Could spot observations be helpful in any of the examples? How?

a. What are the lives of runaway teenagers like?

b. What do Hopi parents consciously try to teach their children?

c. What characterizes social interactions between special education and regular education students?

d. How does young children's play reveal their developing gender-role identities?

e. How do teachers of adult ESL students provide support to their students in dealing with a new culture?   ■

Teachers as Researchers

Some qualitative researchers have begun to stress the importance to education of research by teachers. Having roots in action and applied approaches, the concept of teacher-as-researcher is part of a movement to bring new voices into the educational research enterprise. This movement is driven by perceptions of discontinuity between university-based research and what actually occurs in classrooms. Cochran-Smith and Lytle (1992), among others, suggest that this discontinuity makes university-generated research inaccessible and not useful to most classroom teachers.

The concept of teachers researching themselves certainly challenges the traditional view that university-based theory can and should drive school-based practice. But teacher research has certain obvious advantages. First, it can provide rich data, located in actual schooling contexts. In addition, it can encourage teachers to perceive and think about their teaching in new ways. This kind of reflection can lead to important changes in individual teachers' practices.

But it would not be a good thing if important changes were based on invalid research. Not all university-based research is valid, but most professional researchers

FIGURE 9.3 The researcher's presence in the setting at various levels of immersion.

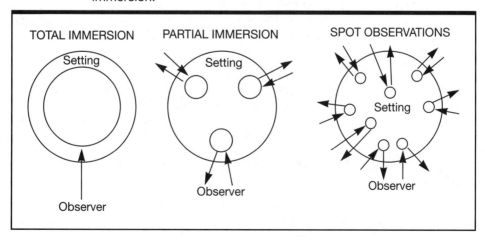

have been trained to conduct valid research, while many teachers have not. A collaborative approach, in which academic researchers and practitioners are research partners, has been suggested as a good and more moderate alternative.

Recording Data

Qualitative observers usually record their observations in the form of field notes. Field notes contain the raw data of the project, analogous to the variable values that quantitative researchers record. The notes document each visit to the setting or each day in the setting in full. Ideally, anything that occurs within the selected focus is recorded: the physical characteristics of the setting, words and behaviors of participants in the setting, even self-reflections of the researcher.

It is often inadvisable for qualitative observers to take notes during observations, because note taking can make people feel self-conscious about being watched. Furthermore, it is unrealistic to expect observers to look and listen at the same time that they write things down in a notebook. What usually happens is that observers jot down a few phrases or words as memory cues and then record their full observations from memory as soon as possible after the observation is completed. Depending on their personal preferences, observers write field notes by hand, use typewriters or word-processing computers, dictate their observations onto audiotape, or take what are called *headnotes* (mental notes) to be written up immediately after the observation.

Sometimes, in an attempt to capture it all, observers use video and/or audio recording equipment in addition to field notes, to extend and/or verify the accounts they transcribe from memory. In long-term projects, however, only occasional use can be made of this strategy. Taping an entire year's worth of all-day, every-day observation would be prohibitively expensive and would result in such a massive accumulation of material that it could not be efficiently analyzed.

When field researchers write their field notes, they attempt to reproduce the entire period of observation. It is not enough for them to summarize events or conversations. It is important to capture the characteristics of the setting and the language and behavior of participants as they actually occurred. Reproducing characteristics fully and accurately, conversations word for word, and behavior fully and in chronological order takes practice.

Here is a small excerpt from the field notes of an extended study in a school (Golez, 1995, p. 58). This study focused on a teacher-training program. This excerpt was recorded during a site-based seminar in which the preservice teachers argue the use of grades to motivate elementary-school students. Note how the dialogue or script provides detail of the interaction.

> *Preservice teacher seminar*
> Lynda questions, "is grade a primary motivator?" If we are using [grades] to motivate we should speak to effort. Motivation doesn't have a place in certain cases.
>   Charles responds, "[that] of course you can [because] the children see grades as achievement. If you pad the grades you end up with eighth graders who can't spell. . . ."
>   Dr. M interjects, "I wouldn't give grades, I'd give mastery [scores] to show where kids are." She adds that the "ABCD thing is antiquated in today's world; [it is] always subjective."
>   Charles asks, "How is it subjective if I add up the scores?"
>   Lynda asks Charles how he would "score first graders learning to read. . . ?"
>   Judy (preservice teacher) states that, "we [teachers] need to deal with intrinsic and external motivation; we cannot judge who will succeed." She does not want grades to be primary motivators. . . . "Noticing what [a child] is doing and how they invest self

is a valid conversation because it values. . .[a] bigger picture." [She asks], "Who are grades for and what are they really saying?"

Qualitative observers try to behave as if they were audiovisual recorders, reproducing the sights and sounds they observe in vivid detail. In practice, observers make decisions about how much detail to include in their descriptions. If a boy's shirt is red, is it important to know what shade of red? If a girl is described as tall, is it important to know her exact height? The answers to this kind of question depend on the purposes of the study. When the level of detail no longer informs the research objective, it makes sense to stop. For example, research to understand peer groups among middle-schoolers would require more attention to details of clothing style than would a study of their political awareness. Training increases researchers' capacity to remember events in detail and chronologically. Although perfect recall is an unrealistic goal, it is important to describe as fully and accurately as possible who did or said what, to whom, and under what circumstances. Memory improves with practice. Researchers discover that a good memory depends on how intently they look and listen. New field researchers are sometimes amazed at their capacity actually to remember entire conversations word for word with only a few lapses.

Writing accurate descriptions also requires describing events without evaluating them. To evaluate is to impose one's opinions on the data. Good qualitative descriptions let the events speak for themselves. In the following account (Henry, 1976, p. 172), notice the detail the observer was able to capture and the non-evaluative nature of the record, which allows the events to speak for themselves.

> Charlie reads a story he made up himself: "The Unknown Guest." One dark, dreary night . . . on a hill a house stood. This house was forbidden territory for Bill and Joe, but they were going in anyway. The door creaked, squealed, slammed. A voice warned them to go home. Spider webs, dirty furniture. . . . Bill wanted to go home. They went upstairs. A stair cracked. They entered a room. A voice said they might as well stay and find out now; and their father came out. He laughed and they laughed, but they never forgot their adventures together.
>
> *Teacher:*   Are there any words that give you the mood of the story? . . .
>
> *Lucy:*   He could have made the sentences a little better. . . .
>
> *Teacher:*   Let's come back to Lucy's comment. What about his sentences?
>
> *Gert:*   They were too short. . . .
>
> Charlie and Jeanne are having a discussion about the position of the word "stood."
>
> *Teacher:*   Wait a minute, some people are forgetting their manners. . . .
>
> *Jeff:*   About the room: the boys went up the stairs and one "cracked," then they were in the room. Did they fall through the stairs or what?
>
> Teacher suggests Charlie make that a little clearer.
>
> *Lucy:*   If he fell through the step. . . .
>
> *Teacher:*   We still haven't decided about the short sentences. Perhaps they make the story more spooky and mysterious.
>
> *Gwynne:*   I wish he had read with more expression instead of all at one time.
>
> *Rachel:*   Not enough expression.
>
> *Teacher:*   Charlie, they want a little more expression from you. I guess we've given you enough suggestions for one time.
>
> (Charlie does not raise his head, which is bent over his desk as if studying a paper.)

Teacher: Charlie! I guess we've given you enough suggestions for one time, Charlie, haven't we?

(Charlie half raises his head, seems to assent grudgingly.)[2]

In writing field notes, qualitative researchers have traditionally tried to describe events without evaluating them or imposing their opinions on the data. This stance is currently being challenged by some methodologists, who argue that this practice results in only a simulated objectivity. Researchers have feelings, opinions, and experiences that affect what they record, even if the record seems objective. It may be preferable for researchers to record their interpretations openly, being explicit about their biases, rather than foster an illusion of objectivity.

Some researchers keep a field "diary" of observer comments separate from their formal field notes. In these intuitive records, they record their feelings, opinions, and information about events that might affect or enhance their observations. The diary may be simply a column in each margin of the field notes. Such diaries help researchers reflect on subjective impressions that might affect their objectivity in recording and/or analyzing their observations.

In designing research projects, observers have to allow sufficient time in their schedules for writing field notes. The process of writing such notes is a kind of debriefing or "emptying your head." The importance of this aspect of the research is such that some observers determine the amount of time they will spend in the setting according to their estimates of time available for writing field notes. It can require twice as much time to write the notes as it takes to do the observations. However, one reward for the time and effort is that the data can reproduce the richness and complexity of real-life settings.

Observer Effects

The quality of data collection depends, in part, on characteristics of the observer. Ethnicity, gender, age, and physical appearance are some of the characteristics that can affect data collection. Imagine that the purpose of a research project is to study social interactions among boys on a football team in a locker room after winning a game. Would a male or female researcher be more likely to collect good data? In designing qualitative studies, researchers must allow for the influence that observer characteristics can have on data collection. Either observers must be employed who are more likely to obtain good data—for example, a male observer would have to be employed in a boys' locker room study—or the objectives of the study must be accommodated to the limitations placed on data collection by the available observer's characteristics.

Characteristics of the researcher also influence his or her attitudes and orientations toward the events being studied. Researchers bring their preconceptions with them when they first enter the field setting. Observers' religion, ethnicity, gender, and age predispose them to certain expectations about the groups they study. It is likely, for example, that a Black researcher will have different perceptions in a multicultural classroom than a White observer will; and age affects perceptions of people who are younger or older than the observer.

---

[2]From J. Henry. "Attitude Organization in Elementary School Classrooms." *American Journal of Othopsychiatry,* Vol. 27, No. 1 (January 1957), 117–123. Copyright © the American Othopsychiatric Association, Inc. Reproduced by permission.

Personality traits influence data collection as well. Some researchers are shy and find it difficult to initiate conversations with people they hardly know. At the other extreme, some observers have such dominant personality styles that they intimidate the people they are observing. Backgrounds and personalities of researchers, like those of other people, are varied, and it is often necessary for observers to adapt their behavior to the characteristics of the setting they study. One researcher, for example, was accustomed to addressing teachers as Ms. or Mr. However, when she conducted field research in a school setting where informality and casual exchange between students and teachers were the norm, she was expected to call both students and teachers by their first names. This minor adjustment was also instructive about the way the place operated (Pollock, 1979).

■ EXERCISE 6

In what ways could such observer characteristics as age, gender, and ethnicity affect the quality of data collected in the following settings? If you were the observer, how could your characteristics be advantages or disadvantages?

a. a bilingual-education program in a middle school
b. a continuing education class in a retirement community
c. an orientation session for new principals
d. a history class in a suburban high school
e. interactions in a multicultural classroom   ■

A major problem for observers is the fact that their presence can alter the behavior of the people they are observing. As a student you probably remember feeling somewhat self-conscious and distracted when an observer was present in your classroom. Researchers learn to expect some initial curiosity about their presence because people ordinarily notice a stranger in their midst. Temporary disruption of ordinary behavior is predictable when researchers first enter a setting. Researchers try to minimize the impact of their presence by becoming part of the scene. Anything the observer does that inhibits or interrupts the flow of everyday conduct is an obstacle to the collection of good data. Fortunately, what often happens is that those who are being observed soon forget the researcher is present and return to business as usual. In fact, observations are conducted so routinely in some schools that both teachers and students are quite accustomed to observers in their classrooms.

The following excerpt from Douglas Foley's work exemplifies how a researcher's presence influenced participants' behavior (Foley, 1990, pp. 208–209).

> At school, my persona was a curious mixture of serious researcher and down-home jock. Being an ex-college basketball and tennis player, I worked out regularly with both teams. Not infrequently, I was running around the high school campus in shorts and a t-shirt. I went to all the extra-curricular sports events, even the out-of-town games. I also hung around the field house and rode on the player bus to games. I became identified as an "ex-college player," and kids used to ask me questions about college sports. I also helped the "father of North Town tennis," a retired coach, give his proteges a few pointers as we played.
>
> My acceptance by the kids was an interesting progression. Initially the rumor went around school that I was a narcotics agent. The year before, a number of high school kids had been busted for drugs in an undercover operation. When I went to my

first football game, the entire student section chanted "narc, narc, narc" when I walked by. Needless to say, this amused the adults and turned me a pale shade of red. It was a good-natured taunt, but there was some suspicion. Many students came up to me in school and asked directly if I was a narc. For a month or so, that was a source of endless joking.

Gradually, however, I began being invited to Anglo student drinking-dope smoking parties after football games. Some of the dope smoking kids also made a practice of letting me know they were stoned. They would come up in the halls and show me their joints, and ask if I had noticed how "ripped" they were in class.[3]

Another characteristic of the observer that can affect data collection is the degree of the observer's familiarity with the research setting. Educational researchers have spent many years in schools, as students and perhaps as teachers. How can impartial observations take place under these circumstances? On one hand, familiarity facilitates the initial phase of fieldwork. Researchers already know that there is a person known as "the principal," others who are called "teachers," younger people who are "students," groups called "classes," an activity known as "junior prom," and so forth. The same familiarity, however, can also impose constraints in the form of attitudes or expectations about what occurs in school. A researcher who remembers high school as a successful, happy time will tend to perceive a high-school setting in a positive light and think of it as a good place; a researcher who remembers high school as unhappy and unsatisfying will probably approach the institution with a negative bias.

Observations that are bias-free are beyond human capability. Bias poses an especially serious threat in qualitative observation, which is by nature a subjective activity. Because researchers are the instruments of observation, they often interact with the people they observe and react to events as human beings in a real place. Qualitative data collection is interactive, selective, and long-term. As a result it is very difficult for the observer to perceive the people being studied as objects. The human tendency to empathize—to put ourselves in the place of another—reinforces a subjective relationship with participants in the research setting. This issue involves what is called the researcher's positionality with respect to the assumptive mode of subjectivity/objectivity. How much should a researcher's personal knowledge influence her data collection and analysis? Some methodologists have suggested that suppressing one's knowledge and beliefs creates an artifice of objectivity. Anthropologist Renato Rosaldo (1989) suggests that personal experience can give one a deeper understanding of cultural practices. He could not understand the headhunting practices of the Ilongot (a non-Western culture that he studied) as a bereavement practice until he felt the force of anger possible in bereavement after his own wife's death.

Objectivity, in the literal sense of regarding what we study as external to ourselves, is neither likely nor desirable in qualitative research. Although the researcher's goal is to be dispassionate and impartial, part of the purpose of the research is to describe a social scene from the perspective of the people who participate in it. The characteristics of qualitative research tend to reduce the distance between observer and observed. In fact, for many qualitative observers, this very human and dynamic experience is the most compelling and sustaining aspect of their work.

Qualitative observers attempt to compensate for observer bias by making their beliefs and biases explicit at the outset. In their field notes, they might write: "I was a social outcast in high school. I hated sports and spent most of my time in the physics lab." Or they could acknowledge: "I was president of the Swank Club and had lots of

---

[3]From D. Foley, *Learning Capitalist Culture: Deep in the Heart of Tejas.* © Copyright 1990 by University of Philadelphia Press, Philadelphia. Reprinted with permission of the Publisher.

friends. I was lucky enough to attend a school that offered many opportunities and challenges." They also use extended observations to confirm or reject their previous beliefs. Qualitative observation is often a long-term project that requires the accumulation of vast amounts of day-to-day observations. Data gathered in this way tend to overcome personal bias because observations of real life do not necessarily conform to the experiences of the observer. In fact, researchers often use their previous experiences and assumptions to formulate their research objectives. For example, the first researcher in the example above might want to investigate the social status of science-club members in a high school. The second observer might explore the relationship between popularity and school achievement.

Qualitative observers also try to suspend personal beliefs temporarily. Most difficult of all in the case of educational research is the attempt to act as if you are a naive stranger when you are not. Familiarity with schools makes a truly naive orientation impossible, of course, but professional observers are trained not to take anything for granted. They insist that people they study explain the words they use and provide reasons for the events that occur there. "What does homework consist of?" "Why does that child have to sit alone in the back of the room?" "What happens if you don't show up for school in the morning?" Qualitative observers conduct themselves as if the ordinary conventions and norms of life were unfamiliar phenomena.

Many qualitative researchers conduct what are called *reflexive exercises* to address this issue of researcher effects. Reflexivity consists of the researcher's examining how her person, including her knowledge and beliefs, affects the research setting and participants and the researchers' perceptions and conclusions. Researchers' positionality on the objectivity/subjectivity continuum affects how they choose to treat researcher effects once they are discovered. What needs to be examined in a reflexive exercise, regardless of one's positionality, is how the researcher has affected the setting and the research.

Sometimes the goal of a researcher is to impact directly the setting, normally for purposes of social action. This kind of research is termed *applied research* or *action research*. It is often conducted by or in collaboration with a participant insider. For instance, Golez (1990) studied the academic perceptions of Chicano elementary-school students while simultaneously searching for a way to improve the academic standing of his own fourth-grade Chicano students. In this case, the researcher needed to examine closely the influence on his research of his being a teacher and a Chicano student advocate.

Figure 9.4 summarizes the process of qualitative observation. The data analysis referred to in the figure is interim analysis, not final analysis. The figure emphasizes the fact that qualitative observers conduct ongoing, interim analyses of data during the data collection process. These interim analyses inform the direction of the next phase of data collection. Final analysis of data, which we will deal with in chapter 10, takes place after observation has been completed and the observer has left the setting.

INTERVIEWS

Interviews are the second common way that qualitative researchers collect data. Qualitative interviews are essentially guided conversations between researchers and the people they are studying. They can be unscheduled, off-the-cuff interactions that occur informally as part of everyday life in the setting, or they can be scheduled, formal arrangements with specific people for particular purposes. The form and content of interviews are guided by the questions or topics that the researcher wants to explore.

You have already seen how different qualitative observing is from quantitative observing; qualitative interviewing differs from quantitative interviewing in much the same way. Quantitative interviewers must ultimately reduce what their subjects say to variable values—to one of a few possibilities. Qualitative interviewers are interested in exploring the richness and complexity of what their subjects have to say. Here are some research topics that have been studied using qualitative interviewing:

- Whether educational campaigns designed to lower the birth rate in Mexico affected the fertility decisions of a group of women in Cuernavaca (Dixon, 1990).
- The reasons a group of American Indian women give for their success or failure in school (Vierra and Ford, 1990).
- How multicultural education can alter the learning environment of a school and thereby influence students' relationships, attitudes, and behaviors (Jacob, 1995).
- The moral dimensions of high-school students' interpretations of historical films (Seixas, 1994).

FIGURE 9.4   The qualitative observer's process.

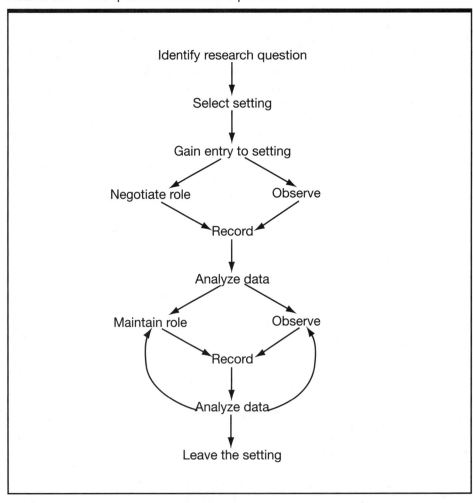

Sometimes interviewing is the only strategy used in a particular qualitative research project; at other times it is used in conjunction with observation. A qualitative researcher's decision about whether to use observation, interviewing, or some combination is based on both heuristic and practical concerns. For example, if a researcher wants to know what it was like to be a child in a traditional Hopi community, observation will be of little value—contemporary Hopi communities have been too impacted by Anglo culture. On the other hand, older living members of the Hopi tribe can be interviewed about their childhood experiences.

Even when observation is the primary strategy in a project, interviews can provide data that are not accessible by observation—for example, historical background. Interviews can also be used to verify, clarify, or amplify field observations. In the course of observation at a school, for example, a researcher may notice that a parent-teacher conference attracted only a small number of parents. Subsequent interviews with teachers might yield the information that attendance is usually poor at such conferences and that teachers have difficulty getting parents to come to school to discuss their children's work. Or perhaps teachers would report that normally most parents attend school conferences, but on that particular occasion the conferences happened to conflict with an important community meeting about local property taxes.

While interviewing is typically less time-consuming than observation, some interview projects are quite extensive. Sometimes the same subject is interviewed on many different occasions that can take place over an extended period of time. In their study of adult men's development, Levinson and his associates (1978) interviewed 40 men. Each man was interviewed on several occasions, for a total of about 12 hours of interviewing per subject. This project thus required about 500 hours of interviewing time. In her study of student-teacher initiation rites, Head (1992) individually interviewed key student-teacher informants weekly for an hour throughout their teaching semester. She also conducted informal and focus-group interviews with the other members of the 19-person group of student teachers over the same semester.

Focus

The focus of interviews, like the focus of observation, depends on the researcher's driving interest. The greater the range of interests, the broader the interview focus; the more narrow the range of topics to be explored, the more specific the focus of the interview. A narrow focus tends to allow the interviewer to probe areas of interest in more depth.

The following is an example of open-ended, broad-focus questions for a qualitative evaluation project for a Minnesota Outward Bound school course for the disabled (Patton, 1990, pp. 363–364). There was a series of three interviews: before the project, after the project, and a six-month follow-up.

Precourse Interview: Minnesota Outward Bound School Course for the Disabled

1. First we'd be interested in knowing how you became involved in this course. How did you find out about it?

   a. What about the course appealed to you?

   b. What previous experiences have you had in the outdoors?

2. Some people have difficulty deciding to participate in an Outward Bound course, and others decide fairly easily. What kind of decision process did you go through in thinking about whether or not to participate?

    a. What particular things were you concerned about?

    b. What is happening in your life right now that stimulated your decision to take the course?

3. Now that you've made the decision to go on the course, how do you feel about it?

    a. How would you describe your feelings right now?

    b. What lingering doubts or concerns do you have?

4. What are your expectations about how the course will affect you personally?

    a. What changes in yourself do you hope will result from the experience?

    b. What do you hope to get out of the experience?

Here are examples of interview questions with a more specific focus from a study of high-school students' perceptions of films portraying revisionist historical themes (Seixas, 1994, pp. 282–283).

- How long ago did you see *Dances with Wolves?*

- What did you see in that [film] segment?

- Did any questions occur to you during that segment?

- Tell me about the main differences you saw between the segments from *Dances with Wolves* and *The Searchers?*

- Which is the more accurate picture in its picture of

    a. life for Natives in the 1860s

    b. life for Whites in the 1860s

- Have you discussed Native-white relations in school?

- Have you seen other films which show Native-white relations?

Structure

Interviews can be more or less structured. In more structured interviews, the interviewer asks each subject the same predetermined questions, and each question tends to have a fairly narrow focus. Although subjects are typically permitted to formulate their responses in any way they choose, they tend to reflect the structuredness and focusedness of the interviewer by responding in a fairly brief, "on-task" way. This type of interview resembles a written questionnaire.

Here is an example of a more structured portion of an interview transcript (Vierra and Ford, 1990):

Sharon: So how old are you now, Jennie?
Jennie: How old am I now? I'm 22.
Sharon: And you belong to what tribe?
Jennie: San José pueblo.
Sharon: And you're full-blooded San José?
Jennie: No, I'm not full-blooded. I'm half. My mother's full-blooded, my father's Anglo.
Sharon: How many kids do you have now?
Jennie: I've got one and he's two and a half years old and he's a rough one.

In less structured interviews, interviewers may have a set of predetermined topics to explore, but they have considerable latitude in conducting the interview, including the freedom to change focus as necessary to follow up on leads that arise during the interview. In less structured interviews, interviewers are guided by some of the same considerations that guide observers. They may begin the interview with a broad focus, shift and perhaps narrow focus as new information arises, and change focus as a topic becomes saturated.

Less structured interviews tend to be characterized by more spontaneity between researcher and subject and to promote lengthier responses from subjects. They also tend to produce both broader and deeper coverage than do more structured interviews.

The following excerpt from an interview transcript with a student is an example of a less structured format (Goetz and LeCompte, 1984, pp. 132–133):

Goetz: Would you go to school if you didn't have to?

Nancy: Sometimes I would go to school when I was in the mood, and the other times—when I wasn't, when I wanted to go horseback riding or something like that—I wouldn't. But sometimes when I felt I was in the mood to go, I would.

Goetz: Do you like school?

Nancy: Sort of, sometimes.

Goetz: What are some of the things you like about school?

Nancy: Well, sometimes I like school because we have extra recess or art or something like that, and other times—when we have to go to music—I don't like it because I don't like music.

Goetz: What are some other things you don't like about school?

Nancy: When we have a whole lot of work—like we have English, spelling, and handwriting, all kinds of stuff like that in the morning and stuff. Then we have about 42 problems in math, like we did that one time.

Goetz: If you didn't go to school, what would you miss?

Nancy: Sometimes—like if there was laws and stuff that we don't have to go to school and they changed things around—then I might miss art one day and something [else] the next day and something like that, and I wouldn't even know what day we're supposed to have them on.

Goetz: What do you think you'd miss the most about school?

Nancy: Well, the most thing I would miss would be work, I guess.

Goetz: What kind of work?

Nancy: (shrugging) I don't know. Any kind of work. Some play work and some hard work.

Goetz: What would you miss out on learning?

Nancy: Like if we was just starting to do division, but we've already did it—if we was starting to learn it that one day when I was, when I missed school because I didn't want to go or something—then I wouldn't know how to do it when I came back, and if they was stingy and stuff, they wouldn't help me. Then I would probably get all of my answers wrong if we had a test.

■ EXERCISE 7

What seems to be the focus of the following portion of an interview transcript (Vierra and Ford, 1990)? Does this portion seem more or less structured?

Valerie: I can't remember what you said about when your father moved out.

Amy:	It was my mother that moved out and it was—I had already finished high school. I was at the university. I think it would have been like my second year when I was at the university.
Valerie:	So all the time you were growing up he was an alcoholic in the home?
Amy:	Uh-huh.
Valerie:	Was that any kind of problem for you in school?
Amy:	During my elementary school years it was and mainly because everybody looked at my dad as the town drunk. He was the one on the road, he was the one on the highways just with all these people drinking. And basically I would say we basically isolated ourselves from the community. Kids used to pick on me. I mean if I had a good argument going and that person wanted to win so bad, all that person would have to say is your dad's a drunk and I would keep my mouth shut for the rest of the time. And in that way yes that was a problem. I grew up in a violent family in that sense. My dad tends to get very violent when he's drinking. But it was my mom that kept the family together.

Consultants

The people the researcher interviews are sometimes called *consultants*. Researchers usually try to select consultants who are both reliable and representative. A reliable consultant is one who is likely to be truthful and accurate. Sometimes researchers try to become familiar with potential consultants before interviewing them, so that they can evaluate their reliability; at other times they may decide not to use interview material from a particular consultant or to use it selectively and cautiously, because they do not feel the consultant was reliable.

Another consideration in selecting consultants is how representative they are. As with quantitative research, representativeness is related to the research question. If a researcher's goal is to understand a setting, such as a school, then the researcher would want to select consultants who represent the wide range of roles and perspectives that are likely to exist in such a real-life setting—students of both genders and of various ages and backgrounds, teachers and other staff members, parents, administrators, and perhaps even cafeteria workers and maintenance personnel. On the other hand, if the researcher's goal is to understand children's attributions about their success or failure in school, then the researcher would want to select as consultants only those children who are clearly succeeding or failing in school.

Inherent in the process of selecting consultants is the issue of consultant bias. Bias is a part of real life. It occurs as a result of people's roles and vested interests. Teachers and students, for example, probably have different perspectives on final exams. People who have worked in a school for 20 years may have attitudes about changes in administrative policy that differ sharply from those of people who were hired after the policies were implemented. A school superintendent is likely to express opinions different from those of union activists regarding a proposed teachers' strike.

While it is neither possible nor desirable for researchers to find truly unbiased consultants, researchers must try to minimize the possibility that consultant bias will impair the validity of the research results. This can be done, in part, by first identifying the range of opinions that exist on issues to be explored in the project and then talking to representatives of the various factions and interests that have been identified. Failure to take into account the range of representative opinions undermines the credibility of qualitative interview data.

In addition, however, to attending to the possibility of consultant bias, the researcher must attend to the possibility of her own bias—of what has been called a virtuous subjectivity. In excluding information from consultants who are thought to be biased, the researcher may really be excluding information that does not concur with the researcher's positionality or the research project's objectives.

■ **EXERCISE 8**

In the following examples of research projects, what are some of the perspectives you would need to account for in selecting consultants?

a. the impact of federal funding on a school district
b. the impact of sex education on adolescent sexual behavior
c. reactions to the reorganization of a school district
d. racism in Native American education
e. exercise of authority in a private boys' school ■

Recording Interview Data

Interviews are usually tape-recorded and then transcribed. The advantage of this strategy is that it provides a verbatim record of the data. If the nature of the interview precludes this strategy—if, for example, the interview was unplanned and no recorder is available, or if using a recorder would make subjects uncomfortable—interviewers write up notes of each interview as soon after the interview as they can, much as observers write field notes. Some researchers video-record interviews. Working with video can be quite difficult as transcription services often are not available. The capturing of visual cues, however, makes this an option worth considering. Researchers sometimes do their own transcription of audio- or videotapes because subtle effects are otherwise lost in transcription.

Quality of Interview Data

The quality of interview data depends on the interviewer's skill and the interpersonal dynamics of the interview itself. Interview skills, like observation skills, must be learned and improve with practice. Interviewers learn how to ask questions and to probe responses. They learn to let the consultant do most of the talking. They learn how to establish trust and maintain rapport with consultants.

Extensive fieldwork provides opportunities for trust and rapport to develop over time; the personal relationships that often occur between researchers and informants in long-term projects facilitate candor in interviews. When researchers must conduct interviews without the opportunity to first establish a trusting relationship with informants, techniques are available to enhance rapport.

These techniques include such things as beginning the interview with straightforward, nonthreatening questions, such as the consultant's age, marital status, number of children, and so forth. As consultants become comfortable answering these kinds of questions, the interviewer moves to more complex and revealing questions. To maintain the consultant's comfort with the interview process, interviewers learn to be nonjudgmental in their reactions to consultants and to affirm consultants' responses and sponsor or validate consultants' feelings. These "familiarization" practices are sometimes implemented in a preliminary interview, conducted specifically to establish rapport and to evaluate the individual's suitability as a consultant. Ethical practice requires that interviewers be sensitive to consultants' feelings and know when to "back off." More than one writer on the subject of qualitative interviewing has observed that it can take on much of the flavor of a counseling session and that the skills required of a good interviewer are much like the skills required of a good counselor.

A further consideration is where the interview takes place, since the location of the interview can affect the data collected. This consideration is often discussed in terms of what is called turf. Who is in control of the turf? Is the interview taking place on the researcher's or consultant's turf? Is it shared turf—e.g., a coffee shop? If a student is interviewed in a principal's office, the data may have a different quality than if the interview took place in a local fast-food restaurant because the student may be more relaxed in the restaurant. The interview setting can also interfere with the quality of audio- or video-taping. For example, the noise level in a fast-food restaurant is sometimes high.

As with observation, characteristics of interviewers can affect the data they obtain. Some of these characteristics are beyond the interviewer's control. In a study of adolescent boys' sexual behavior, for example, a male interviewer might obtain better data than a female interviewer would. A younger interviewer might also have more success with these subjects about this topic. Larger projects often employ more than one interviewer; this gives researchers some leeway to attempt to match interviewer and consultant characteristics in ways that will enhance the accuracy and completeness of the data. The scope of smaller projects, on the other hand, sometimes is determined by probable limits on interviewer-consultant rapport. Figure 9.5 summarizes the qualitative interview process. As with qualitative observing, the analysis referred to in the figure is interim analysis, not final analysis. The figure emphasizes the fact that qualitative interviewers tend to conduct ongoing, interim analyses as they complete each interview. These interim analyses inform the direction of subsequent interviews and sometimes affect the selection of subsequent consultants.

ARCHIVAL DATA

As with quantitative research, archives or records provide data for qualitative researchers. Historical research, or historiography, is an established enterprise; in education, it is a specialty in its own right. We include it in this chapter because it is a form of qualitative research (although historians can also employ quantification in reporting results, as you learned in chapter 3). We also include it in this chapter because many qualitative researchers, while not primarily interested in historical events, utilize archives to provide part of their data. Archives are often valuable, for example, in understanding the background for a contemporary setting or issue that will be studied by observation and/or interviewing.

Schulte (1987), in her qualitative study of an adult learning center in a small community, made extensive use of observation and interviewing, but she also obtained and used many kinds of records pertaining to the center—including students' individualized prescription sheets; daily sign-in sheets; a telephone log; administrative

FIGURE 9.5   The qualitative interviewer's process.

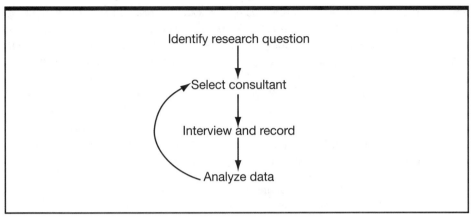

memoranda; the center's newsletter; monthly, quarterly, and annual reports; mission and goal statements; and articles from the local newspaper. Qualitative research that is explicitly historical can span the entire field of education, from biographies of individuals who have been important in educational enterprises to analyses of educational movements in the contexts of the social periods in which they occurred.

Researchers who use archival data evaluate the evidence they gather by assessing the validity of their sources. They examine the authenticity of the source; they scrutinize the author's credibility, competence, and possible biases; and they cross-reference one source with other records of the same event or issue.

A problem in the use of archives as data sources is that the researcher does not participate in the setting or with the subjects and thus has no personal sense of the data, nor can the researcher directly verify the data. In contrast, the researcher personally experiences data that are derived from observation and interviewing, and these data can be verified during the research by both the participants and the researchers.

Another problem with archival evidence is that it can be vast and time-consuming to sift through. In the field of education it would be difficult to exhaust all the relevant archival material concerning almost any topic of interest. For example, it might be possible, though formidable, to review most of the information bearing on the history of British influences on American secondary schools. But it would be impossible for even a large team of researchers to do this for the history of British influences on education in all the British colonies, which would include India, China, Africa, the United States, and the Middle East. As a result of the sheer quantity of archival evidence, researchers must usually select a sample from all the available sources.

Figure 9.6 illustrates the process of collecting qualitative archival data. As with qualitative interviewing and observing, the figure emphasizes the use of interim analyses of data to inform subsequent data collection.

■ **EXERCISE 9**

Think of a historical topic or problem in education that interests you. Try to imagine what the relevant sources of data about the topic might be. How might you sample the available sources?   ■

SELF-REPORT DATA

Self-report data are similar to archival data in that the data record is not generated by the researcher but by the research participants. Self-report data can take a variety of forms: journals or other writings of participants, responses to survey questions, and self-recorded audio- or videotapes, for example. Self-report data are often useful for particular research purposes. If one were studying preservice teachers, the teachers' professional-journal entries probably would provide useful data. The following is an example of such self-report data (Mann, Strong, and Golez, 1995, pp. 37–38).

> For the most part, my diploma will come as the result of accumulating enough credits in the right courses. Still the final grade, the grade that will culminate all of [the] long nights, will be an exhibition of this last year's knowledge.
>
> A diploma by exhibition.
>
> The wind increases. I hear autumn's last leaves rustling signaling their determination to stay the course. We are much alike the leaves and I. I have stayed the course, too.
>
> I have learned much in the last six weeks. Much about this idea of exhibiting one's knowledge. I have planned two vastly disparate units for forty children of vastly disparate abilities. I have asked them to exhibit their knowledge.
>
> And I have seen many of them, most of them passionately assail their tasks. I have seen them use the skills they have the most faith in. I have seen success where I would have predicted failure.
>
> So while my own children sleep, and the win[d] and I keep each other company. I wonder whether I will perform well.

The use of self-report data is most common in what is called collaborative research, where members of the research setting participate with the researcher as co-researchers. There is considerable controversy surrounding the use of participants as co-researchers. One of the concerns involves the credibility of self-report data, which has been criticized as highly susceptible to participant embellishment. On the other hand, without a dialogical or collaborative researcher-participant research effort, the data may lack an insider perspective. Often, too, researchers have limited time and money; in such cases, collaboration can make the research possible.

FIGURE 9.6   Steps in the archival research process.

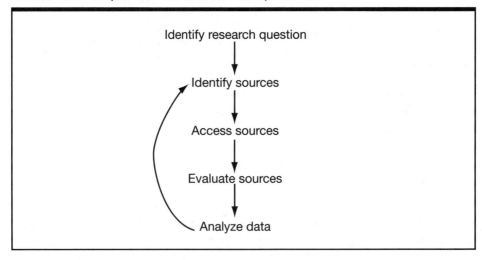

Identify research question

Identify sources

Access sources

Evaluate sources

Analyze data

SUMMARY

There are important methodological distinctions between qualitative and quantitative research. These methodological distinctions are grounded in the difference between quantity and quality reflected in researchers' assumptive modes. Qualitative research topics tend to be broader and more open-ended than do quantitative topics. Qualitative researchers use a number of data sources, often in one study: observation, interviewing, archives, and self-report.

Qualitative researchers choose foci and settings for observation. The focus of observation depends on the research question; both the question and the focus often change as the research progresses. Settings are chosen for their heuristic value and accessibility. Access to settings can be a serious problem for qualitative observers, since their research tends to be intrusive. Subjects are less willing to commit to the long-term observation that often characterizes qualitative research; as well, they often find the open-ended nature of qualitative observation threatening. Including the participant in a collaborative role sometimes alleviates these concerns.

Observers must establish a role in the settings they study. These roles may be participant and/or nonparticipant. Participant observation enhances the observer's ability to understand the setting from the perspective of an insider; however, it can also serve to identify the observer with one faction in the setting, which then tends to limit the observer's access to information about other factions. In practice, especially in long-term projects, observers tend to adopt participant roles in some contexts and nonparticipant roles in others.

Observers' degree of immersion in the setting varies with research objectives and with practical considerations. Getting valid answers to some qualitative questions requires that the observer be totally immersed in the setting—that is, that the observer live the research. Often, however, partial immersion is adequate. Spot observations can also be useful, to establish productive directions for research and to verify and extend the results of long-term observation.

Although shorter projects can make use of taped records, most qualitative observers record their observations in the form of field notes. These notes document each observation in full, describing everything that occurred within the selected focus in a way that is as complete, accurate, and unbiased as possible. Doing qualitative observation and writing field notes can be an extremely time-consuming process, but the resulting data are our best way to capture the richness and complexity of real-world settings.

Characteristics of the observer, including demographic characteristics, personality, and attitudes, can affect the quality of data. Observers must be matched to settings if good data are to be obtained. Total objectivity is neither possible nor desirable in qualitative observation; the empathy that observers often develop for their subjects can provide valuable insights into the setting. However, qualitative observers attempt to limit deleterious effects of observer bias on data.

Qualitative researchers also employ interviewing to obtain data. Sometimes interviewing is the only strategy used in a project; sometimes it is used in conjunction with observation. The focus of interviews depends on the research question. Qualitative interviews tend to be loosely structured, allowing the interviewer considerable latitude in such matters as how and when to pose questions and what topics to pursue.

The people who are interviewed are sometimes called consultants. Researchers try to select consultants who are both reliable and representative. Consultants are biased (as, of course, are researchers). Researchers compensate for this fact by selecting a variety of consultants, who represent the range of roles and interests that are relevant to the research question. Interviews are usually tape-recorded and transcribed, which provides a verbatim record of the data.

The quality of interview data depends in large part on interviewer-consultant rapport. As with observation, characteristics of interviewers can affect the data they obtain. Demographic characteristics are beyond the interviewer's control, but characteristics such as empathy can be learned.

Qualitative researchers also use archival data. Historical research in education, which is a specialty in its own right, relies primarily on archives. In projects based primarily on observation and/or interviewing, archives can be important sources of data on such things as the background of a contemporary setting or issue. Researchers who use archival data evaluate the evidence they gather by assessing the validity of their sources. Archival data, unlike data resulting from observation and interviews, cannot be verified directly by the researcher.

Related to archival research is the use of self-report data. Self-report data are generated by or in collaboration with participants. The use of self-report data is controversial.

SUMMARY EXERCISES

1. Save your responses to this exercise; you will need them for a later exercise.

a. Find any educational setting that affords you easy access. Once you have gained entry to the setting, think of a topic or some aspect of the place which interests you. Choose a focus of observation. Spend an hour watching and listening to everything that goes on within your area of interest. Try not to take notes during the observation. Then, when you write your field notes, record everything you can possibly remember about the physical setting, what people said and did, and what you experienced while you were there.

b. What have you learned about the topic you were interested in? Which events and conversations were especially informative? Did your focus shift during the observation? What would you observe next if you were going to pursue this project?

2. Read the following three excerpts from published research. You will notice that each observation takes place in a classroom. How would you describe the researcher's role in the setting? Where do shifts of focus occur? What events occur during the observation? What information does the dialogue contain? What type of research project might the data be useful for?

a. Dumont and Wax (1976, p. 213):

> They are reading about important men in history and have just finished with a section about adult educators. Teacher (referring to the observers): We have two distinguished educators here. Does this make you feel proud?
>
> It is quiet for the first time in the room. It is likely that the students are all thinking, how could we be proud of educators! As observer, I am uneasy and expectant; I wonder who will break the silence and how he will handle the delicate situation.
>
> *John:* I don't like schools myself.
> *Teacher:* Would you quit school if you could? (He's asking for it!)
> *John (a firm answer):* Yes.

Teacher: Suppose that your dad came and said you could quit, but he brought you a shovel and said, Dig a ditch from here to Brown's house, since you weren't going to school.

John: Okay.
Another student: He might learn something.

Everyone finds this humorous; the class is in good spirits and is moving along.

John, too, is quick to reply: "Might strike gold." The topic has been discussed earlier in class. (The interaction develops and others become involved, including the most reticent students.)

b. Moore (1976b, p. 244): The Afternoon Session

During the afternoon another person came to observe Mrs. Auslander's class. She came after the lunch period was over and the children were back in their room.

As the new observer came in the door, Mrs. Auslander greeted her, saying, "You see that child over there? She clings all the time. That's all she does, cling." She was referring to a Hispano girl who has a piece of cloth which she is rubbing up and down a steam pipe at the side of the room. The new observer next notices a boy sitting in the front of the room, sucking his thumb. The teacher audibly continues her discussion of the class: "This is a class of low intelligence. They have taken all the worst children in this grade and formed this class. I'm a new teacher! What do you think of the fact that I was given a class like this? All of these children are terrible problems." The observer sees the teacher has a lesson on the board but notes that there is a great deal of activity among the children. One boy is crawling on the floor looking for a nickel. Allen, the Negro youngster with crossed eyes, is sitting in the front of the room, but maintaining constant activity from his seat. Many of the children are hitting one another; a child will get up from his seat, go over to another child for no apparent reason and slap him in the face, or perhaps push him or strike his body before rushing back to his seat. These are all initial impressions made after the first few minutes in the classroom.

One boy, Angel, runs over to Allen, throws him on the floor, and jumps up on his back with both feet. Allen quite naturally screams and yells. The teacher screams too: "Get away from there!" She continues to scream and we learn the names of the two brawlers. Many children are calling out and shouting to one another across the room. As the observer looks around the room, she sees many children hitting each other on the head with pencils.[4]

c. Foley (1990, p. 86): Mexicano Views of Race Relations: Rebellious Vatos

The other group of Mexicano kids that were more hostile towards Anglos was the *vatos*. The following comments were collected during a rap session with four kids in the auto mechanics class. We had just finished tearing down the engine of my van, and I offered to buy everyone a cold drink. After much pleading for "cold ones" (a six-pack of beer) they settled for cokes. This spirited conversation ranged over many topics, but the essence of what was said about *gringos* was the following:

"We don't like *gringos* man. They act like they are superior. They ain't no better than we are. . . . Ya, they always fucking get their way in school. They get whatever like getting out of class, or detention, or something. They always got an excuse that the teachers buy. I get tired of them [he enacted a kind of whimpering, whining behavior] getting breaks. . . . They don't like us either. Most of them just put up with us. . . .

---

[4]From G. Moore. *Realities of the Urban Classroom.* Copyright © 1964, 1967, by Alexander Moore. Reprinted by permission of Doubleday and Company.

The chicks, most of the chicks aren't very friendly either. They won't go out with you. Up north Anglo chicks will go out with Mexicans. Here very few will. . . . If you drink at the Dairy Queen, Anglos will give you shit, shoot you the bird [give you the finger]. But if they come over to Hector's, we don't say nothing. . . . Naw, not many come over. We go to Dairy Queen a lot more than they come to Hector's. . . . Shit, man, they are afraid they'll get their asses kicked, if they come over to Mexican Town. It's better, really, if we each have our own place.[5]

3.   A portion of two interview transcripts follow. What does the focus of each portion seem to be? Does the portion seem to you to be more or less structured? Where does the interviewer seem to shift focus to take advantage of a lead the consultant gives? Where does the researcher show empathy?

a.   Vierra and Ford (1990)

Jeanne: Did you like school when you started in kindergarten?

Marge: Yes, a lot.

Jeanne: And did you like it by the time you finished in high school?

Marge: Yes, I think that was built up by my father cause even though he only went to third grade, he gave us newspapers to read and then he was also [a leader in the community] so we had visitors coming in and I acted as a translator also for the other people. Like now we have all kinds of people working with us, the welfare workers, social workers, and at the time I was growing up they didn't have anybody to translate for them and most of the people in the village who were receiving aid didn't speak English or barely spoke English so when those social workers came in then they would take us along. I don't know how well I did translating.

Jeanne: But you were a child. It had to be before you were ten.

Marge: Uh-huh.

Jeanne: That's a lot of responsibility.

Marge: Yes, but I liked it because I would get 50 cents or a quarter. We had all sorts of visitors I guess, and then my father would take me along on selling trips.

Jeanne: Where did you go then?

b.   Jacob (1995)

Student: The Black culture has been distorted so much that, you know Black kids go to these Hispanic things and they get upset because the Hispanic culture is a culture that hasn't been distorted. . . . So they [Hispanics] have something to believe in. We, I mean Blacks, don't have that.

Interviewer: How do you think language affects this?

Student: It's another wall to get over. . . . I think if they taught everybody. . . these languages, I don't think anybody would have a problem. I think right now it's a barrier because Black kids feel offended because none of them can speak the language that they did speak when they were in Africa or whatever you call it. None of them can speak "their" language. None of them can say that they have a language. And I can understand that, and that's what I call frustration. Because they want something to call theirs, but everything that they had, that was theirs, has been taken away.

Interviewer: Do you think that Hispanic kids have "more" culture?

Student: They have more heritage. I mean we have a heritage, but it's not as strong as the Hispanic kids 'cause they know. We don't exactly [know] where this person came from or that person came from or how Africa [started].

4. Imagine that a researcher wishes to study the growth of women's athletic programs at a major university over the past 25 years. What archival sources might provide data of interest to this researcher? What considerations might arise for the researcher in trying to evaluate the credibility of the sources? How might the researcher compensate for possible bias in the sources?

5. In examining this self-report excerpt, how would you imagine that it was used in a published report? There are several misspellings and grammatical errors in the excerpt. Should the researcher correct these? (Shethar, 1993, p. 366)

> Racism iside the system and especially in jail
> is something as I see will never end.
>   The reason being, is that because we are so
> closely confined with one another, we automatically
> tend to congragate with our own race or in some instance
> with those of our own religion
>   I also believe that the establishment use racism
> as a tool to keep us fighting among ourselves.

10

Analyzing Qualitative Data

Raw data are the immediate result of the data collection phase of research. In quantitative research, raw data are variable values. In qualitative research, raw data are such things as field notes of observations, transcripts of interviews, or notes from archival material.

Raw data, whether qualitative or quantitative, are usually too voluminous to be directly or immediately intelligible. Staring at 1,000 variable values, or 2,000 pages of field notes, or 500 pages of interview transcripts cannot tell researchers what they want to know. Raw data must be analyzed to make the information they contain accessible to researchers.

To analyze raw data means to examine them critically so as to determine their essential characteristics. As you have seen, quantitative researchers usually use statistics to do this. Qualitative researchers occasionally use statistics, too, but since most of their raw data are not quantified, statistics cannot help with the bulk of the analytic task. How, then, do qualitative researchers determine the characteristics of their data?

The answer to this question is complex. On one level, qualitative data analysis is not as programmatic as quantitative data analysis is. Qualitative researchers have many approaches to choose from for a given analytic problem, and which approach to use is often a matter of opinion. Some of the data analysis strategies that qualitative researchers use are "seat of the pants"—they feel their way as they go along and do what seems to make the most sense at a given time. Two equally competent researchers might well choose very different methods of analyzing the same qualitative data set.

In fact, many qualitative researchers have described the analysis stage of their research as the most difficult. A rule of thumb is that analyzing qualitative data can require about twice as much time as collecting the data; and, as you saw in chapter 9, collecting qualitative data is itself typically a time-consuming process. Researchers can feel overwhelmed by the sheer quantity of essentially undifferentiated raw-data material and by the lack of prescriptions for analyzing qualitative data. They often have to take some time off between data collection and analysis to achieve some perspective on the data collection experience and to restore their energy for the analysis phase. Despite the lack of standard procedures for qualitative data analysis, most analyses share some common features. In this chapter, we will concentrate on describing these common features.

INTERIM ANALYSIS

In most quantitative research the data are analyzed after all of the information has been collected. In qualitative research there is a tendency toward regular, frequent, interim analyses of data during the data collection process. During the course of data collection, qualitative researchers continually examine their notes or transcripts in an effort to avoid bias, check facts, examine their data for consistencies and inconsistencies, and discover the most salient features of their data. Data collection and interim analysis are interactive in the sense that they inform and guide one another. This interactive activity is often called a preliminary inductive analysis. One method of this continual process is termed *constant comparative analysis* (Strauss, 1987). In the constant comparative method, data collection and analysis are a continuous process.

For example, in one fieldwork project at an experimental program in a suburban high school, the researcher assumed that the teachers there would function as authorities for the students in the program. The researcher assumed that teachers would have the final say about policies such as grading, attendance, requirements, and other typical issues in high schools. Extended field observations and interviews forced the researcher to revise that assumption. The observer discovered that adult personnel refused to accept traditional role expectations and instead wanted the students to be self-directed learners and to make decisions by consensus. The issue of authority turned out to be one of the most salient and complex aspects of the setting. The researcher's assumption that teachers are necessary authorities in an educational program required radical revision as a result of data collection (Pollock, 1979).

Interim analysis informs subsequent data collection. By periodic comparison of new data with previous observations a researcher learns what areas of interest have been saturated, what shifts in focus are now appropriate, and what other areas are still in need of investigation. Questions that drive the researcher throughout this process include the following. What do I know? How can I make sure this knowledge is accurate? How do I seek out other explanations for the events I have observed? What question do I want to answer next? These questions continue for the duration of the project until the last draft of the final report is completed. In the following example, such questions led to the recognition of a significant constructed category as the interim data analysis unfolded (Golez, 1995, pp. 59–61).

> In my initial analysis of the program I had failed to recognize an embedded progressive, experiential quality. Superficially this program seemed to have all the components of a disorganized traditional teacher education program with the specialized agenda of isolated inservice and methods training. . . . My initial evaluation of these training sessions [suggested] that they illustrated the throwing of information at teachers, which I had often experienced when going through teacher training. . . . I did not recognize the undercurrent of "choice" flowing through what seemed to be just another twist on the typical teacher training program. . . . What began to emerge was that none of the participants, including myself, [was] accustomed to working in an educational setting which embraced "choice." It was difficult for me, as a researcher/former teacher, to sift through the rhetoric of a progressive pedagogical agenda. I had never really seen an experiential model in action. . . . My first inclination was to examine the program from a perspective of questioning control variables. Who exactly was in control of the program? I knew that something was different regarding the control factor in the program. As I became more familiar with experiencing a shifting paradigm, I came to realize that no one was in control, yet we all were.

Interim analysis is useful for dealing with bias that may result from spending considerable periods of time in the field setting. Submitting interim reports to impartial reviewers and colleagues helps to control the tendency to exaggerate the significance of events in the field that the researcher finds personally compelling and meaningful. Debriefings and interim reports also reduce the problem of role conflict that tends to occur in participant observation.

An option in such collaborative analysis efforts is to include the participants in what is termed a *dialogical analysis* component. The following is an example of such a dialogical approach emerging from the preliminary recognition of "choice" in the excerpt just above (Golez, 1995, p. 61).

Post program interview

Felipe: Now did you feel that it [the program] was a little bit different, that you were allowed to have input into your own [learning], not allowed but encouraged. . . ?

Elaine: Oh yeah, it was different and some students had a hard time with that. . . . I mean you go to college, you get your syllabus, this is what you do, do it this way, 250 words, blah, blah, blah, 6 pages, however and it's due and all of a sudden we're doing [anything] anyway we want. What do you mean anyway we want?

One interesting issue for qualitative researchers is when to terminate the data-collection phase of the research. Many qualitative projects are such that researchers could continue data collection almost indefinitely. Researchers' decisions to terminate data collection thus are often based on such practical considerations as having run out of time, money, opportunity, or energy for further data collection.

Typically, just at the end of the data-collection phase of their research, qualitative researchers review the data they have collected, partly to assess whether there are gaps in the data. After taking care of these gaps as they can, they formally terminate the data-collection phase of their research. This final pass through the entire set of data before terminating the data-collection phase is also the first stage of the researcher's final analysis of data; it gives the researcher a preliminary, overall sense of what the raw data have to say.

CODING, CONSTRUCTS, AND PATTERNS

In qualitative studies, large quantities of data are typically collected. Sometimes there are hundreds or even thousands of pages of notes and/or transcripts. These data usually are not organized according to a prearranged format, as in a quantitative study. Instead, they are intended to be naturalistic representations of the research context. Researchers need a systematic means of organizing and interpreting this information.

Coding

Most qualitative researchers begin analyzing this mass of material by identifying constructs, topics, or themes in the data. They examine small portions of their data and ask themselves, "What is this portion about?" Some topics emerge from the data themselves; others are predetermined by the researcher. At this early stage of analysis, researchers try to make their topics as descriptive and non-evaluative as possible, to avoid biasing the raw data.

When they begin this process of identifying topics in their data, researchers may have a predetermined set of possible topics in mind. Some of these topics are derived from the research questions and objectives; others grow out of interim analyses. In examining each small portion of the data, researchers ask themselves whether this bit of data is relevant to any of the predetermined topics or suggests new ones.

Qualitative researchers are aware that focusing exclusively on predetermined topics can cause them to overlook important topics that they could not predict. In identifying topics in their raw data, qualitative researchers usually want at least some of their topics to be suggested by the data themselves. Thus, in addition to searching for examples of predetermined topics, qualitative researchers also try to examine each small portion of their data with an open mind. They ask themselves such questions as: "What was going on here?" "What were these people doing or saying?" "What was important in this setting at this time about this small piece of data?" As topics occur in the raw data, the researcher usually notes each occurrence in some way, often by making an entry in the margin of the notes or transcript. To save time, researchers usually develop a brief code to represent each topic. Here is a coded excerpt from a transcript of an interview in a study of 20 American Indian women's perceptions of their formal educational experiences (Vierra and Ford, 1990). Note that the same material in the transcript is sometimes given more than one code.

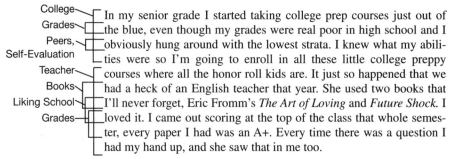

College
Grades
Peers,
Self-Evaluation
Teacher
Books
Liking School
Grades

In my senior grade I started taking college prep courses just out of the blue, even though my grades were real poor in high school and I obviously hung around with the lowest strata. I knew what my abilities were so I'm going to enroll in all these little college preppy courses where all the honor roll kids are. It just so happened that we had a heck of an English teacher that year. She used two books that I'll never forget, Eric Fromm's *The Art of Loving* and *Future Shock*. I loved it. I came out scoring at the top of the class that whole semester, every paper I had was an A+. Every time there was a question I had my hand up, and she saw that in me too.

Field notes from observational studies are also coded. Here is a coded excerpt from field notes from an observational study of fourth-grade classrooms (Goetz and LeCompte, 1984, p. 186). There are several elements to this coding system. First, teacher talk is designated in quotation marks; student talk and behavior are designated in parentheses; second, a system of letters and numbers identifies the locations of the actors; finally, the type and time of activity are indicated in the left margin.

(Children are playing outside the classroom; a few are standing on the porch. The teacher arrives.)

8:55		"Come in, girls first." (There's some messing around before they line up.) (They come in and move toward
8:57		their seats.)
	T2A	(T2A) "Mrs. Smith is ready to start."
getting settled	R1A	(She's sitting on the desk in the front of the room.)
	R2B	(R1A) "Mrs. Smith is waiting." (R2B) "I like the way
	R1A	Bernie is sitting down, and Atocha." (R1A) "Please, people, do not throw snowballs at one another."
	R4B	(R4B) "There isn't enough snow on the ground and you pick up rocks with it. If we have a lot of snow we'll have a snowball fight, but please don't throw the snow when
	R4A	there isn't much—" (R4A) "If you go along with me and don't throw now, as soon as there's good stuff we'll have
	R4B	a snowball fight." (R4B) "It isn't just that you hurt people, but you'll get in trouble too."
9:03	T2A	(T2A) "All right, the girls will go to bake cookies at recess." (W1B) "Boys, come back here if you aren't done; if you can't work alone you can go into Mrs. Dvorak's game room."

getting	W2B	(W2B) "I expect if you come in here to work I expect
organized	R1A	you to work." (R1A) "I want everybody to bring a nickel
		by Monday." (Is it for the girls' surprise?) "No, it's for
		everybody."

■ EXERCISE 1

a. Here is an excerpt from published field notes. Code the excerpt in the margin to identify the type of behavior (verbal or nonverbal) and the actor (teacher or student). Code each unit of behavior as *SV* (student verbal), *SN* (student nonverbal), *TV* (teacher verbal), or *TN* (teacher nonverbal).

Lilly stands up out of her seat. Mrs. Caplow asks Lilly what she wants. Lilly makes no verbal response to the question. Mrs. Caplow then says rather firmly to Lilly, "Sit down." Lilly does. However, Lilly sits sideways in the chair in order to see the writing on the blackboard. Mrs. Caplow instructs Lilly to "turn around and put your feet under the table." This Lilly does. Now she is facing directly away from the teacher and the blackboard where the teacher is demonstrating to the students how to print the letter "O." There is no way that Lilly can now see what the teacher is writing. (Rist, 1973, pp. 161–162)

b. A portion of an interview transcript is presented below. Do any of the following predetermined topics come up in this portion?

- financial matters
- activities
- peers
- romantic relationships

Does the excerpt suggest other topics that were not on the predetermined list? Code the excerpt in the margin as fully as possible, using topics from the predetermined list as well as additional topics that are suggested by the data.

I did most of my sports in high school. I was into basketball and volleyball and track. They took us all over the place and that was fun, going to compete at all these schools. When I went to my first year at Utah State we formed a girls' basketball team up there. We had a great coach from Oklahoma and we had a lot of fun, too. Down in California I was a Candy Striper, I did volunteer work at an old age home. I must have been a tenth grader and I would go after school to these old age homes and spend a couple of hours there during their dinner time helping them, feeding them, taking them here and there, things like that. Sports is actually the only thing I've been into. I don't have any kind of musical talent, just dancing, that's just about it. That's one thing if I could turn back time I would have liked to specialize in a certain instrument but I think because of my background it was never a priority. (Vierra and Ford, 1990)

c. Conduct an initial wide-lens observation of a public area where people interact: e.g., the student union, a grocery store, or a laundromat. Take observational field notes, mapping the area and recording an overall census. From these field notes, conduct a preliminary analysis of this data. Design a coding system to conduct this analysis. What categories, patterns, and constructs emerge from your analysis? If a classmate conducts an observation in the same setting, compare your data and initial findings to examine the credibility of your findings. An alternative to this would be to work in observational teams. ■

Constructs

Once topics have been identified in the raw data, researchers begin to organize these topics into constructs. Researchers ask themselves such questions as, "What topics seem to be recurring? What topics seem to belong together?" These constructs can be characteristics of the setting or informants, types of activities, kinds of participants, attitudes, or anything else that seems to characterize a set of similar topics. As with topics, constructs can emerge from the data, or researchers can have a set of predetermined constructs that they search for examples of in the data.

From field-note excerpts like the following, Lortie identified a construct: how teachers decide what works for them in the classroom (1975, p. 78):

> This is the only valid way of learning how to teach—by getting in and doing it. You can observe and watch to see what someone else is doing but it doesn't mean it is going to work for you. [#38 F-35-3d]

> Really, trial and error. . . and then asking others and talking and listening to them. I like to listen because they are so completely different and I try to take what I think will help me from each of them. [#9 F-23-2d]

> I don't think there's any way around trial and error . . . not that you do it any old way. . . . But you have to experiment and find a way to teach which is best for you so that you're not under strain and that's easiest for the children. . . . No one can give you a lesson plan and say go to it this way because what works for one may be poor for another. [#47 F-32-1st]

> Thinking of some of the successful teachers, teachers who appeal to me and who also fit my personality or at least I think fit my personality. Observing methods that other teachers use and my own application of them, fitting them to my personality. [11 M-41-Science]

In her interview transcripts, Ford (1989) found examples, including the following, of a construct: negative feelings in adolescence about parents' sexuality.

> I heard [my parents having sex] one time when I was sneaking out of the house, and I was about 14 years old. I found it very upsetting. . . . For two or three days after that, you know, looking at them, and my heart would start to race, and I thought, "Oh, no." (p. 170)
>
> So when I finally realized that [my parents] did [have sexual intercourse]. . . I was 12 years old. . . . Somehow it's like it all came together, and I remember I got up from the dinner table and went out in the back yard and spent a long time out there by myself thinking. . . . [I]t freaked me out. I didn't like it. (p. 171)

The following interviewing and field-note excerpts from Spatig and Bickel (1993) indicate how difficult it is for students in a college course to understand their professor.

> My impression is that Bill. . . . is talking so fast and is talking about issues so complex and using vocabulary so sophisticated that most students feel unable to meaningfully participate on a regular basis. (2-17-89) [fieldnote]

> . . .[I]n class he used a large vocabulary. Some words I knew, but sometimes I didn't understand to be quite honest. . . . [Did you ask about it?] Sometimes I did, but I usually just tried to figure it out. I think someone said something about it once and he said that he would try to fix it, and he did a little. (Interview: 5-12-89)

> He talks on a level that's above your head and that's a good thing. . . . He shows his education. He speaks above your head and makes you pay attention. I think I could sit down and have a conversation with someone in higher education now and maybe not be lost, after spending a semester with him. (Interview: 5-1-89)

Triangulation

An important technique in qualitative data analysis is called *triangulating*. Triangulating refers to the researcher's checking topics and constructs derived from one source against another source or sources. If two participants independently mention something, that topic seems more likely to be valid than if only one participant had mentioned it. For example, if two teachers independently refer to the principal's unavailability, then it seems more likely that the principal is, at least under some circumstances, unavailable to faculty. If, in addition, the researcher has observed the principal's unavailability, the existence of this phenomenon is further validated.

Qualitative researchers are encouraged to triangulate. A common form of this is sometimes known as member checking or member identification (Hammersly and Atkinson, 1992, p. 51). As the researcher develops topics and constructs, it is wise to check them out with the research participants. A researcher who is coming to believe that the principal is unavailable might ask other faculty, or the principal herself, about this. Not only can such member checking confirm or disconfirm the validity of a suspected construct, but additional information often can be obtained—e.g., information about the particular circumstances under which the principal is and is not available to faculty, and perhaps even reasons for this.

Emic–Etic Distinctions

Constructs that researchers use to organize data can be described as either *emic* or *etic*. *Emic* refers to an insider's view. An emic construct would include folk concepts and explanations that are distinctive to that setting. *Etic*, on the other hand, pertains to the outsider's view of a scene. An etic construct would contain the observer's concepts and scientific explanations.

Qualitative researchers tend to have an emic emphasis in collecting data, because the goal is usually to represent the situation from an insider's point of view. In developing topics and constructs to analyze qualitative data, researchers sometimes attempt to continue to employ the participants' ways of thinking to describe and explain what takes place. This could include a dialogical component, where the participants are actively involved in an aspect of data collection or analysis, or it might mean triangulating, where emerging constructs are checked against the participants' own interpretations. Emic constructs are explanations of what an event or some other phenomenon means to the participant.

In grouping raw-data topics into categories, Parrott used an emic approach; the following categories represent how second-grade children in Parrott's study described the things they do in recess (1972, p. 214):

Recess Activities

Games	*Goofing Around*	*Tricks*
Keepaway	Runnin' around	Getting someone
Hot box	Making faces on trees	Tripping someone
Relay races	Sucking icicles	Looking under a
Races	Fighting	girl's skirt
Fire red	Talking	Splashing someone
Kick the can	Making fun of people	Smashing a
Ditch	Somersaulting into	snowball on
Chase	snow	someone's head

Frisby	Jumping into piles of	Tapping someone
Girls catch the boys	snow	and hiding
Catch (2)	Sliding down the slide	Stealing a stocking
Avalanche	into snow	cap
Catch (1)	Sliding down the slide	
Throw sweater at wall	when it is covered with ice	

In other research using an emic approach to data analysis, an observer asked "kindergarten children to tell her all of the things they thought they and their teachers could do in kindergarten. From their responses, a typology of children's perceptions of student and teacher roles was developed" (Goetz and LeCompte, 1984, p. 123).

Educational researchers who are interested in cognitive development frequently ask children to sort items, group objects, and put similar things together. The purpose of the activity is to discover emic constructs, or conceptual frameworks, that exist in the children's minds.

In contrast, an etic construct reflects what an event or phenomenon means to the researcher. Etic constructs are explanations that researchers take with them into their field settings. These constructs are part of the observer's own baggage of personal and cultural experiences—e.g., work, school, play, or family. They also include concepts from a researcher's academic orientation, such as culture, social role, neurosis, and underachievement. Etic constructs are imposed on the data by outsiders.

Doyle wished to develop a set of etic constructs of activities that took place in a third-grade classroom (1972, pp. 150–151). Here are the constructs that were found in the raw data. Note the difference between these etic classroom constructs and the emic recess constructs that were identified by Parrott in the example above.

Activities or Actions

A. Working
  1. Doing science
  2. Doing social studies
  3. Doing reading
  4. Doing math
  5. Doing music
  6. Doing spelling
  7. Correcting morning papers
  8. Doing writing
  9. Taking a speed test
B. Doing extra activities
  1. Doing art
  2. Making scrapbooks
  3. Making pictures
  4. Making things for the room
  5. Writing poems
  6. Writing stories
C. Playing games
  1. Playing 7-Up
  2. Playing Eraser-Pass-Back
  3. Playing Eraser-on-the-Head
  4. Playing Hangman
  5. Playing Flying Dutchman
  6. Playing kickball
  7. Playing baseball
  8. Playing Dog Catcher
  9. Playing Changers
D. Having lunch
E. Having lavatory break
F. Having gym
G. Having show and tell
H. Choosing new officers
I. Reading *Reader's Digest*

Etic constructs are determined by the researcher, and data are organized around them. For instance, an etic approach would find the researcher requesting children to put round objects in a pile or to distinguish jungle animals from household pets. Similarly, students in education are sometimes asked to observe nurturing behavior or examples of emotional disorders or social interaction. In these cases, essential characteristics of each construct are determined beforehand. The task of the observer is to find examples which have those characteristics.

Although qualitative field research is primarily concerned with emic constructs in data collection, etic explanations are important in data analysis. Etic constructs are employed in the design of the project and in the interpretation of results. Etic explanations belong to a larger universe than do emic constructs and, thus, are essential for making a distinctive social setting comprehensible and meaningful to people outside. Emic constructs enable researchers to understand how people within an organization perceive their world, and they help researchers explain those perceptions to other people.

■ EXERCISE 2

Read the following excerpts from field notes[1] (Lortie, 1975, pp. 138–139). What constructs can you derive from these examples?

> Of course I test a great deal. In arithmetic, I test very often. I see each child work at the board every single day and then we have a test, if not every day, every other day so that I know what they can do. [#660 F-59-6th]

> If I give an examination and I find 40 or 50 percent of my class didn't get it, I know I should do more teaching. [#40 M-46-Eng., Hist.]

> I test, see if they're making improvement. . . . I'm never satisfied with normal improvement. I'd like it a little more because if you teach it right, they will do better than normal. [#21 F-56-Reading]

> How well they respond, when they do their work papers and I ask questions and they answer them intelligently—then I know—well, I guess I'm getting it across. . . . We compare notes with other teachers, what they're doing, how well advanced they are, what their first group is doing and so on and so forth. [#20 F-24-1st]

> One way, of course, is tests. Almost any questions the students ask. If they volunteer to come in after school. A lot of little things. [#24 M-33-Business]

> If the class is not attentive I feel that I'm not doing a good job . . . perhaps I am not making it as interesting as it could be. [#87 F-52-English]

> I think if I have a quiet, busy roomful of children. I think if they're happy in their work and everybody is really accomplishing something then I feel that I have had a good day and I've really accomplished something . . . the fact that children can settle down and work by themselves and . . . be happy in their work and their room. [#59 F-58-1st) ■

Patterns

As constructs develop, researchers look for patterns or relationships among them. In searching for patterns, researchers try to understand the complex links between various aspects of people's environment, mental processes, and behavior. They ask themselves how constructs affect and are affected by other categories. In the following excerpt the author explains how he perceived a pattern (Grindal, 1974, p. 368).

---

[1]From D. Lortie, *Schoolteacher: A Sociological Study.* Chicago, IL: University of Chicago Press. Copyright ©1975. Used with permission of the Publisher.

The following statements demonstrate the relationship between the student's awareness of his poverty and his desire to achieve:

"When I have finished my schooling, I will sit down and think of the time when I was in middle school. And when I think of how poor I was and how I suffered, I will laugh at myself. For now I will have left the university. I will be a very rich man, and I will be sending some of the money home to my family. And there were those people who laughed at me when I was poor. But someday they will see me driving in a fine car, and they will be sorry. Maybe too, they will also be poor; and when they see me, they will ask for money. But I was as poor as anything once and God helped, so I will help anyone as poor as I was."

In her study of an adult learning center, Schulte found the following patterns in the students' first contact with the center (1987, p. 80):

Students often entered the Coalsville Adult Education classroom appearing uncertain and confused. A teacher usually approached the individual student and offered help. Frequently, the student was seeking information about the classes or about what services were available. Quite often new students came in with friends, and it was quite common for enrolled students to bring in friends and family members to register. Other students were brought in by social workers or counselors.

In the following example the authors describe their perceptions of a recurring pattern (Spatig and Bickel, 1993, p. 56). Note that the authors indicate that their pattern identification is validated by participants—i.e., "consistent with. . .the students."

Our understandings, based on classroom observations and course material, were consistent with those of the students. A major focus of class discussion and readings concerned the relationship between what goes on in schools and social inequalities. The following excerpt is typical of countless fieldnote entries:

"Bill began to talk about the impact of schooling on social inequalities. He read an excerpt from the Coleman report which states that 'schools bring little influence to bear on a child's achievement which is independent of his background and general social context.' Bill went on to talk about the school's inability to sever ties between socially-ascribed traits and achievement. Then he asked about the implications of this for our view of American society as a meritocracy."

Vierra and Ford (1990) found a number of patterns in their study of high-school dropouts and college graduates. One of these patterns was that pregnancy was often associated with dropping out of high school, but that the dropouts already had a long history of difficulty with school by the time they became pregnant and dropped out.

■ EXERCISE 3

Read the following three excerpts from published field notes from a study of students at the beginning of college (Geer, 1969, pp. 151 and 156, respectively) and students interacting in a college class (Spatig and Bickel, 1993, p. 58). What patterns do the researchers believe exist in their data?

a.   I think that this one afternoon and evening has given us some idea of the friend-making process at the beginning of college. When you see it happening under your nose this way, it seems so natural that I wonder why we ever had any questions about it. I think you could make a typology somewhat as follows: There are the students who come from the same high schools or nearby towns and have some acquaintance with each other, and if there is a small number of these they get together and stay together, at least at the beginning of school. It is probable, for instance, that Tom, Dick, Harry . . . from (a small town) will room together in some combination. Those students who come from Kansas City can get together rather easily, although they have come from different schools, by placing each other by means of country clubs, addresses, and boys they have dated.

b. It is quite clear that the . . . students are unprepared for this wealth of competition for their time, this wealth of choice, and I would say that probably only the ones with something very specific in mind are going to get over the realization of this variety as a painful and difficult thing when it comes to them after they arrive. This is really a prediction, I suppose, and I feel that it is reinforced by their earnestness and wanting to do well in their studying and have their family be proud of them, which is going to set up a conflict between all these fascinating things and their rather weak direction in themselves. They want to study, but they don't know what and they don't know how much. They are earnest and sincere, but they have no guideposts. They look to me at the moment like . . . a bunch of very sweet lambs being led into a slaughter of decisions to make, pressures to withstand, and moral fiber to reinforce. And yet many of them speak regretfully of their casual high-school years, and you get the strong flavor of missed opportunities and lack of foresight.

c. The fieldnotes below describe a typical class session:

"As Bill pushed for a comment about the Lortie article, the silence became more and more noticeable. 'What about the Lortie article? Did it make sense?' Silence. 'Was it consistent with what you know?' Silence. 'What does it say about teachers as a group?' Silence. (2-3-89)"

■

For qualitative researchers, the process of identifying topics, constructs, and patterns in their data is akin to the quantitative researcher's process of statistical analysis of variables. The purpose is to reduce large quantities of data to manageable, intelligible units and to discern relationships among these units. Figure 10.1 illustrates the process of analyzing qualitative data that we have outlined in this chapter: identifying topics in the raw data, then constructs of topics, and finally patterns among constructs. The detail which this process reflects can vary widely. It is highly dependent on the researcher's position along an enumerative-constructive continuum. Researchers can approach qualitative analysis with intensive detail, coding every element in field notes and discourse. These elements can be tabulated for frequency to establish constructs and patterns, giving the analysis an enumerative quality. Or researchers can look at broader constructs, or *chunks* of significant interactions. In this case, though patterns may be recurring they have a broader quality, with often overlapping significance. This broader construct analysis is not specific or precise. This is said to mirror the nature of human behaviors and interactions, which rarely unfold into precisely broken down linear pieces. In this case, coding and analysis are considered *open*.

Computers

For many years, computers were the province of quantitative researchers and were rarely used to assist in the analysis of qualitative data. Now, however, there are a number of computer programs that allow qualitative researchers to enter their raw data and codes.

FIGURE 10.1   Topics, constructs, and patterns.

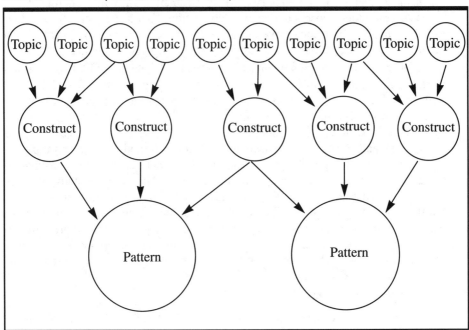

Computers can expedite a qualitative researcher's task of finding categories in topics and patterns in categories. Using a computer, a qualitative researcher can sort an entire raw-data file according to topic codes. The researcher can look, for example, at what every informant had to say about a particular topic, or at every context in which a particular behavior occurred. This makes the researcher's job of discerning constructs and patterns in large amounts of material considerably easier.

You may at this point be seeing similarities between qualitative and quantitative research. Qualitative researchers deal with topics, constructs, and patterns; quantitative researchers deal with variables, values, and relationships. Certainly there is a similarity between qualitative researchers' constructs and patterns, and quantitative researchers' variables and relationships: Qualitative researchers seek to understand how constructs pattern; quantitative researchers seek to understand how variables are related. Both enterprises can yield greater understanding of real-world events, including cause and effect.

However, there is an important difference between the two approaches. Quantitative research typically starts with a theory or at least a hypothesis about the relationship between variables. These variables are identified and isolated for study before the data collection begins. In qualitative research, topics, constructs, and patterns more often emerge from the data.

REPORTING RESULTS

Quantitative researchers use statistical techniques to discover patterns in their data—for example, that students in program *A* like school more than do students in program *B*. In reporting their research results, quantitative researchers describe the patterns they found and support their conclusions by providing tables that summarize their statistical analyses of data.

Qualitative researchers use other techniques to discover patterns in their data. Like quantitative researchers, they report the patterns they found. To support their conclusions, they typically provide examples of the raw data that led them to these conclusions.

The results of a single qualitative study are usually lengthy and complex. But the following excerpts from qualitative research reports will give you some idea of the kind of reporting and defending of conclusions that is typical in qualitative research.

The first excerpt is from a study by Elizabeth Eddy (1976, pp. 430–431) of beginning teachers. This excerpt has to do with the influence of the new teachers' student-teaching experience on their first year of teaching.

> The formal socialization provided by courses in education is culminated by student teaching, which is intended to facilitate the transition of students from those who think and act like students to those who think and act like teachers. Student teaching is a cooperative venture between the teacher training institutions and conveniently located school systems. The students are placed in a particular school or schools on a full- or part-time basis for a period of several months. In the school, they work under the direction of one or more cooperating teachers, with occasional supervisory visits from a faculty member in the training institution.
>
> During this transitional period of student teaching, the students observe and act out the behaviors they are eventually to assume as teachers. Clerical work, lesson planning, practice teaching, classroom management, and other tasks which teachers perform are assigned to them in varying degrees. The students are observed while teaching, evaluations of them are recorded, and suggestions for improvement of teaching techniques are given to them in supervisory conferences. The students nearly always do well enough that the teacher training institution officially states that they are prepared to teach and declares them deserving of a new status in the educational system.
>
> The circumstances under which student teaching eases the transition from the role of student to that of teacher, and the extent to which it does so, are not empirically known. Yet it seems clear that important learnings about the role of teacher do occur during student teaching and that this time may be particularly useful for the transmission of written and oral traditions about teaching from one generation of teachers to the next. As the following examples indicate, the handing down of written materials, teaching techniques, and classroom management procedures provides a means for the communication of the traditions, beliefs, and customs of the more experienced teachers in the school.
>
>> I had Mrs. LaSalle as a cooperating teacher when I student taught in the school, and she gave me a copy of her plan book, and I've been using this as a guide. It just happens to be a very good plan book, and she happens to be an excellent teacher, so I have talked with her, and I'm copying her style of doing it.
>>
>> I'm using this method of teaching reading now because when I student taught it was the method the teacher was using, and naturally because I don't know any other really. You know, you copy their methods because you're there to learn from these teachers and it worked well with her.
>>
>> Last year when I student taught, the teacher gave me a whole bunch of rexographs that she had used, and I took them home. I've been using some of them.
>>
>> It's from the school that I developed my methods of teaching—from the student teaching. I watched how the other teachers did it, and the assistant principal told me how she wanted it done.

It is very important for a teacher to always be on her guard and to be very, very strict the first weeks of school. This is something which many people will tell a young teacher, or this is something that we have heard constantly while we were student teaching. This is not to smile for the whole first month of school, not even to smile at all, not to let them get away with anything, and to hold on very tight. Only after you have the children disciplined can you begin to let go. . . .

There is one thing I learned about a slow class from my student teaching experience. You absolutely cannot teach a slow class anything until you have complete control of that class. I saw my cooperating teacher take period after period just to tell her class and yell at them that they should be quiet, and that they should really obey the rules of the school. This lecturing really did pay off because the class knew she meant business, and she followed up everything she said, and they worked for her.

I learned from my cooperating teacher that it's a good idea to have everything removed from the desks, because this way they can concentrate on you. If there are any notebooks or papers or pens or pencils, they tend to start playing with them. This way they have nothing to do but keep their hands on their lap or on their desks and look at you.[2]

The second excerpt is from a study by Harry Wolcott (1976, pp. 452–453) of the elementary-school principalship. Wolcott conducted the study by focusing on a principal whom he called Ed. In this excerpt, Wolcott deals with how new principals are selected.

The candidate who aspires to the principalship has already tacitly demonstrated that he recognizes and accepts the authority system of the school. The process of socialization into teaching tends to assure that candidates who can survive can live with the educational hierarchy. Advancing up the "ladder" requires more than simply acquiescing to the system, however. One must actively demonstrate willingness and aptitude for assuming greater responsibility. In the parlance of educational administration, such people are sometimes referred to as GASers.

GASing behavior, or Getting the Attention of Superiors, describes a style of teacher behavior characteristic of the teacher seeking to move up and out of the classroom. GASing refers particularly to a teacher's taking additional school-related but nonteaching assignments as a strategy to increase his visibility from among the teacher group at large. The consequence of being a successful GASer is that one becomes known to those people who are in a position to make or directly influence promotions or to lend indirect support as sponsors. . . .

The GASing syndrome appeared to be quite familiar to principals and to would-be principals alike, although the term itself was not used in the district. . . .

Ed and his colleagues recognized and discussed the GASing behavior exhibited by aspiring candidates among the district's elementary school teachers. Ed was appointed to a Principal Selection Committee to recommend to the superintendent and school board the "best people" among the eligible candidates for three principalships opening up the following fall (Wolcott n.d.). During the deliberations of the committee, comments were frequently made indicating a sensitivity toward the amount of GASing behavior each candidate had engaged in as well as an assessment of whether the extent of GASing was appropriate for the particular candidate. For example, Ed's assessment of one candidate, a young man who had attained considerable visibility and was suspected of seeking too much power in the internal organization of the school district, was, "I see too many people ahead of him myself." Ed had stated a similar opinion in more detail a few months earlier after attending a meeting in which that teacher had taken a domineering role:

> He's already a resource teacher, and I think this is only his third year in the district. This fellow just doesn't want to wait his turn, that's all. He's trying to get in good with Boggs [the superintendent]. It's not that there is actually a seniority system in selecting principals, but there are a lot of qualified fellows who have been around longer than he has.

Of another candidate apparently not in high favor, one principal's assessment hinted that too little talent in personal dynamics had been exhibited: "I worked closely with him on that big evaluation project. He wasn't loud and forceful, but he did do a good job." Still other candidates were perceived as having tried too hard. The written recommendation of one woman principal reviewed by the selection committee warned that the candidate had done "too much of the business of the local teachers' association" when he should have been attending to his responsibilities as the school's resource teacher. Another woman principal expressed concern about a candidate from her staff: "I think his one big problem is relating to people because he tends to want to move too fast."

Some candidates had apparently managed to exhibit the appropriate degree of GASing. Ed offered this appraisal in support of a candidate whom he felt would be an excellent principal: "He has dealt with some difficult situations very well as the committee chairman in the Teachers Association. He has a real ability to make his leadership felt." The other members of the committee joined in unanimous agreement regarding the candidate in question, capped by an endorsement from the Director of Elementary Education, "I used to think of him as a guy who just 'went along,' but I see him differently now." From the candidate's point of view, her comments could be interpreted as the successful culmination to all his efforts as a GASer, not only to getting the attention of superiors, but to getting that attention to the proper extent and for the right reasons.[3]

The third excerpt is from a study dealing with how ethnicity is a flowing, negotiated social process in academic settings. Davidson, Yu, and Phelan (1993, pp. 80–81) examine how a high-school student negotiates ethnicity at home and school.

Carla, a Mexican/Cuban American sophomore, moves between two sociocultural worlds. At home and during her freetime at school, Carla spends time with her working-class family and Mexican-descent peers, speaking Spanish and English. According to Carla, talk with her Latino friends centers around relationships, feelings, and personal affairs. School is rarely discussed. Carla says that she feels most comfortable around these friends, because their values are similar to her own:

> "We listen to the same music, you know, we talk about the same things, like on a similar subject kind of. . .I don't know, I guess how our parents, you know, had brought you up. It's different and stuff. It's a different life that we live."

During school, Carla moves into high track classes dominated by European- and Asian-American students. Carla's conversations with her class friends center on school: how to get on a teacher's good side, what needs to be done to prepare for the SAT, how to best complete a homework assignment, teacher characteristics and

---

[3]From H. Wolcott. "Maintaning the System: The Socialization of a Principal." In J. Roberts and S. Akinsanya (Eds.). *Schooling in the Cultural Context.* Copyright © 1973 by Holt, Rinehart and Winston, Inc. Used by permission of the Author.

personalities. Grades on assignments and tests are often compared. Carla's behavioral shifts and conformity to classroom norms have helped her succeed in a highly competitive environment. She earned a 4.0 GPA during her freshman year and 3.5 GPA during the first semester of her sophomore year.

For Carla ethnicity is an eddy in which she rests and recharges emotionally, but which she leaves to succeed academically. On the one hand. . .Carla conceives of her ethnicity primarily in terms that are oppositional to others' low expectations. When asked how she feels about her heritage, she replies:

"Well, I'm proud of it. I feel that, you know, that Latins aren't stupid. I'd like to be one of them that could achieve something. Cause most people think that Latins aren't—you know, that they can't do nothing, that they're just going to become like in the lower class. And, I think that that's not true. I think that everybody's the same. You can do anything you want to."

Achieving academically is a strategy Carla uses to prove what she knows by experience—that Latinos "aren't stupid." However, Carla does not equate aspects of her Latina self with her academic success, nor does she reveal her ethnic self in the classroom. Over the 15 months that we knew Carla, lunch time was the only time where she revealed the linguistic aspects of her cultural background or talked about her home life and personal concerns. While Carla believes that "you can work among white people without being white," she leaves her ethnicity outside the classroom door, adopting a "situated" (Spindler and Spindler, 1989) classroom persona that speaks standard English, works individually, and divorces her personal experience from the classroom:

"You don't really share your personal life with them, cause you really aren't, you know, the culture isn't quite [the same]. We don't talk about that. We just talk about school or school things. We just talk about school."[4]

THE CREDIBILITY OF QUALITATIVE RESEARCH METHODS

Quantitative researchers have long concerned themselves with the credibility of their research methods. They have formalized credibility concerns in such terms as reliability, validity, and generalizability, and they routinely criticize their own and others' methods with respect to these kinds of considerations. Qualitative researchers have tended to be less concerned with formalizing issues surrounding the credibility of their research methods. This is partly because qualitative methods themselves are less formalized than are quantitative methods. However, as qualitative approaches gain wider acceptance, qualitative researchers are increasingly turning their attention to formalizing their approaches; this in turn fosters increasing attention to formalizing discussion of the credibility of qualitative research approaches.

As Goetz and LeCompte (1984) point out, addressing the credibility of qualitative research methods overall and of the particular methods employed in a given study requires a different approach from that taken by quantitative researchers. However, the ultimate issues are similar. The first issue is whether the conclusions drawn from a given piece of empirical work are essentially valid conclusions for the situation that was studied; in quantitative terms, this relates to the internal validity of the study. The second issue is how the conclusions drawn from a given piece of empirical

---

[4]From A. Davidson, H. Yu, and P. Phelan. "The Ebb and Flow of Ethnicity: Constructing Identity in Various School Setttings." *Educational Review*, Vol. 7, pp. 65–87, ©1993. Used by permisssion of Carafax Publishing, P.O. Box 25, Abingdon, Oxfordshire OX14 3UE, United Kingdom.

work relate to a wider context than the one that was studied; in quantitative terms, this relates to the external validity of the study.

With respect to internal validity, the involvement of qualitative researchers with the research context is usually much broader and deeper than that of quantitative researchers. For this reason, one of the major threats to the internal validity of qualitative research is often the researcher himself. The researcher's personality and mere physical presence affect the participants and thus the data that are collected, and the researcher's positionality affects his perspectives on those data. Most qualitative researchers try to minimize these constraints, to the degree possible, and to keep them in mind when analyzing their data. The breadth and depth of their involvement with the setting and participants also provides qualitative researchers with opportunities that quantitative researchers typically don't have to discover and remedy threats to the internal validity of their conclusions.

Imagine a quantitative study in which a research assistant spends a half hour in each of a number of classrooms in a high school administering a test. Unknown to the researcher, a number of students who dislike taking tests and have no stake in the outcome of this testing have hatched a plot to answer the multiple-choice questions randomly. The research results will thus be invalid; but it is unlikely that the researcher will be aware of this.

A qualitative researcher in a similar situation would have spent most of the year in the school. She would have established relationships with many teachers and students and would thus be likely to hear about such a plot. She would also be attuned to the students' normal behavior and therefore in a position to see their behavior around this testing as deviating from normal. In this way, she might just discover the plot herself.

Qualitative methods do not lend themselves to the kinds of highly structured controls of internal validity (e.g., random assignment) that are possible in some quantitative research. However, techniques are available to qualitative researchers for strengthening the credibility of their conclusions about patterning in their data. Typically, qualitative researchers attempt to verify the internal validity of patterns by triangulating and by searching their data carefully for information that would disconfirm the pattern.

This is one of the reasons that qualitative researchers often employ multiple methods of data collection and analysis. If field notes suggest a pattern, then interview transcripts can be reviewed to see whether they offer information that would tend to confirm or disconfirm the existence of this pattern. Additional interviews and observations may also be conducted to check on this. Suppose that during classroom observation a researcher notices that the teacher speaks more harshly to girls than to boys. Further observation reinforces the researcher's suspicion of a pattern of differential treatment of students by the teacher on the basis of gender. Later, from interviews with other students and teachers, the researcher learns that this teacher has a reputation for being tougher on girls than on boys. A follow-up interview with the classroom teacher reveals that she believes that "girls have always been treated too leniently, and not enough has ever been expected of them in school. In my class they will have to toe the mark."

The researcher next examines her data carefully for information that is contrary to this interpretation—information that this teacher does not treat girls and boys differently. No such negative data are found. The researcher is now able to suggest with some confidence that preferential treatment based on gender exists in that teacher's classroom.

When a qualitative researcher begins to see a pattern in her data, she will try to obtain confirmation of her thinking from other people. If others have been involved in the collection of data, they can be asked for their perspectives. Or an insider informant could be consulted. Or a colleague could be asked to review and critique the researcher's conclusions. With respect to external validity, wide generalizability of research results is rarely attainable in any single study and is typically achieved only after many separate studies have been done on similar issues. In fact, the findings of any single study are usually too narrow to generalize widely; rather, in further studies, we learn under what conditions the results of a single study apply and under what conditions they do not apply. This is as true of quantitative as of qualitative research and will be discussed more fully in chapter 11.

In considering the external validity of any single study, two separate issues must be considered. The first is replicability of research methods; the second is replicability of findings. These must be distinguished because even when methods are replicated, findings can be different; and we are not surprised when different methods yield different findings.

Quantitative methods are easier to replicate than qualitative, and quantitative findings are more often replicated than qualitative. This is at least partly due to the relative simplicity of quantitative approaches and findings. Quantitative studies typically require less investment of resources than qualitative studies do. For this reason alone, it is reasonable to expect more efforts to replicate quantitative than qualitative studies.

With respect to findings, the research questions asked by qualitative researchers and the kinds of answers they get tend to be more complex than those of quantitative researchers. When so many factors are involved, they complicate the issue of replicability of findings. Qualitative findings tend to generalize less widely than do quantitative findings; however, due to the greater complexity of qualitative findings, qualitative replications have the potential to provide richer information on the conditions under which particular findings do and do not apply.

Evaluating Qualitative Methods

Qualitative researchers have tended not to be explicit in their research reports about the methods they used to collect and analyze their data. This makes it impossible for a reader to evaluate these methods. Qualitative methodologists have begun to call for more reporting of methods by qualitative researchers, so that methodological issues can be evaluated for a given study and discussed more widely by the profession.

As yet, no widely accepted standards exist for evaluating the appropriateness of the methods of data collection and analysis used by qualitative researchers. However, Goetz and LeCompte (1984) have suggested the following model (p. 233).

They identify five concerns at the data collection and analysis stages:

1. The overall design that characterized the endeavor
2. The group that provided the data
3. The experiences and roles of the investigators
4. The data collection methods used
5. The analysis strategies developed

They suggest that each of these categories be evaluated on each of five bipolar scales:

1. Appropriate/inappropriate
2. Clear/opaque
3. Comprehensive/narrow

4. Credible/incredible

5. Significant/trivial

But they also caution that:

> As components of studies are evaluated in accordance with these scales, the primary referent should be the intent of the investigators and the research questions they claim to address, rather than what the reviewer thinks should have been done.

SUMMARY

In qualitative research, data collection and data analysis are interactive processes. Interim analysis takes place throughout a project and informs subsequent data collection. Interim analyses and reports permit revision of working hypotheses, verification of facts, and generation of categories. Researchers typically begin final analysis of qualitative data by searching for topics or themes in the raw data and coding small units of raw data as examples of these topics or themes. Some topics emerge from the raw data; possible topics are predetermined by the researcher as well. Raw data are usually coded to reflect examples of topics.

Recurring topics are then examined for possible constructs of data. Constructs may be emic or etic. Emic constructs are "native" and are used to describe data in terms that are meaningful to the subjects of the study; etic constructs are imposed by the researcher and are used to interpret data in universal terms and to relate research results to existing theories.

As constructs evolve, patterns among them are sought. Patterns refer to the complex relationships that exist among people's environments, mental processes, and behavior. Patterns in qualitative research are analogous to relationships between variables in quantitative research.

Qualitative researchers report the patterns they have found in their data. They typically provide evidence for the existence of these patterns by providing examples from the raw data. Issues surrounding the credibility of research findings have not been addressed as systematically by qualitative as by quantitative researchers, although there is now a trend in that direction. It can be argued that qualitative research has more potential for internal validity than does quantitative research, because qualitative researchers are more immersed in their research contexts and thus have more opportunity to identify and remedy threats to internal validity. Qualitative researchers use triangulation and the lack of negative examples to verify their conclusions. Currently, dialogical methods in which participants collaboratively collect and analyze data are providing a means of checking the validity of researcher constructed findings. In essence, an insider-member researcher provides an emic triangulation component.

Replicating qualitative research methods requires more resources than does replicating quantitative methods; thus, fewer replications are attempted. The complexity of qualitative findings means that the findings themselves are also less often replicated than are quantitative findings. However, the typical richness of qualitative findings means that additional studies have the potential to yield more information about the conditions under which findings do and do not generalize.

Qualitative methodologists are currently attempting to refine standards for evaluating methods of collecting and analyzing qualitative data. These standards need to be different from those applied to quantitative methods.

SUMMARY EXERCISES

1. This is a follow-up exercise for Summary Exercise 1 in chapter 9. After you have collected data and written field notes, complete the following steps:

a. In the margins of your field notes write key words or topics that best describe each segment.

b. Try to find topics that are similar, and then organize them into constructs.

c. Do you see the possibility of any patterns in your data? What specific examples from your data support the possibility of these patterns? Are there any negative examples in your data that cause you to question your interpretations?

d. Formulate a question to answer in subsequent data collection.

2. Read the following excerpts, which appear in *The Invisible Children: School Integration in American Society* (Rist, 1978, pp. 115–130), and answer the following questions:[5]

a. What pattern do you feel is suggested in each excerpt with respect to the influence of teacher behavior on children's behavior?

b. What specific examples of teacher-student behavior support the existence of the pattern you see? Are there any negative examples that would call into question the interpretation you have made?

Mrs. Brown

Mrs. Brown comes to where I am seated and apologizes to me, saying she is going to have to take the remainder of the morning to administer a series of tests to the class. She says she is sorry there will be no class activities for me to observe. I ask if I can stay to watch the testing, and she says I can, but answers in a way implying that there will be nothing of interest to me. Before she leaves, she adds, "Every fall I have to give this damn test. There is no need for it because I know what all these kids are doing. But it's required and I guess I have to go along."

She goes to the front of the room, tells the class to put everything off their desks except a pencil. She tells them they have to get ready to take a test. "How many of you understand that this test doesn't matter? It really doesn't matter, but you should still try to do your best. How many of you really understand it doesn't matter?" Only a few hands go up. She starts walking through the room moving the desks apart, telling the class she knows they will not look at anyone's paper, but she does not "want any eyes to wander by mistake." When she comes by my seat, she hands me the test record sheet with the scores of the two tests the class completed yesterday. The scores suggest a bimodal distribution. Donald scored toward the bottom of the lower distribution.

Mrs. Brown is back in the front of the room. "OK, I am waiting." Mary calls out, "Mrs. Brown, will you move Donald away? He wants to look at my paper." Mrs. Brown replies, "Oh no. Donald would not do that." But she moves his desk anyway. She asks Mary if everything is now all right and Mary says, "Yes."

"OK, I want you all to listen. Open your tests to page 6, where we will do test three. There is a blue line across the middle of the page. Donald, what does that line mean?" Donald responds, "It show you." "It shows you what?" "What to do." "No, that's not it. Tim, do you know?" "It tells you the problem." "No, but you're close. What it tells you to do is to concentrate on only those problems above the line and

[5]Reprinted by permission of the publisher from *The Invisible Children: School Integration in American Society* by Ray C. Rist, Cambridge, Mass.: Harvard University Press, Copyright ©1978 by the President and Fellows of Harvard College.

none of those below it. Do you all understand?" No responses from the class. "OK, I'll get ready and you get ready and we'll all try to start together." She finishes her directions and tells the class to begin.

She comes to the back of the room and tells me that yesterday the test got so frustrating for the class that she had to end early. She says many of the children cannot read well enough to complete the items and they become very upset. She begins walking through the class talking to the students, telling them not to worry and just to do what they can. She speaks to me again, "I know talking to them during the test is not supposed to happen, but I don't like to see them so frustrated. Isn't this all a waste of time." She seems quite agitated. I note that one of the boys, David, has closed his book and is drawing circles on the cover. At the end of the fifteen-minute test period, Mrs. Brown tells Craig to collect the papers. Ian begins to cry. He says he could not do the test and he did not answer a single question. He is crying quite loudly. Mrs. Brown goes over to him and puts her arm around him. She tells him it is OK and she knows he tried to do his best. Ian, still sobbing, says, "But I couldn't get even one." Mrs. Brown leaves him and comes to the front. "OK, we'll take a break and have recess." Ian is still sobbing. "I know how you feel Ian, we all felt that way yesterday. Just do the best you can." She continues. "By the way, boys and girls, we have some more tests to take this afternoon. How many of you think taking the test is fun?" Two hands go up. She looks at me and frowns. Lori calls out, "It's no fun 'cause I can't read the questions." Several other children voice their agreement with Lori, including Brad, Kim, and Donald. Mrs. Brown dismisses the class to the playground.

Mrs. Wills

Jeff is out of his seat looking at the supply box brought by Kurt. A girl sitting next to Kurt says to Jeff, "You're not supposed to use anyone's things but your own." Jeff picks one of the crayons from the box, breaks it, and puts the pieces back. The girl gets up from her seat and goes to tell the teacher what happened. Mrs. Wills comes and quietly tells Jeff he should keep his hands off other people's supplies. She says Jeff has his own supplies and should use them.

Jeff is up out of his seat. He goes to the front blackboard and calls out to Don, "Don, this say black?" pointing to one of the words on the board. Don says yes. (The class had gone over this and the three other words on the board, but Jeff was not paying attention at the time. He was drawing on the sole of his tennis shoe with a pen.) He goes back to his chair, and pushes it far back so it is up against the desk of the student behind him. He watches her for a short while and then is up again and back at the board. He calls out to this girl, "Ellen, this say black?" She says yes and Jeff comes back to his chair. He now begins to draw on Ellen's paper, and she pushes his hand away, telling him in an irritated voice that he should be doing his own work. He stops drawing on her paper but does not turn around.

Mrs. Wills, who has organized a reading group on the right side of the room, has observed part of this exchange. She calls out in a quiet voice, "Excuse me, I believe it is now time for everyone to be working on their own papers." Jeff pushes his chair back to his own desk, but gets up again. He goes to the teacher and says, "Teacher, teacher." She responds. "What?" "Watch me." He goes to the board and asks if the word at the bottom says "black." She says it does. Jeff goes to his seat and gets out several crayons. He starts playing with them by rolling them together across his desk. Soon he is writing on his desk with one of his crayons. Mrs. Wills, who has come to her desk for a paper, sees Jeff and comes over to him. Again in a soft voice: "Jeff, we are not to write on our desks, only on the paper." With no other comments she goes back to her reading group. Jeff takes one of the crayons and begins to print his name on his paper.

Part IV
Summing Up

Parts II and III introduced you in some detail to the processes researchers use in collecting and analyzing data. Part IV is about how all this detail fits into a bigger picture: the gradual emergence and use of scientific knowledge about matters of concern to educators. Part IV contains one chapter, which deals primarily with how individual studies contribute to bodies of knowledge.

The chapter takes up the matter of theory, which was introduced in chapter 1, and relates the acquisition of knowledge to theory building. It also discusses the paradigmatic differences between qualitative and quantitative research approaches and relates the two approaches to theory building. The goals of the chapter are to help you read individual research reports with an understanding of how they contribute to overall knowledge in an educational field and to help you understand the complexities of knowledge acquisition and use.

The chapter concludes with a set of summary exercises that reflect the big-picture focus of the chapter. The exercises consist of the complete texts of published research reports, on which you can simultaneously practice all the skills you have acquired in reading educational research.

11

Evaluating Research

COMPLETE RESEARCH PROGRAMS

No study is methodologically perfect; every study has some methodological weakness. Many studies have more than one. Qualitative research by its nature almost always has very limited generalizability; it is not practical for one researcher to study a wide variety of people, places, and things with the kind of depth and intensity that characterizes qualitative research. Quantitative researchers also face formidable obstacles. The kinds of variables that educational researchers are interested in do not usually lend themselves to precise measurement; operational definitions thus often have questionable validity. Many of the independent variables in which educational researchers are interested are impossible or impractical to control; this precludes random assignment and places causal argument in real jeopardy. Even quantitative researchers are rarely able to study truly representative samples of large populations of interest.

How, then, do scientists ever really learn anything? The answer to this question lies in broadening our focus from single studies to whole research programs. Comprehensive knowledge can never be based on a single study, precisely because any single study must have limitations. Comprehensive knowledge emerges over time, as a result of the accumulated information provided by many studies—sometimes hundreds or even thousands of individual studies.

But that doesn't mean that all research is equally valuable, or that all individual studies make equal contributions. Some studies are much more valuable than others. This depends in part on the study's methodological strengths and weaknesses, but also on how the study fits in to the state of knowledge in a field. Different fields embody different knowledge states at different times. The kinds of knowledge that are most needed in particular fields at particular times differ. We cannot, therefore, evaluate the contribution that a study makes to knowledge in a given field without knowing what the state of knowledge is in that field at that time.

In some fields, the state of knowledge is so primitive that almost any new information is welcome. However, we often value studies in such fields not for the knowledge they add per se but because they set the stage for productive work in the future. An excellent example is provided by the field of addiction. This is an area of great applied interest, but until the recent past little was understood about it. In the past decade, research, especially qualitative research, has begun to shed important new light on this subject. This qualitative research strongly suggested that the earlier focus in addiction research was too narrow. Addiction needed to be much more broadly defined than it had been in the past. People are addicted not only to alcohol and other, sometimes illegal, substances; people are also addicted to food, to work, and even to personal relationships.

When the definition of addiction is broadened to include these kinds of behaviors, it can be seen that addiction tends to run in families: that the children of alcoholics, for example, are not only much more likely than the children of nonalcoholics to become alcoholics themselves, but that those who escape this manifestation of addictive behavior are still much more likely to manifest addiction in other ways—for example, to marry alcoholics or to have eating abnormalities such as bulimia (compulsive overeating) or anorexia (inability to eat). Thus, addiction is part of a personality dimension that is very basic and may even be genetically influenced.

Interestingly, some of the most heuristically useful work in this field was done not by professional researchers but by practitioners (e.g., Forrest and Gordon, 1990). Practitioners, whether they conceptualize themselves in this way or not, are in a real sense doing qualitative research: empirically immersing themselves in the topic. They can thus be more likely to discover previously unsuspected patterns than are researchers, especially if the researchers have a quantitative bias and only collect data on variables they have previously defined as relevant.

These practitioners' qualitative data were not collected to test hypotheses; their suggestions about causal relationships in addiction were only that—suggestions. And their samples were very biased; generalizability of their observations was thus very limited. However, due to their work, research in addiction took a new and more productive direction. We probably have learned a great deal more about addiction in the last 10 years than in the 50 years previous to that.

Sometimes the major barrier to acquiring knowledge in a field is measurement. The field of intelligence is a current example (Hernstein, 1996). Intelligence is thought to have genetic components and to reside in the morphology (structure) and physiology (function) of the brain. We do not presently have direct ways to measure these brain characteristics adequately. To measure intelligence, we rely on observations of behavior from which we infer intelligence—for example, people's responses to IQ tests. However, learned behavior tends to confound our inferences. There are cultural differences, for example, in the ways that people respond to these kinds of instruments, and efforts to develop "culture-fair" IQ tests have so far been only moderately successful.

Thus research on intelligence that suggests improvements in methods of measuring intelligence might make a valuable contribution, even if the study has limited generalizability, while research on intelligence that has good external validity but the usual measurement problems might make a less valuable contribution.

In some fields, causal argument is the major barrier to acquiring knowledge. The field of gender differences in behavior is a good example (Hoyenga, 1993). The question currently of most interest in this field is whether gender differences in behavior are genetically determined or learned through differential childhood socialization. Neither of these causes is controllable by researchers, so random assignment is not possible. And these causes involve packaged variables, which almost always occur together; that is, biological females are almost always socialized as females, and biological males are almost always socialized as males. In any study of biological causes, except those done on newborns, socialization is almost certainly a confounding variable; and in any study of social causes, biology is almost certainly a confounding variable. It is therefore almost impossible to distinguish biological from social causes.

Occasionally, however, there are naturally occurring "experiments." An example is provided by individuals who suffer from a rare genetic anomaly. When these individuals are born, they appear to belong to one sex; at puberty, however, they begin to take on the appearance of the opposite sex, which is their true biological sex. These kinds of natural occurrences provide researchers with subjects who are biologically one sex but socialized as the other. These subjects have some behavioral characteristics that are typical of members of their biological sex and other characteristics that are typical of their social gender. This kind of evidence strongly suggests that the former characteristics are biologically determined, while the latter characteristics are socially determined.

However, such studies typically have internal validity problems; for example, the biological determinants must be assumed to affect the children's behavior, even though the children and members of their social groups are unaware of the children's biological sex. This may, in turn, elicit treatment from members of the social group that is not typical of the treatment accorded other children in the child's socially defined gender group. These studies also usually have very small sample sizes and other extreme limitations on generalizability. Such studies, however, may make a much more valuable contribution to knowledge than do studies with large, representative samples that document the existence of gender differences in behavior without adding to our knowledge of the causes of these differences.

In fact, generalizability has a way of taking care of itself. In the early stages of knowledge acquisition in a field, researchers tend to worry about measurement and causal argument problems; these kinds of problems have to be worked out before it is particularly worthwhile even to worry about generalizability. If studies are not valid for the samples on which they are done, then there is not much point in worrying about whether the results will generalize.

As more and more studies are done by researchers working on these problems, generalizability evidence is also accumulating. The studies tend to be done by different researchers, working with different samples, in different contexts. By the time the state of knowledge in a field is well enough advanced that researchers have largely solved the measurement and internal validity problems, enough research has usually been done in enough different contexts that a great deal is already known about how the results generalize.

Meta-Analysis

In recent years quantitative researchers have explored the use of statistical techniques to assist in evaluating the state of knowledge in a given research area. The techniques involve analyzing the results of a number of different studies which focused on the same or similar independent and dependent variables, in order to determine what the group of studies taken together have to say about the relationship between the variables. As these techniques have been formalized, they have come to be known as *meta-analysis.*

The first step in meta-analysis involves a literature search to locate relevant research reports. Sometimes all the reports that can be located are included in the analysis; at other times, the reports are sampled for analysis: For example, methodologically weaker reports may be eliminated; or, if there are many reports, a random sample may be taken.

The particular statistical technique employed is usually one that estimates the average effect size of the various studies. As you learned in chapter 8, *effect size* refers to the magnitude of the effect that the independent variable of interest has on the dependent variable of interest. The effect size is first estimated for each study; then an average effect size is calculated across all the studies. Partly because meta-analysis is relatively new, there are a number of unresolved issues surrounding its use; however, it can provide information of value in synthesizing the results of a number of studies of similar research questions.

Theory Building Revisited

In chapter 1, in discussing research questions, we related research to theory building. It is time now to return to that discussion.

Theory is one of the most powerful tools that scientists have for advancing causal understanding because theory is comprehensive causal explanation that goes beyond what is already widely accepted to be true. Because theory is such a powerful tool, fields lacking good theory are likely to be fields in which causal understanding is developing at a relatively slow rate, while fields with several promising theories on which most scientists are actively working are likely to be fields in which causal understanding is developing at a fairly rapid rate.

Research is the empirical part of theory building. Scientists do inductive research to generate theory, and they do deductive research to test theory. When research is done to generate theory, the research is usually relatively unfocused. Inductive researchers observe a wide range of events that may bear on what they want to know about. In observing and in analyzing their observational data, they try to be alert to the possibility of patterning in the observed events—patterning that may reflect the systematic operation of cause and effect.

When researchers detect patterns that may reflect causal relationships, they try to formulate these relationships in theoretical terms: to propose fairly comprehensive causal explanations of the observed patterns. Their research strategy then shifts from induction to deduction. Instead of observing everything that might bear on the issue, they restrict their empirical work to tests of the theoretical propositions. Now their data collection is focused on one or a few possible causal relationships that they wish to test empirically. If these tests tend to confirm the theory, then our confidence in the explanatory power of the theory is increased; if these tests tend not to confirm the theory, then our confidence is decreased.

Typically, these kinds of tests result in neither definitive acceptance nor definitive rejection of the theoretical propositions. Rather, they yield information that is used to revise and refine the theoretical propositions. The revised theory is then subject to further empirical work. This new work may be inductive—perhaps the previous research suggested the need for new work in a largely unexplored area; or the new research may be deductive—perhaps the previous work narrowed the field of possible causes to two, and the need is for further research to determine which of the two is operative. Figure 11.1 illustrates this view of research as the empirical part of theory building.

Much research in education that is published in well-respected nationally distributed journals is conducted for the contribution it can make to theory building. Understanding an individual research report depends in part on understanding how the research fits into theory. The questions researchers ask, the methods by which they

FIGURE 11.1   The roles of research in theory building.

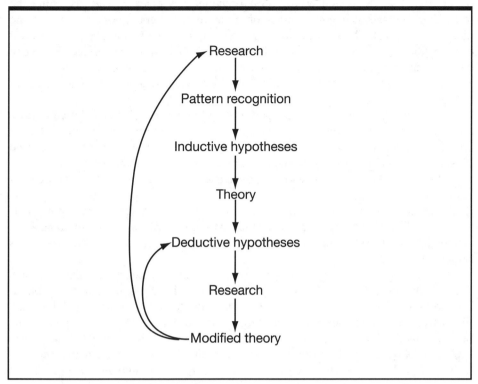

collect empirical data, and the value of the answers they get depend importantly on the state of theory in the field of knowledge to which the research contributes.

This is a more systematic way of making the point that was made by example in the first part of this chapter. There are differences between studies in the contributions they make to theory building. All studies have methodological weaknesses, but the value of a given study does not depend on its methodological strength alone, or sometimes even primarily. The value of a study depends ultimately on how it contributes to theory building. Evaluating the contributions that a study makes requires knowledge of the state of theory building in the field. Studies cannot be evaluated in isolation. Methods that are productive for testing deductive hypotheses may not be productive for generating theory. Answers that would be unsatisfactory to researchers testing hypotheses may be satisfactory to researchers generating hypotheses.

■ Exercise 1

A good example of a complete research program—that is, of a complete process of theory building—in a fairly compact time frame is provided by Legionnaire's disease, which you may remember from the popular press (e.g., *U.S. News & World Report,* 1983). In 1976, a number of people attending an American Legion convention in Philadelphia became ill; 29 of them died. The disease initially could not be identified. This set off an alarm in national medical circles: An apparently contagious disease was killing people, and the medical profession did not know what was causing the disease.

Medical researchers had an urgent theoretical problem: to understand the cause of this new malady, which was dubbed Legionnaire's disease. The first thing the researchers did was to begin empirical observation of the entire context in which the disease had struck. This work was relatively unfocused. Comprehensive medical examinations of victims, both deceased and surviving, were performed. Everyone who had any role in the context—survivors, family and friends of victims, and persons providing service to the convention—was interviewed about anything that might be relevant.

Resulting data were analyzed and the following conclusions drawn. Those affected had had certain physical characteristics and symptoms, stayed in a particular hotel, and eaten at a particular restaurant. Thus the disease might have been caused by some environmental agent in the restaurant, possibly something that the Legionnaires had ingested, or by some environmental agent in the hotel where the Legionnaires had stayed.

The next stage of research was highly focused, on the hotel and restaurant. This research indicated that the relevant context was the hotel, not the restaurant. Ultimately, it was discovered that a virus living in the ventilation system of the hotel was responsible for the disease.

This was a very dramatic and compact example of theory building. In most fields, including education, the same general process is employed, but theory building takes a much longer time and the results tend not to be as definitive and dramatic. Fit this example into the theory-building model in Figure 11.1. What part of the research involved pattern searching? What patterns were discovered? What causal explanations were induced from this pattern search? Were these explanations considered proposed or "proved"? What part of the research involved the testing of hypotheses that were deduced from these inductively generated causal explanations? What was the purpose of testing these hypotheses?   ■

The Example of Learning Theory

Educational researchers who wish to understand a phenomenon about which little is known begin much as the Legionnaire's disease researchers did. They observe in empirical contexts relevant to what they want to know and collect data on a wide variety of events that may have some relevance to the issue. As they collect and analyze these data, they search for patterns. If patterns can be detected, scientists in the field try to formulate causal explanations for them. These explanations must then be fleshed out and tested on independent bodies of data. This more focused research yields information, which permits scientists to discard, accept, or (most usually) modify the original explanations. This, in turn, gives direction to future research.

Over time, theories are refined and retested until a substantial body of knowledge exists and is widely accepted. States of knowledge in educational subfields vary with the stages of theory development in the field. The field of learning psychology provides an excellent example.

Half a century ago, B. F. Skinner was a relative unknown in the field of psychology, working on a new theory of learning involving what he called *operant conditioning*. The general idea of operant conditioning is that learning is caused by the consequences of behavior: that organisms learn to do things that have pleasant consequences and learn not to do things which have unpleasant or no consequences (Skinner, 1959).

Research tended to confirm this theory. More researchers thus became interested in it. Over time literally thousands of studies were done that tended to confirm the proposition that learning is caused by the consequences of behavior. Questions of detail about the theory were raised and, over time, answered: For example, how do the frequency and dependability of consequences affect learning? We now know that behavior that is always followed by a pleasant consequence is learned quickly but also extinguished ("unlearned") quickly, while behavior that is sometimes followed by a pleasant consequence and sometimes by no consequence is learned less quickly but is also more resistant to extinction.

Subjects of these thousands of studies included many species, from pigeons and mice to humans. Some of the studies were laboratory experiments, some were field experiments, and some were nonexperimental studies. We now know that reinforcement learning theory generalizes widely: that the learning of many kinds of organisms, in many contexts, is shaped by the consequences of behavior. Thus it is now widely accepted as true, not just by psychologists but also by such practitioners as teachers and parents, that reinforcement learning theory is correct, and that one of the important causes of learning is the consequences of behavior.

However, in the course of their work, some psychologists found evidence that other forces shape learning as well. For example, reinforcement learning theory predicts that an infant who is held when she cries will learn to cry more often; however, it was discovered that infants who are held when they cry usually cry less often. There is also empirical evidence that observed behavior is sometimes imitated in the absence of any apparent reward. And young children consistently draw the wrong conclusions from certain data even when they are rewarded for the right conclusions. For example, young children insist that a tall, slender container holds more water than a short, wide container, even when they have just seen the same amount of water poured from the first container into the second. Reinforcement learning theory does not, therefore, explain all learning. These kinds of observations, which were not initially systematic or focused, gradually led some psychologists to induce other causal explanations of learning, which complemented reinforcement learning theory; for example, attachment theory, social learning theory, and cognitive learning theory.

Attachment theory (Klaus, 1995) says that human (and other) infants are born with the propensity to attach to one or a few individuals in their environments, and that after this attachment takes place the infant will behave in ways to secure proximity to this attachment figure. Infants whose attachment figures are readily available become secure in their attachments and less insistent in their proximity seeking, while infants whose attachment figures are not readily available become insecure in their attachments and more insistent in their proximity seeking. This explains the data on crying of infants who are and are not held.

Enough work has now been done on attachment theory that its basic validity is generally accepted by developmental psychologists. We know, for example, the major dimensions of how attachment figures are chosen: They are the persons who are most socially responsive to the infant during the latter part of his first year of life. Some details of the theory, including how it articulates with such other theories as social learning theory, remain to be worked out.

Social learning theory (Bandura, 1986) explains learning in terms of observation and imitation of models. People (and other species) observe and imitate the behavior of other individuals who are selected as models. This explains the data on imitation in the absence of reward. Social learning theory is gaining wide acceptance, although many details remain unknown. Some of the factors that affect an individual's choice of models have been identified—for example, modelers are more likely to choose models whom they perceive as similar to themselves, and rewarding either the model or modeler increases the probability that a behavior will be imitated.

The Piagetian branch of cognitive learning theory (Wadsworth, 1996) explains learning in terms of biologically determined cognitive maturational processes. These processes unfold in a predictable sequence at predictable times. Very young children have not entered the second stage of development, which involves the ability to conserve in time and space; thus they insist that a tall, thin container holds more water than a short, wide container.

The broad outlines of Piagetian theory are also widely accepted, although recent work has necessitated some revision of Piaget's original conception. Piaget thought that most normal individuals attain the final, formal operational, stage of development, but research in the last decade indicates that most individuals probably remain concrete-operational.

Interest in cognitive psychology, however, has recently moved away from more specific maturation theory to a broader perspective on human cognition, which includes how people think—that is, how we process information for memory storage, how memory is encoded, what happens to information in storage, and how it is retrieved and manipulated (Strube, 1993). Rough outlines of a theory are emerging (e.g., we apparently classify in order to store), but our knowledge about cognitive processes is very primitive compared with our knowledge about reinforcement, or even attachment and modeling.

As an active research area in learning psychology, then, reinforcement theory has waned and cognitive theory is ascending. For the foreseeable future, cognition will probably be the area in learning psychology in which knowledge is developing at the most rapid rate. Over time, as knowledge of cognition becomes established, research will raise new questions, new theories will be proposed, and researchers will turn their attention to building these new theories.

■ EXERCISE 2

Having had this brief lesson in learning theory, imagine that you now read two research reports, one on cross-cultural differences in classifying objects and one on the effectiveness of classroom reinforcement. The research on classification had fuzzy operational definitions, imperfect control of potentially confounding variables, and a very restricted sample; results were so mixed as to be uninterpretable. The only firm conclusion the researcher reached was that certain variables which could have been controlled, did, in fact, confound the study's results. The research on reinforcement had good operational definitions, good control of potentially confounding variables, and a useful sample. The researcher was able to conclude that classroom reinforcement is effective. Which study is more worthwhile?   ■

Evaluating Research in Its Theoretical Context

With even the sketchy overview of learning theory that you have read in the last few pages, you would now be able to read research on learning with more understanding than before you began this chapter, unless, of course, you already had some understanding of learning theory. The brief lesson in learning theory was provided to make the point that it is impossible to read the research literature in most fields with real depth of understanding unless one already has a fair understanding of the state of theory in that field.

A caution is required here, however. In chapter 1 we pointed out that educational research questions can spring from either applied or basic knowledge concerns. Applied research is conducted for its potential to provide information of use in meeting an immediate perceived need of practitioners; basic research is conducted for its potential for contributing to basic knowledge, although basic knowledge can and often does prove of ultimate use to practitioners. We pointed out in chapter 1 that one of the reasons theory is valuable is because it offers the scientific community a standard for judging the contribution that a particular study makes to basic knowledge.

Our discussion thus far in this chapter has been limited to research that springs from theoretical concerns, since much of the research in education is theoretical in its orientation. The interesting thing is that this is true of applied as well as basic research. Applied researchers often make use of theory, but the way they deal with theory is sometimes different from the way basic researchers deal with theory.

Education is an applied field, similar to medicine and engineering. Knowledge issues in applied fields are different from those in basic fields such as biology, sociology, chemistry, and psychology. In basic fields, knowledge is valued in and of itself, whether or not it has any immediate, perceived applicability to solving practical problems. In applied fields the situation is just the opposite: Knowledge is valued precisely and primarily for its usefulness in solving practical problems.

Researchers in applied fields can and do develop their own theories relevant to their applied fields, but they also tend to rely heavily on theory borrowed from basic fields. Thus, much medical knowledge comes from such basic fields as biology, chemistry, and physics, while much educational knowledge comes from such basic fields as psychology, sociology, and anthropology. However, in pursuing knowledge specific to applied concerns, medical or educational researchers often are not concerned with contributing to theory building in the basic field in the way that a biologist or psychologist would be. Applied researchers sometimes are not as interested in the contribution that their research can make to basic theory building as in the contribution that existing basic theory can make to their applied concerns. Thus, their approach is often to identify theories that seem relevant to a given practical problem and then to apply these theories in trying to understand and solve the problem. Their results may or may not also function to generate or test theory in the basic field, but this is not their primary concern. Evaluating a theoretically based study in terms of the contribution it makes to theory building is thus appropriate in basic knowledge fields but may or may not be appropriate in applied fields. If a researcher in an applied field is interested in building theory relevant to that field, then evaluating the study's contribution to theory building is appropriate. If, on the other hand, a researcher in an applied field is interested in testing whether theory borrowed from a basic field can help in understanding and solving practical problems in the applied field, then the study should be evaluated in terms of how well it meets that goal rather than how well it contributes to theory building in the basic field.

No single study ever stands alone; all research is part of a much larger endeavor to acquire knowledge. Whether the larger endeavor is primarily basic or applied, you cannot evaluate individual research reports without reference to the larger endeavor of which it is a part. No single study is methodologically perfect; all studies have some methodological weakness. Evaluating a research report is not a matter just of being able to spot the methodological limitations of a study but also of being able to judge the contribution the study makes in spite of its weaknesses. That kind of decision depends in part on the state of knowledge in the field to which the study contributes. Reading and evaluating research reports requires the kinds of knowledge that you have acquired from earlier chapters, but your understanding of research depends also on your ability to place the study in the context of knowledge in the field to which the study contributes.

■ EXERCISE 3

Learning psychology is one of the most exemplary of all fields of interest to educators with respect to theory building. In most subfields in education, theory building has not been as impressive. However, theory building goes on at some level in all fields of knowledge that are of interest to educators. Look through back issues of books and journals that review research in your field—for example, the *Review of Educational Research* and the *Review of Research in Education*. Identify a review article that seems relevant to theory in your field and read it. (If you have trouble identifying theory in your field, ask one or more professors in your field what they think are two or three of the most interesting theoretical issues in the field.) Choose two or three of the research reports that are cited in the article. Locate and read them. Did the review article give you a perspective on the research reports that you would not otherwise have had?   ■

Discussion Sections in Research Reports

The final section of a research report is usually a discussion section. The researcher has, at the beginning of the report, indicated what the research question is and why it is worth answering. This typically involves a literature review, in which the researcher documents the contribution this study can make to an issue of applied interest or to theory building. In the second section of the report, the researcher has described what he did to answer the question—what his research process was. This involves explaining such things as who his subjects were, in what contexts he studied them, and how he collected data—through testing, interviewing, observing, and so forth.

In the third section, the researcher has presented his results. If the research was quantitative, this involved presenting the results of statistical analyses of the data. If the research was qualitative, the results were presented in narrative expository form.

In one sense, the researcher's task is now complete. However, after presenting their results, researchers usually go on to discuss the results. Sometimes, for example, results were mixed. Perhaps the null hypothesis was rejected for boys but retained for girls. Or perhaps the dependent variable had several operational definitions, and the null hypothesis was rejected for some but retained for others. The researcher will usually speculate about why this happened.

Most studies also have limitations, such as problems with measurement, confounding variables, or sampling. The researcher usually discusses how these limitations affect the results—what cautions the reader should keep in mind when interpreting the results.

Researchers also tend in this section to refer to the applied or theoretical rationale that they provided for the research in the introductory section of the research report.

They may, for example, discuss how they think their results contribute to theory building. A common inclusion at this point is a discussion of what questions this research leaves unanswered and what directions this research suggests for further applied or theoretical work. Sometimes, however, this kind of discussion is omitted and it is up to you to do this kind of analysis for yourself.

■ EXERCISE 4

Examples of discussion sections from several published research reports follow. What do the researchers have to say about limitations of their studies? How do they deal with mixed results? How do they relate their findings to applied or theoretical issues?

a. Baxter et al. (1985) studied the content of music video. Here is part of their discussion (p. 336):

> Consistent with Levy's (1983) observation, MTV videos stressed sexual content. However, like other studies of televised sexual content, music video sexual content was understated, relying on innuendo through clothing, suggestiveness, and light physical contact rather than more overt behaviors.
>
> Thus, music video sexual content may have a decidedly adolescent orientation, suited to its audience; fantasy exceeds experience and sexual expression centers primarily on attracting the opposite sex. Sexual behavior, as portrayed in music videos, may reflect actual or desired adolescent courtship behavior, or the expression of attraction impulses. This issue is beyond the scope of this study. The study's results indicate, however, that sexually oriented, suggestive behavior is portrayed frequently in music videos. Questions regarding the impact of this portrayal on adolescent socialization, peer relationships, and modeling are raised.
>
> The frequency of instances of violence and crime content also merits further attention. Frequent content elements in the violence and crime category also exhibited understated characteristics. The most frequently coded content elements were physical aggression, not the use of weapons, murder, or sexual violence. Violent action in music videos often stopped short of the fruition of the violent act.

b. Warren (1982) did a qualitative study of a bilingual, bicultural program in "Campbell School," his pseudonym for an elementary school in Southern California. His purpose in doing the study was to focus "on the role of schooling processes in structuring, reinforcing, *or* muting a bicultural experience" (p. 384; emphasis in original). His conclusions follow (pp. 404–405).

> In the introductory section two interrelated questions were posed as a focus for the organization, presentation, and analysis of data. One question concerned the relationship of cultural differences to schooling processes; the second concerned the effects of ethnic/cultural characteristics of pupils on classroom practice and teacher behavior. These questions have been answered primarily through a description and analysis of curriculum systems and extra-classroom activities.
>
> Curriculum systems have been presented as prototypical instructional processes and have been found to be culturally "Anglo" in their socializing effects oriented toward individualistic achievement values—and (whether presented in English or in Spanish) eliciting from pupils common patterns of adaptive behavior. Certainly the attributes of these systems are not characteristic of all classroom and school activities. Through social studies units, literature, drama, song, and festivities, ethnic heritage is

studied, reinforced, and celebrated. Nevertheless, curriculum systems represent a powerful influence on the life of Campbell classrooms and on the values and teaching practices teachers believe to be fundamental to success. Although the systems serve the objective of individualized instruction, they impose on classroom life a required structure and sequence of teacher and pupil behavior.

To understand the role of curriculum systems and extra-classroom activities in structuring, reinforcing, or muting a bicultural experience, it is important to view them within the context of the language-maintenance bilingual education model used at Campbell. Unlike major alternative program models (transitional or immersion), the maintenance model assumes the continuing importance of bilingual competence to the present and developing needs of Campbell pupils. At every grade, pupils can express these needs in that language which provides them the most meaning. Hence the constant availability to pupils of their mother tongue affords them a more open relationship with teachers and more freedom in their evolving adaptation to a bicultural environment. Of more importance, the maintenance model affirms the equal worth of ethnic backgrounds and the inseparability of language and culture.

c. Vierra (1984) studied reading test scores of Chicano children. She found no statistically significant difference between the reading gains of Chicano children who had Anglo teachers and those who had Hispanic teachers. Here is her discussion (pp. 287–289).

Limitations
The major limitation on this study's internal validity is that students were not randomly assigned to teachers. Controlling for pretest scores in the analyses of covariance partially alleviates this problem. However, it is still possible that it has an effect. For example, it is possible that differences in the groups' pretest scores affected their gains. To check on this possibility, an analysis of variance was calculated at each grade level; there was no significant difference in pretest scores between the two groups of children in either grade (third grade $p = .57$; fourth grade $p = .82$).

The major limitation on this study's external validity is the absence of a random sample. Although all third- and fourth-grade Chicano children in the district's Title I schools were originally identified for the study, subject attrition was high. Out of an original number of 3,191 subjects, complete data were available on only 2,129 children. The unavailability of data on teachers' ethnicity was probably an effectively random occurrence. However, when test data were unavailable, something systematic might have been going on. It seems likely, for example, that less able children had a higher rate of absenteeism on test dates and a higher rate of unusable tests. This study's results may not, then, be representative of all third- and fourth-grade Chicano children in the district's Title I schools. Another limitation that should be discussed involves the study's definitions of ethnicity. Children identified as Chicano include children whose families have long resided in the city; children whose families have recently moved to the city from predominantly Hispanic, rural communities throughout the state; and children whose families have recently emigrated from Mexico. Researchers have consistently found psychometric and behavioral differences between such groups of children (e.g., Kagan, 1981; Madsen & Shapira, 1970).

Teachers identified as Hispanic for the purposes of this study also differ in their backgrounds, as well as in a number of variables that may be related to teaching effectiveness—e.g., teaching experience.

The definitions of ethnicity in this study thus gloss over a number of factors that may well be relevant to children's school achievement. Matching student and teacher ethnicity seems to be ineffective when ethnicity is broadly defined, but it is still plausible that Hispanic children's achievement is enhanced when their teachers in fact have backgrounds similar to those of the students and/or self-identify with their students' ethnicity, for example.

Conclusions

This study provides a needed test of the academic results for Chicano students of matching student and teacher ethnicity. For this sample of public school children, there is no statistically significant relationship between teacher ethnicity and student achievement. There may, of course, be other non-academic effects: teacher ethnicity may affect such things as minority students' self-concepts or liking of school. These are matters which can be empirically tested. On the basis of this and other studies, however, it seems that there is neither an academic advantage nor an academic disadvantage to matching student-teacher ethnicity when ethnicity is broadly defined.

d. Rosenfeld and Jarrard (1986) studied "Student Coping Mechanisms in Sexist and Nonsexist Professors' Classes." Here is their concluding discussion (pp. 160–161):

Prior research established that liked and disliked classes may be distinguished with respect to their climate for both female and male professors (Rosenfeld & Jarrard, 1985). Differences in climate, however, appear to affect self-reported student coping mechanisms only for male professors. While no coping mechanism distinguished female professors' liked from disliked classes, six coping behaviors distinguished the two types of classes for male professors. The most important coping mechanisms likely to be employed in male professors' disliked classes were: daydreaming in class, not doing what the teacher asks, and hiding feelings. These findings corroborate Rosenfeld's (1983) earlier conclusions, but only for male professors. In that earlier study, six coping mechanisms distinguished liked from disliked classes; separating male and female professors reveals that those same six mechanisms distinguish the two types of classes only for male professors. Inspection of the means on the Coping Mechanisms instrument indicates that the coping mechanisms examined in this study are not used in classes with female professors.

The second series of analyses focused on coping mechanisms associated with perceived professor sexism in male and female professors' liked and disliked classes. Coping mechanisms associated with perceived sexism in male professors' liked classes revealed passive strategies—not doing what the teacher asks, and hiding feelings—while the one associated with perceived sexism in the disliked classes revealed an active strategy—forming alliances against the teacher. Perceived sexism in a liked class, described as having a supportive climate (Rosenfeld, 1983; Rosenfeld & Jarrard, 1985), evoked a nonhostile defensive reaction, whereas in a disliked class, described as having a nonsupportive climate, it evoked a hostile defensive reaction.

Although perceived sexism in male professors affected students' descriptions of their coping behavior, no parallel conclusion may be posited for female professors. While students perceived variations in sexism in their female professors (Rosenfeld & Jarrard, 1985), these were unrelated to any of the coping mechanisms studied in this investigation. The failure to find effects for female professors may be a result of the low power associated with tests conducted with small sample sizes (Cohen, 1977), the general non-use of coping behavior in classes with female professors (regardless of sexism), or the perceived lower level of sexism in female professors. Concerning this latter explanation, it may be necessary for perceptions of sexism to surpass a particular threshold before consequences for coping behavior become evident.

Taken together with the findings of the earlier investigation (Rosenfeld & Jarrard, 1985), results suggest that sexism in the college classroom may be a "male disease," a disease which affects perceptions of the class, the social-psychological environment in which class members interact, and the selection of particular coping behaviors only for male professors. Awareness of nonegalitarian behavior in female professors appears to have no consequences for descriptions of classroom climate or coping behaviors, indicating that the relationship between sexism and classroom behavior supported by research in the elementary schools (e.g., Serbin, O'Leary, Kent, & Tonick, 1973) may not be generalizable to the college level for female professors. The long list of subtle and not-so-subtle nonegalitarian attitudes and behaviors observed on the college level (Hall, 1982; Tetreault & Schmuck, 1985), and the important negative reactions they provoke, may be relevant only for male professors.

e. Greenbaum (1985) did an observational study of communication differences in American Indian and Anglo classrooms. Here is his concluding discussion (pp. 110–113):

Erickson (1977) suggested that the integration of qualitative and quantitative methods will enable an expanded understanding of everyday life in the classroom. Questions examined in this study were based on prior ethnographic descriptions of nonverbal differences between Native American and Anglo classrooms; quantitative measures were used to corroborate and further specify the nature of these differences. The overall pattern of results tends to support the ethnographically derived hypotheses. During classroom switchboard participation, Choctaw students, at a magnitude approximately twice the rate of the non-Indian students, exhibited shorter utterances when speaking individually, spoke individually (as compared to chorally) less frequently, and interrupted the teacher more often in unsuccessful floor-taking attempts. Compared with non-Indian students, Indian students at both Choctaw and Lawrence spent more time gazing at peers when the teacher was talking. Taken together, these findings seem to reflect cultural differences that could well involve functional difficulties in classroom interaction between Indian students and their non-Indian teachers.

Reduced duration and frequency of individual speaking by the Choctaw students is in line with prior ethnographic reports that have indicated that Indian students avoid individual participation. Increased choral responding and higher rates of peer-directed listener gaze among Choctaw students are consistent with an affinity for group rather than individually oriented behavior. This tendency has been cited as characteristic of Indian (specifically Choctaw) cultural values and tribal life (e.g., Bigart, 1974; Brown, 1980; Dumont, 1972). More specifically, King (1967), in an ethnography of an Indian boarding school in Canada, described a similar relatively high incidence of student choral speaking and a dislike for individual response:

A group conversation can be initiated among them if the children are allowed to speak in unison or several at a time, in disconnected spurts of utterances (or in more formalized choral speaking). As soon as attempts are made to narrow such discussions down to one speaker, silence and embarrassment prevail. . . . As a result, teachers come to be satisfied with simple, minimal recitations (p. 81).

Peterson (1975), based on her experiences as a speech teacher of Mississippi Choctaw adults, noted a similar apparent preference for group, rather than individual, orientations in classroom behavior. Unlike Anglos, Choctaws would neither compete against each other for grades nor criticize their classmates.

Although probably rooted in the students' cultural experiences, the functional effects of the observed differences apparently represent difficulties in classroom interaction that would presumably obstruct learning. As Cazden and Leggett (1981) point out, "Verbal participation in classrooms is important for all children as one indicator of engagement as well as one kind of demonstration to the teacher of what has been learned" (p. 81). Moreover, the Indian students' greater peer directed gaze while the teacher is speaking may influence the teacher's judgment concerning the students' attention. Cappella (1981), in a recent review of nonverbal behaviors (including gaze) that serve an expressive function, notes that these behaviors "will be the behavioral basis for assessments of involvement with another and involvement with the situation" (p. 101). In addition, this difference in listener-gaze is considered to provide speakers with an important cue for the regulation of their own performances (Kendon, 1967).

The Choctaw students' higher rates of teacher interruptions and choral speaking are consistent with previous reports of cultural differences in the regulation of talk. Moreover, increased teacher interruptions and choral responding, inasmuch as they are violations of the teacher's turn-taking rules, would seem to impede classroom exchanges and conversational flow. Ferguson (1977), in a laboratory study of conversations, distinguished four types of mutually exclusive interruptions. Ferguson found that the type of interruption observed in the Choctaw classroom, butting-in interruptions, reflects a lack of social skill rather than an attempt to dominate. While other types of interruptions have been associated with increased status and dominance (i.e., overlap and silent interruptions; Beattie, 1981; Ferguson, 1977), butting-in interruptions probably reflect the Indian students' misassessment of when the teacher's speaking turn has ended and the floor is open. This perhaps suggests that the Choctaw students are comparatively less familiar or comfortable with switchboard participation.

It should be noted that in some respects the observed student behavior profile seems inconsistent with some reports of Indian classroom behavior. Unlike Philips (1983), who found that Warm Springs elementary students were reticent and unresponsive, or Wax and his colleagues' (1964) descriptions of "walls of silence" in Pine Ridge Sioux and Oklahoma Cherokee classrooms, Mississippi Choctaw students spoke often and were sometimes quite animated. They were less responsive only in that their utterances were comparatively shorter. The higher rate of failed floor-gaining interruptions and choral responses among Choctaw students, which gave the classroom a somewhat chaotic atmosphere, would appear to contradict typifications of Indians as being overly polite or shy. However, disorderly classrooms are commonly associated with minority education; and as Au and Mason (1981) have pointed out, disorder and silence may both represent characteristic student responses to cultural discontinuities in the rules for interaction. Moreover, Wax et al. noted that in the Sioux classrooms observed in their study, it was not until the seventh grade that student silences were all-pervasive. In the intermediate grades (fourth-sixth), both silence and disorder were common, with disorder being more frequent. Darnell (1971) noted a similar dichotomy. It should also be noted that efforts to generalize about "Indian" classroom behavior are complicated by the fact that there are more than 300 American Indian tribes, which probably exhibit various differences in conversational etiquette, as opposed to a single pan-Indian pattern. Tribes also vary in the extent to which they control their own school systems. Students' reactions to the classroom setting may vary accordingly. Currently, no systematic research has been done on the extent of intertribal variation in nonverbal cues and conversational etiquette.

Among the teachers included in the study, those in the reservation classrooms, compared with those in the public school, showed differences in behaviors that may be functionally associated with the observed behavioral differences in the Choctaw students. For instance, when the Choctaw students delivered shorter utterances, their teachers tended to exhibit longer turn-switching pauses. In considering the potential for cross-cultural interference in Indian education, Mohatt and Erickson (1981) suggested that the amount of time the teacher allows for the children to respond is an important aspect of culturally patterned teacher behavior, reflecting the tempo and directiveness of classroom interaction. Their study showed that an Odawa teacher paused longer for student replies than his non-Odawa counterpart. The longer pauses by the reservation teachers might therefore reflect an adaptive accommodation to the Indian students. Conversely, however, the Anglo teachers may possibly have been pausing longer for student replies, reflecting uncertainty that the students had completed their utterances; or perhaps they were taking additional time to formulate a response to a shorter-than-expected reply. The reservation teachers also posed more questions than did the public school teachers. Increased teacher questioning could reflect an attempt to secure more feedback than occurs in the relatively shorter Choctaw student replies. The reservation teachers' questions were also of shorter durations when compared to their public school counterparts, suggesting another possible response-matching adaptation on the part of the teachers in the Choctaw classrooms.

In summary, the goal of this study was to quantify, under switchboard participation conditions, differences in nonverbal behaviors of students in reservation and public school classrooms. Observed differences in the gaze and talk-silence behavior between Indian and Anglo students are consistent with interference theory. The present study looked at differences between students operating within the switchboard; future research should investigate whether these differences are more global, as opposed to being restricted to switchboard participation. Additional data on the degree to which students and teachers find these differences problematic would help extend the present findings. Are misattributions common, with teachers seeing students as inattentive, laconic, and dull-witted, while students see their teachers as too directive and bossy? Evidence cited by Blanchard (1981), Guilmet (1979), and Key (1975) suggests the existence of such misattributions. Answers to these questions would more fully establish the relevance of sociolinguistic interference in the American Indian classroom as a factor associated with educational failures of Indian children.

■

QUANTITATIVE AND QUALITATIVE RESEARCH

Quantitative research methods in education are based primarily on a natural or "hard" science model, which was essentially borrowed from such fields as physics, chemistry, biology, and, especially, experimental psychology. The quantitative model has dominated educational research until very recently, primarily because experimental psychology dominated education for most of the last century.

Although qualitative methods have been around for a long time, in such fields as anthropology, clinical psychology, and, to some extent, sociology, there was almost no qualitative research in education until the late 1960s. Initially, the educational research establishment was very suspicious about qualitative methods, and qualitative researchers struggled to gain a foothold in the mainstream of educational research. As qualitative researchers persevered, increased in number, and succeeded in illuminating some educational issues, the qualitative-quantitative distinction became polarized. Educational researchers took sides, arguing that one or the other approach was superior. The two approaches were seen by their proponents as incompatible outgrowths of philosophically different stances toward the nature of knowledge and knowledge acquisition.

The basic approach is to characterize positivist [quantitative] and alternative [qualitative] paradigms respectively in terms of various dichotomies—facts versus values, objectivity versus subjectivity, fixed categories versus emergent categories, the outsider's perspective versus the insider's perspective, a static reality versus a fluid reality, causal explanation versus understanding. . . . Insofar as qualitative research gets associated with an epistemological paradigm that rejects things like facts and objectivity, it becomes vulnerable to the familiar charges that it is hopelessly subjective, unscientific, relativistic, and is virtually without any standards at all (Howe and Eisenhart, 1990).

In very recent times, however, the literature on educational research methods has begun to move away from this oppositional stance toward what promises to be a more realistic view of educational research methods. Consensus seems to be emerging that the quantitative or positivist view of knowledge—that there is something called Truth, and that knowledge of Truth is attainable by an objective science—needs to be replaced by a post- or neo-positivist view—that there are many truths with respect to any issue, that science cannot be truly objective, and that at any point in time science can provide only limited or partial knowledge of these many truths.

Social theorist Jurgen Habermas (1973) identifies three ideological paradigms to classify researchers' positions. The Empirical/Analytical tradition has been the dominant paradigm of most physical and social scientists. The scientific method for gathering and analyzing data and reaching conclusions is firmly embedded in this tradition.

But Hermeneutic and Critical thinkers, to use Habermas's terms, are challenging this Empirical/Analytical tradition. Hermeneutical thinkers suggest that classroom teachers may know as much about teaching as educational researchers do—or perhaps even more. Critical thinkers suggest that scientific knowledge cannot be divorced from sociopolitical issues—that traditional science has served dominant political interests, and that a new science can and should concern itself with alleviating social inequities.

In some research circles, the distinction between qualitative and quantitative research approaches is increasingly being seen as at least a partially false opposition. Qualitative researchers do strive for objectivity in analyzing their data and interpreting their results, and at times they even quantify their data; and quantitative research is not truly objective or value-free—researchers' personal biases and theoretical perspectives influence their choices of measurement instruments, confounding variables to be controlled, research contexts, analytic techniques, and interpretations of results. In other research circles, however, the line dividing qualitative and quantitative research has never been more firmly drawn.

Clearly, there are differences between qualitative and quantitative approaches in the kinds of questions that are asked, the processes that are employed in pursuing empirical answers to these questions, and the kinds of answers that are obtained. But the pursuit of knowledge is at best difficult; the educational research community needs to welcome alternative strategies and judge them not on the basis of a priori notions of correctness but on the value of the results that a given approach yields. Some issues of interest to educational researchers can best be investigated through qualitative methods; others lend themselves to quantitative approaches; still others can be validly pursued from either perspective. The research question thus ought to drive the choice of method. A researcher should choose the method of collecting and analyzing data that is best suited to the issue that will be investigated. Too often, however, the choice of method is determined by the researcher's bias for a particular approach.

Part of the problem lies in the fact that most researchers are trained in either qualitative or quantitative methods but not both. Becoming competent in even one of these approaches is a formidable undertaking; few researchers can afford the resources that would be necessary to become competent in both. For this reason, there may continue to be a dichotomy of sorts in educational research. Researchers will tend to utilize the methods in which they feel most competent. However, it is a mistake to scorn useful information that is provided by other researchers working with different methods.

A conventional approach to finding room in the educational research enterprise for both qualitative and quantitative approaches is to see them as useful at different stages of theory building. We took this approach in chapter 1, when we introduced the notions of qualitative and quantitative research and of theory and pointed out that qualitative methods are often more appropriate in theory-generating research and quantitative in theory-testing research.

This statement should have more meaning to you now than it did then. Theory-generating research is done when our knowledge base is very limited—so limited that we do not even know the variables on which we might profitably focus. Qualitative methods, with their emphasis on holism, on detail, and on using all reasonable sources of knowledge in a research context, are ideally suited to the generation of theory.

Quantitative methods, on the other hand, are ideally suited to the testing of theory. Quantitative methods require that we focus on one or a few variables and that we measure these variables with at least some precision; quantitative methods also permit very precise knowledge of the generalizability of results through the use of inferential statistics.

There is, of course, some overlap. Quantitative methods are also useful in generating theory, especially when we have some ideas about the directions in which we need to go. And qualitative research is, on occasion, used to test theory, especially when the theory involves constructs that are difficult to measure with the kind of precision that quantitative research implies.

This view, of qualitative research as primarily suited to induction and theory generation and quantitative research as primarily suited to deduction and theory testing, is not inaccurate, but it is limited. Relegating qualitative research to theory generation ignores other contributions it can make to the research enterprise.

This is particularly true in educational research, partly because education is an applied field. Earlier in this chapter we discussed approaches to theory in applied fields. Qualitative methods have an important role to play in applying borrowed, basic theory to applied issues. Well-developed theory from basic fields can provide information about the processes that should produce particular outcomes. The task of applied researchers is then to explore to what extent and under what conditions these theoretical predictions are useful in applied settings. Qualitative research, with its emphasis on process rather than product, can be particularly useful in this kind of research.

KNOWLEDGE VERSUS PRACTICE

Research, like any other human enterprise, is not perfectly conducted, and there is a great deal about education that we do not understand. But when we consider the difficulties involved in building and testing good theory, especially in a field like education, in which the phenomena that most interest us are extraordinarily complex and often not directly observable, it is astonishing not that we know so little but that we know as much as we do.

Educational practice is limited by what we don't know, but also, and sometimes more frustratingly, it is limited by what we know but don't practice. Practice tends to follow knowledge, but the process is often slow. This is because changing practice on a wide scale requires social change, and social change depends on more than knowledge.

The slowness of social change can be a good thing. We cannot always foresee the far-reaching results of immediate change. An example is the almost total shift that occurred in this country several decades ago in infant-feeding practices. The germ theory of disease suggested that feeding infants sterilized milk from sterilized equipment was superior to breast feeding; conscientious mothers and pediatricians everywhere implemented this recommendation.

But human milk had been adapted over literally millions of years of biological evolution to meet the needs of human infants; and the changes bottle feeding would make in infant-holding practices were not foreseen and their consequences not anticipated. Breast feeding requires physical contact between mother and infant, contact that is necessary to normal development. The medical community now recommends breast over bottle feeding, unless there is some compelling reason to bottle feed. Conservatism in its generic sense provides a safety net. Too rapid change can be dangerous.

On the other hand, change is also inevitable. Full consideration of the determinants of social change is beyond the scope of this book, but knowledge gained from research has played a role in social change in the past and will continue to do so in the future.

SUMMARY

All studies have methodological weaknesses. Understanding the contribution that a single study makes to knowledge is partly a matter of assessing its methodological limitations. However, studies must also be evaluated in terms of the state of knowledge in the field to which they contribute. A study may make a valid contribution despite methodological weaknesses if its strengths address important unresolved issues in the field.

In some fields the need is for good measurement. Studies with methodological weaknesses can make a worthwhile contribution in such fields if they improve on measurement. In some fields the need is for good causal argument. Studies that have methodological weaknesses can make a contribution in such fields if they add to causal understanding. External validity concerns are not appropriate until measurement and causal argument have been dealt with. Studies that are not valid for the subjects on whom they are done cannot be generalized. In the course of conducting many studies to work out problems of measurement and causal argument, researchers often cover such a wide range of subjects and contexts that generalizability has a way of taking care of itself. By the time researchers have achieved good measurement and causal argument, they have often also established generalizability.

Building good theory ultimately makes the most valuable contribution to knowledge. However, in primarily applied fields such as education, theory is often borrowed from basic fields such as psychology. The purpose of an educational study may be to test the extent to which borrowed theory can inform applied issues, rather than to contribute to theory building in the basic field. Studies with a theory-building orientation need to be assessed in terms of the contribution they make to theory building; but studies of the usefulness of theory in applied settings need to be assessed in terms of their own goals. In discussing their results, researchers usually address the methodological limitations of their studies and the contributions their studies make to applied or basic knowledge.

Educational research has been characterized by a sharp dichotomy between qualitative and quantitative approaches. The assumption has been that the two methods represent competing and incompatible ways of understanding the nature of knowledge and of approaching knowledge acquisition. Now the climate seems to be ripe, however, for a new view of qualitative and quantitative approaches as having important contributions to make to the admittedly imperfect process of acquiring knowledge about education. In a given study, the method or combination of methods should be chosen for their potential to provide useful information about the issue being investigated.

Qualitative and quantitative research typically make different kinds of contributions to theory building. Qualitative research tends to contribute most to fields lacking good theory or in which the development of theory is very primitive. Quantitative research is more appropriate for testing theory, although it can be used to generate theory as well, especially when researchers already have some productive focus. However, relegating qualitative methods to theory-generating situations does not take advantage of their full potential. Qualitative methods can also be extremely useful in exploring the relevance of theory to applied concerns.

Educational practice does not always follow knowledge. Implementing research findings on a large scale often requires social change, and social change is determined by more than knowledge. Because our knowledge processes are imperfect, this lag between our acquisition of knowledge and our practice can be useful.

SUMMARY EXERCISES

The complete texts of three published research reports are included in appendix A. Evaluate each of these reports using all of the skills you have learned. What questions were the researchers asking? Were their methods qualitative or quantitative? Does the choice of approach seem appropriate? If the methods were quantitative, what variables were studied? Were these variables validly measured? Evaluate causal argument if applicable. Evaluate external validity. How did the researchers analyze their data? What conclusions did they reach? Were these inductive or deductive conclusions? What contributions does each report make to knowledge? If the methods were qualitative, is the voice of the participants evident in the research project? Is there evidence that the findings emerged from the collection and analysis of the data? Are the conclusions triangulated? Is the positionality of the researcher evident and appropriately examined?

Responses to this exercise appear at the end of Appendix C, "Responses to Exercises," following the responses to the exercises in Chapter 11.

A

Research Reports

The complete texts of three published research reports follow. See the Summary Exercises section of chapter 11 for questions pertaining to these reports.

(1)
The Ethnography of Children's
Spontaneous Play (Finnan, 1982)

Introduction

One girl made a mock lunge at another girl. The second girl ran a few feet and stopped, taunting the chaser to try to catch her. The chaser responded with another lunge, and the other player again ran only a few feet. This continued for several minutes; the girls moved away from the school building. Suddenly the chasee ran several yards to hide behind a woman and child standing near the edge of the playground. The players ducked and circled around the woman, laughing as they played. They eventually worked their way back to the building, darting and teasing. Finally, the chasee sat down near a group of girls and refused to continue playing. [Third grade, 3/19/74]

A quick glance at any school playground in the United States shows the prevalence of this kind of spontaneous play. It is brief, seemingly chaotic, often rough, and little understood by adults. A closer look, though, shows that it has a structure which gives children[1] freedom rather than imposing rules. These chase games are unlike formal games, such as Tag, because there are no preestablished rules and roles. In fact, rules from the nonplay world are often overturned and mocked. Rules are replaced by signals that announce that anything goes because "This is play."

Insights into children's behavior and development can be drawn from observations of spontaneous play. This kind of play flourishes away from adult influence, expectations, and approval. Children participate for their own enjoyment, not for adult sanction. Spontaneous play reflects behavioral patterns of the children's nonplay world. Insights drawn from analysis of spontaneous play are applicable to problems children have outside of the play framework.

Observations of spontaneous play lead one to ask why groups of children participate differently in spontaneous play when there are no rules or roles to adopt. I will focus on two examples of how play preferences and style differ in spontaneous play. First, I will explore sex differences in play style. In a study of white American children's play, I found that girls' and boys' styles of play differ. Boys' play is aggressive and girls' play is halting and teasing. Boys are proud of their role on the playground, while girls are dissatisfied with their role unless they can involve boys. I suggest that these differences reflect children's general attitudes toward future sex roles.

In my second example, I will show that children must possess a degree of cultural knowledge to enjoy spontaneous play. This work is based on observations of Vietnamese refugee children's play on American playgrounds. I found that they generally play highly structured, rule-governed games rather than participating in free-flowing spontaneous play. I hypothesize that they are using play to learn the rules of the playground and society, while their American peers choose spontaneous play because they know these rules so well they enjoy breaking them.

What Is Spontaneous Play?

Spontaneous play is activity created for the moment, without the rules and roles that dominate more formal games. Self-structured chase games[2] are perpetuated through their own adaptive structure rather than through preestablished rules. Spontaneous play involves the basic elements of more highly structured activities—chase-elude, attack-defend, and capture-rescue (Sutton-Smith 1992)—but there are no restrictions on the when, where, how, and whom of these activities.

There has been little research on children's spontaneous play, in part because most research methodologies are not suited to studying anything so seemingly chaotic. Surveys, interviews, and short-term observations uncover activities that are named and replicable. Most of the research on children's play has either (1) directed children into adult specified activities, (2) elicited game preference by asking for the names of games, or (3) compiled collections of games (Avedon 1971, Herron and Sutton-Smith 1971, I. and P. Opie 1969). Activities that do not have rules, roles, purpose, and a result are lumped into a category "pastimes" (Avedon 1971: 422).

Structures of Behavior

One must look for structures more fundamental to activity than formalized rules and roles to understand children's spontaneous play. These patterns and structures emerge only after extensive observation. They cannot be assumed *a priori* and cannot be elicited through surveys, tests, interviews, or brief observations.

Gregory Bateson's translation of behavior as communication stimulated interest in underlying structures of behavior. Bateson introduced the idea that activities are "framed" or set off from each other through signals. In play, we transcend normal boundaries of appropriate behavior because we frame behavior as play. Through signals, we say, "It is OK for us to scream, hit wrestle, and pinch because we are playing." Framing gives a minimal structure to activity. Players are freed from society's rules and its emphasis on order as long as the frame is maintained. When the frame is broken, however, the players no longer read a message "This is play," but ask the question "Is this play?" Play cannot continue if this question remains (Bateson 1972).

Why has so little attention been focused on the process of signaling boundaries between play and nonplay behavior? In part it is because the signals are so much a part of play that they disappear into its structure.

All players can read and send signals that set play behavior off from nonplay behavior. However, signals are rarely verbalized in a player's description of play and even less often in adult research on play. Signaling is "just one of those things we do" in play. It is something all players do, but they do not think about why, or what it means. This creates a dilemma; researchers cannot ignore what players cannot pay attention to. Players cannot play if they analyze their own actions, and researchers cannot analyze behavior if they do not understand what the players take for granted. The solution to this dilemma lies in the researcher's orientation and methodology. Both must be geared to discovering patterns of behavior central to the activity. Anthropological ethnography is well suited to this task because of its emphasis on structural interaction. The following is a description of how I used anthropological ethnography to study children's spontaneous play.

Methodology

This chapter is based on data gathered in two separate research projects. The first study was conducted in conjunction with a children's folklore project undertaken by the Southwest Education Development Laboratory in Austin, Texas. This laboratory contacted several local folklorists to record children's natural playground activity. Each of the researchers chose a group of children or a kind of activity to observe. I chose the play of white girls. Observation took place from January to May 1974.

The second project focused on the role of play in the social adaptation of culturally different children, in this case Vietnamese children had been in the United States for a little over one year. I chose four schools differing in their racial composition and their treatment of students with limited English. There were 22 Vietnamese children enrolled in the four schools: 12 in the fourth to sixth grades.[3]

My observations in both studies were nondirective. I tried to stand on the periphery of activity and made no attempt to influence the play. I talked to children when they came up to me, but I never drew children out of their play to interview them. I was looking primarily for the signals children

used to set the frame "This is play" and to record what occurred within the frame. I tried to record as much detail as possible on movements, vocalization, and players' flow into and out of games. In both studies, I relied primarily on note-taking to record play behavior; however, I also used a tape recorder in the first study. Before entering the playgrounds, I would make note of weather conditions, time, date, and anything that might affect the children's play (holidays, changes in school schedule, etc.). I arrived at the playground before the children were let out for recess, so that I could watch play groups form. In the first project I did not focus on specific children, but on kinds of play. In the second project, however, my focus was on specific children.

I developed an informal code for participants and movements. I used an abbreviation of their names if I knew them; otherwise, I relied on their most obvious physical characteristics, such as race, size, hair, color, and sex. Notes such as "blo. b." or "fat w.g." are sufficient to bring back an image of a blond boy or a fat white girl. I also made note of the time, in at least five-minute intervals. When I used a tape recorder along with notes, I wrote down verbalizations as well as behavior, so that my notes and the tape would coincide.

The most important part of note-taking is immediate transcription. I tried to transcribe my notes into full, typed field notes as soon as I returned from the playground. Otherwise, scribbled notes lose their meaning and unrecorded activity is forgotten.

Although I used a tape recorder in the first project, I did not in the second. I felt it would be more distractive than useful, since my focus was on a specific group of children. I did not want to shun other children, but I was more interested in watching Vietnamese children than in talking to others. From my experience in the first study, I did not want to draw attention to myself through the tape recorder, and I found that I was able to write down most of the verbalization I could hear. I suggest that before using a tape recorder in recording playground behavior, researchers should be sure it warrants the distraction it creates. Often, when one is not directly involved in the activity, there is enough time to record behavior and verbalization through notes. Also, it is often difficult to make sense of the layers of talk picked up by a tape recorder, and important speech can be lost in a garble of screams and shouts.

The Continuum of Chase Games

All chase games share several basic features. They depend on communication of the message "This is play," as all spontaneous play does, and they are based on the elements chase and elude. Chase games, however, are not all simple dashes across a playground. They differ according to the sex of the participants, the ratio of chasers to chasees, type of flight, purpose of the game, provocation, and use of space.

The following outlines the continuum of chase games from simple spurts across a field to complex fantasy-based interactions. This illustrates what occurs within the frame "This is play" and how seemingly chaotic activity shares a common structure with other self-structured chase games.[4]

The preceding outline shows both the similarities and the differences of these

---

TYPE A

1. Number of participants	Two
2. Sex of the pair	Same sex or girl/boy
3. Ratio of chasers to chasees	1:1
4. Type of flight	A long spurt
5. Purpose of the game	The purpose is to capture the chasee or for the chasee to outdistance the chaser.
6. Provocation	1. The chasee attacks the chaser and retreats.
	2. The chasee takes a possession from the chaser.
	3. The chaser or chasee gives a verbal or nonverbal signal of aggression.
7. Use of space and territory	The chase is usually into space that is not occupied by other children. The territory covered in the chase is rather large. In some cases the chasee can flee to a safety area.
8. Fate of the captured chasee	*Boy/boy*—the chaser pins the chasee to the ground.
	Boy/girl—sometimes she is pinned to the ground, but usually only for a few seconds.
	Girl/boy—she holds the boy as long as possible, but often needs help from a friend or a prop (jumprope) to hold him.
	Girl/girl—the chaser holds the chasee for a few seconds.

Example. Three second-grade girls showed a fieldworker how to perform a hand clap game. When they finished, they stood up and played with a wad of paper, trying to push it into each other's clothes and hands. Barbara[5] tried to push it up Cathy's sleeve, but Cathy ran away. Cathy ran toward a building across the field, but was captured before reaching it. Barbara held her for a few seconds before Cathy ran back to where they had been playing. Barbara did not follow Cathy again, and walked away in another direction. [Second grade, 3/8/74]

TYPE B

1. Number of participants	Two if girl/boy; 2, 3, or 4 if same sex
2. Sex of the group	Girl/boy or same sex
3. Ratio of chasers to chasees	1:1, 2:1, 3:1
4. Type of flight	Short, evasive movements
5. Purpose of the game	The chasee tries to evade the chaser. If the chaser is not a skillful runner, the chasee will taunt him/her, usually

nonverbally. For girls, the main purpose is to tease each other. For boys, the chase seems to be secondary to wrestling.

6. Provocation	The provocation is similar to that in Type A, but usually the chaser and chasee share the desire to participate in this game.
7. Use of space and territory	The chase usually takes place in a space that is occupied by other people or playground equipment. They are used to shield the chasee from the chaser. Since there is little distance between the chaser and the chasee, the chasee does not have a safety area.
8. Fate of the captured chasee	*Boy/boy*—the object of the game is to wrestle on the ground. The chasee is almost always knocked down by the chaser; roles are often reversed when the game resumes.
	Boy/girl—she is sometimes knocked down, but they do not wrestle. Usually, the boy playfully hits the girl, or grabs her for a few moments.
	Girl/boy—this situation is rare, but when it occurs the chaser slaps or grabs at the boy but rarely captures him.
	Girl/girl—the chaser generally only pokes at the chasee or grabs her by the arm or around the shoulders.

Example. Three second-grade boys were engaged in a wrestling-type chase game. They were playing in an area occupied by a group of kindergarten children. The chaser would catch the chasee from the back, and usually tried to knock him down by pushing his knees forward. When the chasee fell, he was immediately pinned to the ground. Soon the victim was up and another boy was captured and knocked to the ground. The three boys switched roles throughout the games and never tried to escape from the chaser. They seemed to enjoy the capture more than the chase. [Second grade, 2/15/74]

TYPE C

1. Number of participants	Three to six
2. Sex of the group	Girl/boy
3. Ratio of chasers to chasees	3:1, 4:1, 5:1, 2:2, 3:2, 4:2
4. Type of flight	The flight flows between long spurts and short evasive movements. The short movements are most common.
5. Purpose of the game	The purpose is to inflict some kind of punishment on the chasee. It is important for the chasers to establish their superiority over the chasee.
6. Provocation	These games are often offshoots of Type A or B, with the same provocation. However, the chasers often initiate the game without provocation from the chasee.
7. Use of space and territory	These games are played in both open and occupied space. There are rarely safety areas.
8. Fate of the captured chasee	The chasee is almost always punished when captured. He/she is either detained by the chasers or knocked down, hit with a ball, robbed of clothing (shoes, coat), etc.

Example. It was a hot afternoon, and the children clustered in the shade. Two girls ran out from the shade of the second-grade building, chasing after a blonde boy. He got about halfway to the bar that separated the school from the street when the girls caught up with him. They encircled him with their arms and hauled him back to the shady area. They held him for several minutes as he squirmed and pulled and finally escaped. By this time, some other girls joined their friends, and when the original two chasers brought him back again, the whole group pinned him to a tree and hit at him. A few minutes later, I saw the boy running after one of the girls, and he soon captured her. [Second grade, 3/19/74]

TYPE D

1. Number of participants	Five or more
2. Sex of the group	Either all male or all female
3. Ratio of chasers to chasees	*Boys*—more chasers than chasees. *Girls*—more chasees than chasers
4. Type of flight	*Boys*—these games involve long runs; they are actually similar to very simple ball games.
	Girls—the flight is short, on the whole, and is often terminated when the chasee darts into a safety area.
5. Purpose of the game	*Boys*—they usually use some equipment, such as a ball, and the object is to catch the person who has control of the ball. The chaser/chasee roles are more fluid than in kickball, and there are no preestablished rules.
6. Provocation	Provocation is not especially important in these games because no players have to be coerced to play.
7. Use of space and territory	*Boys*—the boys cover the entire playing field and have no safety area.
	Girls—the girls' games are played primarily in a mandatory safety area, and a semi-safe territory.
8. Fate of the captured chasee	*Boys*—he becomes a chaser. He may be knocked down in the process of the capture, but that is secondary to the chaser's wish to become the chasee.
	Girls—often nothing happens. The girls may take on a similar role to the chaser (witch or vampire). Sometimes a chasee is captured and held hostage or punished by the chaser.

Example—Girls' games. Several boys briefly joined a girls' chase but soon lost interest, leaving a group of 8–10 girls under their shelter (a piece of play equipment resembling a lean-to). This shelter served as a safety zone when witches or monsters attacked. Karen assumed the role of witch and, with a friend, captured another girl, pinning her to a tree. She announced, "She's still tied 'til the wicked witches come." Karen then yelled to a girl across the playground, "All right, Connie, Witchie-poo, get her." Connie left her game and became a witch. A small girl tapped one witch and the prisoner on the shoulder, saying "I'm a fairy, bing." Karen sloughed this off saying, "Oh, that's what you think." With Connie as wicked witch, Karen and her friend became protectors of the other players. Karen yelled, "My children, my children, come here!" They took the girls under the shelter. Connie announced, "I'll get you, you little rats!" Karen: "No, you won't; no, you won't." The game became rather chaotic as girls enacted scenes from the film *The Wizard of Oz* (shown on television that week). Brief chases between two and three girls ensued. Several boys invaded the safety zone, but by this time the play group had splintered into many small disconnected groups. [Third grade, 2/28/74]

Example—Boys' game. A large group of boys ran past me in a pack. They were pursuing one boy who had control of a kickball. He was grabbed by several boys after being caught, but was not knocked down. Another boy captured the ball, and the chase resumed with the pack chasing the boy with the ball. [Third grade, 3/12/74]

TYPE E

1. Number of participants	Five or more
2. Sex of the group	Girl/boy
3. Ratio of chasers to chasees	The chasees outnumber the chasers.
4. Type of flight	The game includes both short spurts and long runs.
5. Purpose of the game	One purpose is for the girls to be chased by the boys. Another purpose is to gather a large group of players to act out a group fantasy.
6. Provocation	The girls tease and taunt the boys until they join the game. Boys may also be attracted to the role they can play in the game (monster, vampire).
7. Use of space and territory	Most activity revolves around the safety zone (a piece of play equipment). Eventually boys ignore the sanctity of the safety zone and the children cover more territory.
8. Fate of the captured chasee	The chasee can either return to the shelter, be held hostage, or be transformed into a monster or a vampire. This often involves a ritualized imitation of bloodsucking.

Example. A chase began when Tony chased Karen, Vickie, and two other girls into the lean-to shelter. The girls screamed, "Can't come into our house" to the nearby boys. Karen and another girl ran in and out of the house, taunting the boys by chanting, "Na, na ne, boo, boo." The girls began to play house in the shelter. Tony knocked on the door, and said, "Hey, I need some dinner for me and my pal here." One girl pestered Tony about his pal's name, until he replied, "His name is Jesus." Another girl began shooting at the boys with an imaginary shotgun. Tony said, "You put that down. That's what, what makes me mean, people who shoot guns all the time." Tony affected a "monster stance" and stormed through the shelter, sending the girls screaming into the open field. Soon, about 20 children were playing. Eventually all of the girls were caught by monsters or vampires and they too became threatening creatures. The game moved away from the now abandoned safety zone. The game became chaotic, with many small groups chasing and capturing each other. One girl insisted she was a ghost, but when other players challenged her power as a ghost, she left the game in tears. The chasing became more aggressive as the boys experimented with their monster or vampire roles. Eventually, most of the girls wandered away from the game, leaving it to the boys. [Third grade, 3/29/74]

TYPE F

These are rule-governed chasing games, such as Touch or Tag. I did not record any of these games during my first project, but they also fit in to the chase game continuum. For example, the game of Touch is outlined below (Opie, 1969:62).

1. Number of participants	Generally more than four
2. Sex of the group	Same sex or girl/boy
3. Ratio of chasers to chasees	Chasees outnumber the chasers
4. Type of flight	The flight is long unless the chaser is an unskillful runner or the chasee is very confident.
5. Purpose of the game	To chase and evade and to become or remain a chasee

6. Provocation   Desire to play a simple rule-governed game.

7. Use of space and territory   Games usually take place in open space. Some versions have a safety area built into the rules.

8. Fate of the captured chasee   He/she becomes the new chaser until someone is captured or until everyone is captured.

---

self-structured chase games. All games are set off as play. They revolve around the basic elements of chase and elude, and they become more complex as the number of players increases, as boys and girls play together, and as new elements, such as fantasy roles, are added. Despite the complexity of some activities, children do not rely on rules to hold the games together. What holds the games together is the maintenance of the frame "This is a play."

The play frame gives players freedom to act as they please, as well as freedom to remove responsibility for their actions, especially aggressive acts. Within the play frame, a player can "cremate" a friend without fear of punishment or a sense of guilt. In the context of the self-structured chase games, a player can become intensely involved in the play until eventually the play frame breaks. He or she then asks, "Is this play?" and is frightened by the consequences of a negative answer. The following occurred during the Type E game described earlier. Vickie's play frame broke and she retreated to the teacher and to the comfort of the rule-governed world:

Vickie: I'm already a vampire. I'm a vampire already, Gilbert.
Other: I'm not . . . growl!
Vickie: I'm a dying soul.
Gilbert: You what?
Vickie: Tony, Tony, I'm a ghost! I'm a ghost! (Earlier in the game, Vickie was Tony's "helper.")
Gilbert: He's a vampire.
Gilbert: You're invisible so you can go through anything. (Vickie now clings to my waist.)
Gilbert: We can see you. (He chases her around me.)
Vickie: Quit it!
Gilbert: You can't see a ghost.

Vickie: No, Gilbert! (She begins to whine.) Why don't you (?) Teacher!
Other: Growl.
Vickie: Leave me alone!
Boys: He's already a vampire.
Vickie: Tony, Tony, I'm a ghost.
Tony: A vampire could kill a ghost. (Vickie becomes very upset and leaves in tears.) [Third grade, 3/28/74]

Differences in Children's Participation in Spontaneous Play

The intent of the previous discussion was to show how a structure emerges from seemingly chaotic activity. Once the basic elements of an activity are known, differences in children's involvement in the activities become obvious. The following sections will show first, how there are sex-typed differences in children's spontaneous play, and second, that cultural knowledge is required for these games.

Sex-Typed Differences

Three boys raced toward me, with two girls in close pursuit. The boys stopped, wheeled around, and lunged at the girls. The girls fled in mock terror to the other end of the playground. They huddled together, giggling, anticipating the boys' possible retaliation. Meanwhile, another boy explained, "This school is weird. Usually the boys chase the girls, but here, the girls chase the boys." [Sixth grade, Redwood City, CA, 2/19/77]

Contrary to this boy's opinion, there is nothing unusual about his school. In fact, it is more common for girls to chase boys than the reverse. The continuum of chase games points to numerous examples of differences in boys' and girls' style of play and play preferences. Several examples of girls coercing reluctant boys to join their games were also given. This may seem like a sign of changing sex roles on the playground, but closer observation reveals that girls still act out traditional feminine roles in their play.

Male and female roles are clearly marked in many traditional rule-governed games (Sutton-Smith and Rosenburg 1960, 1961; Sutton-Smith, Rosenburg, and Morgan 1963). The labels "boy's game" or "girl's game" follow many activities through generations of players. For example, marbles is a boy's game; jacks, a girl's game. Boys' games are traditionally aggressive and competitive; girls' games are passive and accommodating. Boys and girls play differently, even when they participate in the same game.

Distinct boys' and girls' chase styles exist, even in the simplest self-structured chase game. Basically, boys' chase style is aggressive and physical and girls' style is passive and teasing. A simple chase between girls will be quite different from one between boys, and when boys and girls play together, they combine the most powerful elements of their respective styles. The disorder and chaos created in large girl/boy self-structured chase games gives girls a rare opportunity to transcend the restraints traditionally inhibiting them in their play.

Boys' self-structured chase games require a great expenditure of physical energy. They are a test of boys' physical strength and consist of competition in running, wrestling, and tackling. Two boys' games were used as examples under Type B and Type D. These examples illustrate the importance of physical strength in boys' self-structured chase games. The emphasis in small games is on the capture; in the large games, it is on the chase. In the small games, the players create a mock fight in which they attempt to "cremate" each other. The large games resemble kickball, but the self-structured games have no preestablished rules or winners.

Four elements characterize the boys' self-structured chase games. First, aggression is a key component. The boys claim to kill, cremate, and destroy each other. A non-aggressive participant has no place in these games. Second, there is a great deal of physical contact. Bodies are pressed together during the capture. The players separate only during the chase. Third, boys enjoy freedom of movement in their chase games. No safety zones are established, so the chaser is always free to pursue his victim. Fourth, no roles are permanent. The roles of chaser and chasee are constantly fluctuating. No player has the power to dictate the flow of the game, i.e., one boy cannot tell another to keep a role permanently.

These elements of boys' chase games stand in contrast to the girls' style of play. The girls have a teasing, halting style of chasing. Physical strength is not a key element. In small games (those involving two or three players), the chasee teases the chaser; prolonged running chases are not found. In large games, girls assume fantasy roles such as witch, fairy, and slave. A dominant player establishes the roles and sets the flow of the game, in contrast to the free flow of boys' chase games. Girls' small-scale chase games find the players keeping their respective roles throughout the game (i.e., the chaser and chasee never exchange roles), while in large-scale games roles are exchanged after a chasee is captured by the chaser. In contrast to large-scale boys' games, however, role changes in large-scale girls' games are relatively structured, with changes permitted only after capture. Examples of girls' games appear on the first page and as an example of Type D games.

Girls' self-structured chase games are characterized by five basic elements. First, all chases are short and halting. The object is to tease, not to overpower the opponent. There is little or no wrestling. Second, roles are often permanent. In the small games, one girl remains the chaser and the other the chasee. In the large games, there is more flexibility, but witches are usually permanent and the victims only change roles when captured. Permanent roles are often maintained because one girl directs the movement of the game. Third, a safety zone must be respected. The safety zone can be a person, or a stationary object. The fourth and fifth elements are most frequently found in the large games. They are the use of fantasy roles and the underlying desire of the players to eventually involve boys as participants. The aggressive fantasy roles serve to attract boys who are otherwise disinterested in girls' games.

Behavioral differences found in boys' and girls' chase games are similar to differences observed in their nonplay behavior (Mussen, Conger, and Kagan 1969; Whiting and Edwards 1973; Maccoby and Jacklin 1975; Barry, Bacon, and Child 1957; D'Andrade 1966). According to cross-cultural studies, boys tend to be more aggressive than girls, while girls are more nurturant and supportive than boys (Whiting and Edwards 1973; Maccoby and Jacklin 1975; Barry, Bacon, and Child 1957). Children's attitudes toward their play reflect their sex role satisfaction. Studies of American children's attitudes toward feminine and masculine roles outside of play show that boys are happier with their sex role than are girls (Maccoby 1966; Stein, Pohly, and Mueller 1971; Rabban 1950; Brown 1957; Smith 1939; Gardner 1947).

On the playground, boys are proud of their games and their status. They express no desire to include girls in their play or to play girls' games. During an aggressive all-boy game, a third-grade boy offered his opinion:

> *I:* We're trying to figure out how you play your games. We want to teach other kids the games you're playing.
> *Boy:* I don't think the girls would like this one.
> *I:* Why not?
> *Boy:* Because we get cremated.
> *I:* They'll get what? [I didn't understand him at first.]
> *Boy:* They'll get cremated. That's the whole idea of the game, is getting killed. [Third grade, 3/1/74]

Girls, on the other hand, are discontented with their role on the playground and are envious of boys' play. Three third-grade girls express both a longing to play traditional girls' games and an attraction to boys' play:

> *I:* Why are they chasing the boys? [referring to several other girls]
> *Karen:* Because the girls like to chase the boys.

> *I:* Do you have to play with the boys?
> *Pam:* No, they [other girls] like to.
> *I:* Oh, they like to?
> *Pam:* And they don't like to play jumping rope, so there's hardly any girls to play jumping rope.
> [skip one minute]
> *Pam:* They [the boys] play too rough. They knock you down on purpose and get all dirty and all muddy and all that.
> *I:* Yeah, what kind of games do you play when you play with the boys?
> *Karen:* Boys catch the girls, um, whatever.
> *Gina:* Yeah, boys chase the girls or the girls chase the boys, or the boys knock down the girls or the girls knock down the boys.
> *I:* Sounds pretty good. Do the girls chase the boys more than the boys chase the girls or [interruption]
> *Girl:* The girls chase the boys more than the boys chase the girls.
> *I:* Really? Why?
> *Girl:* Because, I don't know [interruption]
> *Pam:* Because they don't want to chase us, and we want to play a game, and so we chase them and hit them, and knock them down.
> *Karen:* And then whenever we [interruption]
> *Pam:* And they they get mad and start chasing us. [Third grade, 3/1/74]

These second- and third-grade girls resemble other 9-year-old girls described by Rosenburg, Sutton-Smith, and Morgan (1963) in another study on play. The girls they studied exhibited ambivalent play preferences. The researchers noticed that the girls were attracted to immature games such as jump rope and hopscotch and also to mature games such as basketball and soccer. The 9-year-old boys described by Rosenburg,

Sutton-Smith, and Morgan were only interested in mature games. The researchers credit boys' clear play preferences to the traditional involvement of men in sports and the ambivalence of girls to the absence of a similar tradition of women's participation in adult competitive sports (1963).

Why are some girls this age so interested in involving boys in their play? One reason may lie in the impact of boys on girls' games. When boys and girls play together in self-structured chase games, the games take on aspects of both boys' and girls' games, but most importantly, they lose the order and conformity characteristic of girls' play. Most girls quickly accept the absence of rules and lack of organization. There is little protest from girls when boys ignore their safety zone, even though it is rarely violated in the all-girl games. No rules exist once chasers have driven all the players out of the safety zone. At this point, girls can no longer cling to the safety of a home and conformity to rules. All players, both boys and girls, must use aggression to protect themselves, since they are no longer protected by rules. On the other hand, girls as well as boys can assert themselves forcefully, since no rules restrain them.

Rather than assuming this aggressive, seemingly chaotic play is nonproductive, one can see it as the response of children preparing for a changing society. Games of disorder address the dialectic between the order created in society and the disorder associated with the environment and with new societal demands. These games do not equip children to be mommys or daddys or doctors and nurses, but help children cope with change and uncertainty in a nonstatic society. Games of disorder are found in diverse societies, but are more prevalent in complex societies and are played more frequently today than in the past (Sutton-Smith 1977, Sutton-Smith and Rosenburg 1961).

Involvement in the girl/boy self-structured chase games is a rare opportunity for girls to play aggressively with disorder. Girls are adept at fantasy play but rarely permit disorder to override order. Even in children's storytelling, girls tell stories of deprivation (disorder) followed by reward (order), while boys reverse the order in their stories, leaving the characters in a state of disorder (May 1966). The fantasy play in girl/boy self-structured chase games, however, is pure disorder; players must leave the game to find order. It is significant that girls initiate the play in these games despite their preoccupation with order.

There are three possible reasons why girls initiate these particular games of disorder. First, boys and girls generally adopt sex-typed play styles. The girls' style is relatively restrictive; girls are encouraged to "be nice" even when they play. Their play is often closely connected with nonplay situations, such as playing house or playing school. Janet Lever found that white American girls play indoors with fewer playmates in less competitive activities lasting a shorter time than boys. She concludes that play patterns perpetuate traditional sex-role divisions by preparing boys for occupational interactions and girls for familial interactions (1976). Reports of play in other cultures usually mention gender segregation in play groups and the role of play in sex-role acquisition. Boys are generally more free to play, because they are away from adult supervision, while girls assume household duties at an early age (Mead 1928, 1930; Deng 1972; Schwartzman and Barbera 1976). Girls' conventional play permits little room for impulsive or aggressive behavior. Only in the self-structured games are American girls free to abandon these restrictions and act as they please. They find the disorder in the girl/boy self-structured chase games unusual and compelling.

Second, girls are in limbo in their play choice. By the age of 8 or 9, they are no longer satisfied with immature games, such as jump rope, but are not preparing for mature sports, as are boys at this age. Boys are also in a transition period, but are offered an alternative to their earlier play styles. The girls' play world is disjointed, with little promise for a satisfying future play role.

Third, girls are not satisfied with the traditional feminine sex role, and they are presented with few alternatives to it. In a sense, their image of themselves as women is in disorder. They want respect and status, but there are few models to emulate.

The sex roles ascribed to boys and girls above may seem outdated in light of the changing role of women. It would be too speculative at this point to draw strong connections between changes in the status of women and the play of third-grade girls. Girls' play will change as the status of women changes. Playground activities will reflect the increasing interest in women's professional sports. Girls' participation in organized sports such as Little League will affect their status on the playground. These changes will be superficial, though, unless children also learn different sex role behavior. Boys are, at present, encouraged to play aggressively and competitively, while girls are encouraged to be accommodating and thoughtful in their play. Boys and girls must learn to be both accommodating and competitive to function successfully as adults. Children are now using self-structured chase games to experiment with disorder and the challenges of a changing society. If the role of women in the adult society continues to change dramatically, girls must necessarily utilize self-structured play to develop the skills relevant to a new status.

Cultural Knowledge and Self-Structured Play[6]

It should already be clear that spontaneous play serves a positive role in children's development. However, not all children choose to participate in spontaneous play. Observations of Vietnamese refugee children's play showed that these 9- to 12-year-olds have more restricted play preferences than their American papers. Vietnamese children tend to choose highly structured games, even though their American peers often choose spontaneous play.

I found two patterns in the play of Vietnamese children. First, Vietnamese boys have very different patterns of play involvement than Vietnamese girls. All Vietnamese boys play actively, while few girls participate in play activities. Second, Vietnamese children play rule-governed games almost exclusively. They rarely participate in the spontaneous, free-flowing play created by their peers.

It was no surprise that Vietnamese girls and boys adopted different play patterns; however, the differences were more marked than I expected. I attribute the girls' lack of participation to the lack of fit between their play in Vietnam and games played by their American peers. When asked what they played in Vietnam, most girls said badminton and jump rope. Neither game is played by fourth- to sixth-graders at the four American schools. Most of the girls alternate between talking to friends and joining rather aggressive games during their recess periods. Vietnamese girls have few minimally verbal play options.

All Vietnamese boys play during recess, but they limit their play participation to rule-governed games. When Vietnamese girls play, they also play rule-governed games. Free-flowing, spontaneous play exists on all of the playgrounds, but the Vietnamese children choose rule-governed games instead. Since they are free to choose their play activity, there must be a reason why they prefer rule-governed games to spontaneous play. It seems that the security of rule-governed games is attractive to Vietnamese children. Vietnamese children choose play forms with well-defined boundaries and well-defined roles. They rely on the game's structure to clarify and define their position in relation to the other players. It is not clear if they are retreating from the confusion of learning a new culture into the safety of rules, or if they are pulled to a structure they can work within. According to Caillois, all game players try to eliminate confusion: "The confused and intricate laws of ordinary life are replaced in this fixed space and for this given time by precise, arbitrary, unexceptionable rules that must be accepted as such and that govern the correct playing of the game" (Caillois 1961:7).

The children who are fairly sure of their status on the playground and understand the social rules create novel play situations by transcending and overturning social rules. In contrast, children unfamiliar with American culture find rule-governed games novel because they learn new social rules. D. E. Berlyne writes that we are most responsive to an intermediate degree of novelty. We are indifferent to situations that are either too remote or too familiar (1960:21). Different criteria for novelty influence the play patterns of Vietnamese children and their American peers. A novel situation for an immigrant child may seem boring to an American child because it is too familiar, while a novel situation for an American child may be too foreign for an immigrant child.

Previous discussions of spontaneous play have not recognized the importance of a shared cultural base. New social structures and interactions intrigue those who are so secure in their culture they can think about changing it. If children do not fully understand the social structure and rules spontaneous play turns against, play boundaries and signaling will not be strong enough to hold children in spontaneous play. Vietnamese children avoid spontaneous play with American peers because they are still trying to establish boundaries and understand social relations in their everyday world. They engage in play forms that strengthen social relations and clarify social rules rather than participating in play that breaks down the social structure they are trying to build.

Children do not participate wholeheartedly in spontaneous play unless they are sure of the social rules they violate. Vietnamese children will gain this security by first mastering rule-governed games. I do not mean they must become good athletes; rather, they must understand the rules along with what lies beneath the rules. A parallel development of rule manipulation occurs in children's riddling.

Children go through three stages in learning to riddle. They begin with learning the structure and linguistic rules and end with transcending and distorting the rules. First, children learn the linguistic code, in this case, the question/answer sequence. They enjoy asking riddles such as "What two letters do Indians live in? T.P." Once the code is learned, they play with and distort the linguistic sequence by demanding answers that do not follow as clearly from the question, for example, "What is black and white and red all over? A bloody zebra." Children eventually subordinate the linguistic code to their interpersonal relations and substitute victimization as the proper response to the question. They ask a question such as "Do you want a Hawaiian punch?" and follow it by punching the child in the face (McDowell 1974).

The development of riddling skills is analogous to the development of play skills.

Rules of proper speech or play behavior are learned in the first stage. At this time, children enjoy mastering rules they will use in daily life. Learning rules loses its novelty once children are proficient in them. Children then begin testing the sensation of rule distortion. Players are not bound by the rules, because they are playing, either physically or linguistically. Eventually, the riddles or games transcend the limits of their codes. Communication in both cases goes beyond verbalization or patterned interaction into what Bateson calls "metacommunication" or communication about communication (Bateson 1972:191).

Vietnamese children are essentially in the first stage, learning the linguistic and social codes. Vietnamese girls are at a disadvantage because they are avoiding both spontaneous play and rule-governed games. They are like the child who never tells a riddle. They stand back and observe the social interactions of play, but they do not learn what it is like to participate in the play. The girls learn the social rules, just as the nonriddler learns the question/answer sequence, but they do not learn how to play with the codes. In contrast, Vietnamese boys are learning social rules through play and may eventually know them well enough to play with them. These data suggest that Vietnamese boys will gain a deeper understanding of American culture than will Vietnamese girls, because of their participation in play.

Vietnamese boys are learning American cultural roles through the informal channel of play. They will learn to play with the rules and adapt to changes in American society if they go beyond rule-governed games. Vietnamese girls, in contrast, are learning social rules through the more formal channel of school and adults. They may be less prepared for change than Vietnamese boys, because school and adults do not give children an opportunity to play with the rules they have learned.

Significance

Most educational research focuses on aspects of schooling that adults hope to improve. To improve a situation, one must manipulate it. Researchers interested in children's play are torn between a desire to influence play and the realization that children's play should remain their own domain. The kind of play described in this chapter does not lend itself to adult intervention, but is a rich source for insights into child development and social interaction. I discourage any attempts to tap spontaneous play for improving classroom learning, but I offer the following to support my belief that spontaneous play is an important expression and outlet or children.

Spontaneous Play Offers a Positive Learning Environment

On playgrounds where violence is a problem, it is difficult to see spontaneous play as anything but potentially destructive behavior. However, if adults learn to read the signals for "This is play," the distinction between playful interactions and real fighting is evident. Children often resent adult interference into what they know is play, but what looks like a fight to the untrained observer. Adults often see spontaneous play as potentially dangerous, but from my observations it is no more dangerous than formal games.

Spontaneous play should not be discouraged among children of any age. It is not childish regression to an earlier stage of development, but a level of play that demands knowledge of both rule-governed play and societal rules. Children involved in spontaneous play are like clowns in ice-skating shows. They know how to play or skate so well they can play with the structure of the activity. Children respond to pressures from the nonplay world in their spontaneous play. They know how to follow rules, but they also know that the rules constantly change. Spontaneous play gives them an opportunity to disregard rules.

Children's Involvement in Spontaneous Play Reflects Sex-Role Acquisition

Historical and cross-cultural accounts of children's play usually mention differences in the play patterns of girls and boys. (Sutton-Smith 1961, Schwartzman and Barbera 1976). Generally, boys play in preparation for competitive, aggressive roles in society, while girls' play is geared to nurturant, accommodating roles. Girls' involvement in spontaneous play exemplifies an attempt to break from traditional play patterns. Unfortunately, few ethnographies and

cross-cultural studies of play describe children's spontaneous play (Schwartzman 1976), so it is impossible to show comparable sex-specific behavior in other cultures. However, I speculate that many of the patterns described above do not characterize black American girls' play. Black girls proudly perpetuate many traditional games, such as hand claps and ring play (Jones and Hawes 1972) and do not seek boys' involvement in their play (Brady 1975). Black girls' opinions of their future sex-role may be more positive than that of their white counterparts.

Observations of children's spontaneous play will give us a clue to changes in deep-rooted sex-role differences. David Lancy's study of culture change among the Kpelle shows that changes in play were among the first reflectors of culture change (1976). Changes in play preference may also reflect changes in sex roles. Other influences on both sex roles and play behavior are adults' efforts to expand athletic opportunities for women through increased exposure of women's sports on television and the availability of Title IX funds. Girls will have both role models and financial encouragement to pursue more competitive sports. These efforts will succeed only if girls' early play behavior changes. I see their interest in more aggressive self-structured chase games as an indicator of such change.

Spontaneous Play Demands a Degree of Cultural Knowledge Some Children Do Not Possess

Adults cannot assume that all children are capable of enjoying the same activities. Often the games that seem the easiest to join, such as spontaneous play, are not suited to the needs or desires of culturally different children. Culturally different children need to learn the rules of play and society before they can enjoy breaking them. This may also be true in the classroom. Culturally different students may excel in clearly structured environments but flounder in loosely structured classes. Rule violations are probably due to ignorance rather than to a desire to test the teacher.

The Normal Flow of Children's Play Must Remain Unaltered for Relevant Research

Ethnography is well suited to this task because it is both unobtrusive and nondirective.

Ethnographers try to blend into the background and watch children play as they normally play rather than recording what they say, what they play, or what they will play if asked. Anthropological ethnography is especially useful because anthropologists are trained to draw their assumptions from the data, rather than coming to the site with *a priori* assumptions about the nature of children's play. Through cross-cultural experiences, anthropologists realize that one must not look for what should be there, but should try to understand what is there.

Notes

1. Children referred to in this paper are between the ages of 7 and 12.
2. I use "game" because the children call their play "games." The activities, however, do not conform to a format definition of games (Avedon 1971).
3. In the first study, permission to conduct research at the school was obtained by SEDL. In the second, I obtained permission from the school principals.
4. Data are drawn from the first study in Austin, Texas.
5. Names have been changed.
6. An account of this research also appears in *Play: Anthropological Perspectives,* edited by Michael Salter (Cornwall, NY: Leisure Press, 1978).

References

Avedon, Elliot. 1971. "The Structural Element of Games." In Elliot Avedon and Brian Sutton-Smith, eds., *The Study of Games.* New York: John Wiley and Sons.

Barry, Herbert, III, Margaret K. Bacon, and Irvin L. Child. 1957. "A Cross-Cultural Survey of Some Sex Differences in Socialization," *Journal of Abnormal and Social Psychology,* 55:327–332.

Bateson, Gregory. 1972. "A Theory of Play and Fantasy." In *Steps to an Ecology of Mind.* New York: Ballantine Books.

Berlyne, D. E. 1960. *Conflict, Arousal and Curiosity.* New York: McGraw-Hill Book Company.

Brady, Margaret K. 1975. "This Little Lady's Gonna Boogaloo: Elements of Socialization in the Play of Black Girls." In *Black Girls at Play: Folkloristic Perspectives on Child Development.* Austin, TX: Southwest Education Development Laboratory.

Brown, D. G. 1957. "Masculinity and Femininity Development in Children," *Journal on Consulting Psychology,* 21:197–202.

Caillois, Roger. 1961. *Men Play and Games.* New York: Free Press of Glencoe.

D'Andrade, Roy G. 1966. *Sex Differences and Cultural Institutions: The Development of Sex Differences.* E. E. Maccoby, ed. Stanford: Stanford University Press, 174–204.

Deng, Francis. 1972. *The Dinka of the Sudan.* New York: Holt, Rinehart and Winston.

Gardner, L. P. 1947. "An Analysis of Children's Attitudes Towards Fathers," *Journal of Genetic Psychology,* 70:3–28.

Herron, R. E., and Brian Sutton-Smith, eds. 1971. *Child's Play.* New York: John Wiley and Sons.

Jones, Bessie, and Bess Lomax Hawes. 1972. *Step It Down.* New York: Harper & Row.

Lancy, David. 1976. "The Play Behavior of Kpelle Children During Rapid Cultural Change." In D. Lancy and B. A. Tindall, eds., *Problems and Prospects in the Study of Play.* New York: Leisure Press.

Lever, Janet. 1976. "Sex Differences in the Games Children Play." In *Social Problems,* 32(4) (April) 478–487.

Maccoby, Eleanor E. 1966. *The Development of Sex Differences.* Stanford: Stanford University Press.

———, and Carol N. Jacklin. 1975. *The Psychology of Sex Differences.* Stanford: Stanford University Press.

McDowell, John. 1974. "Interrogative Routines in Mexican-American Children's Folklore." *Working Papers in Sociolinguistics* 20.

May, Robert. 1966. "Sex Differences in Fantasy Patterns," *Journal of Projective Techniques,* 30(6):464–469.

Mead, Margaret. 1928. *Coming of Age in Samoa.* New York: William Morrow & Co., Inc.

———. 1930. *Growing Up in New Guinea.* New York: William Morrow & Co., Inc.

Mussen, Paul, John Conger, and Jerome Kagan. 1969. *Child Development and Personality.* New York: Harper & Row.

Opie, Iona, and Peter Opie. 1969. *Children's Games of Street and Playground.* Oxford, England: Clarendon Press.

Rabban, M. 1950. "Sex Role Identification in Young Children in Two Diverse Social Groups," *Genetic Psychology Monographs,* 42:81–158.

Rosenburg, B. G., Brian Sutton-Smith, and E. F. Morgan. 1963. "Development of Sex

Differences in Play Choice," *Child Development,* 34:119–126.

Schwartzman, Helen. 1976. "The Anthropological Study of Children's Play," *Annual Review of Anthropology,* 5:289–328.

——, and L. Barbera. 1976. "Children's Play in Africa and South America: A Review of the Ethnographic Literature." In D. Lancy and B. A. Tindau, eds., *Problems and Prospects in the Study of Play.* New York: Leisure Press.

Smith, S. 1939. "Age and Sex Differences in Children's Opinion Concerning Sex Differences," *Journal of Genetic Psychology,* 54:17–25.

Stein, Aletha, Sheila Pohly, and Edward Mueller. 1971. "The Influence of Masculine, Feminine and Neutral Tasks on Children's Achievement Behavior; Expectances of Success and Attainment Values," *Child Development,* 42(1):195–207.

Sutton-Smith, Brian. 1972. "A Syntax for Play and Games." In R. E. Herron and B. Sutton-Smith, eds., *Child's Play.* New York: John Wiley and Sons.

——. 1977. "Games of Order and Disorder." In *The Dialectics of Play.* Schorndorf: Verlag Karl Hofmann.

——. 1961. "Sixty Years of Historical Change in the Game Preferences of American Children," *Journal of American Folklore,* 74: 17–46.

——, and E. P. Morgan. 1963. "The Development of Sex Differences in Play Choice During Preadolescence," *Child Development,* 34:119–126.

——, and B. G. Rosenburg. 1960. "A Revised Conception of Masculine-Feminine Differences in Play Activities," *Journal of Genetic Psychology,* 96:165–170.

Whiting, Beatrice B., and Carolyn P. Edwards. 1973. "A Cross-Cultural Analysis of Sex Differences in the Behavior of Children Aged 3–11," *Journal of Social Psychology,* 9:171–188.

(2)
The High School Environment: A Comparison of Coeducational and Single-Sex Schools (Schneider and Coutts, 1982)

Subjects were a total 2,029 Grade 10 and 12 students from five coeducational, four all-female, and four all-male high schools. They completed measures of value climate and environmental press (High School Characteristics Index) in order to permit an evaluation of the hypotheses that compared with single-sex schools, coeducational schools would be perceived by their students as placing (a) less emphasis on scholarship and achievement, (b) greater emphasis on affiliation and pleasurable, nonacademic activities, and (c) less emphasis on control and discipline. Support was attained for Hypotheses 2 and 3, whereas the evidence relevant to Hypothesis 1 was inconsistent. The results were interpreted as confirming those of other studies in suggesting that, at least from the perspective of most students, coeducational schools enjoy an advantage both in terms of attending to social-emotional needs and minimizing the necessity of regimentation and discipline.

In North America, as in most regions of the world, the recent trend has been away from sex-segregated education toward coeducation (Greenough, 1970). Whereas many of the arguments in support of coeducation have considerable intuitive appeal (e.g., coeducation provides a more normal or natural social environment), those against it seem equally compelling (e.g., coeducation neglects the existence of sex differences in interests and aptitudes). Indeed, a number of professionals recently have called for a thorough examination of the relative merits of coeducation and single-sex education (e.g., Kolesnik, 1969; Lockheed, Note 1). In Great Britain, for instance, Byrne (1978) has called for a national debate on the issue.

A major assumption underlying the debate on coeducation versus single-sex education is that there are critical differences between the social psychological environments of the two types of institution (Feather, 1974). It stands to reason that in order to achieve an understanding of the effects of the two kinds of institution on their students, a thorough analysis of their respective environments is required. Yet, strikingly little research, particularly in North America, has been conducted, a state of affairs that undoubtedly is related to the declining availability of single-sex schools. The purpose of this investigation was to extend the comparison of the environmental perceptions of students from coeducational and single-sex high schools to the North American educational context and to do so in a more systematic and thorough manner than has heretofore occurred. Consideration of the research literature led to three hypotheses.

Hypothesis 1

Compared with their single-sex school counterparts, coeducational school students perceive their schools as placing less emphasis on scholarship and achievement. This hypothesis stemmed from Coleman's (1961) suggestion that coeducation may have a negative impact on the academic achievement and social adjustment of students because status among peers at the high school level may depend more on nonacademic factors than on scholastic achievement. Coleman's thinking was based on the responses of students from predominantly coeducational high schools in the United States to questions about their perceptions of those factors that contribute to the attainment of status among their schoolmates. For example, for both sexes popularity was seen as depending more on nonacademic attributes and accomplishments (e.g., being an athlete and having a nice car) than on academic success, and, suggestive of the

disadvantages of coeducation, this was particularly so for popularity with members of the opposite sex. A study conducted in New Zealand by Jones, Shallcrass, and Dennis (1972), using Coleman's "value climate" measure, provided some support for Coleman's thinking. On the other hand, Feather (1974) found no support for Coleman's view when he had Australian students rank values (from Rokeach's Value Survey; 1973) according to the emphasis given them by their schools.

Hypothesis 2

Students perceive coeducational schools as placing greater emphasis than single-sex schools on affiliation and more pleasurable, nonacademic activities. Hypothesis 2 likewise is consistent with Coleman's analysis. It also has received some empirical support in the aforementioned study by Jones et al. (1972) and, particularly, in the research of Dale (1969, 1971) in Great Britain. Dale, in the most extensive investigation of the environments of coeducational and single-sex schools to date (12 schools in each category were included), found that coeducational-school students were more likely than single-sex school students to agree with the statement that the atmosphere of their schools was pleasant. In fact, Dale highlights the atmospheric difference as a factor that particularly differentiated the two school types. In characterizing the pleasantness of their school atmospheres (using a free-response technique), the coeducational-school students focused on the following three themes: (a) friendliness of peers and good social life, (b) positive student-teacher relations, and (c) normal boy-girl relations.

Hypothesis 3

Students perceive coeducational schools as placing less emphasis than single-sex schools on control and discipline. This hypothesis directly accords with the perceptions of both students and exstudents in Dale's (1969, 1971) research, as well as the evidence from Feather's (1974) study that single-sex schools were seen as attaching greater emphasis on being clean, helpful, and polite. Also suggesting that coeducational schools place less stress on order and control are the results of a study by Schneider and Coutts (1979) in which Ontario coeducational and single-sex high school teachers rated the acceptability of stereotypically feminine and masculine traits. There was a tendency for coeducational teachers to be more tolerant of masculine traits (e.g., rebellious and inattentive) and less insistent on the display of feminine traits (e.g., obedient and neat).

In the present investigation, as in Coleman's (1961) and Jones et al.'s (1972) research, a measure of value climate was used. However the main focus of the study was an analysis of the environmental press of the institutions involved. The term *press* may be attributed to Murray (1938), who proposed that one's behavior is a function of the combination of needs and presses. In defining press, Pace and Stern (1958) say "just as needs are inferred from the characteristic modes of response of an individual, so press are reflected in the characteristic pressures, stresses, rewards, [and] conformity-demanding influences of the . . . culture" (p. 270). Central to the notion of press is that the environment includes factors that may either facilitate or interfere with the gratification of needs. In the present investigation, scales from the High School Characteristics Index (HSCI; Stern, 1970) were used to measure environmental press. Respondents indicated whether or not each statement comprising a scale (e.g., achievement scale) was characteristic of their schools, thereby indicating the extent to which they perceived their school environment as contributing to the satisfaction of the relevant need (e.g., need for achievement).

Method

Subjects

The subjects were high school students representing five coeducational schools, four all-male schools, and four all-female schools. Among the coeducational-school students were 210 Grade-10 males, 215 Grade-10 females, 211 Grade-12 males, and 212 Grade-12 females. Among the single-sex-school students were 294 Grade-10 males, 295 Grade-10 females, 295 Grade-12 males, and 297 Grade-12 females. All of the schools were separate schools; that is, they were Roman Catholic and, therefore, attended primarily by Catholics.[1] The percentages of

lay teachers in the coeducational, all-male, and all-female schools were 77 (range = 51 to 91), 75 (range = 57 to 83), and 71 (range = 48 to 87), respectively; the percentages of female teachers in the coeducational, all-male, and all-female schools were 36 (range = 22 to 45), 7 (range = 0 to 11), and 86 (range = 75 to 100), respectively. The schools were located in urban centers of Southwestern Ontario (minimum city population = 80,000). A School Type (coeducational and single-sex) $\times$ Sex $\times$ Grade (10 and 12)[2] analysis of variance (ANOVA) on Blishen's (1967) index of socioeconomic status (based on father's occupation) revealed no significant differences in social class among the various categories of student.

Procedure and Questionnaire

The scales relevant to this study were included in a questionnaire administered to

---

[1]Up to and including Grade 10, Roman Catholic separate schools in Ontario are publicly funded, and for Grades 1 to 8 approximately one third of all Ontario students are enrolled in separate schools (*Education Statistics, Ontario, 1980*, 1980). After Grade 8, about a third of the separate school students enroll in separate high schools. However, in urban areas the proportion tends to be considerably higher; in the four areas from which the present sample of schools came, the percentages are 46, 48, 69, and 73. Through Grade 10 separate schools are classified not as private but as publicly supported schools and are administered by local separate school boards. After Grade 10, separate schools are classified as private, operating outside of the publicly supported school system. However, it is important to recognize that the vast majority of students remain the in the same schools throughout their secondary education. This description of the Ontario Roman Catholic Separate School System has been provided in order to underscore the differences between it and what are commonly regarded in the United States as private schools.

[2]In respect to grade level, the schools represented at Grade 12 were not entirely the same as those at Grade 10. Data from one all-male school were available on Grade 10 students only; thus only three schools are represented in the Grade 12 all-male sample. Also, data from one coeducational school were available only at the Grade 10 level and from a second coeducational school only at the Grade 12 level; thus, for the coeducational data, only three schools were the same at Grades 10 and 12.

students on a group basis at their schools. For the measure of value climate, the students were asked the following: "Among the items below, what does it take to get to be important and looked up to by the other girls (boys, in the case of male students) here at school?" Subjects then rank ordered (1 being most important) the following six items: "being a leader in activities," "having money," "getting high grades, honour roll," "being an athletic star," "being good looking," and "having a good personality."

For the measures of environmental press, scales from the HSCI were used. The HSCI consists of thirty 10-item scales in true-false format. Eight scales were selected on the basis of Mitchell's (1968) factor analysis of the HSCI, which yielded four independent factors. Two scales from each of the four factors were selected. Below are listed Mitchell's four factors and their corresponding two HSCI scales. Each scale is accompanied by a brief identifying phrase provided by Stern (1970, p. 16) and a sample item.

1. Strong Intellectual Orientation. Achievement: "striving for success through personal effort." Sample: "There is a lot of competition for grades." Humanities, Social Science: "interests in the humanities and social sciences." Sample: "Many teachers and students are involved with literary, musical, artistic, or dramatic activities outside the classroom."

2. School Activities. Affiliation: "group-centered social orientation." Sample: "It is easy to make friends in this school because of the many things that are going on that anyone can participate in." Play-Work: "pleasure seeking versus purposefulness." Sample: "Everyone has a lot of fun at this school."

3. Strong Environmental Control. Impulsiveness-Deliberation: "impulsiveness versus reflection." Sample: "Students who tend to say or do the first thing that occurs to them are likely to have a hard time here." Deference-Restiveness: "respect for authority versus rebelliousness." Sample: "Teachers go out of their way to make sure that students address them with due respect."

4. Negative Attitude Toward the Environment. Abasement-Assurance: "self-depreciation versus self-confidence."

Sample: "The teacher very often makes you feel like a child." Objectivity–Projectivity: "objective detachment versus suspicion." Sample: "Everyone has the same opportunity to get good marks here because the tests are marked very fairly."

Results

The design of the study entails three factors: school type (coeducational and single-sex), grade (10 and 12), and sex. Because our focus is on possible differences between coeducational and single-sex schools, primary attention is given to reporting the findings relevant to the effects of school type, including its interactions with grade and sex. The results concerning school type are reported first, and then a selective review of the results regarding grade and sex is presented. In view of the large sample size, $p < .01$ is considered to signify statistical significance, and $.01 < p < .05$ to signify marginal significance.

Effects of School Type

Value climate. Recall that students were asked to rank order six items in terms of their relative importance in contributing to status among their same-sex peers. The students' rankings of the six items of the value-climate measure were first subjected to a School Type × Grade × Sex multivariate analysis of variance (MANOVA). The three main effects and the School Type × Sex interaction were significant ($p < .001$). Then a separate univariate ANOVA was carried out on the rankings given to each of the six items. The mean rankings are presented in Table 1.

Main effects of school type indicated that students from single-sex schools ranked "being a leader in activities," $F(1, 1980) = 11.46$, $p < .001$, and "getting high grades, honour roll," $F(1, 1980) = 11.46$, $p < .001$, and "getting high grades, honour roll," $F(1, 1980) = 107.06$, $p < .0001$, as contributing more to the attainment of status among their peers than did coeducational-school students.[3] On the other hand, coeducational-school students ranked "being good looking," $F(1, 1976) = 160.35$,

---

[3]The degrees of freedom vary slightly among the various analyses because of missing information on small proportions of subjects.

Table 1   Mean rankings of value-climate items (collapsed across grade).

Item	Coeducational Schools		Single-sex Schools	
	Males	Females	Males	Females
Good personality	1.87	1.39	1.76	1.38
Leader in activities	2.94	2.90	2.85	2.61
Athletic star	2.61	4.05	2.84	3.71
Good looking	4.36	3.21	4.86	4.20
High grades	4.24	4.15	3.50	3.62
Money	5.00	5.31	5.15	5.46

Note: Low number signifies item was seen as contributing highly to achieving importance among same-sex peers at school.

$p < .0001$, and "having money," $F(1, 1976) = 8.47\ p < .01$, higher than did the single-sex school students. A School Type × Sex interaction, $F(1, 1983) = 25.85, p < .0001$, indicated that among males, coeducational-school students perceived "being an athletic star" as more important than did single-sex-school students ($p < .01$), whereas among females, the reverse was true ($p < .001$). The above value-climate results provide support for Hypothesis 1, that single-sex-school students would perceive their environments as placing greater emphasis on academic achievement. This is clearly suggested by the fact that single-sex-school students ranked getting high grades much higher than did coeducational-school students, whereas the latter ranked nonacademic factors—good looks and money—higher.

Environmental press. Students were asked to respond to eight scales based on Mitchell's (1968) factor analysis of the entire HSCI. Scores on the HSCI scales initially were analyzed by a School Type × Grade × Sex MANOVA showing that all main and interaction effects were significant ($p < .01$). A subsequent univariate ANOVA also was carried out on each of the eight HSCI scales. The mean scores are presented in Table 2.

In regard to the two scales that loaded on Mitchell's (1968) Strong Intellectual Orientation factor, the results showed that

for the Achievement scale, the School Type × Sex interaction, $F(1, 2021) = 7.58, p < .01$, and the School Type X Grade X Sex interaction, $F(1, 2021) = 7.75, p < .01$, were significant; for the Humanities, Social Science scale, no effects involving school type were significant. Analysis of the three-way interaction on the Achievement scale revealed that school type was not a significant factor among Grade 12 students; however, among Grade 10 students, whereas achievement press was higher for coeducational-school females than for single-sex-school females ($p < .001$), there was a tendency for it to be lower among coeducational-school boys than among single-sex-school boys ($p < .05$). These results, coupled with the nonsignificance of school type for the Humanities, Social Science scale, indicate that, unlike the value-climate data, the environmental-press data do not support the first hypothesis, that single-sex-school students would perceive greater emphasis on scholarship and achievement in their schools.

For the two scales related to the School Activities factor, the results indicated that for the Affiliation scale, school type, $F(1, 2021) = 266.00, p < .0001$, and the School Type × Grade × Sex interaction, $F(1, 2021) = 10.87, p < .001$, were significant; for the Play-Work scale, school type, $F(1, 2021) = 351.10, p < .0001$, and the School Type × Grade interaction,

Table 2 Mean environmental press scores (collapsed across grade).

High School Characteristics Index Scale	Coeducational Schools		Single-sex Schools	
	Males	Females	Males	Females
Achievement	5.73	5.87	5.89	5.56
Humanities, Social Science	3.46	3.29	3.38	3.23
Affiliation	7.01	6.70	5.49	4.81
Play-Work[a]	7.49	7.19	5.99	5.68
Impulsiveness-Deliberation[a]	6.21	6.33	5.90	5.59
Deference-Restiveness[a]	4.00	4.01	3.75	4.66
Abasement-Assurance[a]	3.92	3.89	4.36	4.71
Objectivity-Projectivity[a]	6.39	6.41	6.10	5.54

[a]High scores signify the characteristic on the left.

$F(1, 2021) = 10.78$, $p < .001$, attained significance. The very sizeable effect of school type for both the Affiliation and Play-Work scales, an effect that is maintained at each grade-sex combination ($p < .001$), strongly supports Hypothesis 2. As predicted, coeducational-school students perceived their school environments as being more affiliative and pleasure oriented than did single-sex-school students.

For the scales related to the Strong Environmental Control factor, the analyses revealed that for the Impulsiveness-Deliberation scale, school type, $F(1, 2021) = 46.11$, $p < .0001$, and the School Type $\times$ Sex interaction, $F(1, 2021) = 8.04$, $p < .01$, were significant. Similarly, for the Deference-Restiveness scale, school type, $F(1, 2021) = 8.50$, $p < .01$, and the School Type $\times$ Sex interaction, $F(1, 2021) = 39.24$, $p < .0001$, were significant, whereas the three-way interaction approached significance, $F(1, 2021) = 4.42$, $p < .04$. Subsequent analyses of the interactions indicated that both single-sex-school males and females described their schools as being lower on impulsiveness than did either coeducational-school males ($p < .01$) or females ($p < .001$), and single-sex-school females (but not males) described their schools as placing more emphasis on deference ($p < .01$). These results, then, generally accord with the third hypothesis, that single-sex-school students would view their schools as placing greater emphasis on control and discipline.

The results concerning the scales associated with the Negative Attitudes Toward Environment factor revealed that for the Abasement-Assurance scale, school type, $F(1, 2021) = 39.30$, $p < .0001$, and the School Type X Grade interaction, $F(1, 2021) = 9.15$, $p < .01$, were significant; for the Objectivity-Projectivity scale, school type, $F(1, 2021) = 25.65$, $p < .0001$, and the School Type $\times$ Grade $\times$ Sex interaction, $F(1, 2021) = 9.30$, $p < .01$, were significant. Analysis of the interactions showed that school type had its greatest effect at the Grade 10 level, wherein single-sex-school students described their schools as being higher on abasement and lower on objectivity than did their coeducational-school counterparts ($p < .001$). At the Grade 12 level, there was a similar marginal tendency for single-sex-school students to perceive higher abasement press ($p < .05$) and a significant tendency for single-sex-school females, but not males, to perceive lower objectivity press ($p < .001$).

Effects of Grade and Sex

In addition to the ways grade and sex moderated the influence of school type (as reported above), some other findings concerning their effects are noteworthy.[4] In respect to value climate, whereas grade was

_____

[4]A complete review of the results for grade and sex is available from the first author.

a significant factor for only one item (Grade 12 students ranked leadership in activities higher than did Grade 10 students), sex was a significant source of variance for all but the importance of high grades. Females gave higher rankings than did males to leadership in activities, $F(1, 1980) = 6.72, p < .01$, good looks, $F(1, 1976) = 237.12, p < .0001$, and good personality, $F(1, 1984) = 76.18, p < .0001$. In contrast, males gave higher rankings to having money, $F(1, 1976) = 36.50, p < .0001$, and being an athletic star, $F(1, 1983) = 429.32, p < .0001$.

Regarding environmental press, a finding of interest relates to the comparison of the responses of males and females from single-sex schools to the scales associated with the Strong Environmental Control factor, the Impulsiveness-Deliberation and the Deference-Restiveness scales. The School Type × Sex interactions showed that, compared with single-sex-school females, single-sex-school males described their schools higher in impulsiveness press ($p < .01$) and lower in deference press ($p < .001$). These sex differences, suggesting the perception by females of a greater emphasis on control and discipline, did not pertain to coeducational-school students.

Discussion

Of the three hypotheses underlying the investigation, the results fail to support unequivocally only the first—that the single-sex-school environment would be viewed as placing greater emphasis on scholarship ad achievement than would the coeducational school environment. Some support for the hypothesis was indicated by the value-climate data, which showed that single-sex-school students were much more likely than coeducational-school students to believe that academic excellence is an avenue to the achievement of status among their same-sex schoolmates. However, contrary to the first hypothesis, environmental-press data (i.e., the HSCI Achievement and Humanities, Social Science scales) suggested a marked similarity between the amount of intellectual emphasis in the two types of institution. In seeking to reconcile this apparent inconsistency, it may help to

compare both the conceptual and psychometric properties of the value-climate measure and the two HSCI scales. Conceptually, the value-climate measure taps the prevailing peer-group reward structure, that is, what does one have to do to be esteemed by one's schoolmates. The HSCI scales, on the other hand, focus primarily on the degree to which the *overall* school environment is perceived as providing opportunities for the satisfaction of one's intellectual needs.

Notwithstanding the conceptual differences between the value-climate and environmental-press measures, it is still reasonable to expect greater consistency between the two than is evident. The ipsative nature of the value-climate measure may further help to account for the inconsistency. This measure is based on a ranking procedure in which the score (rank) assigned to one factor is tied directly to the nature and relative importance of the other factors being ranked. On the other hand, the HSCI does not suffer from this limitation; scores on each of its scales are independently derived. Thus, it is possible that a factor, such as academic excellence, may on an absolute level be of equal importance to students in the two types of school but on the value-climate measure may be ranked higher in the single-sex institution because the other factors being ranked are of lower absolute importance in single-sex schools than in coeducational schools. Indeed, the considerably higher HSCI Affiliation and Play-Work scale scores of the coeducational-school students suggest why such nonacademic factors as physical appearance and money are ranked higher in the coeducational schools.

Clearly, we cannot confidently conclude that our data support Coleman's suggestion that coeducation may be inimical to the academic progress of students. Our reluctance is bolstered by the lack of consistent evidence from both the United States (Kolesnik, 1969) and Great Britain (Wood & Ferguson, 1974; Irving, Note 2) that single-sex-school students show an achievement superiority over coeducational students and from the aforementioned Schneider and Coutts (1979) study that revealed a stronger belief among coeducational-school teachers (many of whom taught the subjects in this study) than among single-sex-school teachers in the importance of mastering the actual content of courses.

Notwithstanding the status of the hypothesis regarding school-type differences in academic emphasis, the two remaining hypotheses were firmly supported. In contrast to their single-sex-school counterparts, coeducational-school students described their schools as substantially higher in both affiliation and play press, thus supporting Hypothesis 2, that coeducational schools would be viewed as more affiliative and pleasure oriented. Furthermore, coeducational-school students described their schools as higher in impulsiveness press, and coeducational females, but not males, described their schools as lower in deference press. These results largely support our third hypothesis, that single-sex-schools would be viewed as placing greater emphasis on control and discipline. Last, school-type differences were found for the two scales loading on Mitchell's (1968) Negative Attitude Toward Environment factor. Coeducational-school students, particularly at the Grade 10 level, described their schools as lower on abasement press and higher on objectivity press.

The general picture that emerges, then, is one in which, compared with the single-sex-schools, the coeducational schools were perceived by their students as more gregarious, group-centered, and friendly, more entertaining and enjoyable, more tolerant of noncompliance, spontaneity, and impetuosity, as more conducive to the development of feelings of self-confidence and self-respect, and as reflecting less prejudiced and irrational thinking.[5]

Undeniably, the coeducational-school students provided a considerably more favorable description of the social psychological environments of their schools than did the single-sex-school students. It is noteworthy that the results pertain to both grade levels and sexes, although they tend to be stronger at the Grade 10 level concerning abasement press and objectivity press and for female students concerning deference press and objectivity press.

Although it is essential to acknowledge the possibility that the present findings may have relevance only to the coeducational/single-sex-school distinction in the Separate School System of Ontario or perhaps only to the specific schools sampled, it is significant that the descriptions given by our sample of students are very similar to those that have been given by students in other countries, namely Great Britain (Dale, 1971) and New Zealand (Irving, Note 2). Recall that, as mentioned in the introduction, Dale highlighted the more pleasant atmospheres of coeducational schools as particularly differentiating the two types of school. It is not surprising that he also found attitudinal concomitants of such differences. In general, coeducational-school students and exstudents reported being happier in school; and exstudents from both coeducational and single-sex-schools (including those who had attended both types) indicated a decided preference for mixed-sex schooling. The present students' responses to the scales loading on the Negative Attitudes Toward Environment factor seem to corroborate Dale's results.

It is our contention that the present data veridically reflect major differences in the social psychological environments of coeducational and single-sex high schools inasmuch as we believe that these differences are based on the particular social-structural features of each type of institution. A possible argument against this position is that as a consequence of selective enrollment, the results simply reflect differences in the personalities of the students attending the two kinds of institution. According to such a view, either the environments of the schools are determined by the personalities of their students (Holland, 1973) or the students' perceptions of their schools reflect projections of their personalities. However, the subjects' scores on personality variables relevant to two of the environmental press scales—the Achievement and Affiliation scales—were available and cast doubt upon this alternative interpretation. Contrary to a self-selection argument, no significant differences between coeducational and single-sex-school students were found on Personality Research Form (Jackson, 1965) measures of need for

---

[5]This general description is based on definitions of the HSCI scales provided by Stern (1970).

achievement and need for affiliation. The latter is especially noteworthy in light of the students' perception of a substantial difference in the affiliation press of the schools.

What remains to be explained is precisely what accounts for the environmental differences between coeducational and single-sex-schools, for it is unlikely that they result that they result largely from conscious differences in educational policy. It may not be difficult to understand why schools comprised of a mixture of male and female adolescents have richer social atmospheres. But what is perplexing is the greater stress on control and order that characterizes single-sex-schools. At least three not unrelated explanations may account for this environmental difference. First, as suggested by Dale (1969, 1971), the presence of the opposite sex may have an ameliorating influence on students' conduct, thus making it possible for those in authority to administer a lighter form of control. (Dale reports that teachers tended to agree that girls positively influence the behavior of boys, whereas lesser agreement was found regarding the effect of boys on girls.) This lessened control, according to Dale, would also make it easier for teachers to be friendlier and more helpful toward students, thus reducing barriers between students and teachers. Second, notwithstanding the particular effects of one sex upon the behavior of the other, it is possible that the generally greater enjoyment of the school environment experienced by coeducational school students would create a situation in which less control and discipline are required to maintain a reasonable degree of order. Finally, irrespective of differences in the actual need for such control, to the extent that there exists a widespread belief that single-sex-schools are more authoritarian in nature, our earlier finding suggesting that single-sex-school teachers are less tolerant of rebelliousness, inattentiveness, and disobedience among students (Schneider & Coutts, 1979) may reflect a process of self-selection whereby those individuals who are predisposed toward the exercise of either more or less control seek out teaching positions within the single-sex and coeducational school systems, respectively.

The role of sex also merits comment. Consistent differences, cutting across both school type and grade, were found on five of six value-climate items. Females attached greater importance than males to leadership in activities and, particularly, to having good looks and a good personality as means to achieving peer-group status; on the other hand, males placed greater emphasis than females on having money, and especially, on being an athletic star. It is of interest that the only item on which the sexes did not differ was the one related to the importance of scholastic success. Furthermore, the "high grades, honour roll" item was not viewed as of major importance for any category of student (the highest was a rank of 3, which was given by single-sex-school females). This pattern of findings resembles the academic/athletic popularity syndrome that has been used by some writers to describe Canadian and American adolescent societies (Downey, 1965; Friesen, 1968), wherein academic achievement is valued less than athletics (especially among boys) and popularity (especially among girls).

Last, it is interesting to speculate about why the all-female schools were perceived as placing greater emphasis on control and discipline than were the all-male schools. One explanation for this difference stems from a consideration of the sex composition of the teaching staffs of the all-female and all-male schools. That is, the perception of a differential emphasis on control is consistent with the results of our earlier study (Schneider & Coutts, 1979; see also Johnston, 1970) that showed that female teachers—from both coeducational and single-sex-schools—were more likely than male teachers to encourage students to engage in a constellation of controlled-related behaviors (e.g., to be obedient, quiet, orderly, and cooperative), whereas male teachers were more tolerant of such traits as restlessness and aggressiveness. Moreover, male teachers reported being more inclined to grant students the autonomy and freedom from control necessary for self-directed learning. Thus, in light of the fact that the teaching staffs of the all-male schools were predominantly male and those of the all-female schools were predominantly female, the differential perceptions of the students from the two kinds of school regarding the degree of environmental control may have, at least in part, directly reflected the institutional norms as embodied in the teachers' attitudes and beliefs about appropriate student behavior.

In conclusion, this investigation has confirmed what has long been thought to be true but rarely subjected to systematic examination—that important differences exist between the social psychological environments of mixed-sex and single-sex high schools. Coeducational schools are perceived by most students as having more pleasant atmospheres—both in terms of attending to the social-emotional desires of their students and minimizing the necessity of control and discipline. It remains for further research to ascertain whether or not the apparent advantage enjoyed by coeducational students occurs at the expense of academic achievement and the development of other socially desirable qualities, such as a sense of responsibility and self-control.

Notes

1. Lockheed, M. *Legislation against sex discrimination: Implications for research.* Paper presented at the meeting of the American Educational Research Association, San Francisco, April, 1976.
2. Irving, J. *Coeducational or single-sex schools? A review of the literature* (Set 76, No. 1, Item 9). New Zealand Council for Educational Research, 1976.

References

Blishen, B. R. A socio-economic index for occupations in Canada. *Canadian Review of Sociology and Anthropology,* 1967, *4,* 41–53.

Byrne, E. M. *Women and education.* London: Tavistock, 1978.

Coleman, J. S. *The adolescent society.* New York: Free Press, 1961.

Dale, R. R. *Mixed or single-sex school?* (Vol. 1). London: Routledge & Kegan Paul, 1969.

Downey, L. W. *The secondary phase of education.* New York: Blaisdell, 1965. *Education Statistics, Ontario, 1980.* Toronto Ministry of Education, 1980.

Feather, N. T. Coeducation, values, and satisfaction with school. *Journal of Educational Psychology,* 1974, *66,* 9–15.

Friesen, D. Academic-athletic-popularity syndrome in the Canadian high school society (1967). *Adolescence,* 1968, *3,* 39–52.

Greenough, R. Coeducation as a world trend. *School & Society,* 1970, *98,* 31–32.

Holland, J. L. *Making vocational choices: A theory of careers.* Englewood Cliffs, NJ: Prentice-Hall, 1973.

Jackson, D. N. *Personality Research Form A.* Goshen, NY: Research Psychologists Press, 1965.

Johnston, J. M. A symposium: Men in your children's lives, part 2. *Childhood Education,* 1970, *47,* 144.

Jones, J. C., Shallcrass, J., & Dennis, C. C. Coeducation and adolescent values. *Journal of Educational Psychology,* 1972, *63,* 334–341.

Kolesnik, W. B. *Coeducation: Sex differences and the school.* New York: Vantage Press, 1969.

Mitchell, J. V., Jr. Dimensionality and differences in the environmental press of high schools. *American Educational Research Journal,* 1968, *5,* 513–530.

Murray, H. A. *Explorations in personality.* New York: Oxford University Press, 1938.

Pace, C. R., & Stern, G. G. An approach to the measurement of psychological characteristics of college environments. *Journal of Educational Psychology,* 1958, *49,* 269–277.

Rokeach, M. *The nature of human values.* Riverside, NJ: Free Press, 1973.

Schneider, F. W., & Coutts, L. M. Teacher orientations toward masculine and feminine: Role of sex teacher and sex composition of school. *Canadian Journal of Behavior Science,* 1979, *11,* 99–111.

Stern, G. G. *People in context: Measuring person-environment congruence in education and industry.* New York: Wiley, 1970.

Wood, R., & Ferguson, C. Unproved case for coeducation. *Times Educational Supplement,* Oct. 4, 1974, p. 22.

(3)
The Effect of Time Constraints and Statistics Test Anxiety on Test Performance in a Statistics Course
(Onwuegbuzie and Seaman, 1995)

ABSTRACT. *The performance of students who completed a statistics examination under time limits was compared with that of students under no time limits. Another purpose of the study was to determine whether students high or low in statistics test anxiety were affected differentially by these two examination conditions. Twenty-six graduate students who were enrolled in an intermediate-level statistics course were randomly assigned to the two examination groups, timed or untimed. Both low- and high-anxious students performed better on the final course examination under the untimed condition than under the timed condition. However, the benefit of the untimed examination was greater for high-anxious students than for low-anxious students. The results were interpreted using Hill's (1984) and Wine's (1980) conceptual frameworks. The results suggest that differences between high- and low-anxious students in evaluative situations are caused by differences between them in motivational disposition and attentional focus.*

Courses in statistics are among the most anxiety inducing for graduate students in education and other non-math-oriented disciplines (Schacht & Stewart, 1990; Zeidner, 1991). Many students view statistics courses as a major threat to the attainment of a degree and often delay taking these courses for as long as possible, frequently enrolling in a class just prior to graduation (Roberts & Bilderback, 1980). Some students go so far as to change their academic majors and career choices as a direct result of their experiences in these classes (Feinberg & Halperin, 1978).

Testing appears to be one of the most formidable components of a statistics course. Onwuegbuzie (1993) and Zeidner (1991) have suggested that statistics test anxiety adversely affects students' test performance, self-efficacy, and attitude toward the subject matter. In fact, this negative reaction to the subject matter distinguishes both

mathematics test anxiety (Richardson & Woolfolk, 1980) and statistics test anxiety (Benson, 1989) from general test anxiety, in which adverse reactions usually are limited to the evaluation itself. Addressing the problem of statistics test anxiety is an obvious first step in addressing the more general anxiety problems associated with statistics courses in non-math-oriented programs of study.

One way to reduce test anxiety might be to ensure that students have enough time to complete an examination, thereby eliminating their concerns about performance speed and remaining exam time. However, researchers (Bridgeman, 1980; Caudery, 1990; Evans & Reilly, 1972; Reilly & Evans, 1974; Wild, Durso, & Rubin, 1982; Wright, 1984) have found that increasing examination time has little or no effect on student performance. None of these researchers took into account the students' test-anxiety level.

Some learning theorists (Covington & Omelich, 1985; Osterhouse, 1975; Wine, 1980) believe that high-anxious students do not live up to their potential because they tend to focus less energy and attention on the examination itself, instead letting thoughts of concern interfere with pertinent thought processes. Others predict that the performance of high-anxious students can be facilitated by a relaxed examination atmosphere that reduces such concerns (Zollner & Ben-Chaim, 1988), as well as by a level of anxiety that is neither too high nor too low, but optimal for the particular task (Towle & Merrill, 1975). The results of studies by Hill and his colleagues (Hill, 1977, 1979, 1980, 1984; Hill & Eaton, 1977; Hill, Wigfield, & Plass, 1980) support these predictions. Hill and his colleagues found that third- and fourth-grade students with a high level of anxiety did not perform as well on timed examinations as their low-anxious counterparts did. When time constraints were removed, however, the performance of high-anxious students improved considerably, sometimes even equaling that of the low-anxious children.

The documentation of high anxiety among non-math-oriented graduate students in statistics courses suggests the suitability of this population for further tests of theoretical predictions concerning the effects of anxiety level and time constraints on examination performance. Our purpose in the present study was to investigate how time constraints on testing affect the test performance of students who differ in statistics test anxiety within this population. We hypothesized that both high- and low-anxious students would perform better in an untimed examination condition than in a timed examination condition. We also hypothesized that the test performance difference between students in the timed and untimed conditions would not be as large for low-anxious students as for high-anxious students.

Method

Participants

Participants for the experiment were 26 graduate students from several non-math-oriented disciplines (e.g., education, nursing, and health administration) enrolled in an intermediate-level educational statistics course at a large university in the southeast United States. Students gave their consent to participate in the experiment by signing an informed consent form. Only 2 of the 28 students in the course did not participate in the study. These students expressed a desire to participate but were unable to do so because of scheduling conflicts. Thus, selection bias was not deemed a threat to the validity of the study.

The students ranged in age from 23 to 59, with a mean age of 40.7. Sixty-two percent of the participants were over age 40. The sample included 21 women (81%) and 5 men (19%).

Instruments

We used four instruments: the Test and Class Anxiety subscale of the Statistical Anxiety Rating Scale (STARS), the Background Information Form (BIF), the Mid-Term Examination (MTE), and the Statistics Achievement Examination (SAE).

STARS (Cruise & Wilkins, 1980) is a 51-item, 5-point Likert-format instrument that assesses anxiety in a wide variety of situations involving the academic study of statistics. The Test and Class Anxiety subscale comprises 8 items that measure the level of anxiety experienced in preparing for, and taking, a test. High scores on this subscale indicate high anxiety levels. Normative data for this subscale have yielded an alpha coefficient of .91, item point-multiserial correlations ranging from .66 to .85, and a 5-week test-retest reliability coefficient of .83 (Cruise, Cash, & Bolton, 1985). A validity coefficient of .76 was obtained by correlating students' scores on this subscale and the Mathematics Test Anxiety factor (Fennema & Sherman, 1976).

The BIF was developed specifically for this study. It is a questionnaire designed to collect demographic information from students participating in the experiment.

The course instructor, who was one of the researchers, constructed the MTE. The examination form consisted of open-ended questions of two types, computational (e.g., "Construct a two-sided confidence interval for the comparison of interest") and conceptual (e.g., "Is the equal variance or unequal variance test more powerful for these data? Give reasons for your answer"). All the items pertained to content from the first half of the course and were chosen from the instructor's item bank to ensure that the examination was typical of past examinations given by this instructor. The MTE was administered under untimed conditions. Because we hypothesized a confounding effect of anxiety and performance, time constraints were eliminated in an attempt to reduce anxiety and obtain a measure of past performance that was a more valid estimate of aptitude.

The course instructor also constructed the SAE. The SAE paralleled the format of the MTE, yet covered the complete course content. The course instructor scored both the MTE and SAE on a 100-point scale, using a key that specified the number of points awarded for both correct and partial-credit answers. Throughout the study, the instructor remained blind to student placement in conditions to eliminate the potential threat of scorer bias.

Procedure

The participants completed the STARS and the BIF 2 weeks before taking the SAE. All students were allowed to bring a calculator and three pages of notes for the SAE. On the day of the examination, students were randomly assigned to experimental conditions, with 13 students each in the timed and untimed conditions. The examinations for both groups were identical, began at the same time, and were administered in adjacent, similar rooms. The same instructions were read to both groups except for the phrases concerning time allotment. Students in the timed condition were told they had 90 minutes to complete the examination, whereas students in the untimed condition were told that they had unlimited time. A typical time allotment for final examinations at the university where the study took place is 90 min. The researchers considered the SAE to be sufficiently long to induce anxiety within these time limits, yet not so long that students would fail to complete the examination, thus introducing a separate confounding variable into the experiment. In fact, all students in the timed condition completed the examination within the allotted time.

The SAE was an actual examination that affected course grades. Therefore, to maintain fairness for all students, we intercepted the students in the timed condition as they left the classroom and gave them the opportunity to work further on another copy of the examination form (to keep examination results separate from those used for the study). All students declined this offer.

We performed a series of t tests to determine the equivalence of the treatment groups with respect to important demographic variables. We found no statistically significant differences on the variables shown in Table 1 or in gender ($p = .99$). The largest sample differences were in the number of college-level mathematics and statistics courses taken prior to this course, yet these differences favored the timed group, so that potentially higher SAE scores in the untimed group cannot be attributed to quantitative course experience.

Results

We used a general linear model (GLM) to assess the effects of treatment condition and statistics test anxiety on statistics achievement. The midterm score served as a covariate.

Interpretation of the GLM results is confounded if the covariate is involved in any of the two-way or three-way interactions. Therefore, all interactions were placed in the GLM model and then removed in a stepwise manner. Neither the three-way interaction (Examination

TABLE 1   Means and standard deviations by experimental group for selected variables.

Selected variables	Timed group (n 4 13)		Untimed group (n 4 13)		
	M	SD	M	SD	P
Age	40.5	7.6	41.0	9.5	.87
Number of college-level mathematics courses	7.2	10.1	1.8	1.2	.08
Number of college-level statistics courses	3.6	3.7	1.8	1.3	.11
Number of years since last mathematics course	17.3	10.1	15.2	8.3	.57
Final grade in previous statistics class	3.8	0.3	3.7	0.7	.64
Class and test anxiety	28.2	7.6	23.9	7.5	.15
Midterm examination	66.1	22.8	70.8	21.4	.59

TABLE 2 Summary of the general linear model analysis.

Source	SS	df	MS	F	p
Group	310.2	1	310.2	4.7	.04
Anxiety	368.0	1	368.0	5.5	.03
Group × Anxiety	541.5	1	541.5	8.1	< .01
Midterm	4,913.9	1	4,913.9	73.6	< .01
Error	1,401.3	21	66.7		

Condition × Statistics Test Anxiety × Midterm) nor the two-way interactions (Statistics Test Anxiety × Midterm; Examination Condition × Midterm) were significant.

Condition × Anxiety Interaction

Table 2 contains the results of the general linear model analysis. The effect of primary interest (Anxiety x Group Interaction) was statistically significant. In other words, the examination condition had differential effects for students with different levels of anxiety.

The nature of this interaction effect, after controlling for prior performance with the GLM, is shown in Figure 1. Timed and untimed examination conditions had little effect on the test performance of students with low statistics test anxiety. The timed examination condition caused a substantial decrement in the test performance of students with high statistics test anxiety. To explore this interaction further, we calculated the correlation between statistics test anxiety and statistics performance separately for each treatment group, without controlling for prior performance. This analysis revealed that the relationship between test anxiety and performance was stronger for the timed examination group ($r = -.83$) than for the untimed examination group ($r = -22$). Final examination performance as a function of statistics test anxiety and examination condition, adjusted for prior statistics

Effect of Treatment Condition

The treatment condition effect was statistically significant (see Table 2). The adjusted final examination mean scores of the untimed and timed groups were 76.2 and 69.4, respectively. (The standard error for both

groups was 2.4.) The effect size was defined as the difference between the adjusted mean scores of the two treatment groups divided by the pooled standard deviation of the scores of the two groups (Cohen, 1988, p. 20). We obtained an effect size of .32, using a mean square error (442.9) from a reduced model that only included the group factor.

Effects of Statistics Test Anxiety

We found a significant relationship between statistics test anxiety and performance on the final examination, after adjusting for prior performance (see Table 2). The Pearson product-moment correlation between anxiety and performance was $r = -.57$. Thus, for the entire sample, as the level of statistics test anxiety increased, the level of statistics performance decreased.

Discussion

The findings of this study suggest that students with a high level of statistics test anxiety may have greater statistics ability than their performance under timed examination conditions indicates. Hill and Wigfield (1984) claimed that the examination scores of students tested under timed conditions may represent an invalid lower bound estimate of their actual ability, and indeed the present results support that contention. In fact, using the course instructor's predefined scale for converting SAE scores to grades, we found that the most high-anxious students in the timed condition would have been awarded grades that were one letter grade below the grades awarded the high-anxious students in the untimed condition. Given both the real and perceived

Figure 1   Final examination performance as a function of statistics test anxiety and examination condition, adjusted for prior statistics.

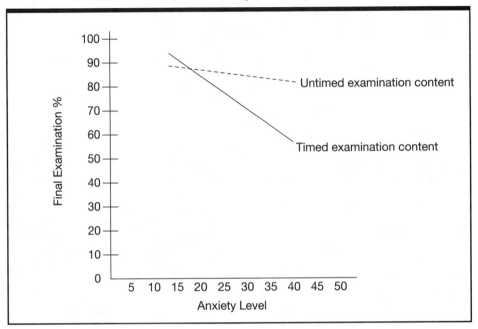

importance of grades for students, this is a strong effect.

Two theoretical models provide potential causal explanations for the findings. The negative motivation model (Hill, 1977) supposes that anxiety reduces one's motivation to contribute all resources to a task, instead shifting the focus from the task to self. The cognitive-attentional interference model (Wine, 1980) elaborates on Hill's model by postulating that information-processing capabilities (memory retrieval processes, problem-solving strategies, etc.) are adversely affected by these task-irrelevant thoughts. In general, the self-preoccupation of test-anxious students interferes with the directed attention required to perform successfully (Hunsley, 1985; Sarason & Stoopes, 1978). In the present context, the debilitating effects of anxiety were compounded by the placement of time constraints on students who were already highly anxious. Conversely, some of their anxiety was reduced when they were informed that time was not a factor in the examination.

One anecdote from the study adds support for cognitive interference theories of

anxiety. Whereas all the students in the untimed examination group recorded their identification number, only one student in the timed examination group did so. This treatment group difference occurred even though both groups were read the same set of instructions concerning identification numbers.

The interactive effect of test anxiety and examination condition on test performance partially explains the seemingly conflicting results in the literature. For instance, after controlling for statistics aptitude, Zeidner (1991) found that statistics test anxiety does not affect performance. Like Hill (1984), we found that anxiety does affect performance. The circumstances of the testing environment had much to do with these differences. After controlling for prior achievement, we found very little relationship between anxiety and performance in the untimed condition, whereas the relationship was much stronger in the timed condition.

Our findings also agree with those of Hill and his colleagues (Hill, 1977, 1979, 1980, 1984; Hill & Eaton, 1977; Hill, Wigfield & Plass, 1980) in that we found examination time to be a factor in assessing performance. These studies can be distinguished from other studies of examination time in that other researchers failed to consider test anxiety a relevant variable. The small differences that we found between the low-anxious students in the two conditions are more in keeping with these latter studies. One might speculate that the differences in the outcomes of the conditions may have been eliminated altogether had we used only nonanxious students. Our sample was such that even the term *low anxious* is a bit of a misnomer because it refers to the relative position of some students on the anxiety scale. With only a few exceptions, the sample was made up of students who suffered from a greater degree of anxiety than they might have if they had been enrolled in courses within their major program of study.

Our sample was small, and the findings of the study were based on a single academic course, though this particular course was chosen for its unique properties. We predict that a replication study in a less anxiety-provoking situation would not result in such a pronounced interaction effect. Conversely, we predict there would be a more pronounced effect in a replication study of a more anxiety-provoking situation. The range of SAE scores in the present study was not as wide as we desired; a test with more difficult questions might create more anxiety, thus intensifying the interaction between treatment condition and statistics test anxiety.

Research findings about the role of statistics anxiety in statistics achievement should be of interest to instructors. Awareness of this finding might cause them to consider teaching strategies that help both low- and high-anxious students reach their full potential. Untimed examinations seem an appropriate strategy, not only because such examinations can reduce anxiety but also because real-life application of statistical knowledge is probably best approximated in a setting without heavy time constraints. Another strategy might be to present a practice examination to familiarize students with examination format, instructions, and question type. Directing students to metacognitive information, such as dealing with self-centered worries, accessing problem-solving strategies, and attending to tasks, also might be helpful.

Note

Correspondence should be addressed to Anthony J. Onwuegbuzie, Administration and Secondary Education, University of Central Arkansas, P. O. Box 4719, 201 Donaghey Street, Conway, AR 72035-0001.

References

Benson, J. (1989). Structural components of statistical test anxiety in adults: An exploratory model. *The Journal of Experimental Education, 57,* 247–261.

Bridgeman, B. (1980). Generality of a "fast" or "slow" test-taking style across a variety of cognitive tasks. *Journal of Educational Measurement, 17*(3), 211–217.

Caudery, T. (1990). The validity of timed essay tests in the assessment of writing skills. *ELT-Journal, 44*(2), 122–131.

Cohen, J. (1988). *Statistical power analysis for the behavioral sciences.* New York: John Wiley.

Covington, M. V., & Omelich, C. L. (1985). Item difficulty and test performance among high-anxious and low-anxious students. In H. M. van der Ploeg, R. Schwarzer, & C. D. Spielberger (Eds.), *Advances in test anxiety research* (Vol. 5, pp. 127–136). Amsterdam: Lisse.

Cruise, R. J., Cash, R. W. & Bolton, D. L. (1985, August). *Development and validation of an instrument to measure statistical anxiety.* Paper presented at the annual meeting of the Statistical Education Section Proceedings of the American Statistical Association.

Cruise, R. J., & Wilkins, E. M. (1980). *STARS: Statistical Anxiety Rating Scale.* Unpublished manuscript, Andrews University, Berrien Springs, MI.

Evans, F. R., & Reilly, R. R. (1972). A study of speededness as a source of test bias. *Journal of Educational Measurement, 9*(2), 123–131.

Feinberg, L. B., & Halperin, S. (1978). Affective and cognitive correlates of course performance in introductory statistics. *The Journal of Experimental Education, 46*(4), 11–18.

Fennema, E., & Sherman, J. A. (1976). Fennema-Sherman mathematics attitudes scales: Instruments designed to measure attitudes toward the learning of mathematics by males and females. *JSAS Catalog of Selected Documents in Psychology, 6,* 31.

Hill, K. T. (1977). The relation of evaluative practices to test anxiety and achievement motivation. *UCLA Educator, 19,* 15–21.

Hill, K. T. (1979, July). *Eliminating motivational testing error by developing optimal testing procedures and teaching test-taking skills.* Paper presented at the Educational Testing Service, Princeton, NJ.

Hill, K. T. (1980). Motivation, evaluation and educational testing policy. In L. J. Fyans (Ed.), *Achievement motivation: Recent trends in theory and research* (pp. 34–95), New York: Plenum.

Hill, K. T. (1984). Debilitating motivation and testing: A major educational program, possible solutions, and policy applications. In R. E. Ames and C. Ames (Eds.), *Research on motivation in education* (Vol. 1, pp. 245–274). New York: Academic Press.

Hill, K. T., & Eaton, W. O. (1977). The interaction of test anxiety and success-failure experiences in determining children's arithmetic performance. *Developmental Psychology, 13*(3), 205–211.

Hill, K. T., & Wigfield, A. (1984). Test anxiety: A major educational problem and what can be done about it. *The Elementary School Journal, 85,* 105–126.

Hill, K. T., Wigfield, A., & Plass, J. A. (1980, April). *Effects of different kinds of optimizing instructions on seventh- and eighth-grade children's achievement test performance.* Paper presented at the annual meeting of the American Educational Research Association, Boston.

Hunsley, J. D. (1985). Test and mathematics anxiety: An examination of appraisal and attributional processes (Doctoral dissertation, University of Waterloo, Canada, 1985). *Dissertation Abstracts International, 46,* 12B, 4402.

Onwuegbuzie, A. J. (1993). *A descriptive study of statistics anxiety—Its nature and cause.* Manuscript submitted for publication.

Osterhouse, R. A. (1975). Classroom anxiety and the examination performance of test-anxious students. *Journal of Educational Research, 68*(7), 247–250.

Reilly, R. R., & Evans, F. R. (1974, September). *The effects of test time limit on performance of culturally defined groups.* Paper presented at the annual meeting of the American Educational Research Association, New Orleans, Louisiana.

Richardson, F. C., & Woolfolk, R. L. (1980). Mathematics anxiety. In I. Sarason (Ed.), *Test anxiety: Theory, research, and applications* (pp. 271–288). Hillsdale, NJ: Erlbaum.

Roberts, D. M., & Bilderback, E. W. (1980). Reliability and validity of a statistics attitude survey. *Educational and Psychological Measurement, 40,* 235–238.

Sarason, I. G., & Stoopes, R. (1978). Test anxiety and the passage of time. *Journal of Counseling and Clinical Psychology, 1,* 102–109.

Schacht, S., & Stewart, B. J. (1990). What's funny about statistics? A technique for reducing student anxiety. *Teaching Sociology, 18,* 52–56.

Towle, N. J., & Merrill, P. F. (1975). Effects of anxiety type and item-difficulty sequencing on mathematics test performance. *Journal of Educational Measurement, 12*(4), 241–249.

Wild, C. L., Durso, R., & Rubin, D. B. (1982). Effect of increased test-taking time on test scores by ethnic group, years out of school, and sex. *Journal of Educational Measurement, 19*(1), 19–28.

Wine, J. (1980). Cognitive-attentional theory of test anxiety. In I. G. Sarason (Ed.), *Test anxiety: Theory, research and applications* (pp. 349–385). Hillsdale, NJ: Erlbaum.

Wright, T. (1984). *The effects of increased time-limits on a college-level achievement test.* (Report No. 84-12). Miami-Dade Community College, FL Office of Institutional Research. (ERIC Document Reproduction Service No. ED 267 867).

Zeidner, M. (1991). Statistics and mathematics anxiety in social science students—Some interesting parallels. *British Journal of Educational Psychology, 61,* 319–328.

Zollner, U., & Ben-Chaim, D. (1988). Interaction between examination type, anxiety state, and academic achievement in college science: An action-oriented research. *Journal of Research in Science Teaching, 26*(1), 65–77.

B

Evaluation Research

In education, evaluation typically means one of two essentially different things: evaluation of individuals or evaluation of programs. Both can involve research in the sense in which we have used the term in this book—an empirical process for answering a question. The evaluation of individuals is sometimes called *assessment* rather than evaluation and is an important field in its own right. Consideration of this field, however, is beyond the scope of this book. Assessment of individuals is essentially a measurement issue and is dealt with in texts on psychological measurement (e.g., Anastasi, 1988).

Program evaluation, on the other hand, can involve the kind of research we have dealt with in this book. Program evaluation research is a subfield in its own right, but a subfield of research writ large. Program evaluation research is an important kind of applied research in education. Its goal is to yield information of immediate use to a group of practitioners—those charged with making decisions about the educational program being evaluated.

Programs are evaluated to provide information about two things—the usefulness of the program as it is currently being implemented and how the program can be improved. Evaluation specialists have terms to distinguish these two foci of evaluation—*summative evaluation* assesses the usefulness of the program, and *formative evaluation* assesses how the program can be improved.

SUMMATIVE EVALUATION

In many respects, formative and summative evaluation researchers' concerns are no different from those of mainstream educational researchers. In summative evaluation research, the research question is usually whether the program being evaluated produced the desired outcomes; internal validity is thus important. Decision makers want to know whether or not desired outcomes were obtained; this is essentially a validity of measurement issue. They also want to know whether the program caused the outcomes; this requires control of potentially confounding variables.

The federally funded Head Start preschool program provides a classic example. Summative evaluation of the Head Start program required information on two issues: first, whether children participating in Head Start went on to be more successful in the regular school program than children who did not participate; and second, if Head Start children were more successful, whether this was due to their participation in the program.

Summative evaluation research is thus subject to the rules we gave in chapters 3 and 4 for operationally defining variables and making causal argument. Summative evaluation researchers, like most quantitative researchers, try to validly operationalize the variables of interest and utilize a design that will control potentially confounding variables. These tasks are difficult for any researcher, but evaluation researchers face special problems.

The biggest problem is causal argument. As you saw in chapter 4, the best causal argument is made when random assignment is done. But evaluation researchers are often unable to effect random assignment. Sometimes they are called in after the program has been implemented—and random assignment has to be done at the outset. Even when they are called in early enough to assign randomly, program regulations or philosophy may preclude random assignment. Programs are often required to serve certain people and not others; even when this is not a problem, program personnel, who tend to be more interested in providing service than in evaluation concerns, may be committed to serving on the basis of need and unwilling to assign randomly.

Then evaluation researchers must fall back on the array of methods for controlling potentially confounding variables that you learned about in chapter 4—all of which involve identifying and measuring the variables. As chapter 4 made clear, this process is always subject to error. Much evaluation research thus leaves the causality of relationships between programs and outcomes in doubt.

FORMATIVE EVALUATION

Those who use evaluation research results are interested in knowing not only whether the program worked as intended, but how the program can be improved. Evaluation researchers are increasingly focusing not only on final outcomes but on the entire process of program implementation. Qualitative methods are often especially useful for formative evaluation research. Qualitative methods are much more suited than quantitative to answering the processual kinds of questions that formative evaluation poses.

GENERALIZABILITY

Perhaps the greatest difference between evaluation research and mainstream research lies in the area of generalizability. In mainstream educational research, whether basic or applied, generalizability is usually an important concern, because mainstream researchers typically aim to reach a wide audience.

Evaluation researchers, however, are employed by program personnel for the express purpose of evaluating a particular program. Typically, program personnel are not interested in the generalizability of evaluation results beyond the program of interest.

RESEARCHER'S AUTONOMY

Another important difference between evaluation research and mainstream educational research involves the researcher's autonomy. Mainstream researchers are essentially free to choose their research questions and methods and to interpret and disseminate their results as they wish. Evaluation researchers, on the other hand, are employed by decision makers to provide desired information and must work within the context provided by their employers.

Decision makers typically delineate evaluation research questions and exercise a great deal of control over the research process. They are primarily interested in the utility of research results for decision making. Decision making, in turn, is part of an essentially political process and is heavily shaped by political concerns.

SUGGESTED READINGS

Rossi, P., and Freeman, H. (1989). *Evaluation: A Systematic Approach.* Newbury Park, CA: Sage.

Rutman, L. (Ed.) (1984). *Evaluation Research Methods: A Basic Guide.* Newbury Park, CA: Sage.

Worthen, B., and Sanders, J. (1987). *Educational Evaluation: Alternative Approaches and Practical Guidelines.* White Plains, NY: Longman.

C
Responses to Exercises

We call this appendix *Responses to Exercises* rather than *Answers to Exercises* to emphasize the fact that in research design there often are not hard-and-fast answers. Some of the exercises do have right answers; when this is true, we provide them. But most of the exercises do not; when this is true, we try to suggest ways to think about the exercises. In these cases, the important thing is not whether you phrased your responses exactly as we did, but whether you got the basic ideas. A few of the exercises are entirely open-ended; for these, no responses are given.

CHAPTER 1

1–1. The first knowledge process you used in deciding what caused your illness was expert opinion. Your doctor informed you that your illness had two possible causes, viral infection or food poisoning. She indicated that symptoms of infection with a contagious virus begin about three days after exposure, while symptoms of food poisoning begin about 36 hours after exposure.

To this knowledge you added empirical evidence. You had directly observed the following real world events: First, you were with a friend who was ill about three days before you became ill; second, you ate some food with an "off" taste a few hours before you became ill.

To these two kinds of knowledge you applied logical reasoning. If symptoms of viral infection take about three days to develop, and if you were with a friend who was ill three days before your symptoms developed, then your illness may be viral. If symptoms of food poisoning take 36 hours to develop, and if you ate some food with an off taste a few hours before you became ill, then your illness is not the result of food poisoning: You became ill too soon after eating the questionable food. Because there were two possible causes, a virus or food poisoning, and you have ruled out food poisoning, then your illness must be viral.

1–2. **a.** Research. The word study suggests that this was empirical work.

b. Not research. The title suggests that this is a philosophical article about research.

c. Research. The title suggests that this is an empirical study of "effects" on a particular groups of students in a particular course.

d. Not research. The title indicates that the article reviews "issues and trends" in the entire field of educating the severely handicapped.

e. Not research, but the title doesn't clearly indicate this. This article reviews the literature on women and minority faculty. However, the title could be appropriate for an empirical article as well.

f. Research. The title suggests that this is an empirically based comparison of how two different interventions "impact" children's behavior and achievement.

1–5. a. The research question is whether radio is more stimulating to children's imaginations than is television. The research process involved exposing children to stories via both radio and TV to determine which medium produced more imaginative responses. The answer is that radio is more stimulating than television. In addition, a carryover effect was found: First hearing a radio story enhanced imagination when a second story was seen on TV. First seeing a TV story depressed imagination when a second story was heard on the radio.

b. The research question is how cognitive/relaxation therapy and study-skills training affect test anxiety and performance. The research process involved exposing students to each treatment alone, both treatments together, and no treatment at all. The answer is complex: skills training had no effect; therapy affected anxiety but not performance; and the combination affected both and had a greater effect on anxiety than did therapy alone.

c. The research question is how the length of the school year affects students' standardized test scores. The research process involved locating a group of students whose school year had been shortened owing to severe weather and comparing their test scores in the shortened year with scores from regular years. The answer is that test scores are not higher in longer school years.

d. The research question involves how women's developmental stages affect their responses to continuing education experiences. The research process involved life-history interviews of five women. The researchers conclude that these women's developmental stages did affect their responses to continuing education experiences, although this brief excerpt does not indicate the nature of the observed effects.

1–7. a. This question involves basic research. Answering this question would be more likely to contribute to theory building about human cognitive processes than to meet an immediate, perceived need of kindergarten teachers. The answer to this question would probably not affect kindergarten teaching in any direct, immediate way, although theory building about human cognitive processes ultimately does have an effect on educational practice.

b. This question involves applied research. Answering this question would be more likely to meet the immediate, perceived need of employers to improve their hiring practices than to contribute to theory building in some area of education.

c. This question involves applied research. Answering this question would be more likely to meet an immediate, perceived need of first-year teachers than to contribute to theory building in some area of education.

d. This is a basic question. Answering this question would be more likely to contribute to theory building about the causes of depression than to meet an immediate perceived need of mental health workers, especially because clinicians have no control over their clients' previous life experiences. Mental health theory does, however, ultimately affect the practice of mental health workers, teachers, and others.

1–8. The first example involves a deductive reasoning process, from the general premise that all men are mortal to the particular conclusion that Socrates is mortal. The second example involves an inductive reasoning process, from the particular observation that Socrates has just died to the general conclusion that all men may be mortal.

1–9. **a.** This question involves deduction and theory testing. The research will not involve a search for patterns or generalizations. Rather, one pattern—one generalization—involving age differences in children's classificatory behavior has already been tentatively identified. The research will test whether this generalization is confirmed in a particular, empirical situation.

b. This question involves induction and theory generation. No generalizations have been made about differences between depressed and nondepressed persons; rather, particular life histories of such persons will be explored in the hope of discovering patterns and possible generalizations.

c. This is a deductive, theory-testing question. A generalization has already been made, about the effects of modeling on children's behavior. The research will test whether this generalization is confirmed in a particular, empirical situation.

d. This is an inductive, theory-generating question. Particular teachers will be observed in the hope of discovering patterns in and possible generalizations about teaching effectiveness.

1–10. **a.** This topic would probably be researched qualitatively. The researcher's objective would be not quantification but description. The research report would describe such matters as who takes care of children of what ages; where children spend their time; what kinds of activities children observe and engage in; what the affective content of adult-child interactions is like; and so forth. Any quantification (e.g., the average number of children per mother) would be secondary to the description of child life.

b. This topic would be researched quantitatively. The results of this research would involve numbers and counting (i.e., the researcher would tabulate children's numerically expressed heart rates before and after exercise). Any description (e.g., of the subjects' willingness to participate in the project) would be secondary to the quantification of heart rates.

c. This research would be quantitative. The researcher would count the number of elementary schools offering fine-arts instruction and express this as a percentage of all schools studied. Any description (e.g., of the quality of instruction) would be secondary to the quantification of instruction.

d. This research could be either qualitative or quantitative. If the researcher set up categories of play content in advance and then counted the number of minutes in which children engaged in particular categories of play, the research would be quantitative. If, however, the researcher observed children's play and then reported in a narrative fashion what had been observed (e.g., who did what, where, how, and with whom), the research would be qualitative.

Summary Exercises

1–1. **a.** Benn's work is research because it was empirical: Thirty mother-son pairs were studied. The work is also quantitative, although there is not much information in this excerpt that tells you so. The best cue is that the work was highly focused on specific factors: maternal integration and mother-son attachment. Later in the article, Benn goes on to say that maternal integration and mother–son attachment were rated—that is, dealt with numerically.

Benn's work is basic, because it contributes to theory building in the field of attachment. The work also has applied elements, however, as you might have guessed from the fact that she focused on employed mothers. This is a deductive study. Benn did not conduct the study to search for patterns; she had already identified a possible pattern. She conducted the study to determine whether the pattern she predicted from theory would in fact be found.

   b. Not research. In the abstract, Gordon makes no reference to empirical work, indicating that he will deal with definitions of diversity and pluralism.

   c. Cusick's book is a research report, because it is based on his own empirical work. Cusick observed events in a high school over a period of six months. The research was qualitative. Cusick did not have a narrow focus, nor did he attempt to quantify; instead, he attempted to observe and describe events in all their complexity. His orientation was basic, not applied. He sought basic knowledge, not knowledge of immediate use to some group of practitioners, although his work might ultimately have application. His work was also inductive. He had not identified one or a few patterns which he wished to test; rather, he sought "a clearer understanding" and hoped to discern patterns in the ways that individuals in the school behaved in their environment.

   d. This work was research because it was empirical; information about real-world events (test scores and college enrollment) was empirically obtained for a particular group of American Indian students. The work is quantitative; what was studied were test scores (which are numbers) and number of quarters of college enrollment. This work is applied because it addresses an unmet need of educational practitioners: more accurately predicting academic success for a particular population of students.

   e. Travis's and Kohli's work is research because it was empirical; 817 real men and women were studied. The work is also quantitative, though you would have to infer this from the information given in the excerpt. The empirical information obtained on birth order and academic attainment was quantified: Birth order is numerical—firstborn, secondborn, and so on. And educational attainment is also usually studied in a quantitative way; in this study, researchers documented the number of years of education each subject had completed.

   The work is theoretical, because it contributes to theory building about the causes of birth-order effects. Previous studies established that birth order often does seem to affect educational attainment. The issue is whether this is because later children do not receive as much intellectual input from their overextended parents, or because parents do not have as much money to invest in each child as subsequent children come along. The findings of this study suggest that the latter explanation is correct.

CHAPTER 2

2–1.   Item *b* (number of months in a year) is always 12; item *i* (number of cents in a dollar) is always 100. These are therefore constants. Item *k* (gender of National Football League players) has always been male to date; however, it is possible (although perhaps unlikely) that there may be female players in the NFL in the future. This item is thus a constant with the potential of being a variable. The remaining items are variables. The number of days in a month can be 28, 29, 30, or 31; the number of days in a year can be 365 or 366; and the number of pesos per dollar varies daily, depending on the exchange rate in international monetary markets. People's test scores, leadership styles, native languages, heart rates, and hair color vary widely.

2–2.   Test score, heart rate, and age are continuous; performance rating from 1 to 10 is semicontinuous. There are a number of ways that these variables could be treated as categorical. Test scores, for example, could be converted to pass and fail; if the cutoff for passing was 50, a student with a score of 60 would have the value *pass* of the converted variable. People's heart rates could be characterized as low, normal, and high; someone with a heart rate of 70 beats per minute would have the value *normal* of the converted variable. Age would be treated as categorical if a researcher labeled her subjects *young adults* (18–35), *middle-aged* (36–55), or *older* (above 55). Performance ratings would be treated as categorical if people with ratings of 3 or below were designated *on probation,* and people with ratings above 3 were designated *not on probation.*

The remaining variables are categorical. Leadership style might have such values as democratic and authoritarian, or distant and accessible. Native language might have such values as English, Spanish, and Navajo or Arabic and Hebrew. Program participation would have such values as yes and no or program *A, B,* or *C.* It may surprise you that years in program, with the values one and two, is a categorical variable. Although years in program could be measured continuously, when such a variable has a very limited number of possible values, as in this case, it is usually treated as categorical.

2–3. **a.** The variables studied involved homemaking experience. The subjects were single fathers.

b. The variable studied was gender, with the values male and female. The subjects were physically active persons.

c. The variables studied were gender, with the values male and female; ethnicity, with the values White, Black, and other; and power, with the values balanced and unbalanced. The subjects were heterosexual dating individuals.

d. The variable studied was type of task, with the values solvable and unsolvable. The subjects were pairs of third-grade children and mothers.

e. The variables studied were type of course, with the values required and elective, and rating of instructor. The subjects were college students.

f. The variables studied were parental employment patterns, school grades, and family characteristics. The values of these variables are unspecified. Subjects were White adolescents living in two-parent families.

2–4. **a.** This question is nonrelational. Only one variable is being investigated: native language.

b. This question is relational. Two variables are being investigated: weight and running speed. There is the suggestion of a causal relationship between these variables: that weight influences running speed.

c. This question is also relational. Two variables are being investigated: job success and leadership style. There is the suggestion of a causal relationship between these variables: that leadership style influences job success.

d. This question is nonrelational. Only one variable is being investigated: IQ test score.

e. This is a relational question. Two variables are being investigated: use of physical punishment and family size. There is the suggestion of a causal relationship between these variables: that family size influences the use of physical punishment.

f. This is a relational question. Two variables are being investigated: hair color and the amount of fun being had. There is the suggestion of a causal relationship between these variables: that hair color influences the amount of fun being had.

g. This is a nonrelational question, or rather two nonrelational questions. Two variables are being investigated: highest degree held and years of teaching experience. However, there is no suggestion of a relationship between these variables.

h. This is a relational question. Two variables are being investigated: board exam score and professional rating. There is the suggestion of a relationship between these variables: that board exam score is related to professional success. There is no suggestion that the relationship is directly causal; exam scores cannot directly cause professional success. However, there is a suggestion of some kind of link between these two variables.

i. This is a nonrelational question. Only one variable is being investigated: the daily exchange rate in December for pesos and dollars. An average value will be calculated for this variable.

j. This is a relational question. Two variables are being investigated: amount of alcohol consumed and clarity of speech. There is the suggestion of a causal relationship between these variables: that amount of alcohol consumed influences clarity of speech.

2–5. **a.** There is a relationship between gender and self-disclosure. Women in the study are self-disclosing, and men are not.

b. There is no relationship between months in program and health behavior. Subjects who were in the program for a short time have mixed health behavior, as do subjects who were in the program for a longer time.

c. There is a relationship between participation in special education and self–esteem. Subjects who are in special education have low self-esteem, and subjects who are not in special education have high self-esteem.

d. There is a relationship, although not a perfect one, between anxiety level and test score. Subjects whose anxiety level is lower have higher test scores overall, and subjects whose anxiety level is higher have lower test scores overall.

e. There is very little relationship between instructional program and test score. There is little difference between the scores of subjects in the old and new programs.

2–6. **b.** Weight is the independent variable and running speed the dependent variable.

c. Leadership style is the independent variable and job success the dependent variable.

e. Family size is the independent variable and use of physical punishment the dependent variable. In this example, family size is probably best considered a proxy variable for the true causes, which involve such factors as pressure on parental time and opportunity for conflict between children.

f. Hair color is the independent variable and amount of fun being had the dependent variable. The companies that use this kind of theme in their advertisements for hair-coloring products seem to want consumers to believe not only that this kind of relationship exists but also that it is a truly causal relationship.

h. Board exam score is the predictor variable and professional rating the criterion variable. This is a clear case of a relationship that is predictive rather then truly causal.

j. Amount of alcohol consumed is the independent variable and clarity of speech the dependent variable.

2–7. Hypotheses may be stated in many ways. For each of the research questions, several possible hypothesis statements follow. If your hypotheses are not exactly like the ones given, don't worry. The important thing is that you made each research question into a statement—into some kind of prediction about the kind of relationship that will or won't be found in the research.

b. Weight affects the running speed of NFL quarterbacks.
Lighter-weight NFL quarterbacks can run faster than heavier ones.

c. Successful school principals are more democratic in their leadership styles than are unsuccessful school principals.
There is no relationship between principals' leadership style and job success.

e. Family size affects the use of physical punishment.
Physical punishment is used less often in smaller families.

f. Blondes have more fun than brunettes.
Blondes and brunettes do not differ in their experience of fun.

h. As the board exam scores of a group of lawyers increase, their professional ratings increase.
Lawyers with higher board exam scores have higher professional ratings.

j. People who drink more alcohol talk less clearly.
Alcohol consumption does not affect clarity of speech.

2–8. **a.** Main effects: of student ethnicity on student achievement; of teacher ethnicity on student achievement. Interaction effect: of student ethnicity and teacher ethnicity on student achievement.

b. Main effects: of type of reinforcement on learning; of strength of reinforcement on learning. Interaction effect: of type of reinforcement and strength of reinforcement on learning.

c. Main effects: of age on teaching skill; of highest degree obtained on teaching skill; of years of experience on teaching skill. Interaction effects: of age and highest degree obtained on teaching skill (first-order); of age and years of experience on teaching skill (first-order); of highest degree obtained and years of experience on teaching skill (first-order); of age, highest degree obtained, and years of experience on teaching skill (second-order).

Summary Exercises

1. **a.** This research was relational. The authors studied one independent variable, type of monitoring, and two dependent variables, performance and attitude. They analyzed the independent variable separately with each of the dependent variables.

b. Mwamwenda's research was relational. There was one independent variable, level of cognitive development, and one dependent variable, academic achievement.

c. Vierra's research was relational. She studied one independent variable: teacher's ethnicity. She also studied one dependent variable: reading achievement. Her study involved a third variable, grade level, but it was not treated as an independent variable; rather, two separate analyses of the independent and dependent variables were performed, one for each grade level.

d. The portion of the work of McCoy and associates that is presented was nonrelational. The authors investigated a number of variables involving the contribution made by snacks to the girls' RDAs of a number of nutrients. But the authors do not attempt to relate these variables. Rather, they describe the state of each in terms of its average value for subjects in the study—for example, 52% for riboflavin.

e. This research was relational. Parkhouse and Williams studied two independent variables: high-school athletes' sex and hypothetical coaches' sex. The interaction of these independent variables on each of four dependent variables was assessed. The dependent variables were the athletes' assessments of the hypothetical coaches' knowledge of coaching, ability to motivate, desirability as a coach, and predicted future success.

f. This research is relational. The primary independent variable is educational program with two values, G & T and regular mixed ability. There are two groups of dependent variables. The first group, involving components of academic self-concept, consists of three variables: Reading, Math, and School. The second group, involving components of nonacademic self-concept, consists, according to the abstract, of four variables. However, only three are named: Physical Appearance, Peer Relations, and Parent Relations. Three additional independent variables are mentioned: gender, age, and initial ability level. Apparently each of the four independent variables was analyzed separately with each of the dependent variables. No interaction effects are mentioned.

CHAPTER 3

3-1. a. Gender is not operationally defined; we do not know the operations that will be performed to determine whether the subjects are male or female.

b, c, g, and h. These variables are operationally defined. We have enough information to replicate the operational definitions if we wished.

d. Anxiety is not operationally defined. We do not know the operations that will be performed to determine the subjects' levels of anxiety.

e. Intelligence is only partially operationally defined. We do not know what test was used, so we could not replicate the operational definition.

f. Feedback is a treatment variable, with the values *feedback* and *no feedback*. We cannot tell from this example what kind of feedback the researcher gave or how the feedback was administered.

3-2. There are many ways to define ethnicity operationally. Subjects could be asked to indicate their ethnicity, or someone who knows the subject—a relative, friend, or teacher—could be asked to indicate the subject's ethnicity. Records could be consulted (e.g., birth, medical, school, police, or military records). Or researchers could observe subjects for evidence of ethnicity in such things as their physical appearance, names, and language use.

3-3. With respect to the operational definitions from Exercise 1, here are some of the validity problems you might have identified.

b. Tests like the CTBS, if used appropriately, are generally considered adequate operational definitions of academic achievement. In a particular study, there might, of course, be problems with the use of such a test (e.g., since the CTBS is written in English, it should not be used to assess the mathematics achievement of children who are not fluent in English).

c. The validity of this operational definition depends primarily on the age of the children. Parents are probably valid reporters of the religious affiliation of young children, although it is possible that they will report what they think is socially acceptable rather than what is actually true. However, parents may not have accurate information about the religious affiliation of older children.

e. It is, of course, not possible to evaluate this operational definition fully without knowing what test was used. However, many people believe that any test is inadequate as an operational definition of as complex a construct as intelligence.

g. There may be problems with this operational definition. Although clients' opinions can be useful, there are known problems with such ratings. If, for example, a client believes that the rating will be used to evaluate the therapist (for job continuation or advancement or for salary decisions), the client may hesitate to rate the therapy as unsuccessful. It is also known that people tend to evaluate highly an enterprise in which they have invested (effort, time, money, etc.), because they wish to believe their investment was worthwhile.

It is possible that clients (especially certain clients—e.g., those whose therapy was court-ordered) are not good judges of therapeutic outcomes. There may also be a problem with collecting the evaluations at the termination of therapy; perhaps clients' evaluations six months after the termination of therapy would have been more accurate.

h. The validity of this operational definition is questionable. Smiling is not always an indication that an individual is having fun, nor is lack of smiling always an indication that an individual is not having fun.

3-4. Items *b* and *e* involve the use of objective tests. Items *a* and *f* involve the use of interviews or questionnaires. Items *d* and *h* involve the use of observation. Items *c* and *g* involve the use of archival records.

3-5. An operational definition of classroom atmosphere using an interview/questionnaire method of measurement would probably involve asking the teacher and/or students whether they feel the classroom atmosphere is informal/unstructured or formal/structured. A strength of this operational definition is that teachers and students have more direct experience of the classroom than any other individuals have. This is also a relatively inexpensive way to operationalize this variable.

A weakness of this definition is that young students would have difficulty understanding and responding to this kind of question and could only provide indirect information. In order for information gained from teachers to be valid, teachers would either have to be anonymous or believe that either answer is acceptable—that they will not be evaluated on the answer they give.

An observational method of measurement would involve sending observers into classrooms. Two conditions would have to be met for this kind of operational definition to be valid. First, observers would have to be competent—well trained and unbiased. Second, steps would have to be taken to compensate for the possibility that the presence of an observer changes the classroom atmosphere. If these conditions were met, this would be a very valid operational definition.

A weakness of this definition is that it is relatively expensive: Observers' salaries would have to be paid during training and data collection.

3-6.   a. This method of measurement is archival. Engelberg and Evans did not identify children's level of achievement; the school system did. The researchers used records of which children were in which kind of class to operationalize this variable.

Although this operational definition is not perfectly valid, it is a reasonable one. It is possible—perhaps even likely—that the school system made a few errors in labeling these children. But a few errors will not greatly affect the research results, and it is unlikely that Engelberg and Evans could have improved on this operational definition without incurring the enormous expense of subjecting each of the children to a full diagnostic workup by an educational psychologist. Catching a few errors does not justify this kind of expense.

The researchers probably chose this operational definition because it was reasonably valid and very inexpensive. Another researcher could readily replicate this method of measurement.

b. This method of measurement is observational: The research involved direct observation of counselor touching behavior. The definition seems valid; it measures the variable of interest—counselor touch—in a very direct and straightforward way. The definition is very explicit and complete. Another researcher could readily replicate this method of measurement.

Stockwell and Dye probably chose this operational definition in part because they used the same observers to operationalize other variables in the study. Observation was a very direct, straightforward, and valid way to measure the variable of interest and, for this variable, was not particularly expensive.

c. This operational definition is observational. From the partially concealed observation site, the experimenter was able to observe directly whether each subject was "invaded" or not.

Although this definition is quite direct and straightforward and could easily be replicated, it may or may not be a valid definition of the variable of interest: personal space invasion. Although many people probably do feel mildly "invaded" when talking on the phone when a stranger is close enough to eavesdrop, this may not be the case for everyone. More obvious personal space invasion would, however, have been likely to create real distress for the study's subjects and would thus have posed ethical problems for the researchers. DeBeer-Keston, Mellon, and Solomon probably compromised on this definition to avoid this problem.

d. Questionnaires and interviews are the most straightforward way to operationalize attitude variables. Interviews are usually much more expensive than questionnaires and would probably not, in this case, have provided as valid an operational definition. On a subject as personal as religion, teachers were probably more likely to respond candidly to a questionnaire than to an interviewer.

e. Self-concept, like other affective variables, is difficult to operationalize validly. The Piers-Harris Children's Self-Concept Scale is a nationally known and used instrument. Sorsdahl and Sanche took advantage of this acceptable and inexpensive method of measuring the variable in which they were interested.

3-7.   **a.** This operational definition presents an interrater reliability problem. The researcher should offer evidence that the three judges agree in the grades they assign. To do this, the researcher would have to do a pilot study in which the three judges actually grade the work of the same children.

b. The publisher's reliability coefficients are based on American samples. Because there may be differences on this kind of instrument between these samples and the group on which this research is being conducted, the researcher should calculate reliability coefficients for the immigrant group.

c. This operational definition is probably reliable. The published reliability coefficients for this kind of test are based on a cross-section of American children. The group on whom this research is being conducted seems very similar to the subjects on whom the published reliability coefficients were calculated.

3-8. **a.** This situation involves predictive validity. The employer uses the test to predict which applicants will be better and which will be worse employees.

b. This situation also involves predictive validity. University officials use the test to predict which students will have difficulty in regular math courses.

c. This situation involves content validity. The professors—"experts"—are asked to say whether the proposed content of the examination seems valid.

d. This situation involves concurrent validity. The researcher/test designer is providing evidence that results obtained using her instrument concur substantially with results obtained using another method of measurement that is probably reasonably valid: the physicians' diagnoses.

3-9. **a.** In order to assess the validity of this operational definition, we would want to know whether the teachers' anonymity was assured and what teachers thought the ratings would be used for.

Strengths of this definition are that teachers are in the best position to know about their principal's leadership ability and that surveying teachers is less expensive than using trained observers, which would be the other likely method of measurement. A weakness is that teachers' ratings may reflect other considerations; teachers may, for example, inflate the ratings of a principal who is well liked, especially if they believe their ratings will affect the principal in some way, or down-rate a principal with whom they are in conflict.

b. First, the reliability of paper-and-pencil tests needs to be established. But even if the test is reliable, important validity issues remain.

A weakness of this operational definition is that creativity is not the most likely candidate for measurement with a paper-and-pencil test. It would be important to know whether the test has concurrent validity with such other measures of creativity as expert judgment. A strength of this operational definition is that paper-and-pencil tests are relatively inexpensive.

c. In order to assess the validity of this operational definition, we would want to know why the fishers came to the lake. If they are there to catch fish, this might be a very inexpensive way roughly to gauge the number of fish in the lake; but if they are there to socialize, commune with nature, etc., this would not be a valid operational definition.

d. If the test is used to measure the general science knowledge of a "typical" group of subjects, we would want to know the test's reliability in the national norming sample. We would also want to know that the test has concurrent validity with other respected tests of science knowledge and that experts in the field of science and science testing feel that the test has content validity (although we might be willing to assume that the test is reliable and valid in these ways, because a publisher could not sell and therefore would not be likely to go to the expense of producing a nationally standardized test that did not have these characteristics). However, if the test is used for some other purpose (e.g., evaluating a science program) or on atypical subjects, we would want evidence that the test is appropriate for these special uses.

The use of an existing instrument is usually much less expensive than developing a new instrument.

e. We would want to know a great deal about the interviews: who conducted them, where, what kinds of questions were asked, how the subjects thought the results would be used, and so forth.

Strengths of this operational definition include the facts that parents know more about their child-rearing practices than anyone except their children (in fact, if the children are old enough, it might increase the validity of this operational definition to interview the children also); and that interviewing is more practical and less expensive than observation, which is the likely alternative.

Weaknesses of this operational definition include the facts that parents may not know the answers to some of the things researchers want to know, because parents do not always have a sophisticated or realistic view of how they deal with their children; and that even if parents do know the answers, they may not be willing to disclose such personal information to interviewers.

f. The validity of this operational definition depends almost entirely on the observers' qualifications and on whether the fact of being observed changes the teacher-student interactions. We would therefore want to know that these concerns had been dealt with.

The strength of this operational definition is that it provides the most direct possible measurement of the variable of interest. Its weakness is that observers would have to be very well qualified to make this kind of assessment validly, and the research would therefore be fairly expensive.

g. Because the sources of information in this example are so patently likely to be biased, there is probably nothing that could convince us of the validity of this operational definition. However, historical researchers have no choice but to use the information that they can locate. Camp commanders' reports may have to be used in the absence of better sources of data, although the probable bias would also have to be taken into account.

Summary Exercises

3–1.   a. Two variables are mentioned: sensation-seeking (the independent variable) and delinquency (the dependent variable). This excerpt provides no information about how sensation-seeking was measured, but the values of delinquency are "levels." These could be categorical—e.g., high, medium, and low—or continuous. Subjects were middle-class adolescents.

The operational definition of delinquency is a questionnaire developed by the researchers. The researchers cite literature indicating that this is the most valid way to operationalize this variable. They also indicate that their results are in line with those in other, similar studies. If we wished, we could check the references. Although it's likely that some subjects did not fully disclose this potentially damaging information, there seem to be few realistic alternatives for getting this information. This operational definition thus seems to be an inexpensive and reasonably valid way to measure this variable.

b. Only one variable is mentioned in this example: the imposter phenomenon. Its measurement was continuous; its values were subjects' scores on a 20-item instrument. Subjects of this study aren't identified in the excerpt.

The imposter phenomenon is operationally defined in terms of Clance's IP Scale. The only information provided on the validity of the IP Scale is that it "has been found to identify imposters in both clinical and non-clinical settings." References are provided. The internal consistency reliability of the scale is given as .96, which is very high.

It is possible that this instrument was chosen because it is the only one available to measure the variable that has known validity and reliability.

c. The research questions refer to three variables: passionate love, adult developmental stage, and anxiety. In the first research question, the independent variable is adult developmental stage and the dependent variable is passionate love; in the second research question, the independent variable is anxiety and the dependent variable is passionate love. The only thing we know from this excerpt about the subjects is that they are adults.

In this excerpt, one of the variables, passionate love, is operationally defined. The operational definition is the Passionate Love Scale. The authors' discussion of this scale reveals that it actually yields information on three subscales involving the cognitive, emotional, and physical dimensions of passionate love. Thus there are really three dependent variables as operationally defined, and each will need to be analyzed separately with each of the two independent variables, which means there are really six research questions.

Since the PLS is a 30-item instrument and has 3 scales, it seems reasonable to assume that there are ten items per subscale. Subjects' responses to each item range from 1–9. Thus, the possible range of subjects' scores on each subscale is from 10–90. Each subscale is thus a continuous variable.

This instrument is an objective test. Subjects' responses are summed, yielding a subscale score; higher scores represent more of the quality being measured (e.g., the cognitive dimension of passionate love).

The developers of the PLS did several things to check its validity. First, they showed that it has high reliability. Second, they knew that a common problem with this kind of instrument is that subjects often respond in terms of what they think they should say rather than what is really true of them. To check on this, they correlated the PLS with another instrument called the Social Desirability Scale; the fact that this correlation was very low indicates that subjects' answers on the PLS are not driven by social desirability concerns. (This is a kind of concurrent nonvalidity argument.) To support their argument that the PLS measures passionate love rather than mere liking, they report that the PLS correlates more highly with an existing love scale than with a liking scale. They label this a construct validity argument, though it might also be called a concurrent validity argument with respect to the loving scale and a concurrent nonvalidity argument with respect to the liking scale.

The authors of the research report state that there have been other (factor analytic) validity studies as well, and, although they don't describe them, we are provided with the reference.

The researchers probably chose the PLS to measure their dependent variable of interest because it is a relatively quick and inexpensive way to operationalize this variable, and it has been validated in several ways.

d. Only one variable is mentioned in this excerpt: behavior. This variable is continuous; its values are children's total scores on a 10-item instrument, each item being scored on a 5-point scale. Subjects were fourth-graders.

Sorsdahl and Sanche operationally define children's classroom behavior with an observational rating scale that was developed for this study. Direct observation is the most appropriate method of measurement for this kind of variable. Classroom teachers were the observers. Although using teachers was less expensive than hiring and training outside observers, it may also be less valid: Teachers are not necessarily highly skilled in observation and, because they knew some of the children they observed, they might have been somewhat subjective in their ratings. However, the kinds of behaviors that were observed (e.g., attentiveness) do not seem to involve a great deal of observer inference and are the kinds of behaviors that teachers probably attend to normally. Overall, the use of teachers as observers does not seem to be a serious drawback in this study. The instrument's reliability (.88) is very good.

e. Three variables are mentioned. Time of learner's questioning is categorical; its values are while learning and while trying to demonstrate learning. Tutor's response is also categorical; its values are response and no response. The third variable is actual learning; we don't know whether this variable is categorical or continuous. No information is provided in this example about the subjects of the study.

Two of the variables are independent: time of questioning and tutor's response. Learning is the dependent variable. Two main effects can thus be studied: for the independent variable *time of questioning* and the dependent variable *learning;* and for the independent variable *tutor's response* and the dependent variable *learning.* One interaction effect can be studied, for both independent variables and the dependent variable.

Tutor's response was not operationally defined; it was a treatment variable. No information is given here about how the researchers knew that the tutors did what they were supposed to do—respond or not respond.

Time of questioning is not discussed, but its measurement seems straightforward. Subjects' questions occurred at one of two times: while they were working with the tutors to learn, or while they were trying to demonstrate their learning.

The dependent variable learning is not operationally defined in this example.

f. The independent variable is type of classroom. This is a categorical variable with the values American Indian and Anglo. Six dependent variables, all involving classroom conversation, are mentioned in this excerpt: Durations of teacher utterance, class turn-switching pause, class utterance, teacher turn-switching pause, and student gaze duration are continuous, with values measured in seconds—e.g., 1.32 seconds or 16.81 seconds; gaze direction is categorical, with the values *teacher-, peer-,* or *object-directed.* There are thus six research questions, one for each of the dependent variables with the independent variable.

This excerpt provides no information about the measurement of the independent variable. Subjects were students in upper-elementary classrooms.

Greenbaum used transcripts and observation of videotapes of classes to operationalize his dependent variables. Observation provides the most direct method of measurement of this kind of variable. The use of videotapes provided a record of observed events that could be used to review the events and thus increase the validity of their measurement. Two cameras were used: one to provide context and one to permit focus on individuals. Initial recordings were not used, because of the possibility that subjects' initial awareness of being filmed would change their behavior.

Two observers were employed for each observation; this provided a check on all observations. The observers' use of stopwatches increased the accuracy of measurement of the duration variables. Each dependent variable (e.g., duration of teacher utterance) was carefully and thoroughly defined. Interobserver reliability was excellent: .97 to .99.

The operational definitions of the dependent variables thus seem valid. This was a very expensive way to measure these variables, but no other method of measurement would have been appropriate for the variables in which Greenbaum was interested.

g. Subjects were students who were high school seniors in 1965. There were nine predictor variables and one criterion variable. The criterion variable, collective action, was categorical (yes or no). Six of the predictor variables were also categorical: leadership, college preparatory courses, urban school, gender, race, and political efficacy. Grades and student participation were semicontinuous. Socioeconomic status was continuous.

The method of measurement was archival. Paulsen analyzed data collected earlier by other researchers and made available through a research consortium. Although Paulsen describes the original research in some detail in his article, this excerpt provides no further information about the operational definitions of the variables. Thus you cannot assess the validity of measurement in this study.

h. Three variables are mentioned: feedback strategy, incentive condition, and achievement in computer-based instruction. Feedback strategy is categorical and has the five values listed in the excerpt; incentive condition is categorical and has two values, task and performance. CBI achievement is probably continuous (test scores), though we are given no information about that in this excerpt. Subjects were undergraduates enrolled in one of two required introductory courses in teacher education. Feedback strategy and incentive condition are independent variables, and CBI performance is the dependent variable. The researchers studied how the two independent variables interacted to affect the dependent variable.

Only the incentive condition variable is operationally defined in the excerpt. Its operational definition primarily involves which of two courses subjects were enrolled in. Subjects in the technology course were considered to be operating under what the researchers called performance incentives—the important distinction being that their grade in the course would depend in part on their performance on the CBI task. Subjects in the educational psychology course were considered to be operating under what the researchers called task incentives—the important distinction being that their performance on the CBI task had no consequences external to the task itself.

This seems to validly operationalize something that might better be called extrinsic and intrinsic motivation, but this is a terminological quibble. It does seem clear that the two groups were indeed functioning under different incentive conditions.

The other independent variable, feedback strategy, was manipulated by the researchers, but in this excerpt we are given no information about what constituted each of the five feedback conditions and cannot therefore judge the validity of the manipulation.

CHAPTER 4

4–1. This relationship is obviously not causal. Rather, both variables—shoe size and reading ability—are related to a third variable, age. Older children tend to have larger feet and better reading ability than do younger children.

4–2. **a.** Not controlled

b. Controlled by matching

c. Controlled by being held constant

4–3. The values of the variables you came up with need not be exactly like the following examples; the important thing is that you kept gender constant (either male or female) in example *a* and matched IQ in example *b*.

a.

Degree	*Style*	*Gender*
M.A.	Democratic	M
M.A.	Democratic	M
Ph.D.	Authoritarian	M
Ph.D.	Authoritarian	M

b.
Language	SAT	IQ
Spanish	400	110
Spanish	450	115
English	450	110
English	500	115

4–4. a.
Computer	Learning	Grade	Teacher
Yes	More	5	Vincent
Yes	More	5	Vincent
No	Less	3	DiMarco
No	Less	3	DiMarco

Grade level was a confounding variable that stemmed from subject characteristics. Perhaps the fifth-graders learned more than the third-graders because the material was easier for them, not because the computer helped them learn. Teacher was a confounding variable in the research situation. Perhaps Mr. Vincent's students learned more than Ms. DiMarco's because he is a better teacher.

b.
Health Ed	Health Practice	Volunteer
Yes	Better	Yes
Yes	Better	Yes
No	Worse	No
No	Worse	No

Volunteering was a confounding variable that stemmed from subject characteristics. Perhaps the volunteers were more concerned about their health than the non-volunteers, which is why they volunteered. This concern might have caused them to improve their health practices whether or not they had the health education program.

c.
Reinforced	Time on Task	Time of Day
Yes	Same	Afternoon
Yes	Same	Afternoon
No	Same	Morning
No	Same	Morning

This is a particularly interesting problem. Typically, the existence of an undiscovered confounding variable leads us to believe, perhaps falsely, that differences in the dependent variable are caused by differences in the independent variable. But in this case, ignoring the confounding variable might cause us to believe, perhaps falsely, that the independent and dependent variables are *not* related. In this situation it is possible that, without reinforcement, children would have spent less time on task in the afternoon than in the morning, because they were fresher and less tired in the morning than in the afternoon. Perhaps there is a relationship between reinforcement and learning, but it is obscured by the existence of this confounding variable.

4–5.   Blood type, native language, and intelligence must be studied nonexperimentally. Blood type and intelligence are genetically controlled; even if researcher control of these variables were ethical, researchers do not know how to change people's genetic makeup. Native language is learned over time in early childhood; it would be nearly impossible and highly unethical for researchers to control this variable.

Teaching method may be studied either experimentally or nonexperimentally. It is reasonably practical to study this variable experimentally, and if subjects' interests are protected there would not be serious ethical problems with doing so.

Test anxiety and self-esteem can be experimentally manipulated, although they are in part fairly basic and stable aspects of personality and so cannot be entirely controlled by researchers. Mild and brief manipulation of these variables by researchers may be justifiable, but any attempt to raise test anxiety or lower self-esteem as more basic components of personality would be unethical.

4–6. There are 14 females in group 1 and 16 females in group 2; that is, for all but two of the females in group 2, there is a matching female in group 1. There are 11 males in group 1 and nine males in group 2; that is, for all but two of the males in group 1, there is a matching male in group 2. All but four of the 50 subjects are matched on gender. Random assignment thus matched gender very closely.

There are 16 Anglos in group 1 and 17 Anglos in group 2; that is, for all but one of the Anglos in group 2, there is a matching Anglo in group 1. There are nine Hispanics in group 1 and eight Hispanics in group 2; that is, for all but one of the Hispanics in group 1, there is a matching Hispanic in group 2. All but two of the 50 subjects are matched on ethnicity. Random assignment thus also matched ethnicity very closely.

There are 17 noncollege graduates in group 1 and 17 noncollege graduates in group 2; that is, for every noncollege graduate in group 1, there is a matching noncollege graduate in group 2. There are eight college graduates in group 1 and eight college graduates in group 2; that is, for every college graduate in group 1, there is a matching college graduate in group 2. Random assignment thus matched educational level perfectly.

4–8. In this study, teachers' determination of served and nonserved children creates a serious confounding variable problem. A critically important question is how teachers make these decisions. If, for example, they select for service those children who they feel have the most potential for benefiting from the service, they may be selecting the more able children. If children who are served show more improvement in school achievement than do children who are not served, this may be due to the fact that these were more able children to begin with, not because they received special services.

4–9. Your response should look something like the one below.

Subject	Imaging	Pairs Remembered	IQ	Difficulty of Pairs
a	No	3	100	Harder
b	No	4	105	Harder
a	Yes	7	100	Easier
b	Yes	7	105	Easier

Most potentially confounding subject variables have been controlled by this procedure; because the subjects were the same individuals, such things as their IQ, gender, and cognitive style did not differ when they were in the imaging and nonimaging conditions. However, other confounding variables might have been created by the research procedure.

It is possible, for example, that the 10 nonsense-syllable pairs that the subjects were asked to memorize in the nonimaging condition were harder to learn than the 10 pairs that they were asked to memorize in the imaging condition. It is also possible that the subjects learned about the task of memorizing nonsense-syllable pairs the first time they tried, in the nonimaging condition—that they learned something about how to learn this kind of information. This would have helped them remember more pairs in the imaging condition.

4–10.   a. Keating and Bai used the same person to depict both values of each of the independent variables: brow position (lowered or raised) and smile (present or absent). Suppose they had used different people in the lowered and raised brow photographs, and children had attributed dominance to the individual with the lowered brow. This might not have been due to the brow position; it would have been possible that the individual who was photographed with the lowered brow had facial characteristics that the children perceived as more dominant than those of the individual who was photographed with the raised brow.

b. Hong and O'Neil wanted to present part of the regular content of introductory statistics courses in several different ways, to see whether the kind of presentation made a difference in students' learning. Somewhat arbitrarily, they chose as the particular content introductory hypothesis testing. Had some of the students in their study already covered this material in class, they would have had no way of knowing whether differences in the students' learning were due to their presentation of the material or to the students' prior exposure to the material. Thus they made sure that their presentation took place before this material was covered in the regular classes.

Summary Exercises

4–1.   a. King's and Cooley's variables were gender, family of origin achievement orientation, and two achievement-related behaviors (GPA and time spent on academics); their dependent variable was the imposter phenomenon. They found a main effect for family achievement orientation and an interaction effect for gender and each of the two achievement behaviors.

The researchers could not conduct an experiment: It would be impossible to control subjects' gender and impractical as well as unethical to try to control subjects' family-of-origin achievement orientation, GPA, or time spent on academics. Nor could the researchers use a within-subjects design: Subjects cannot be first male and then female or have first one and then another family-of-origin environment.

The authors could have identified and controlled (by holding constant, matching, etc.) individual variables with the potential to confound the study, but elected not to. Causal argument in this study is thus weak. The researchers were aware of this and thus referred to "associations" between variables rather than causal relationships.

b. The independent variables were learning condition (with two values, individual and cooperative) and reward condition (with three values, task, performance or none). The dependent variables were posttest performance and continuing motivation. Subjects were randomly assigned to conditions and within the cooperative condition to triads. Thus, it is probable that subject confounding variables were effectively matched. The researchers were then careful to treat all subjects the same during the conduct of the research, primarily by having all subjects work on the same video. This prevented the introduction of confounding variables in the research situation.

c. Jowett's independent variable was type of preschool; her dependent variables were children's behavior, achievement, and adjustment to school. Although it would have been possible for Jowett to assign children randomly to preschool types and thus control potentially confounding subject variables, this was apparently not practical. She therefore had to rely on identifying and controlling these variables. She elected to control some of them (which she considered "significant" but did not specifically name) in a rough way by matching schools; others (gender, age, etc.) were precisely controlled by matching children.

d. The independent variable was caffeine ingestion, and the dependent variable was submaximal endurance performance. In order to control expectancy effects, Butts and Crowell employed a double-blind design.

e. One independent variable was type of intervention with three values—two intervention types plus a control condition of no intervention. The dependent variables were aggressive and shy behaviors and achievement.

If all of the control classrooms had been in different schools from the experimental classrooms, this would have created a very threatening confounding variable. The researchers therefore included control classrooms from the "intervention" schools. However, this in turn created a potentially confounding variable: Since some of the control classroom were in the same schools as the intervention classrooms, it was possible that teachers in the control classrooms would learn about and adopt some or all of the intervention strategies. The researchers added control classrooms from schools with no intervention classrooms to counteract this possibility.

f. The independent variable was maternal support; the dependent variables were child behavior and child competence. The independent variable, maternal support, could not be studied experimentally or as a within-subjects variable. The researchers attempted to control potentially confounding variables by measuring maternal background, child intelligence, child risk, and child gender. There are, of course, other potentially confounding variables—e.g., maternal personality—which they did not identify or attempt to control.

They used two different methods of control. First they statistically controlled the four variables that they'd measured out of the analyses to see how maternal support alone related to the child variables. Then they treated three of the potentially confounding variables as independent variables of secondary interest, to see how they interacted with maternal support in relationship to the child variables.

Their causal argument is strengthened by the controls they employed, but relative to experimental research causal argument in this study is still weak. The authors acknowledge this by using the term predictor variable rather than independent variable when referring to maternal support.

g. Hebbeler's independent variable was Head Start participation; her dependent variable was later school performance. Although Hebbeler could have randomly assigned children to receive and not receive the compensatory preschool program and then followed them through the fourth, eighth, and twelfth grades to collect data on their school performance, this would have cost a great deal of time and money. She elected instead to do nonexperimental research. In an effort to keep such potentially serious confounding variables as ethnicity and socioeconomic status roughly constant, she defined the control group as students who were eligible for but were not admitted to or did not attend the program. This, however, leaves a critical question unanswered: Why were these students not admitted to or why did they not attend the program?

Perhaps teachers admitted students who they thought were more competent and therefore more likely to benefit from the program; if Head Start students performed better than controls in later grades, this might then be due to their greater competence, not to their Head Start participation. Or perhaps children were not admitted because their parents did not deal successfully with the application process; if control students performed worse than Head Start students in later grades, this might then be because their parents were less adequate models of successful functioning in a middle-class Anglo environment, not because they were excluded from Head Start. Or perhaps children did not attend the program because they left the community for a time; this kind of residential instability may be associated with other factors that depress school performance. If control students performed worse than Head Start students in later grades, this might then be due to these other factors, not because they missed Head Start.

h. The primary independent variable was birth order; the dependent variable was educational attainment. Birth order could not be experimentally manipulated or treated as a within-subjects variable. A potentially confounding variable, social origin, was added as a secondary independent variable. There was an interaction between the two independent variables, such that birth order affected educational attainment only in the comfortable group.

i. Leak's independent variable was method of counseling; his dependent variables involved counseling effectiveness. He was able to use random assignment to control potentially confounding subject variables. The effects of maturation were controlled by the waiting-list group; however, this introduced an expectancy variable into the research. If both treatment groups did better than the controls, it might have been because they expected the treatments to affect them, not because anything about the treatments themselves were actually effective.

Fortunately, Leak's results showed differences in effectiveness between the two treatment groups, so this did not turn out to be a problem. The use of the same counselor for both treatment conditions also introduced an expectancy variable. It is possible that the two treatment groups differed in effectiveness because the counselor expected them to differ. However, using different counselors would have created other kinds of confounding variables.

j. The independent variable was learning context with the values cooperative (experimental) or traditional lecture (control). The researchers initially claim to have randomly assigned subjects to cooperative or lecture treatment conditions. This, of course, would have maximized the probability that any subject confounding variable was effectively matched. However, when more detail is provided we can see that students were not in fact randomly assigned; if the attempted "random" assignment caused a scheduling conflict, then it was abandoned.

If scheduling conflicts were effectively random this would not have been a problem, but in fact scheduling conflicts might not have been effectively random. Suppose, for example, that the time for one of the algebra sections in the study conflicted with an honors class. Brighter students would then have been systematically excluded from that treatment group, biasing the study in favor of the other treatment condition. The researchers understood and compensated for this possibility by administering a pretest; since the cooperative and lecture groups did not differ on this pretest (i.e., they were effectively matched), they considered this potentially confounding variable to have been controlled. To be on the safe side, they also statistically controlled it out of their final analysis by treating it as a covariate.

CHAPTER 5

5–1. Examples *a* and *c* involve random sampling: subjects were chosen randomly to participate in the studies. Example *b* involves random assignment: Subjects were randomly assigned to values of the independent variable.

5–2. **a.** This sample consisted of 70 white, middle-class, suburban kindergarten children and included approximately equal numbers of girls and boys.

b. Subjects were all students in Catholic and Protestant schools in Northern Ireland who had taken state examinations. Because these examinations are state required, we can assume that data were available on very nearly all students. The FEA was interested only in Catholic and Protestant students in Northern Ireland; this is therefore an example of research done on an entire population of interest.

5–4. **a.** The topic of this study is of interest to arithmetic teachers of children as well as adults. However, it is known that there are differences in the cognitive developmental levels of pre-adolescents and (at least some) adults, differences that would be likely to affect people's problem-solving strategies. This sample may not, therefore, represent the entire population of interest with respect to this research question. It seems wise to limit generalizing of this study's results to college students, or at least to adults.

b. This seems to be a very good sample for the researchers' purposes. It is quite large and from a variety of types of classes at two universities over a fairly long period of time.

c. Subjects' gender, socioeconomic status, and membership in a church group may limit the generalizability of this study's results. It seems likely that women tend to respond differently from men to TV commercials; it is also possible that lower- and middle-class women respond differently, and that churchgoers tend to respond differently from nonchurchgoers.

d. Since introductory statistics are most often taught at either the undergraduate or graduate level, it seems safe to generalize the results of this study to most introductory statistics students.

5–5. The actual sampling sequence in this study is a bit difficult to tease out. The researchers' first sampling level was schools: Three schools with cooperative teachers were chosen to represent three different social classes. The second sampling level was grade: Parents of an entire grade level in these schools were then surveyed. This resulted in a third-level sample, comprised of children of survey respondents. At the fourth sampling level, survey data were used to classify respondents' children into two groups: working class and middle class. To this a third group was added, identified by the staff at one of the schools: children for whom English was a second language. This set the scene for the fifth and final level of sampling of 24 children from each of the three groups. See illustration page 330.

5–6. The identified population was seventh-grade students at a particular high school. The population was stratified into three groups: those in the below-average English class, those in the regular English class, and those in the accelerated English class. These groups were sampled independently to provide three subject groups of roughly equal size.

Results from each sample group should generalize to that group in the population, since each population group was sampled randomly. For example, whatever the researchers find out about self-esteem in the sample of average children is probably also true of the population of average children. However, results from the entire sample cannot be generalized safely to the entire population. What the researchers find out about self-esteem in their entire sample may not be true of the entire population, because the entire sample does not represent the entire population.

5–7. Although this sample size may seem impressive, this is an entirely self-selected sample that may not be at all representative of "most Americans" with respect to this research question. The interesting issue is what kinds of people, first, read this column and, second, were motivated to respond to this kind of question. It is possible that people who did not like school tended to be motivated by this opportunity to vent their negative feelings, while people who liked school tended not to be stirred by the question and thus not to respond. This sample cannot provide information on whether most Americans like school.

5–8. This researcher has a fairly challenging internal validity problem: to convince people who take an easy test that the test is actually hard, and to convince people who take a hard test that the test is actually easy. In order to obtain informed consent from prospective subjects, she must warn them that she may not be entirely candid with them about all aspects of the research in which they are being asked to participate. This, of course, tends to give subjects a somewhat suspicious mindset while they participate in the research. This makes the validity of the perception variable even more questionable.

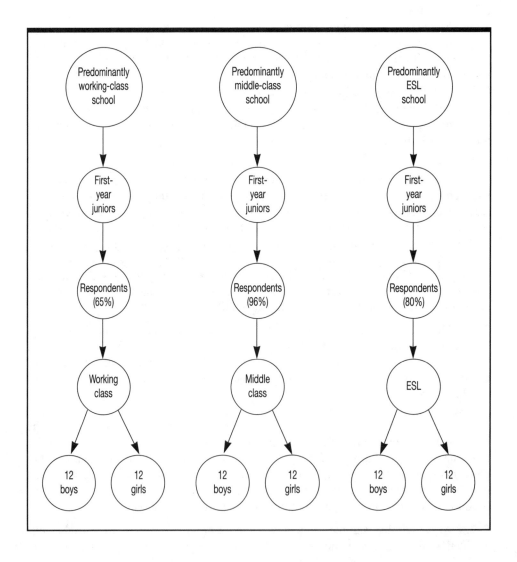

5–9. The major external validity problem in this study is presented by the fact that the study's subjects were long-term residents of Montgomery County. Head Start is designed to improve the later school performance of low-income children, who frequently have trouble in school. Residential stability (especially among low-income families, whose moves are unlikely to reflect upward occupational mobility) may be associated with other characteristics that affect children's school performance. Low-income families who are residentially stable may have more effective support networks, be more emotionally stable, be more committed to socially acceptable behavior, and so forth. Residentially stable low-income children thus probably grow up in better environments than do their residentially unstable peers and may not need the kind of help that Head Start is intended to provide. Head Start's effects on residentially stable children thus may not be the same as its effects on residentially unstable children. If this study shows Head Start to be ineffective, this result may not generalize to less stable children.

Or perhaps there is something special about Montgomery County. Perhaps low-income families in Montgomery County are not isolated in ghettos but interspersed throughout the community. Their children may thus have an opportunity to learn successful middle-class behavior from neighborhood models, an opportunity that is not available to low-income culturally diverse children in more typical communities. They thus may not need the kind of help that Head Start is intended to provide. If this study shows Head Start to be ineffective, this result may not generalize to other communities. Notice that the matter of residence also came up with respect to internal validity. We pointed out in the response to Summary Exercise 1g in Chapter 4 that the comparison group included children who did not attend Head Start because they did not reside in the county during that year; this kind of residential instability may be linked to the causes of their subsequent poor performance.

Summary Exercises

5–1. **a.** Thompson and Zerbinos sampled multiple episodes of all children's cartoon shows in a local viewing area during February 1993. Since the researchers work in Dayton, Ohio, it seems likely that this was the locale for the study. Our interest in the results is not restricted to this locale or time; we would like to be able to consider this sample to be representative of some larger population, which we would probably define as all children's cartoons aired nationwide in recent years. This is probably safe; there seems to be no obvious reason that children's cartoons aired in Dayton in February 1993 differ substantially from children's cartoons aired nationwide in recent years. It is possible, of course, that we are overlooking something. Perhaps, for example, programming in metropolitan areas with large, culturally diverse populations includes types of cartoons that are not shown in Dayton.

b. Although this sample was randomly selected, it was selected from a highly specialized population. This population does not, in turn, represent the general population of counseling clients with respect to a characteristic that seems likely to affect the research question: their enrollment in a course on personal growth and the building of interpersonal communication. If the course is elective, it seems likely that students who take such a course are especially interested in interpersonal communication. Even if the course is not elective, students who take such a course acquire knowledge of these matters. This must be assumed to affect their response to counselor touch. The results of this study should not be generalized to a less interested or knowledgeable population.

c. This research provides a good example of the difficulty of obtaining truly random samples. The researchers' stratified random sampling procedure was a good one, designed to yield a manageable sample size that would be representative of the entire population of the U.S. school districts. However, only 39% of the sampled districts returned the survey. It seems likely that districts that did not respond differ from districts that did respond in ways that might well affect the answers to the research questions. Perhaps districts did not respond because they did not have testing policies or did not have testing policies that require accommodating students with disabilities. The researchers' findings, that about 60% of school districts do have such policies, would then provide an inflated estimate of the true national picture.

d. These researchers' original sample consisted of all children born in a particular community in one year, spanning 1972 and 1973. The size of the original sample is not mentioned, but when the children were assessed at age three, the sample size was large (1,037). When the children were 18 and the study was completed, almost all of the original sample (1,008 individuals) seems to have been available for study. This is an amazingly high retention rate for such a longitudinal study. And the researchers argue that whatever attrition occurred was effectively random; the ultimate sample was representative of the original population of Dunedin births in the given year.

Since most of us are probably not interested in this particular community, we would, of course, like to know whether this original population is itself representative of some larger population. All we know of the Dunedin subjects is that they are predominantly of European ancestry. It may be that results of the study would generalize to other populations, especially populations of European ancestry, including much of the Anglo population of the United States. This probably would depend primarily on whether early childhood and young-adult traits are similar across such populations.

e. Leak used a convenience sample: all inmates of a particular prison who volunteered for counseling. The most salient characteristic of this sample that may affect its generalizability is the fact that all subjects volunteered. It is known that persons who voluntarily receive counseling are more receptive to the process. The results should thus not be generalized to nonvolunteer populations. The fact that Leak's subjects were incarcerated felons must also be assumed to affect the sample's representativeness greatly. The results also should not be generalized to nonprison populations.

Leak reports the attrition rate, which seems unlikely to affect the study's external validity: It was not extremely high, and attrition did not seem to be systematic but occurred for "numerous reasons." Leak's research context was very specialized: Counseling sessions were held at the prison, and only one counselor was employed. Physical surroundings are likely to affect counseling, so it would not be safe to generalize his results to nonprison contexts. And it is likely that characteristics of the counselor also affected the results. Leak did not focus on counselor characteristics. Other studies that did could help us understand how counselor characteristics affect the usefulness of this counseling method. Leak's choice of a convenience sample promoted internal validity by holding constant a number of potentially confounding variables in the research situation and by making random assignment much more practical.

f. Green's and Stager's study has good external validity. They drew a random sample from a list that probably contained the names of most educators in Wyoming. The sample can thus be considered representative of that population. Those of us who work outside of Wyoming are, of course, interested in being able to consider their population to be a representative sample, in turn, of some larger population that is of interest to us. There seems to be no obvious reason that we should not do so. Can you think of a reason that educators in other parts of the country would respond differently from the Wyoming educators to the questionnaire variations that Green and Stager employed?

g. Although we know very little about the subjects in this study, including how they were selected, the only obvious problem is with the sample size, which is small. The dependent variable being studied—oxygen demand while running—is not likely to be affected by such things as the subjects' place of residence, educational levels, and so forth. These subjects seem likely to be fairly representative of healthy, well-trained male distance runners with respect to the variable of interest.

The research context also seems reasonably representative of real-world contexts. Subjects were acquainted with the research procedures and had run considerable distances in the test shoes before the data were collected, so that any novelty effects of the research situation were reduced. Subjects probably functioned in the research situation much as they would have if they had been running for their own purposes.

h. Travis's and Kohli's topic had been researched fairly extensively before they conducted their study, and findings were interesting enough to warrant investing some resources in generalizability. It was thus important that they use as good a sampling strategy as their resources would permit. They chose a cluster sampling strategy, which is the next best thing to true random sampling. They randomly sampled city blocks from a cluster of census tracts. The census tracts were chosen to represent class and race distributions in the California city where the research was done, and the sample size was large. At this stage their sampling strategy thus provided good generalizability; this strategy should provide a sample that represented the entire population of the California city. However, this is not the entire population of interest to researchers in this area. In considering the generalizability of this study's findings, we need to consider whether this California city in turn represents other populations of interest.

But there is another problem with the generalizability of this study. Travis and Kohli could not, of course, force people in the sampled blocks to respond, and nonresponse is often a source of serious attrition in such studies. They needed to do what they could to increase the probability that individuals would agree to cooperate in the study. They thus made two personal visits to each identified household. Seventy-four percent of the sampled households remained in the final sample. Although this is a good rate for studies like this, the attrition was probably not random and thus limits generalizability. People who refused, were ineligible, or were never at home might well differ from respondents in ways that would affect the research question, and there were enough of them that, if they did differ, the study's results would be affected.

CHAPTER 6

6–1. **a.**

Type of Counseling	n	%
Directive	2	50
Nondirective	2	50

b.

Test Score	n	%
51	1	11
53	1	11
54	1	11
55	3	33
56	2	22
57	1	11

c.

Rating	n	%
1	1	14
2	1	14
3	1	14
4	2	29
5	2	29

6–2.

a. Type of Counseling	**b.** Rating	**c.** Score
Directive	Low	50
Directive	Low	51
Directive	Low	52
Nondirective	Low	52
Nondirective	Low	52
Nondirective	Low	53
Nondirective	Average	53
	Average	53
	Average	53
	Average	53
	Average	54
	Average	54
	Average	54
	Average	54
	High	55
	High	55
	High	
	High	
	High	
	High	

6–3.

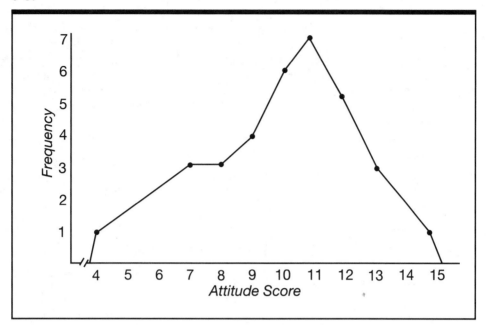

6–4. **a.** X
3
4
4
5
5
5
6
6
8

The median of this data set is 5. The mean is calculated as follows:

$$\bar{X} = \frac{\Sigma X}{n} = \frac{3 + 4 + 4 + 5 + 5 + 5 + 6 + 6 + 8}{9} = \frac{46}{9} = 5.11$$

Because there are no outliers in this data set, the mean and median are similar, and the mean is a more appropriate measure of central tendency than the median.

b. X
30
50
51
52
53
53
54
54
55

The median of this data set is 53. The mean is calculated as follows:

$$\bar{X} = \frac{\Sigma X}{n} = \frac{30 + 50 + 51 + 52 + 53 + 53 + 54 + 54 + 55}{9} = \frac{46}{9} = 50.22$$

This data set has an outlier: 30. The mean is thus lower than the median; it is pulled in the direction of the outlier. In this case, the median is a more appropriate measure of central tendency than the mean.

    c. X
          1
          1
          2
          3
          4
          5

The median of this data set is 2.5. The mean is calculated as follows:

$$\bar{X} = \frac{\Sigma X}{n} = \frac{1 + 1 + 2 + 3 + 4 + 5}{6} = \frac{16}{6} = 2.67$$

This data set has no outliers. The mean and median are thus similar, and the mean is the more appropriate measure of central tendency.

6–5.

X	x	x^2
2	–4	16
4	–2	4
6	0	0
8	2	4
10	4	16

$$S = \sqrt{\frac{\Sigma x^2}{n}} = \sqrt{\frac{16 + 4 + 0 + 4 + 16}{5}} = \sqrt{\frac{40}{5}} = \sqrt{8} = 2.83$$

6–6. 0.1% of people score between 60 and 70; 2.2% score between 70 and 80; 13.6% score between 80 and 90; 34.1% score between 90 and 100; 34.1% score between 100 and 110; 13.6% score between 110 and 120; 2.2% score between 120 and 130; and 0.1% score between 130 and 140. If your score is 122, only about 2% of the people score higher than you.

6–7.
$$z = \frac{X - \bar{X}}{S}$$

For an X of 2:

$$z = \frac{2 - 6}{2.83} = \frac{-4}{2.83} = -1.41$$

For an X of 8:

$$z = \frac{8 - 6}{2.83} = \frac{2}{2.83} = .71$$

6–8. The two kinds of transformations give you identical information.

$$z = \frac{X - \overline{X}}{S} = \frac{34 - 32}{4} = \frac{2}{4} = .5$$

Since z-scores always have a mean of 0 and a standard deviation of 1, your z-score of .5 indicates that you scored half a standard deviation above the mean—that is, your score is well above average.

$$50 + 10z = 50 + 10(.5) = 50 + 5 = 55$$

Since you know that the mean is 50 and the standard deviation 10, your score of 55 indicates that you scored half a standard deviation above the mean—again, well above average.

Summary Exercises

6–1. **a.** Because locus of control is a categorical variable, the appropriate data-reduction statistic would be frequency distribution.

b. Because course grade is a categorical variable, the appropriate data-reduction statistic would be frequency distribution.

c. Because reading ability test score is a continuous variable that (usually) distributes normally, the appropriate data-reduction statistics would be the mean and standard deviation. However, if in a given study the distribution of this variable departed substantially from normal, the median would be more appropriate.

d. Because ratings from 1 to 5 reflect a semicontinuous variable with a restricted range, frequency distribution could be used. The median could also be used. And it is not unusual to see a mean calculated on data like these, although we would want to interpret such a mean with caution.

e. Because gender-role identity is a categorical variable, the appropriate data reduction statistic would be frequency distribution.

f. Because height is a continuous variable that (usually) distributes normally, the appropriate data-reduction statistics would be the mean and standard deviation. Again, however, the median would be more appropriate if a given data set departed substantially from the normal distribution model.

6–2. **a.** These authors reported the minimum, maximum, mean, and median of a single variable. These statistics tell us that subjects spread out over the entire possible range of scores on this variable; that overall, subjects had fairly good ability to discriminate; and that there are no extreme outliers in this data set, because the mean and median are very similar.

b. These authors calculated a frequency distribution for the variable, principal companions and caretakers, which had 10 categorical values, peer group (single sex) being one value. The most frequent value in this sample was mixed-sex peer group. In approximately a fourth of these societies, young children are cared for primarily by peers.

c. The median PPVT-R standard score was 101. This was used to split the children into high and low groups.

d. The frequency distribution of subjects' gender was 28 boys and 33 girls. Their mean age was 11 years, 1 month; their standard deviation for age was 3.5 months. If age distributed normally, this means that about two-thirds of the subjects were from 10 years, 9.5 months to 11 years, 4.5 months old.

e. The measure of central tendency that was used is not specified, but it was probably the mean rather than the median. Average ages for the two groups were 11.87 and 13.08. The median age would have been the age of the middle child in the distribution, and it is unlikely that children's ages were expressed in decimals like 11.87 or 13.08.

6–3. Since scores on the support variable were transformed, we can compare the groups' means. The two older groups of children had similar support scores, while the youngest group's score was somewhat lower. First- and second-graders in this study had less social support than did upper-elementary and middle-school children. For the loneliness variable, we can compare the two older groups' scores, since they took the same form of the test; again, their scores are similar. But we have no way of knowing whether the youngest group's score reflects more, less, or the same amount of loneliness as the older groups, since they took a different form of the instrument and scores were not transformed.

CHAPTER 7

7–1. a. There will be a difference in the grade-point averages of subjects with internal and external locus of control orientations.

b. There will be a difference in the locus of control orientations of men and women.

c. As college grade-point average increases, starting salary in first job increases.

d. As IQ test score increases, achievement test score increases.

e. There will be a difference in time on task of students who are rewarded for being on task, students who are punished for being off task, and students who are ignored when they are off task.

7-2. a. The categorical independent variable is place of residence, with the values *rural, urban,* and *suburban.* The dependent variable, reading ability test scores, is continuous and usually distributes normally. The appropriate relationship-assessing statistic would thus be the mean and standard deviation of the reading ability test scores of each of the groups of children: rural, urban, and suburban.

b. The categorical independent variable is women's age, with the values *older* and *younger.* The dependent variable, gender-role identity, is also categorical, with the values *feminine, masculine, undifferentiated,* and *androgynous.* The appropriate relationship-assessing statistics would thus be the frequency distribution of gender-role identity for each of the groups of women: older and younger.

c. The categorical independent variable is tenure status, with the values *tenured* and *untenured.* The dependent variable, students' ratings, is semicontinuous with 10 values. This is a large enough number of values that frequency distribution might not provide adequate data reduction. The appropriate relationship-assessing statistics would probably be the median student rating of each of the groups of professors: tenured and untenured.

d. The categorical independent variable is participation in a computer course, with the values *participated* and *did not participate.* The dependent variable, attitude toward computers, is also categorical, with the values *positive* and *negative.* The appropriate relationship-assessing statistic would thus be the frequency distribution of attitude for each group of subjects: those who have and those who have not taken a computer course.

7-4. All possible main and interaction effects are present: the main effect of teacher gender on student performance; the main effect of student gender on student performance; and the interaction effect of student and teacher gender on student performance. However, because the interaction effect is present, the main effects cannot be interpreted directly. That is, although the overall performance of boys and girls in this study differs in favor of girls, we cannot simply conclude that girls do better than boys; and although the overall performance of the students of male and female teachers in this study differs in favor of male teachers, we cannot simply conclude that male teachers are better than female teachers.

The interaction effect tells us that student gender and teacher gender interact in their effects on student performance—that teacher gender makes no difference for girls but does make a difference for boys; and that student gender makes no difference when the teacher is male but does make a difference when the teacher is female. There are several plausible explanations of this result; social learning theory, with its emphasis on the importance of role models, provides one. It is possible that, in this society, girls find men and women to be equally acceptable as models, while boys find men to be more acceptable than women as models.

7–5.   a., b., and c. See art on the following page.

7–6.   a. Negative: As alcohol consumption increases, clarity of speech decreases.

   b. Positive: As time spent studying increases, exam grade increases.

   c. Positive: As children's age increases, their height increases.

7–7.   a. $r^2 = .36$; the relationship is moderate and positive.

   b. $r^2 = .09$; the relationship is weak and negative.

   c. $r^2 = .81$; the relationship is strong and positive.

7–8. For correlation coefficients ranging from .51 to .65, r^2 ranges from .26 to .42. Thus, for hearing-impaired children in this study, there are moderate, positive correlations between measures of intelligence and academic achievement. This means that there is a moderate tendency for children with higher IQ scores also to have higher achievement scores.

7–9.   a. $r^2 = .02$. When years of education completed is controlled, there is almost no relationship between grade-point average and income.

   b. $R^2 = .09$. There is a weak relationship between the two independent variables, years of education completed and grade-point average, and the dependent variable, income.

   c. These authors were primarily interested in two variables: field independence and computer competence. They analyzed these variables in two ways for each groups of Zimbabwean girls—Black and White.

First they correlated the variables. Coefficients were .47 ($r^2 = .22$) for the Black girls and .33 ($r^2 = .11$) for the White girls. There was thus a moderate, positive relationship between the variables for the Black girls and a weak, positive relationship between the variables for the White girls. Next they calculated partial correlation coefficients between the two variables, controlling for the influence of intelligence by partialling intelligence out of the analyses. This reduced the strengths of the relation-

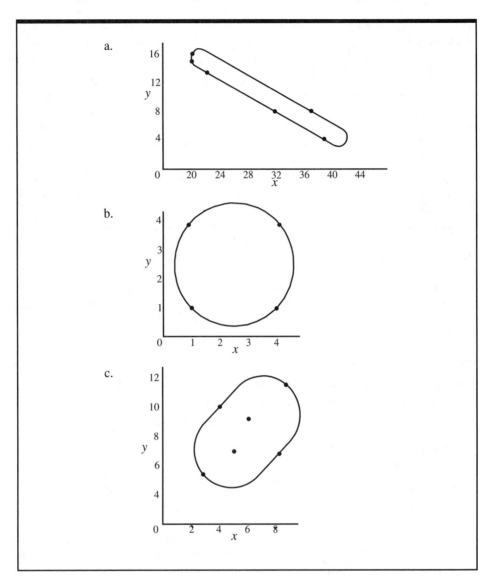

ships, more for the Black girls ($r^2 = .29$; $r^2 = .08$) than for the White girls ($r^2 = .27$; $r^2 = .07$). Thus, when the influence of intelligence was controlled, the relationships between field independence and computer competence were weak and positive for both groups of girls.

Summary Exercises

7-1.   a. Ryska reported means and standard deviations for each of the dependent (perceived coach support) variables, separately for each of the four independent variable (anxiety) groups. There are lots of data in the table, but over all of the dependent variables the repressive group perceives the most coach support, and the low anxious group perceives the least coach support.

Differences involving the two high anxious groups exist but do not pattern in as clearcut a way. The standard deviations of each dependent variable tend to be similar across the independent variable groups; thus the anxiety groups differ in their average perceived coach support but tend to spread out similarly around their respective averages.

b. Pianta and Ball calculated r^2 for each of their independent/dependent variable pairs, separately for low and high risk children. They reported the coefficients as r^2 rather than r to show the amount of variance accounted for. The r^2 between maternal support and behavior was lower than the r^2 between maternal support and competence for both risk groups; thus, the amount of support the mother has seems to be more strongly associated with child competence than behavior. However, the r^2 for both dependent variables is higher for the high risk children; thus, the amount of support the mother has seems to be more strongly associated with both child outcomes, behavior and competence, for high than for low risk children.

c. Scale scores are the transformed scores used by the publishers of the Stanford Achievement Test. You will remember that transformed scores are based on z-scores. Publishers provide transformed scores because raw scores have no intrinsic meaning. Vierra uses both raw and scale scores. She provides scale scores because raw scores are difficult to interpret across levels of the test.

Vierra is interested in the relationship between teacher ethnicity and student achievement at each of two grade levels. She presents mean reading-test gains over the school year for two groups of children at each grade level: those with Anglo teachers and those with Hispanic teachers. There seems to be no relationship between the variables *teacher ethnicity* and *student reading gain* in this sample of children; mean raw- and scale-score gains for both groups of children—those with Anglo teachers and those with Hispanic teachers—are the same or nearly the same at each grade level.

d. The statistic used was the mean.

In the sample, males in the control condition had a lower mean survey score than did females; that is, without experimental intervention, males' "rape-supportive" beliefs were lower than those of females.

But intervention had opposite effects on males and females. Females in the control condition had higher survey scores than did females in either experimental condition; thus, both kinds of advertisements depicting females seem to have decreased female subjects' "rape-supportive" beliefs. The result for males was different: Males in the control condition had lower scores than did males in either experimental condition; thus, both kinds of advertisements seem to have increased males' "rape-supportive" beliefs.

Within the context of higher post-intervention scores for men and lower post-intervention scores for women, the type of intervention had similar effects on males and females. Viewing females in progressive roles caused both male and female subjects to have lower "rape-supportive" beliefs than did viewing females in sex-object roles.

CHAPTER 8

8–1. The alternative hypothesis is that there is a relationship in the population between preschool attendance and first-grade reading readiness. The p value says that there is a 13% chance that the null hypothesis is true—i.e., that there is no relationship between these variables in the population. If there is a 13% chance that the null hypothesis is true, then there is an 87% chance that the alternative hypothesis is true—i.e., that there is a relationship between these variables in the population.

8–2. The policy implication of rejecting this null hypothesis would be to increase teachers' salaries (or at least to have to acknowledge that we're not willing to pay for higher-quality education!). The policy implication of retaining this null hypothesis would be not to increase teachers' salaries. The consequence of a Type I error would be wasted resources—paying more without getting more quality. The consequence of a Type II error would be having lower quality teachers than we could have.

8–3. **a.** Using the .05 criterion, the researcher will reject the null. This makes a Type I error possible—in fact, 3% probable.

b. The researcher will retain the null. This makes a Type II error possible, but we don't know how probable.

8–4. **a.** Using the conventional criterion of $p < .05$, this researcher will retain the null hypothesis, that there is no relationship in the population between the basis on which school boards are elected and constituents' satisfaction with school boards' performance.

b. In this researcher's sample, there is a weak ($.32^2 = .10$) positive correlation between per-student expenditure and students' achievement. This researcher will reject the null hypothesis, that there is no relationship in the population between these variables, and accept the alternative hypothesis, that there is a relationship between these variables in the population. The inferential statistic does not say what this relationship is; however, based on the sample result, we will conclude that the relationship between these variables in the population is probably weak and positive.

c. All of the p values are significant. The researcher will therefore reject all the null hypotheses and accept all the alternative hypotheses: that there is a relationship in the population between ethnicity and achievement and between neighborhood type and achievement; and that in the population the effects of ethnicity and neighborhood type on achievement depend on the way they operate together. This does not, however, tell us how these variables operate. Using sample results, we can conclude that in the population White students achieve more than Black students do, and students in integrated neighborhoods achieve more than those in segregated neighborhoods; but that these variables operate together such that Black students in segregated neighborhoods are disproportionately affected.

d. Two of the alternative hypotheses may be accepted: that there is a difference in the population in students' check-out rates when they are introduced to the library by a librarian and when they have no introduction to the library; and that there is a difference in the population in students' check-out rates when they are introduced to the library by a teacher or have no introduction. The sample data suggest that both of these differences are in favor of the treatment group, not the control group. One of the null hypotheses must be retained: that there is no difference in the population in students' check-out rates when they are introduced to the library by a librarian or by their teacher.

e. The researcher will accept the alternative hypothesis that there is a difference in the population in the scores on this test of field independent and dependent persons when the effects of IQ on the test scores are controlled. We do not, however, know from the information given whether field independent or dependent persons perform better on this test.

Summary Exercises

8–1. **a.** Turnbull and Bronicki used a within-subjects design to test the following two null hypotheses.

1. If the population of second-graders were given this test without receiving this kind of instruction about mental retardation, there would be no difference between their mean pre- and posttest scores. This was retained (presumably $p > .05$).

2. If the population of second-graders were given this test before and after receiving this kind of instruction about mental retardation, there would be no difference between their mean pre- and posttest scores.

This was rejected ($p < .01$).

The inferential statistic used is the Wilcoxon Sign Test for Related Samples. Sample data show control children's posttest scores as slightly higher than their pretest scores, but this difference is not statistically significant. Sample data show experimental children's posttest scores as higher than their pretest scores, and this difference is statistically significant; it is, therefore, reasonable to assume that posttest scores would also be higher in the population.

b. Rothschild et al. report correlation coefficients between EEG and 24 other variables. The correlation technique used was Spearman's rank order coefficient. Thirteen of these coefficients are significant at the .05 level or less (the name of the inferential test used was not specified). All of the significant coefficients are negative and moderate to strong. Interestingly, the pattern of significance differs over categories of variables. Results for most of the immediate recall and immediate affect variables are significant; results for some of the immediate recognition and delayed affect variables are significant; and almost none of the results for delayed cognitive variables are significant. This suggests the existence of an overall pattern of a stronger relationship between EEG and immediate response than between EEG and delayed response, especially for cognitive variables.

c. In fact, anxiety groups are not statistically significantly different in their mean perceived coach support on the first four coach variables—emotional, informational, companion, and nurturance. For the last coach variable, the composite variable, four of the reported means comparisons are statistically significant. The significant differences are as follows: defensive high anxious students and repressive students perceived more composite coach support than did the low anxious group and the high anxious group.

d. Stephen and Zweigenhaft calculated a oneway ANOVA; $p < .01$. Because they had three independent-variable values, they used a multiple-comparison test, Tukey's Honestly Significant Difference Test, to determine which groups in the population probably differed. The only significant result (no p value given) was for the female-touch versus the no-touch condition. It is thus likely that in the population there is a difference in the tips waitresses get when they touch the female member of a dining pair rather than touch neither member. In the sample, a higher average tip was left in the female-touch condition than in the no touch condition. It is therefore reasonable to assume that the population difference is also in this direction.

e. Descriptive data indicated that all of the seven treatment conditions were about equally effective and that all treatment conditions were more effective than no treatment. An analysis of variance showed that at least one of the treatment-no treatment comparisons was significant. Tukey tests confirmed the statistical significance of the descriptive results with one exception: one of the treatment conditions (AAA) was not significantly more effective than the control condition.

f. The inferential statistical analysis essentially confirms the descriptive statistical results. *F*-tests of grade effects were not significant for the three noncontroversial topics ("convention," "noncontroversial scientific," and "noncontroversial ethical"). This means that for noncontroversial topics, children in grades 1–6 have similar views about whether teachers should espouse the position that the student favors. We know from the descriptive statistics that this view is positive. Thus, we can draw the following conclusion: It is probable that, in the population, students in grades 1–6 tend to think that teachers should espouse the student's position on noncontroversial topics.

However, *F*-tests of grade effects were significant for the two controversial topics. This means that for controversial topics, children in grades 1–6 have different views about whether teachers should espouse the position that the student favors. We know from the descriptive statistics that this view is increasingly negative with grade. We can draw the following conclusion: It is probable that, in the population, students in higher grades are more likely than students in lower grades to think that teachers should not espouse the student's position on controversial topics. Putting these two conclusions together, we can say that it is probable that in the population there is an interaction between topic and grade: For noncontroversial topics, students of all grades tend to agree that teachers should espouse the student's view; whereas for controversial topics, students in higher grades are more likely than students in lower grades to think that teachers should not espouse the student's view.

CHAPTER 9

9–1. **a.** Interviews and archives probably would be the main sources of data in pursuing this question. Archives would contain information on community and school demographics (e.g, the local economy and population and school funding, enrollments, and programs) before and during the decline. Interviews would provide the perspective that local people, including school officials, have on the issue.

b and c. Observation and interviewing probably would be the sources of data in pursuing these questions. One or more librarians or several people with different physical disabilities would be observed, probably during the course of at least several days. The librarians or disabled people also would be interviewed, for their perspective on the observational data as well as for additional information that was not obtained via observation.

d. Observation would be the primary source of data for pursuing this question; interviewing probably would be used as a supplementary technique. One or more classes of third-graders would be observed during the first week of school. Children might be interviewed in a very informal way during and perhaps after the period of observation. Their teacher probably would be interviewed to check the observer's perceptions and conclusions.

9–2. **a.** Probable activities: people serving, eating, standing in line, cleaning up, talking to each other, or "horsing around." Some possible foci: food and people's food-related behavior (e.g., what they eat and how); students' social behavior with other students; interactions of cafeteria personnel and students; interactions of teachers and students; the behavior of socially isolated individuals.

The objectives of the research project would guide the observer's choice of focus at a given moment: If the research questions involved peer relationships of students, then students' social behavior with other students and the behavior of isolated students would be likely foci, but food behavior and students' interactions with school personnel would not. The stage of the project and data already collected would also inform the observer's focus: If data collection were just beginning, the observer probably would have a broad focus; if previous observation suggested the need for more information on isolated individuals, then they would be the focus. Events in the setting would also influence the observer's focus: If a fight broke out, the observer would probably focus on that event, whatever she had been planning to do.

b. Probable activities: parents and children interacting with office personnel, either socially or over "business" issues—e.g., scheduling, paying, describing where it hurts; children playing, alone or with other children; people reading; parents interacting with children, their own or others'; office personnel working and socially interacting.

Some possible foci: business events; medical events; parent-child interactions; children's behavior; social events; behavior of personnel.

As with question **a,** the study's objectives, the stage of the study, previous data, and events in the setting would determine the observer's choice of focus at a given time. (Since this will be true for all the questions in this exercise, we will not repeat this comment for each of the remaining questions.)

c. Probable activities: students working on art projects; students socializing with each other; students interacting with each other about class matters—e.g., discussing lighting or setting up a model; the teacher lecturing the students; the teacher critiquing students' work; the teacher assisting students with technique; the teacher socializing with students.

Some possible foci: students' art-related behavior; students' social behavior; teacher-student interactions; teaching style; students' products; the physical environment and people's use of it.

d. Probable activities: board members sitting, talking, writing; people in the audience listening and speaking; someone writing minutes of the meeting; media representatives interviewing citizens and board members.

Some possible foci: board members problem-solving strategies; the chair's leadership style; the issues raised by members of the audience; the affective content of audience-board interactions; the issues of concern to the media representatives; interactions between board members.

e. Probable activities: children using the playground equipment, playing formal games, playing informal games, standing around, talking with each other, running, crying; school personnel watching children, interacting with children, interacting with each other.

Some possible foci: children's formal games; children's informal games; solitary children; children's language; how school personnel relate to children; children's aggressive behavior.

9–3. **a.** Playgrounds, backyards, parks, homes.

b. Classrooms or other teaching settings.

c. Homes, playgrounds, parks, pediatricians' waiting rooms.

d. The union office, schools, or any other setting where relevant events might be taking place—e.g., the superintendent's office.

9–4. a. Participant observation. It would be difficult to observe the full range of relevant experiences without having a role in the child's life, if only because it would make the child and others uncomfortable to have a nonparticipant observer following the child around.

b. Either. A nonparticipant could have full access to the programs, so there would be no advantage in this respect to participating. But neither would there be a disadvantage. Since the programs take place with all factions present (e.g., teachers, administrators, program personnel), being identified with one faction (e.g., teachers) would not limit the observer's access. It is possible that a participant role would give the observer better insight into what is going on, at least from the perspective of that role.

c. At least primarily nonparticipant. It would be unethical for an observer to participate in the superintendent's professional life unless the observer had an appropriate role. Most such roles would limit the scope of observation—e.g., the superintendent's secretary would not go with him on school visits. The only appropriate participant role that would not limit the scope of observation would be that of the superintendent himself, and the probability of bias in a study focused entirely on oneself is high. In addition, most superintendents are too busy to make the kinds of systematic observations and keep the kinds of systematic records that would be required.

d. Probably primarily nonparticipant, although interesting data have been obtained in studies of this kind from a full-participant perspective. The role of teacher probably would not be a wise choice, since teachers tend to be too busy to make the kinds of systematic observations and keep the kinds of systematic records that would be required. Unless the setting was an adult education program, the role of student would be an unlikely choice, since it would be difficult to find a competent observer who looked youthful enough to be accepted as a student.

e. Probably participant. There would be ethical issues in having a nonparticipant observer in such a group.

9–5. a. Partial immersion. There would be serious practical difficulties in an observer's actually attempting to live the life of a runaway teen. Spot observations could be useful in identifying potentially productive settings for the research and in checking data.

b. Total immersion—i.e., living in a Hopi community—would be advantageous. Relevant events might take place at all times and places in the community. If there were practical limits on total immersion, partial immersion could provide useful data, however. Spot observations could be used in checking data.

c and d. Partial immersion. The contexts in which relevant events take place would probably be limited. Observations thus could also be limited, to these relevant contexts. Spot observations could be useful in targeting observational contexts and in checking data.

e. Since relevant events might take place in any interaction between the teacher and students, total immersion would be desirable. Partial immersion could provide useful data, however. Spot observations could be useful in choosing a setting and in checking data.

9–6. **a and e.** There is no obvious reason that age or gender would be an issue in either of these settings. The observer's ethnicity, however, might. For example, if program personnel and students were predominantly Hispanic, an Hispanic observer might find more acceptance in the setting. The observer's ethnicity would also be likely to affect her perceptions in such a setting.

In observing a bilingual program, it would be important for the observer to be fluent in both languages; otherwise, a great deal of important data would be missed. The observer's professional background could certainly affect both her acceptance and perceptions in these settings. Someone who had taught in a multicultural classroom, for example, probably would seem less threatening to program personnel and would have different perceptions in the classroom.

b. An older observer might find a bit more acceptance in the setting; more importantly, however, an older observer would be more likely to be able to see events in the setting from the perspective of the participants. The observer's gender probably would not affect acceptance in the setting; however, it might affect the observer's ability to see events in the setting from the perspective of a participant. Since retirement communities tend to be predominantly female, a female observer might be preferable. An even better strategy, however, would be to have two observers, one male and one female.

The observer's ethnicity might affect his acceptance in the setting, especially if the setting was not ethnically diverse. And, since cultures differ in their orientations toward aging, the observer's ethnicity would almost certainly affect his perceptions in the setting.

The observer's professional background might affect his acceptance by the teacher and his perceptions of the class. Someone who had taught probably would seem less threatening to the teacher and would have different perceptions of the class.

c and d. There seems to be no obvious reason that an observer's age or gender would affect her or his acceptance in these settings. Ethnicity might affect both acceptance and perceptions, especially if the setting was not ethnically diverse. Professional background also might affect acceptance and perceptions.

9–7. Focus: impact of father's alcoholism on consultant's schooling. Less structured: the informant receives little guidance from the interviewer about what to say.

9–8. **a.** You would want to include consultants who know most about the issue. Personnel whose functions are not impacted by federal funding would, for example, not need to be interviewed, unless they feel that they should have been impacted. Some impacted people probably feel positive about the impact, while others probably feel negative; both kinds of people should be chosen. Consultants should also be from various levels within the district, since perspectives would vary across levels. The superintendent, for example, would have a different perspective from that of cafeteria workers.

b. The adolescents themselves probably would know most about this topic, although personnel who work with the students and the students' parents probably could also provide valid information. Consultants should include people who are in favor of sex education as well as people who are against it and people who are conservative about sexual matters as well as people who are liberal.

c. School administrators, teachers, students, parents, and perhaps other taxpayers should be included, since perspectives of these groups are likely to differ on this matter. Consultants should include those who supported reorganization as well as those who opposed it.

d. Native American students and parents would be the most important consultants, although personnel in schools with Native American students would also have valuable perspectives. A special effort should be made to include personnel who are themselves Native American.

e. Students and school personnel would have different perspectives, and both perspectives would be valuable. Parents might also provide good data. An effort should be made to include students who are characterized as rarely, as well as frequently, "in trouble," and personnel who are characterized as more, as well as less, authoritarian.

Summary Exercises

9–2. In the first two excerpts the researchers are primarily nonparticipant observers. However, in both of these excerpts the observers affect (however unintentionally) the events that take place. Shifts of focus occur anytime there is a new speaker in excerpt *a* and whenever the observer mentions different activities, behaviors, and events in excerpt *b*.

In excerpt *a,* events are introduction of the observers, dialogue between the teacher and John, and interactions among the students. In excerpt *b,* events are the teacher's greeting to the observer, specific activities and actions of the various students, a fight between two boys, and subsequent responses among the other children.

In excerpt *a,* the dialogue contains information about values and attitudes toward school. From a single observation alone, it is difficult to know whether the student's responses reflect their true feelings or whether they reflect the atmosphere in the class that day and the effect of observers.

In excerpt *b* the dialogue contains information about the teacher's attitudes and statements about students and about her expectations as a new teacher. Later, the screaming occurs in a classroom incident involving the students and teacher.

In contrast, in excerpt *c* the observer is very much the insider, participant observer. Interestingly enough, despite the fact that the researcher is Anglo, his consultants feel comfortable enough with his presence to express their critical opinions of race relations among high-school students in the town. The researcher also provides a composite of the students' dialogue instead of an interview transcript.

9–3. **a.** Focus: the consultant's liking school. Less structured: the consultant receives little guidance from the interviewer about what to say. The interviewer shifts focus at the end of this portion of the transcript: Focus shifts from liking school to trips. The interviewer shows empathy in her comments on the responsibility that the consultant had for translating when she was a young child.

b. The focus on the second interview seems to be an examination of tension between African American and Hispanic students surrounding the cultural expressiveness of Hispanic students. The interview is structured to delve into the source of cultural tensions, but actually occurs somewhat opportunistically. There is a slight shift in focus as the interviewee explores how the use of the Spanish language further exacerbates tension.

9–4. Major sources would be university records (on such things as budgets, programs, personnel, and enrollments) and media archives (e.g., past issues of local newspapers and the university's student newspaper). Journals or other similar records kept by involved individuals would also be interesting sources of data if they could be located.

In evaluating the credibility of the sources, the researcher would have to take into account the political climate at the time the source was produced as well as the bias of the source itself. For example, it is a reasonable assumption that the university's press releases would tend to present the university in as favorable a light as possible; this would be an especially important consideration in interpreting press releases made at a time when the university was receiving media criticism for its failure to support women's athletics.

9-5. As you probably guessed, these data were generated by an incarcerated person, one who is contemplating issues of race and institutional power. These particular data were collected by a researcher doing literacy tutoring with a Chicano inmate. The researcher used the data to show how writing and literacy can facilitate one's renegotiation of self-identity and ethnic identity. It is considered unethical to alter self-report data.

CHAPTER 10

10–1.

SN

TV

SN

a. Lilly stands up out of her seat. Mrs. Caplow asks Lilly what she wants. Lilly makes no verbal response to the question. Mrs. Caplow then says rather firmly to Lilly, "Sit down." Lilly does. However, Lilly sits sideways in the chair in order to see the writing on the blackboard. Mrs. Caplow instructs Lilly to "turn around and put your feet under the table." This Lilly does. Now she is facing directly away from the teacher and the blackboard where the teacher is demonstrating to the students how to print the letter "O." There is no way that Lilly can now see what the teacher is writing.

b. We have coded this excerpt for the predetermined topics activities and peers, as well as for travel and disappointment, topics that were suggested to us by the data themselves. Your coding and topics probably will not be exactly the same as ours but should be similar.

ACT

TRV

PRS

ACT

DIS

I did most of my sports in high school. I was into basketball and volleyball and track. They took us all over the place and that was fun, going to compete at all these schools. When I went to my first year at Utah State we formed a girls' basketball team up there. We had a great coach from Oklahoma and we had a lot of fun, too. Down in California I was a Candy Striper, I did volunteer work at an old age home. I must have been a tenth grader and I would go after school to these old age homes and spend a couple of hours there during their dinner time helping them, feeding them, taking them here and there, things like that. Sports is actually the only thing I've been into. I don't have any kind of musical talent. Just dancing, that's just about it. That's one thing if I could turn back time I would have liked to specialize in a certain instrument but I think because of my background it was never a priority.

10–2. The topics we found are tests, examinations, questions, responses of the students, and the ways children work. One major construct could be ways teachers assess learning. All the topics pertain to this construct.

10–3. **a.** At the beginning of college, students' friendships tend to be based on shared high school experiences.

b. At the beginning of college, students have difficulty coping with the new experience of having sole responsibility for structuring their time. This is especially difficult for them because they are also faced with a variety of new choices for how to spend their time.

c. There was a low level of student participation in class discussions.

Summary Exercises

10–2. **a.** Mrs. Brown's behavior with the students tends to exacerbate the difficulties they are having with the testing. This is exemplified by her conflicting messages to the students about the importance of the test—e.g., "It really doesn't matter, but you should still try to do your best"; by her indirect communication to the children about her low expectations for their performance—e.g., the children can probably overhear her comments to the observer; by her agitation; and by her disturbing the students while they are taking the test. There seem to be no negative examples.

b. Mrs. Wills's calmness and ignoring of much of Jeff's acting-out behavior eventually seems to result in his settling down and getting to work. This is exemplified by the fact that she ignores all of his acting-out behavior except when it is directly destructive of other people's property; and by the quietness and directness of her responses to him when he is destructive—e.g., telling him he has his own supplies and should use them and that he is not to write on his desk but on the paper. There seem to be no negative examples.

CHAPTER 11

11–1. The initial phase of this research was inductive. The researchers had only one focus: the context of Legionnaire's disease. Initially, everything in that context was potentially relevant. The patterns that were discovered involved an association between certain physical characteristics and the particular hotel and restaurant that had been visited on one hand, and the onset of illness on the other. The possible causal explanations that were induced from these patterns included some environmental agent in the hotel or restaurant. These explanations were initially considered only proposed, not proved.

The next stage of research involved testing hypotheses that were deduced from these proposed explanations. The purpose of these tests was to provide information about which of the two explanations was correct—or, possibly, about the relevance of both—and to gain more knowledge of the characteristics of the hotel and/or restaurant that were responsible for the disease.

11–2. Given the state of theory building about learning, the research on cross-cultural differences in classifying is probably more worthwhile. Reinforcement is well understood; classifying, on the other hand, appears to be an important part of cognition and is not well understood. Even though the research on classifying does not make a substantial contribution to knowledge, it does provide information that may make future research more productive. Such a study will probably contribute more to theory building than will another study of reinforcement.

11–4. **a.** In this discussion, Baxter et al. summarize the results of their research. Their focus is not theoretical but applied. They do not suggest that their results contribute to theory building; rather, they point out that modeling theory suggests that the kind of content and context they found in music video may affect adolescent behavior in ways that are neither socially desirable nor ultimately healthy for adolescents' personal development.

b. Warren's study was conducted against a background of information that suggested that ostensibly bilingual, bicultural programs in fact promote an "Anglo" system of behavior. Warren draws two conclusions from his study: first, that the underlying structure of life in classrooms at Campbell School does involve some Anglicization. Warren found, however, that the Campbell program, with its emphasis on maintenance rather than transition or immersion, does function to validate and preserve a non-Anglo cultural system.

This study has value as applied research, because the merit of bilingual education is currently receiving a great deal of attention in educational literature. Warren's conclusion is that bilingual programs that focus on maintenance rather than transition or immersion can be effective.

c. Vierra discusses limitations of her study in terms of measurement validity, confounding variable control, and external validity. Her discussion has an applied focus; it is useful for educators to know the academic effects of matching teacher-student ethnicity. Her work, however, also relates to a theoretical issue that she does not discuss in this excerpt: whether achievement in an Anglo milieu is facilitated by having Hispanic models, with whom Chicano children might be expected to identify, or Anglo models, who might be more appropriate models of Anglo behavior.

d. Rosenfeld and Jarrard focus on a discrepancy between the results of their work and those of others working in the same area. They did not find effects for female professors that they found for male professors and that other researchers report for teachers of both genders. They discuss possible explanations for this. One possibility is that the effect does exist for female professors, but their sample size was too small to identify it using the statistical test they used. Another possibility is that their results are correct and that the discrepancy between their findings and those of other researchers is due, in part, to age differences between their sample and that of other researchers. This possibility gives an external validity direction for future research—to elucidate the conditions under which teacher sexism has particular effects on students.

e. Greenbaum addresses primarily theoretical issues in his discussion, although his results have applied relevance as well. He notes that his quantitative study provides deductive tests of hypotheses generated inductively from qualitative work. His results generally support these hypotheses, which are relevant to theory of cross-cultural differences in behavior. He notes, however, that there are differences between his results and those of researchers working with other American Indian groups. He suggests directions for future work, including delineation of differences between non-Anglo cultures.

APPENDIX A

Report 1.

Finnan did a qualitative, inductive, hypothesis-generating study of children's spontaneous play, a topic about which little research has been done. She derived two primary hypotheses: first, that sex differences in children's play are linked to adult sex roles; and second, that spontaneous play requires knowledge of cultural rules, while structured play can function to teach such rules. Both of these hypotheses are relevant to theory: in the first case, theory of sex-role learning, and in the second case, theory of culture acquisition.

Her work has applied relevance as well. She suggests that spontaneous play is important to children's development and that adults generally should adopt a hands-off attitude toward this play; that efforts to change sex-role socialization cannot entirely succeed unless girls change their play, and that evidence of such success should be sought in play; and that non-Anglo students learning to function in an Anglo environment may need structure until they internalize Anglo cultural rules.

Finnan did not begin her work with these foci; they emerged from her data. Nor did she reach her conclusions from quantification of her observations; she cannot, therefore, support her argument with reference to tables or statistical analyses. Rather, she derived her conclusions from qualitative analysis of her observations and supports her conclusions by reproducing some of her observations.

Because these conclusions are inductive, they give considerable direction for future, deductive research. Finnan's study was conducted in a small number of schools. She does not claim wide probable generalizability of her specific results and notes that there are probably differences between the Anglo and Vietnamese children she observed and other groups of children, such as Black children. This also gives direction to future research.

Report 2.

Schneider and Coutts, in a quantitative study, tested main effect and interaction hypotheses involving three independent variables—school type, sex, and grade—and a number of dependent variables, which they categorize as representing emphasis on scholarship and achievement, affiliation and pleasure, and control and discipline. Of the independent variables, they were primarily interested in the school-type variable. They operationalized their dependent variables through a questionnaire. No information is given about the validity of the questionnaire, although it has been used by other researchers, and references are provided to their work.

There do not seem to be any serious problems with measurement validity. The independent variables are straightforward and easy to measure validly. The examples of questionnaire items seem directly related to the dependent variables of interest.

The study was nonexperimental. School type, sex, and grade cannot be controlled by researchers. A potentially serious confounding variable is the types of student who attend coeducational and single-sex schools; perhaps students' perceptions of differences between the two school climates is not due to actual differences in the schools but to differences in the kinds of students who attend the two kinds of schools. Schneider and Coutts address this problem at some length in their discussion of their results. In order to control partially for this problem, they compared the two student groups on personality dimensions that were particularly relevant to this study: needs for achievement and affiliation. They found no differences between the groups. This is reassuring but does not rule out the possibility of other confounding variables.

Generalizability is also a concern. Although their sample size was large, all students attended Roman Catholic schools in southwestern Ontario cities. Schneider and Coutts also address this issue in their discussion, pointing out that their results are essentially in line with those of other researchers working in other countries. We are not, however, told what these other samples consisted of—were they, for example, all urban samples? We are given references if we wish to check this.

This sampling strategy was a good one, although it did introduce restrictions on generalizability. Other available options would have created internal validity problems or restricted generalizability more severely. Most single-sex schools are private rather than public. It would have created serious confounding-variable problems to compare single-sex private schools with coeducational public schools, because any dependent-variable differences might well have been due to socioeconomic differences between the students rather than to school type. Schneider and Coutts therefore restricted their sample to private schools. This could have presented serious generalizability problems, because private-school students tend to be from well-to-do families, so they selected religious schools. They point out in a footnote that religious schools in Canada are state-subsidized and therefore have students who are essentially typical with respect to SES.

A large number of hypotheses were statistically tested. Because large samples tend to be highly representative, very small differences are statistically significant. Schneider and Coutts therefore set the p value for rejecting the null very low—.01— and considered .05 to be "marginal." This makes it more likely that statistically significant results are also practically significant.

Most of the alternative main-effect and interaction hypotheses were supported; the exceptions involved some of the dependent variables related to academic orientation. The authors thus conclude that their results support the hypotheses that single-sex and coeducational schools differ in emphasis on affiliation and pleasure and on control and discipline, but their results do not support the hypothesis that the two school types differ in academic emphasis.

These results essentially confirm the results of other studies in this area, thus contributing to a fairly firm knowledge base in an area of some applied interest. Some of their results have theoretical implications as well, especially their findings on interactions between school type and student sex. It seems possible that all-female environments promote more traditional sex-role behavior. This is a lead that researchers in the area of sex-role socialization may wish to follow up on.

Report 3.

Onwuegbuzie and Seaman studied the relationship between two independent variables, time constraint and statistics test anxiety, and one dependent variable, statistics achievement. Time constraint was a treatment variable; the researchers assigned students to the timed and untimed values of this variable and then created the conditions of treatment. Students in the timed condition were told by their professor (who was also one of the researchers) at the beginning of the exam that they would have 90 minutes to finish the exam. Students in the untimed condition were told that they had unlimited time for the exam. Manipulation of this variable seems valid. The researchers were interested in the effects that students' perceptions of time pressure would have on their performance. The important thing, then, is whether students really believed that they were or were not under time pressure. It seems likely that they did.

The independent variable *test anxiety* was operationally defined as the Test and Class Anxiety subscale of the Statistical Anxiety Rating Scale. Reliability of this subscale was assessed by several different techniques; the test-retest reliability coefficient, for example, was .83, which is acceptable. The only evidence of validity for the sub-scale is that it had moderate concurrent validity (.76) with something called the Math Test Anxiety factor, which seems to be an anxiety subscale of a larger set of tests.

The dependent variable, the Statistics Achievement Exam, was operationally defined as an exam designed and scored by the professor/researcher. We are given a little information about the format of this test. Otherwise, no evidence of the reliability or validity of this exam is provided. The researchers could have calculated a reliability coefficient on the exam after the students took it, but apparently did not.

Scoring of the test involved the scorer evaluating such things as students' reasons for their answers. This opened the door for scorer bias. To prevent this, the scorer did not know the treatment condition of the students when he scored the exam. Interestingly, this precaution did nothing for measurement validity—the scorer may still have scored the tests in an invalid way. But it did help causal argument validity; at least if the scoring was biased, the bias was not systematically in favor of one of the independent variable groups.

The design was experimental with respect to the independent variable time constraint; subjects were randomly assigned to the timed and untimed groups. We can thus consider potentially confounding subject variables to have been controlled for this independent/dependent variable relationship. The researchers also controlled a number of variables in the research situation, by keeping them constant; the exam began at the same time for both groups, in similar rooms, and so forth.

For the treatment to be valid, the exam had to be long enough that the 90-minute limit seemed like a real threat to the students. But the researchers had to be careful not to make the exam so long that the students couldn't complete it in the 90 minutes allowed. If students in the timed condition hadn't been able to complete the exam, this would have introduced a confounding variable in the following way: The researchers predicted that students in the timed condition would do worse on the exam because the time limit increased their anxiety. But if the exam had been too long, the lower scores of students in the timed condition might have been due instead to the fact that they did not complete the exam. The researchers checked on this possibility and found it not to be a problem.

The second independent variable, anxiety, was not an experimental variable. It seems likely that this was a potentially confounding variable of such concern that the researchers elected to build it into the study as an independent variable rather than try to control it out. That way, they could see how it interacted with the experimental variable.

A midterm exam was given and served as a covariate in the statistical analyses that were done. Covariates are potentially confounding variables that are being statistically controlled. The researchers were concerned that students' aptitude, as measured by their prior performance on the midterm exam, might differ between the two experimental groups and thus confound causal argument.

On page 300, the researchers provide a table comparing the timed and untimed groups on a number of variables—e.g., age and number of college-level mathematics courses. As they explain, they used this information "to determine the equivalence of the treatment groups with respect to important demographic variables." In other words, they were trying to demonstrate that none of these was a confounding variable. None of the comparisons was statistically significant, though the table does show some fairly sizable differences between the two groups. However, these differences would have to "favor" the untimed group to affect causal argument in the study. Fortunately for the researchers, they did not.

These demographic variables, as well as aptitude, are subject characteristics; random assignment should have taken care of them. In order for random assignment to work well, however, the sample size must be fairly large. Perhaps the researchers felt that their sample size was small enough that they shouldn't rely on random assignment to take care of these variables, so they took these extra precautions.

Causal argument in this study seems good. There do not seem to be any confounding variables.

The subjects of the study were 26 graduate students from several non-math-oriented disciplines. The majority of subjects were women over 40. This was a convenience sample. It seems unwise to generalize this study's results to men. The study is about a form of math anxiety, and a great deal of literature shows that women have more math anxiety than do men. Time constraints might affect men differently. Similarly, it seems unwise to generalize this study's results to younger people. Younger people have more recent experience with studying math, which might affect their anxiety.

Subject attrition was low; 2 of the 28 students in the course did not participate in the study due to "scheduling conflicts" (p.299). If a larger number of students had dropped out, and these dropouts were due to something that might have affected the outcome of the study—e.g., if the students had dropped out because they were failing the course—this might have affected the study's results. Students who dropped out might have been the most anxious. The results would not then generalize to the most anxious students. But this was not the case, which is why the authors say that "selection bias was not deemed a threat to validity" (p. 299).

The researchers point out aspects of the research context that limit generalizing, as well. These include the particular course and the difficulty of the test. In a more (or less) anxiety-producing situation, subjects might respond differently.

Because this was an experiment, the researchers did not just measure something about their subjects; they actually did something to them. And what they did had the potential to harm subjects. As the researchers point out, "the SAE was an actual examination that affected course grades" (p. 300), and grades are important to students. Students gave informed consent to their participation in the study. The researchers also attempted to compensate students in the timed condition by offering them an opportunity to continue working on the test after their time was up.

The researchers describe the statistical technique that was used to analyze data as a General Linear Model technique. This technique is similar to Analysis of Covariance. On page 301, the researchers say that they were primarily interested in the anxiety by group interaction. This interaction was statistically significant—the effects of time constraints were different for students with different levels of anxiety. The researchers do not provide us with the sample data that they used to interpret this result; but they do tell us what those data looked like. Time constraints had little effect on the final-exam scores of students with low statistics test anxiety; however, students with high anxiety showed a "substantial decrement" in test performance when they were under time pressure. In addition to this null hypothesis test, the researchers calculated correlation coefficients between anxiety and performance, separately for the timed and untimed groups. Both correlations were negative, which makes sense; students with higher anxiety had lower test scores. The correlation was much stronger for the timed group. This provides a sort of effect-size analysis, that confirms the results of the null hypothesis test and shows that the treatment variable had a much greater effect on the high anxiety group.

In this study, both main effects were present; that is, timed students had lower test scores than did untimed students; and high-anxious students had lower test scores than did low-anxious students. As we pointed out in chapter 7, when an interaction effect is statistically significant, main effects are misleading. This study provides an excellent example of this. Were we to focus on the main effects, we would conclude that time pressure lowers performance; but, in fact, time pressure does not lower the performance of low-anxious students.

In their discussion, the researchers point out that the misleading nature of these main effects may explain discrepant findings of previous studies, which focused on only one independent variable.

References

Allender, J. (1986). Educational research: A personal and social process. *Review of Educational Research, 56,* 173–194.

Anastasi, A. (1988). *Psychologoical Testing.* New York: Macmillan.

Bandura, A. (1986). *Social Foundations of Thought and Action: A Social Cognitive Theory.* Englewood Cliffs, NJ: Prentice-Hall.

Baxter, R., De Riemer, C., Landini, A., Leslie, L., and Singletary, M. (1985). A content analysis of music videos. *Journal of Broadcasting and Electronic Media, 29,* 333–340.

Benn, R. (1986). Factors promoting secure attachment relationships between employed mothers and their sons. *Child Development, 57,* 1224–1231.

Bennett, R. (1993). On the meanings of constructed response. In R. Ward (Ed.), *Construction Versus Choice in Cognitive Measurement.* Hillsdale, NJ: Erlbaum.

Berrueta-Clement, J., Schweinhart, L., Barnett, W., Epstein, A., and Weikart, D. (1984). Changed lives: The effects of the Perry Preschool Program on youths through age 19. *Monographs of the High/Scope Educational Research Foundation, 8.*

Bogenschneider, K., and Steinberg, L. (1994). Maternal employment and adolescents' academic achievement: A developmental analysis. *Sociology of Education, 67,* 60–77.

Buros, O. (1995). *The Twelfth Mental Measurements Yearbook.* Lincoln, Nebraska: University of Nebraska Press.

Butts, N., and Crowell, D. (1985). Effects of caffeine ingestion on cardiorespiratory endurance in men and women. *Research Quarterly for Exercise and Sport, 56,* 301–305.

Caspi, A., and Silva, P. (1995). Temperamental qualities at age three predict personality traits in young adulthood: Longitudinal evidence from a birth cohort. *Child Development, 66,* 486–498.

Cochran-Smith, M., and Lytle, S. (1992). Communities for teacher research: Fringe or forefront? *American Journal of Education, 100,* 298–324.

Cohen, E. (1994). Restructuring the classroom: Conditions for productive small groups. *Review of Educational Research, 64,* 1–35.

Cohen, J. (1990): Things I have learned (so far). *American Psychologist, 45,* 1304–1312.

Cook, T., and Campbell, D. (1979). *Quasi-Experimentation: Design and Analysis Issues for Field Settings.* Chicago: Rand McNally.

Corno, L., and Kanfer, R. (1993). The role of volition in learning and performance. *Review of Research in Education, 19,* 301–341.

Cranton, P., and Smith, R. (1986). A new look at the effect of course characteristics on student ratings of instruction. *American Educational Research Journal, 23,* 117–128.

Cusick, P. (1973). *Inside High School: The Students' World.* New York: Holt, Rinehart, and Winston.

Davidson, A., Yu, H., and Phelan, P. (1993). The ebb and flow of ethnicity: Constructing identity in various school settings. *Educational Review, 7,* 65–87.

DeBeer-Keston, K., Mellon, L., and Solomon, L. (1986). Helping behavior as a function of personal space invasion. *Journal of Social Psychology, 126,* 407–409.

Dendato, K., and Diener, D. (1986). Effectiveness of cognitive/relaxation therapy and study-skills training in reducing self-reported anxiety and improving the academic performance of test-anxious students. *Journal of Counseling Psychology, 33,* 131–135.

Diener, E., and Crandall, R. (1978). *Ethics in Social and Behavioral Research.* Chicago: University of Chicago Press.

Dingman, S., Mroczka, M., and Brady, J. (1995). Predicting academic success for American Indian students. *Journal of American Indian Education, 34,* 10–17.

Dixon, W. (1990). Factors affecting Mexican women's fertility decisions: A research proposal. Xerox.

Dolan, L., Kellam, S., Brown, C., Werthamer-Larsson, L., Rebok, G., Mayer, L., Laudolff, J., Turkkan, J., Ford, C., and Wheeler, L. (1993). The short-term impact of two classroom-based preventive interventions on aggressive and shy behaviors and poor achievement. *Journal of Applied Developmental Psychology, 14,* 317–345.

Doyle, J. (1972). Helpers, officers and lunchers: Ethnography of a third grade class. In J. Spradley and D. McCurdy (Eds.). *The Cultural Experience.* Chicago: Science Research Associates.

Dumont, R., and Wax, M. (1976). Cherokee school society and the intercultural classroom. In J. Roberts and S. Akinsanya (Eds.). *Schooling in the Cultural Context.* New York: David McKay.

Eddy, E. (1976). Teachers in transition. In J. Roberts and S. Akinsanya (Eds.). *Schooling in the Cultural Context.* New York: David McKay.

Engelberg, R., and Evans, E. (1986). Perceptions and attitudes about school grading practices among intellectually gifted, learning-disabled, and normal elementary school pupils. *Journal of Special Education, 20,* 91–101.

Evans, E., Craig, D., and Mietzel, G. (1993). Adolescents' cognitions and attributions for academic cheating: A cross-national study. *Journal of Psychology, 127,* 585–602.

Felmlee, D. (1994). Who's on top? Power in romantic relationships. *Sex Roles, 31,* 275–295.

Fenstermacher, G. (1994). The knower and the known: The nature of knowledge in research on teaching. *Review of Research in Education, 20,* 3–56.

Finnan, C. (1982). The ethnography of children's spontaneous play. In G. Spindler (Ed.). *Doing the Ethnography of Schooling: Educational Anthropology in Action.* New York: Holt, Rinehart, and Winston.

Fishbein, H., Eckart, T., Lauver, E., Van Leeuwen, R., and Langmeyer, D. (1990). Learners' questions and comprehension in a tutoring setting. *Journal of Educational Psychology, 82,* 163–170.

Foley, D. (1990). *Learning Capitalist Culture: Deep in the Heart of Tejas.* Philadelphia: University of Pennsylvania Press.

Ford, V. (1989). *Feminists' descriptions and meanings of sexual activity: A social constructionist approach.* Dissertation. University of New Mexico.

Forrest, G., and Gordon, R. (1990). *Substance Abuse, Homicide, and Violent Behavior.* New York: Gardner Press.

Frederick, E., Howley, E., and Powers, S. (1986). Lower oxygen demands of running in soft-soled shoes. *Research Quarterly for Exercise and Sport, 57,* 174–177.

Friedman, L. (1995). The space factor in mathematics: Gender differences. *Review of Educational Research, 65,* 22–50.

Garcia, G., and Pearson, P. (1994). Assessment and diversity. *Review of Research in Education, 20,* 337–391.

Geer, B. (1969). First days in the field: A chronicle of research in progress. In G. McCall and J. Simmons (Eds.). *Issues in Participant Observation: A Text and Reader.* Reading, MA: Addison-Wesley.

Givon, M., and Goldman, A. (1987). Perceptual and preferential discrimination abilities in taste tests. *Journal of Applied Psychology, 72,* 301–306.

Goetz, J., and LeCompte, M. (1984). *Ethnography and Qualitative Design in Educational Research.* New York: Academic Press.

Goldberg, G., and Mayerberg, C. (1975). Effects of three types of affective teacher behavior on student performance. *Child Study Journal, 5,* 99–105.

Golez, F. (1990). Garfield Elementary School and the effects of a fragmented bilingual program. Xerox.

Golez, F. (1995). *Shifting the paradigm in preservice teacher education.* Dissertation. University of New Mexico.

Gordon, E. (1991). Human diversity and pluralism. *Educational Psychologist, 26,* 99–108.

Gottfried, A. (1994). *Gifted IQ: Early Developmental Aspects.* New York: Plenum.

Green, K., and Stager, S. (1986). The effects of personalization, sex, locale, and level taught on educators' responses to a mail survey. *Journal of Experimental Education, 54,* 203–206.

Greenbaum, P. (1985). Nonverbal differences in communication style between American Indian and Anglo elementary classrooms. *American Educational Research Journal, 22,* 101–115.

Greenfield, P., Farrar, D., and Beagles-Roos, J. (1986). Is the medium the message? An experimental comparison of the effects of radio and television on imagination. *Journal of Applied Developmental Psychology, 7,* 201–218.

Grindal, B. (1974). Students' self-perceptions among the Sisala of northern Ghana: A study in continuity and change. In G. Spindler (Ed.). *Education and Cultural Process.* New York: Holt, Rinehart, and Winston.

Gutierrez, K., Rymes, B., and Larson, J. (1995). Script, counterscript, and underlife in the classroom: James Brown versus Brown v. Board of Education. *Harvard Educational Review, 65,* 445–471.

Habermas, J. (1973). *Theory and Practice.* Boston: Beacon.

Hammersly, M., and Atkinson, P. (1992). *Ethnography Principles in Practice.* New York: Routledge.

Hannon, P., and McNally, J. (1986). Children's understanding and cultural factors in reading test performance. *Educational Review, 38,* 237–246.

Head, F. (1992). Student teaching as initiation into the teaching profession. *Anthropology and Education Quarterly, 23,* 89–197.

Hebbeler, K. (1985). An old and a new question on the effects of early childhood education for children from low income families. *Educational Evaluation and Policy Analysis, 7,* 207–216.

Hegarty, M., Mayer, R., and Monk, C. (1995). Comprehension of arithmetic word problems: A comparison of successful and unsuccessful problem solvers. *Journal of Educational Psychology, 87,* 18–32.

Henry, J. (1976). Attitude organization in elementary school classrooms. In J. Roberts and S. Akinsanya (Eds.). *Schooling in the Cultural Context.* New York: David McKay.

Hernstein, R. (1996). *The Bell Curve: Intelligence and Class Structure in American Life.* New York: Simon and Schuster.

Heyward, V., Johannes-Ellis, S., and Romer, J. (1986). Gender differences in strength. *Research Quarterly for Exercise and Sport, 57,* 154–159.

Hildebrand, D. (1986). *Statistical Thinking for Behavioral Scientists.* Boston: Duxbury Press.

Hokoda, A., and Fincham, F. (1995). Origins of children's helpless and mastery achievement patterns in the family. *Journal of Educational Psychology, 87,* 375–385.

Hong, E., and O'Neil, Jr., H. (1992). Instructional strategies to help learners build relevant mental models in inferential statistics. *Journal of Educational Psychology, 84,* 150–159.

Howe, K., and Eisenhart, M. (1990). Standards for qualitative (and quantitative) research: A prolegomenon. *Educational Researcher, 19,* 2–9.

Hoyenga, K. (1993). *Gender-related Differences: Origins and Outcomes.* Boston: Allyn and Bacon.

Jacob, B. (1995). Defining culture in a multicultural environment: An ethnography of Heritage High School. *American Journal of Education, 103,* 339–376.

Jayanthi, M., Bursuck, W., Havekost, D., Epstein, M., and Polloway, E. (1994). School district testing policies and students with disabilities: A national survey. *School Psychology Review, 23,* 694–703.

Jowett, S. (1986). Does kind of preschool matter? *Educational Research, 28,* 21–31.

Keating, C., and Bai, D. (1986). Children's attributions of social dominance from facial cues. *Child Development, 57,* 1269–1276.

King, J., and Cooley, E. (1995). Achievement orientation and the imposter phenomenon among college students. *Contemporary Educational Psychology, 20,* 304–312.

Klaus, M. (1995). *Bonding: Building the Foundations of Secure Attachment and Independence.* Reading, MA: Addison Wesley.

Klein, J., Erchul, J., and Pridemore, D. (1994). Effects of individual versus cooperative learning and type of reward on performance and continuing motivation. *Contemporary Educational Psychology, 19,* 24–32.

Lan, W., Bradley, L., and Parr, G. (1993). The effects of a self-monitoring process on college students' learning in an introductory statistics course. *Journal of Experimental Education, 62,* 26–40.

Lanis, K., and Covell, K. (1995). Images of women in advertisements: Effects on attitudes related to sexual aggression. *Sex Roles, 32,* 639–649.

Leak, G. (1980). Effects of highly structured versus nondirective group counseling approaches on personality and behavioral measures of adjustment in incarcerated felons. *Journal of Counseling Psychology, 27,* 520–523.

LeCompte, M., and Preissle, J. (1993). *Ethnography and Qualitative Design in Educational Research* (2nd ed.). San Diego: Academic Press.

Lee, V., Bryk, A., and Smith, J. (1993). The organization of effective secondary schools. *Review of Research in Education, 19,* 171–267.

Lee, V., and Smith, J. (1995). Effects of high school restructuring and size on early gains in achievement and engagement. *Sociology of Education, 68,* 241–270.

Levinson, D., Darrow, C., Klein, E., Levinson, M., and McKee, B. (1978). *The Seasons of a Man's Life.* New York: Knopf.

Levitt, M., Guacci-Franco, N., and Levitt, J. (1994). Social support and achievement in childhood and early adolescence: A multicultural study. *Journal of Applied Developmental Psychology, 15,* 207–222.

Lortie, D. (1975). *Schoolteacher: A Sociological Study.* Chicago: University of Chicago Press.

Malave-Lopez, L., and Duquette, G. (1991). Language, culture, and cognition: A collection of studies in first and second language acquisition. Multilingual Matters.

Mann, M., Strong, M., and Golez, F. (1995). Experimental site-based learning. Final report to the PNM Foundation. Xerox.

Mann, T. (1994). Informed consent for psychological research: Do subjects comprehend consent forms and understand their legal rights? *Psychological Science, 5,* 140–143.

Marsh, H., Chessor, D., Craven, R., and Roche, L. (1995). The effects of gifted and talented programs on academic self-concept: The big fish strikes again. *American Educational Research Journal, 32,* 285–319.

Mayer, R., and Anderson, R. (1992). The instructive animation: Helping students build connections between words and pictures in multimedia learning. *Journal of Educational Psychology, 84,* 444–452.

McCoy, H., et al. (1986). Snacking patterns and nutrient density of snacks consumed by southern girls. *Journal of Nutrition Education, 18,* 61–66.

Mendelson, M., Aboud, F., and Lanthier, R. (1994). Personality predictors of friendship and popularity in kindergarten. *Journal of Applied Developmental Psychology, 15,* 413–435.

Menges, R., and Exum, W. (1983). Barriers to the progress of women and minority faculty. *Journal of Higher Education, 54,* 123–144.

Moore, G. (1976a). Alternative attempts at instruction in Atchalan. In J. Roberts and S. Akinsanya (Eds.). *Schooling in the Cultural Context.* New York: David McKay.

Moore, G. (1976b). Realities of the urban classroom. In J. Roberts and S. Akinsanya (Eds.). *Schooling in the Cultural Context*. New York: David McKay.

Morrison, G., Ross, S., Gopalakrishnan, M., and Casey, J. (1995). The effects of feedback and incentives on achievement in computer-based instruction. *Contemporary Educational Psychology, 20,* 32–50.

Mwamwenda, T. (1993). Formal operations and academic achievement. *Journal of Psychology, 127,* 99–103.

Nicholls, J., and Nelson, R. (1992). Students' conceptions of controversial knowledge. *Journal of Educational Psychology, 84,* 224–230.

Nichols, J., and Miller, R. (1994). Cooperative learning and student motivation. *Contemporary Educational Psychology, 19,* 167–178.

Onwuegbuzie, A., and Seaman, M. (1995). The effects of time constraints and statistics test anxiety on test performance in a statistics course. *Journal of Experimental Education, 63,* 115–124.

Osborne, R. (1986). Segregated schools and examination results in Northern Ireland: Some preliminary research. *Educational Research, 28,* 43–50.

Parkhouse, B., and Williams, J. (1986). Differential effects of sex and status on evaluation of coaching ability. *Research Quarterly for Exercise and Sport, 57,* 53–59.

Parrott, S. (1972). Games children play: Ethnography of a second-grade recess. In J. Spradley and D. McCurdy (Eds.). *The Cultural Experience*. Chicago: Science Research Associates.

Patton, M. (1990). *Qualitative Evaluation and Research Methods* (2nd ed). Newbury Park, CA: Sage Publications.

Paulsen, R. (1991). Education, social class, and participation in collective action. *Sociology of Education, 64,* 96–110.

Phelps, L., and Branyan, B. (1990). Academic achievement and nonverbal intelligence in public school hearing-impaired children. *Psychology in the Schools, 27,* 210–217.

Pianta, R., and Ball, R. (1993). Maternal social support as a predictor of child adjustment in kindergarten. *Journal of Applied Developmental Psychology, 14,* 107–120.

Pitman, M. (1988). Developmental stages and institutional structure: The case of continuing education for women. *Anthropology and Education Quarterly, 19,* 139–154.

Pittman, R., Cox, R., and Burchfiel, G. (1986). The extended school year: Implications for student achievement. *Journal of Experimental Education, 54,* 211–216.

Pollock, J. (1979). Negotiating and maintaining social order in an alternative educational setting. Dissertation. Northwestern University: *Comprehensive Dissertation Index* DDJ79_27426.

Qin, Z., Johnson, D., and Johnson, R. (1995). Cooperative versus competitive efforts and problem solving. *Review of Educational Research, 65,* 129–143.

Risman, B. (1986). Can men "mother"? Life as a single father. *Family Relations, 35,* 95–102.

Rist, R. (1973). *The Urban School: A Factory for Failure*. Cambridge, MA: MIT Press.

Rist, R. (1978). *The Invisible Children: School Integration in American Society*. Cambridge, MA: Harvard University Press.

Robison-Awana, P., Kehle, T., and Jenson, W. (1986). But what about smart girls? Adolescent self-esteem and sex role perceptions as a function of academic achievement. *Journal of Educational Psychology, 78,* 179–183.

Romero, M., and Schultz, H. (1992). *Identifying Giftedness Among Keresan Pueblo Indians*. Albuquerque: Gifted and Talented Research Project.

Rosaldo, R. (1989). *Culture and Truth: The Remaking of Social Analysis*. Boston: Beacon Press.

Rosenfeld, L., and Jarrard, M. (1986). Student coping mechanisms in sexist and nonsexist professors' classes. *Communication Education, 35,* 157–162.

Rosenthal, R. (1994). Science and ethics in conducting, analyzing, and reporting psychological research. *Psychological Science, 5,* 127–134.

Rosenthal, R., and Jacobson, L. (1968). *Pygmalion in the Classroom.* New York: Holt, Rinehart, and Winston.

Rosenthal, R., and Rosnow, R. (1991). *Essentials of Behavioral Research.* New York: McGraw-Hill.

Rothschild, M., Thorson, E., Reeves, B., Hirsch, J., and Goldstein, R. (1986). EEG activity and the processing of television commercials. *Communication Research, 13,* 182–220.

Rueda, R., and Mehan, H. (1986). Metacognition and passing: Strategic interactions in the lives of students with learning disabilities. *Anthropology and Education Quarterly, 17,* 145–165.

Ryska, T. (1993). Coping styles and response distortion on self-report inventories among high school athletes. *Journal of Psychology, 127,* 409–418.

Schneider, F., and Coutts, L. (1982). The high school environment: A comparison of coeducational and single-sex schools. *Journal of Educational Psychology, 74,* 898–906.

Schulte, P. (1987). Pressures on an adult learning center: An Ecological Perspective. Dissertation. University of New Mexico: *Dissertation Abstracts International* AAC8820692.

Seixas, P. (1994). Confronting the moral frames of popular film: Young people respond to historical revisionism. *American Journal of Education, 102,* 261–285.

Senechal, M., Thomas, E., and Monker, J. (1995). Individual differences in 4-year-old children's acquisition of vocabulary during storybook reading. *Journal of Educational Psychology, 87,* 218–229.

Shethar, A. (1993). Literacy and empowerment? A case study of literacy behind bars. *Anthropology and Education Quarterly, 24,* 357–372.

Shreeve, W., Radebaugh, M., Norby, J., Goetter, W., Stueckle, A., Midgley, T., and de Michele, B. (1985). School prayer—the polarisation potential. *Research in Education, 33,* 63–67.

Skinner, B. (1959). *Cumulative Record.* New York: Appleton-Century-Crofts.

Solomon, R. (1992). *Black Resistance in High School: Forging a Separatist Culture.* Albany: State University of New York Press.

Sorsdahl, S., and Sanche, R. (1985). The effects of classroom meetings on self-concept and behavior. *Elementary School Guidance and Counseling, 20,* 49–56.

Spatig, L., and Bickel, R. (1993). Education for freedom: A case study in social foundations. *Educational Foundations, 7,* 51–64.

Stack, C. (1974). *All Our Kin: Strategies for Survival in a Black Community.* New York: Harper and Row.

Stephen, R., and Zweigenhaft, R. (1986). The effect on tipping of a waitress touching male and female customers. *Journal of Social Psychology, 126,* 141–142.

Stockwell, S., and Dye, A. (1980). Effects of counselor touch on counseling outcome. *Journal of Counseling Psychology, 27,* 443–446.

Strauss, A. (1987). *Qualitative Analysis for Social Scientists.* New York: Cambridge University Press.

Strube, G. (1993). *The Cognitive Psychology of Knowledge.* New York: North-Holland.

Subrahmanyam, K., and Greenfield, P. (1994). Effect of video game practice on spatial skills in girls and boys. *Journal of Applied Developmental Psychology, 15,* 13–32.

Thompson, T., and Zerbinos, E. (1995). Gender roles in animated cartoons: Has the picture changed in 20 years? *Sex Roles, 32,* 654–673.

Travis, R., and Kohli, V. (1995). The birth-order factor: Ordinal position, social strata, and educational achievement. *Journal of Social Psychology, 135,* 499–507.

Turnbull, A., and Bronicki, G. (1986). Changing second graders' attitudes toward people with mental retardation: Using kid power. *Mental Retardation, 24,* 44–45.

U.S. News and World Report (1983). Supergerms: The new health menace, *94* (Feb. 28), 35.

Vierra, A. (1984). The relationship between Chicano children's achievement and their teachers' ethnicity. *Hispanic Journal of Behavioral Sciences, 6,* 285–290.

Vierra, A., and Ford, V. (1990). American Indian women's explanations for their school success or failure. College of Education, University of New Mexico, Albuquerque. Photocopy.

Wadsworth, B. (1996). *Piaget's Theory of Cognitive and Affective Development: The origins of Constructivism.* New York: Longman.

Walker, S. (1984). Issues and trends in the education of the severely handicapped. *Review of Research in Education, 11.* Washington, DC: American Educational Research Association.

Wang, A., and Nguyen, H. (1995). Passionate love and anxiety: A cross-generational study. *Journal of Social Psychology, 135,* 459–470.

Warren R. (1974). The school and its community context: The methodology of a field study. In G. Spindler (Ed.). *Education and Cultural Process.* New York: Holt, Rinehart, and Winston.

Warren, R. (1982). Schooling, biculturalism, and ethnic identity: A case study. In G. Spindler (Ed.). *Doing the Ethnography of Schooling: Educational Anthropology in Action.* New York: Holt, Rinehart, and Winston.

Weisner, T., and Gallimore, R. (1977). My brother's keeper: Child and sibling caretaking. *Current Anthropology, 18,* 169–190.

Wentzel, K. (1993). Does being good make the grade? Social behavior and academic competence in middle school. *Journal of Educational Psychology, 85,* 357–364.

White, H., Labouvie, E., and Bates, M. (1985). The relationship between sensation seeking and delinquency: A longitudinal analysis. *Journal of Research in Crime and Delinquency, 22,* 197–211.

Wilson, D., Mundy-Castle, A., and Sibanda, P. (1990). Field differentiation and LOGO performance among Zimbabwean schoolgirls. *The Journal of Social Psychology, 130,* 277–279.

Wolcott, H. (1976). Maintaining the system: The socialization of a principal. In J. Roberts and S. Akinsanya (Eds.). *Schooling in the Cultural Context.* New York: David McKay.

Glossary

Analysis of covariance (ANCOVA). An analysis of variance (cf.) technique that controls potentially confounding variables, which are referred to as covariates.

Analysis of variance (ANOVA). A family of inferential statistical tests of null hypotheses involving one or more categorical independent variables and one normally distributed dependent variable.

Applied research. Research that is conducted to meet an immediate, perceived need of some group of practitioners (as opposed to basic research).

Basic research. Research that has the potential to contribute to basic knowledge, especially to theory building, but that may not have immediate practical applications (as opposed to applied research).

Cases. Inanimate entities for which variable values are empirically ascertained. A researcher collecting data on the dropout rates at 100 high schools would refer to the schools as the cases in his study.

Categorical variable. A variable that has values (usually named rather than numerical) that represent discrete categories rather than an underlying continuum (as opposed to continuous and semicontinuous variables).

Chi square. An inferential statistical test often employed to test null hypotheses involving categorical independent and dependent variables.

Cluster sample. A sample obtained by successive sampling of subsets. A researcher who first selected a sample of states, then

of school districts within states, then of schools within districts, and finally of classrooms within schools would have practiced cluster sampling.

Concurrent validity. A type of criterion validity based on the similarity between results obtained when the instrument being validated and another (usually well-respected) instrument are administered to the same subjects or cases.

Confounding variable. A variable that confounds attribution of cause to the independent variable(s) being investigated by itself being a possible cause of the dependent variable being investigated.

Constant. A property of subjects or cases that has the same value for all subjects or cases being investigated. For a group of women, gender is a constant.

Construct validity. A type of measurement validity. Based on the correspondence between theory about the construct we are attempting to measure and results obtained using the measurement instrument being validated.

Consultant. In qualitative research, a person who is selected as a probable source of information that the researcher is seeking.

Content validity. A type of measurement validity based on analysis (usually by people thought to be experts in the field in question) of the content of the instrument being validated.

Continuous variable. A variable that has numerical values, the measurement of which is considered to represent an underlying continuum (as opposed to categorical and semicontinuous variables).

Control group. A group of subjects who get no special treatment during the research, whose value of the independent variable is considered to be "leading normal lives." Often used to control possible maturation effects.

Convenience samples. Samples that exist naturally as a group, as opposed to being grouped by the researcher.

Correlation. Loosely, relationship. More specifically, a group of statistics that provide an index of the strength and direction of relationship between variables.

Covariate. In analysis of covariance (cf.), the term used to refer to a variable whose influence on the dependent variable is being controlled out of the analysis.

Criterion validity. A type of measurement validity. Based on the correspondence between results obtained when the instrument being validated and some other instrument are administered to the same subjects (cf. Concurrent validity and Predictive validity).

Criterion variable. A variable for which subjects' values can be predicted from their values of another variable, referred to as the predictor variable. Used instead of dependent variable to denote the absence of causal implication.

Deduction. A logical reasoning process characterized by reasoning from a general proposition to a particular case.

Dependent variable. A variable considered to be the effect of some other, causal variable(s), the causal variable(s) being referred to as the independent variable(s).

Descriptive statistics. Statistics that describe empirical observations (cf. Inferential statistics).

Emic. Refers to explanations of events and behavior that are based on the meaning given to them by participants in the research setting. Also, distinctive to the setting (as opposed to etic).

Empirical. Based on observation of real world events.

Etic. Refers to explanations for events and behavior that are based on the meaning given to them by researchers or other people outside the research setting. Also, universal or widely applicable explanations (as opposed to emic).

Evaluation research. Research done to evaluate an individual or, more usually, a program.

Expectancy effect. A research result caused by the expectations of those involved in the research, rather than by the independent variable(s) being investigated.

Experimental research. Research in which the values of the independent variable(s) are controlled by the researcher, usually by random assignment.

External validity. The extent to which the results of a study are thought to generalize to other subjects (or cases) and to other contexts than those in the study.

Field research. Research that takes place in natural environments and ongoing social settings as opposed to a laboratory.

First-order interaction. The interaction effect involving two independent variables and one dependent variable. Usually reserved for situations in which the simultaneous effects of more than two independent variables are being investigated (cf. Second-order interaction).

Generalizability. The extent to which the particular subjects (or cases) and contexts in a study represent other subjects (or cases) and contexts with respect to the research question.

Heuristic potential. The capacity to be instructive, to add to knowledge, or to stimulate interest in a subject.

Historiography. A description of the past with a narrative presentation.

Holism. Perspective of a social setting as a complex whole.

Hypothesis. A prediction about empirical observation.

Independent variable. A variable considered to be the cause of some other variable, the effect variable being referred to as the dependent variable.

Induction. A logical reasoning process, characterized by reasoning from a particular case to a general proposition.

Inferential statistics. Statistics that assess the probability of an unknown event (cf. Descriptive statistics).

Interaction effect. Denotes a situation in which two or more independent variables have different effects when they operate together from the effects they have when each operates alone.

Interim analysis. Systematic examination of data conducted periodically during data collection.

Internal validity. The extent to which the results of a study are thought to be valid for the subjects (or cases) and contexts on and in which the research was conducted. Usually reserved for studies designed to demonstrate a causal relationship; in this case internal validity refers specifically to the validity of causal attribution(s), which depends on confounding variable control.

Main effect. The effect that a single independent variable has on a dependent variable. Usually reserved for studies in which the simultaneous effects of multiple independent variables are also being studied.

Matching. Refers to the control of a potentially confounding variable by setting up independent variable groups such that each group has the same (or, in practice, very similar) values of the potentially confounding variable; that is, that the groups are matched on the potentially confounding variable.

Maturation effect. Research result caused by the normal development of the subjects over time, rather than by the independent variable(s) being investigated.

Measurement. The process of assigning values of a variable to subjects or cases.

Measurement error. Error in the variable values obtained using a measurement instrument.

Measurement validity. Refers to whether an instrument validly measures the variable it is intended to measure.

Measure of central tendency. A statistic that describes the midpoint of a distribution.

Measure of dispersion. A statistic that describes the range of a distribution.

Meta-analysis. Statistical analysis of the findings from different quantitative research reports involving similar research questions, to determine what is known about the answer to the question.

Multiple-comparison tests. Inferential statistical tests of the null hypothesis for particular pairs of independent variable groups. Usually used (after a more powerful test has shown that three or more groups differ significantly on the dependent variable) to pinpoint the pairs of independent variable groups that differ significantly on the dependent variable.

Multiple regression. A family of statistical techniques for simultaneously correlating (cf.) multiple independent variables with one dependent variable.

Narrative-expository reporting. Presentation of results in the form of stories and with explanation of their central issues.

Naturalistic. Adapted to natural settings. Not contrived or predetermined.

Negative relationship. An inverse relationship between variables, such that subjects or cases having lower values of one of the variables tend to have higher values of the other variable (cf. Positive relationship).

Nonexperimental research. Research in which the values of the independent variable(s) are not controlled by the researcher but occur naturally.

Nonparticipant observation. In qualitative research, a role in which the researcher remains an observer and does not take part in activities in the setting (cf. Participant observation).

Nonrelational research. Research that focuses on the state of some variable(s), rather than on the relationship(s) between variables (cf. Relational research).

Null hypothesis. A hypothesis that predicts the absence of relationship between variables.

Operational definition. An explicit description of the operations that were performed to measure a variable.

Outlier. An extreme or uncharacteristic value in a distribution.

Packaged variable. Variables whose values tend to be packaged—i.e., for which particular pairs of values tend to recur across subjects or cases. Male biological sex and male social gender, for example, are packaged values. Packaged variables present one of the most serious threats to causal argument.

Partial correlation. A statistical technique for correlating (cf.) variables when the influence of one or more other variables has been removed from the analysis. The variables that are removed are referred to as controlled or partialled out. Usually used to control potentially confounding variables (cf.).

Participant observation. In qualitative research, a role in which the researcher takes an active part in the field setting as well as observes it (cf. Nonparticipant observation).

Population. A group of subjects or cases defined in some way. Usually refers to the entire group of interest—that is, the group to whom the researcher wishes the results of the study to generalize—rather than to the subjects or cases on whom the research was actually conducted (cf. Sample).

Positive relationship. A relationship between variables in which subjects or cases having lower values of one of the variables tend to have lower values of the other variable (cf. Negative relationship).

Predictive validity. A type of criterion validity, based on the accuracy with which subjects' values of the instrument being validated predict their values of some other variable of interest.

Predictor variable. A variable the values of which predict subjects' values of some other variable of interest, referred to as the criterion variable. Used instead

of independent variable to denote the absence of causal implication.

Proxy variable. An independent variable that is used in place of the truly causal variable(s) and is understood not to be truly causal. Proxy variables are useful when true causes are poorly understood or difficult to measure.

Qualitative research. Research that attempts to describe events, usually in as much of their complexity as possible, rather than focusing on quantification of one or a few characteristics of events (cf. Quantitative research).

Quantitative research. Research that focuses on quantification of one or a few characteristics of events, rather than attempts to describe events in as much of their complexity as possible (cf. Qualitative research).

Random. Without pattern; according only to chance.

Random assignment. Random determination of subjects' group membership, usually with respect to which subjects will have which of two or more possible values of the independent variable.

Random sample. A sample that has been selected randomly from some population of interest and, if of adequate size, is thus considered likely to represent that population.

Raw scores. Variable values as they were measured (cf. Standard scores).

Relational research. Research that focuses on the relationship(s) between variables (cf. Nonrelational research).

Reliability. Refers to whether a measurement instrument is consistent—that is, consistently gives the same answer to the same question.

Replication. The repeating of an empirical study. Sometimes refers specifically to repeated studies that essentially confirm the results of earlier studies.

Representativeness. Refers to whether characteristics of the research sample or context that are relevant to the research question are similar to the characteristics of some population or wider context—usually a population or wider context to which the researcher wishes to generalize the study's results.

Representative sample. A sample whose relevant (to the research question) characteristics are similar to the characteristics of some population—usually the population to which the researcher wants to generalize the research results.

Sample. A subset of a population. Although researchers are usually interested in populations, they usually do research on samples.

Sampling error. A difference between a sample and population that affects the sample's representativeness of the population. Usually reserved for the random error contained in random samples.

Second-order interaction. The interaction effect involving three independent variables and a dependent variable (cf. First-order interaction).

Self-selection. Refers to either of two situations: when the value of an independent variable stems from some naturally occurring characteristic(s) of the subject, as opposed to being controlled by the researcher; or when a subject's inclusion in or exclusion from a sample results from some characteristic(s) of the subject, rather than from a decision of the researcher.

Semicontinuous variable. A variable that has values that represent numerical order but not an underlying continuum.

Significance. In inferential statistics, an obtained probability that meets some predetermined criterion.

Significance of correlation. A family of statistical tests of the null hypothesis that there is no correlation between the variables of interest in the population that was randomly sampled.

Single-subject design. A (usually quantitative) research approach in which the focus of investigation and analysis is individual subjects rather than groups of subjects.

Standard scores. Variable values obtained by transforming raw scores to fit a distribution with a predetermined mean and standard deviation.

Structured interview. A conversation between a researcher and subject(s) that is strongly guided by a set of specific, predetermined questions. Not off-the-cuff (as opposed to an unstructured interview).

Subjects. Animate entities for which variable values are empirically ascertained. A researcher who collects data on the test scores of 100 children would refer to the children as the subjects of her study.

Theory. Comprehensive causal explanation that goes beyond what scientists already widely accept to be true.

Treatment variable. An independent variable involving the administration of some treatment or procedure to subjects.

Type I error. The error made when a null hypothesis that is in reality true is rejected (cf. Type II error).

Type II error. The error made when a null hypothesis that is in fact false is retained (cf. Type I error).

Unstructured interview. A purposeful conversation between a researcher and subject(s) in which the researcher permits the direction of the conversation to evolve during the course of the conversation (cf. Structured interview).

Value (of a variable). One of the possible manifestations of some property of subjects or cases. Women manifest the value female of the variable gender.

Variable. A property of subjects or cases that has more than one value among the subjects or cases being investigated. In a group of men and women, gender is a variable.

Within-subjects design. A quantitative research approach in which the same subjects have different values of the independent variable at different points in time. (As opposed to the use of different groups of subjects who have different values of the independent variable.)

Index

Analysis of covariance, 179
Analysis of variance, 177–179
   factorial, 178–179
   oneway, 177–178
Anonymity of subjects, 116
ANOVA (see Analysis of variance)
Archives, 53–54, 220–221
Association (versus cause), 35–36
Attrition of subjects, 113–114

Cases, 29
Causal argument:
   defined, 71–72
   confounding variables and, 71–73
Checklists, 53
Chi square, 176–177
CIJE (Current Index to Journals in Education), 9
Coding (in qualitative research), 231–233
Coefficient of determination, 162
Coefficients:
   concurrent validity, 60
   correlation, 161–164
   predictive validity, 61
   reliability, 57
Computer searches of literature, 9–11
Confounding variables, 72–73, 93–94
   control of, 73–77
Constant, 27, 29
Construct validity, 61
Constructs (in qualitative research), 234–237
Consultants, 218–219
Control groups:
   defined, 91
   and the maturation effect, 90–91
Control of confounding variables:
   in experimental research, 80–81

in nonexperimental research, 82–84
   methods of, 73–77
Correlation, 161–164
   multiple regression, 163–164
   partial, 162–163
   Pearson's *r*, 162
   significance of, 179–180
Current Index to Journals in Education, 9

Data banks, 111–113
Data reduction, 129–141
Deception of subjects, 116–117
Deduction:
   defined, 17
   role of in theory building, 17–18, 256–257
Descriptive statistics:
   defined, 129
   use of in interpreting inferential statistical analyses, 182
Deviation score, 137–138
Discussion sections in research reports, 13, 262–263
Dispersion, 136–137
Dissertation abstracts, 8
Double-blind research, 92

Effect-size estimates, 153–154, 256
Emic categories, 235–237
Empiricism, 3, 5
ERIC Clearinghouse, 9
Ethical guidelines, 116
Ethics:
   historical abuses, 115–116
   and validity, 116–118
Etic categories, 235–237
Evaluation research, 305–307
Experimental research:
   advantages of, 80–81